Orcas, Eagles & Kings

Georgia Strait & Puget Sound

For information contact:
Primavera Press
200 West Camino Real
Boca Raton FL 33432

Library of Congress Cataloging-in-Publication Data

Yates, Steve   (Stephen M.)
    Orcas, eagles & kings : Puget Sound & Georgia Strait / Steve Yates
            p. cm.
    Includes bibliographical references and index.
    ISBN 1-882175-00-X   (hardcover : acid-free paper) : $29.95
1. Natural history—Washington (State)—Puget Sound. 2. Natural history—British
Columbia—Georgia, Strait of. 3. Marine fauna—Washington (State)—Puget Sound.
4. Marine fauna—British Columbia—Georgia, Strait of.   5. Coast Salish Indians.
I. Title.   II. Title: Orcas, eagles & kings.
QH105.W2 Y28 1993
508.797'7—dc20   92-29926

Printed and bound in Singapore
First Printing: January, 1993

99 98 97 96 95 94 93   5 4 3 2 1
This book is printed on acid-free paper.

Orcas, Eagles & Kings

Georgia Strait & Puget Sound

Steve Yates

Primavera Press

Boca Raton, Florida • Seattle, Washington

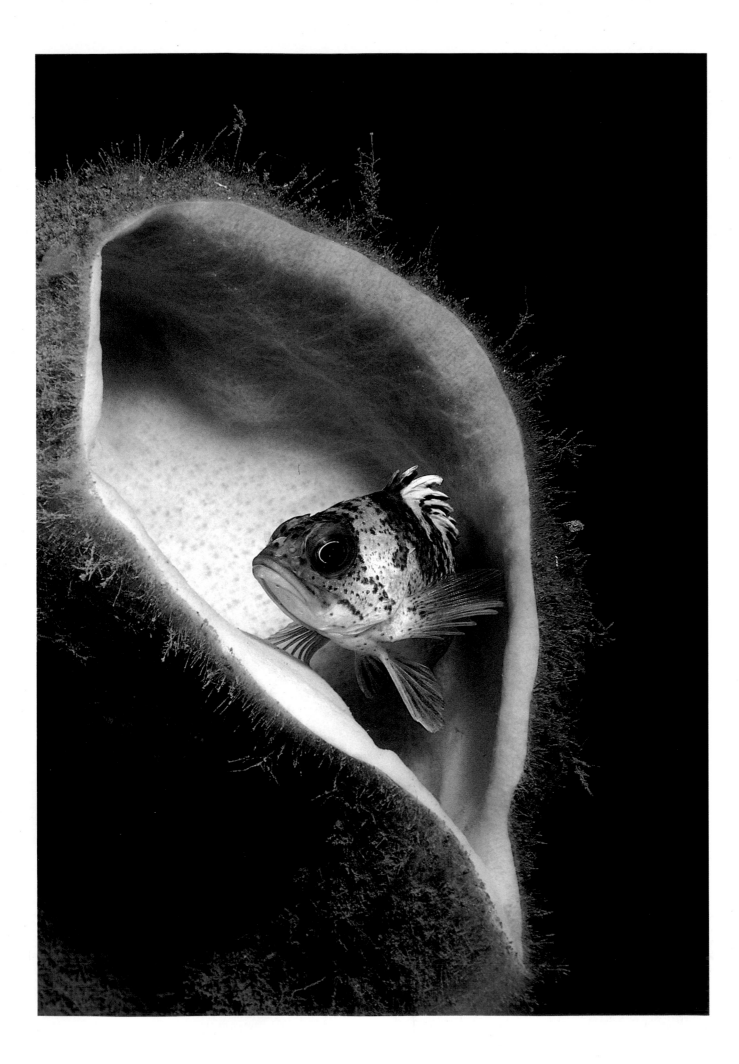

Contents

*A Quillback rockfish
finds shelter within a
chimney sponge.
(Neil G. McDaniel)*

The Olympic Mountains: Looking west from Seattle. (Art Wolfe)

The Salish Sea

Puget Sound, Georgia Strait, and Strait of Juan de Fuca have three separate names and straddle the border of two countries. But in nature they comprise a single sea—a long, brawny arm of the Pacific Ocean terminating in a handful of estuarine fingers gouged into the Puget/Fraser lowlands by sharp glacial fingernails.

Along Puget Sound's populated eastern shore, forested foothills that East Coasters would call mountains pile up into the Cascades, with two snow-capped volcanoes, Mount Rainier and Mount Baker, standing astride this folded range. The North Cascades blend into Canada's rugged Coast Range, forming a continuous wall breached only by the Fraser River, which rushes through spectacular Hells Gate just above the international border. To the west, the Olympic Mountains rise abruptly from Hood Canal, separated by the Strait of Juan de Fuca from Vancouver Island's Insular Mountains.

Autumn through spring, stationary low pressure centers in the North Pacific generate wave after wave of storm fronts borne inland on prevailing southwest winds. Constant rains on the southwest side of the Olympics and Insular Mountains water a mossy rainforest of giant spruce and cedar. By wringing out so much of the oceanic moisture, though, these westernmost mountains spread a dry rainshadow over much of the inland waters. The eastern Strait, the San Juans, and the rugged "Sunshine Coast" north of Vancouver belie the region's otherwise well-deserved reputation for year-round drip.

The picket fence of surrounding peaks still manages to catch enough rainfall to cover the Cascades and Coast Mountains with robes of fir and hemlock, and even darker green undergarments of swordfern, vine maple, and huckleberry. During much of the year, weeks of rain

Opposite:
A Great blue heron in breeding plumage hunts patiently along the shore. (Ervio Sian)

alternate with sunny polar air masses moving south from inland Canada. When these fronts clash, stationary occlusions cover the region's skies with layers of leaden clouds.

Sailboats on Puget Sound. (Bill Thompson/Earth Images)

Throughout the huge watershed, glacier-fed rivulets, milky with rock flour, dance down steep mountainsides into rain-swollen, log-strewn creeks. The streams flow in the shade of sheltering conifers or run naked through checkerboard clearcuts. Leaving the National Forests behind, many are transformed into long green pools imprisoned between narrow rock walls behind dams at towns called Electron or Concrete. Free again, they snake past small logging villages at the edges of state and provincial forest land.

Ten thousand forest creeks merge into a hundred large streams, and then into a dozen major rivers. These meander through the outwash plains of rural valleys amid mushrooming sub-divisions. At the sea's edge, brackish sloughs braid through saltmarsh sedges and rushes, then empty into tidal mudflats. Most of the deltas were diked off long ago for farm and pasture. Others have been covered with cities, channeled and dredged for shipping, lined with factories and shipyards. But a fortunate few have been saved as wildlife refuges, providing stopovers for migrating ducks and geese.

Though most of the rivers originate within the bowl of mountains, the basin's watershed actually includes all of the Fraser's enormous reach—twice the area of the basin itself—the entire southwest quarter of British Columbia. The Fraser, Skagit, Snohomish, and other flood-prone rivers inject torrents of fresh water into the inland sea, diluting the top layer of water. This lens of fresher, less dense water spreads out over the oceanic inflow, floating seaward atop the upwelling tides.

A purse-seiner scoops salmon from Georgia Strait. The annual Fraser River Sockeye run is a cornerstone of the region's economy and lifestyle. (Neil G. McDaniel)

The Salish Sea's Bald eagle population is one of the densest in North America. (Mark Newman/ Earth Images)

If an estuary is a semi-enclosed bay in which seawater is diluted by rivers, this inland sea is clearly a "super-estuary."

This vast network of ocean tides, saltmarshes, rivers, streams, and aquatic wetlands is unimaginably full of life. So fertile are the sea's waters that local scuba divers wait for breaks in the opaque plankton blooms the way surfers await good waves. No one has yet counted all the plants and animals, but scientists estimate more than 2,000 invertebrate species.

Bald eagles nest more densely here than anywhere else in the lower 48 states, along with Tufted puffins, Rhinoceros auklets, and Black oystercatchers. Huge flocks of seabirds, shorebirds, waterfowl, and waders cover shallow bays and saltmarshes.

Two hundred kinds of fish have been caught in these waters—three times that of San Francisco Bay—including massive annual runs of six species of Pacific salmon. Orca pods track the salmon herds. Minke whales rise up to gulp herring as gulls scatter. Dall's and Harbor porpoises feed on huge schools of herring, sand lance, and squid. Harbor seals and sea lions haul out on log booms and rocky islets.

For thousands of years this cornucopia of fish, shellfish, and seabirds supported a large Native American population. Individual tribes identified with the watershed (Duwamish, Snohomish, Nisqually, Cowichan...) in which they constructed winter villages of large, cedar-plank longhouses, but they are known collectively as Coast Salish—a subgroup of the Salishan-speaking tribes inhabiting much of western North America.

Connected by trade, intermarriage, shared environment and technology, Coast Salish people developed a remarkable culture that endures to this day.

Recognizing the Salish's primacy on these shores—and the ecological unity of the three convergent fjords—this international waterway is increasingly being called the Salish Sea.

The Salish Sea moderates our weather, determines settlement patterns, and in many ways defines a unique regional lifestyle. It directly provides many of us with a livelihood, and offers all of us recreation, seafood, and striking scenic beauty.

So scenic, in fact, are the Salish Sea's mountainous surroundings that it is easy to spend years appreciating its viewpoints, strolling its beaches, or crossing it on ferries with hardly a thought to the dark, mysterious world below the waves.

Our image of Puget Sound or Georgia Strait is of a dark, windswept meadow blooming with boats. Sailboats race downwind with billowing spinnakers. Aluminum skiffs mooch for Silvers and Kings. Gillnetters speed out for Sockeye openings. Tugboats tow huge rafts of logs or barges of sand. Container ships steam in and out of major ports lined with massive loading cranes. Pleasure boats funnel between spar buoys marking channels into busy harbors and crowded marinas.

The field is sometimes glassy smooth, at other times white-capped. But it is always a relatively flat surface at the base of the surrounding vertical cliffs, tall trees, mountain peaks, or city skyscrapers.

Waterfall on a Cascades mountain stream. (Peter M. Roberts)

An Orca swims through Elliott Bay, past the Seattle skyline. In few other places do marine mammals and people interact so intimately as on the Salish Sea. (Ken Balcomb)

The water seems impenetrable—too murky to see into, too cold to swim in. Its surface reflects mountains, storm clouds, pastel sunsets, tall glacial cliffs. Increasingly, it mirrors ourselves and our creations—houses, marinas, industrial ports, and city skylines.

Like our conscious mind, the world above the waves is moody and changeable. Steel-gray clouds move in from the Pacific, turning the waters leaden, depressing activity. A cool north wind brings clear continental air and exhilarating sunshine; sailboats spill out from sheltered marinas, people walk the beaches, seabirds soar along the thermal updrafts. Winds pause; the sun beats down on glassy waters, disturbed only by wakes of passing freighters. Inevitably, rainclouds return on southwest winds, lifted against flanks of forested mountains to recharge our rivers and alpine snowpacks.

The Salish Sea's marine world, though, lies almost entirely beneath the waves, invisible and out of mind. Like our subconscious it is there, working all the time, but only glimpsed in dreams:

A seal's head emerges for a moment to stare at us with huge, liquid eyes and disappears without a ripple.

A fish flips out of the water once, twice, fleeing an invisible predator.

Sea lion flippers, disembodied, stick up like stiff brown sails, catching the sun's rays.

A seaduck pops up from nowhere and calmly preens its feathers.

An orca leaps from the water and lands in a fountain of spray—leaving an indelible memory of a whale in flight, despite the rational mind's "this does not compute!"

Only during lowest tides—especially the very lowest daytime tides of May, June, and July—do we glimpse the edge of this extraterrestrial world. And even then we see only those plants and animals adapted to tidepools or periodic exposure, or the immobile creatures unable to retreat or too slow to hide. The vast majority move deeper or, if attached to the bottom, live beyond the lowest tides.

Though the Salish Sea lies just beyond our front yards and just below our boats, it was not until the recent development of submersibles, sonar, scuba gear, and underwater cameras that we began true exploration of the world beneath the waves. How sea creatures lived and interacted in the depths could only be guessed. The sea was as foreign as outer space.

In many ways it still is.

But unlike empty space, the extra-terrestrial world beneath the waves is full of life—its communities more varied and colorful, and far more ancient than those on land. The sea is the matrix from which we evolved yet in many ways it is far more relevant to our future than "futuristic" space. And exploring underwater is a bit more accessible than rocketing into outer space.

Any of us can explore Salish Sea's beaches and tidepools armed with a growing number of handy field guides. Vancouver, Seattle, Victoria, and Tacoma have excellent public aquariums. As well as offering a window into the sea, these—and private groups such as Greenpeace, Victoria's International Cetacean Watch Society, and Port Townsend's Marine Science Center—sponsor beach walks, kayak tours, and nature cruises throughout the year.

Container ships cross in Boundary Pass along the Canada–U.S. border. A juvenile orca surfaces in front, with Mount Baker in the background. (Kelley Balcomb-Bartok)

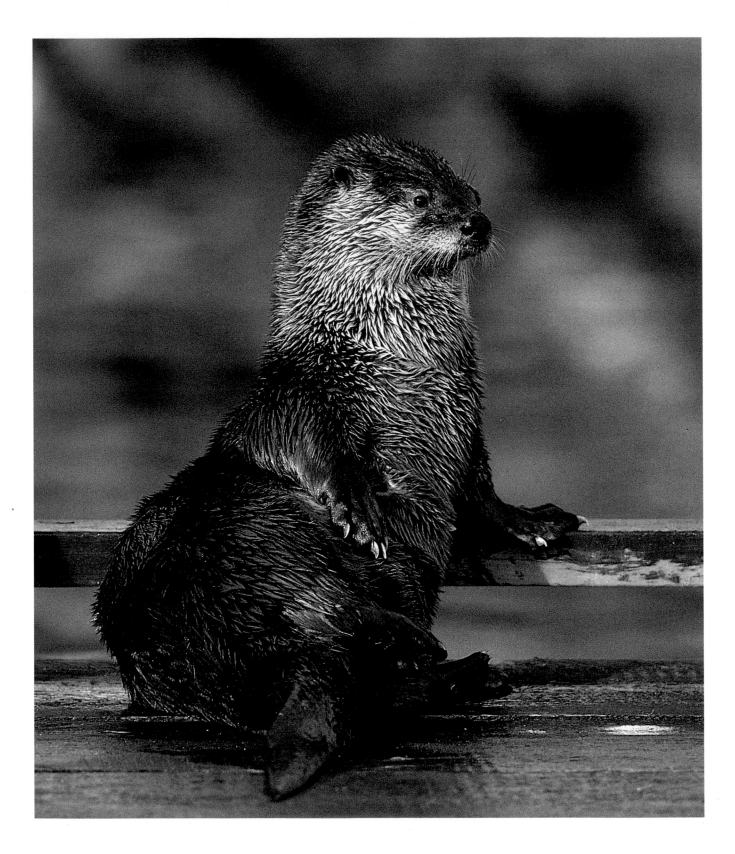

A River otter lounges on a seaside pier. (Timothy W. Ransom)

Above:
Northern and California sea lions haul out on an islet in the San Juan archipelago. Isolated islets are critical to marine mammals and seabirds. (Ken Balcomb)

Below:
Though Harbor seals are graceful in the water, their short foreflippers and webbed rear flippers make them awkward when hauled out on shore. (Neil G. McDaniel)

*A Tiger rockfish defends its home cre–
vice in a rocky reef. (Doug Wechsler)*

All of us can scan the water from the decks of a dozen ferries. Most of us have access to outboards or kayaks. And anyone willing to take a week-long course and spend the initial outlay for scuba gear can follow the shoreline down below the tides.

Someday we might have artificial gills to draw dissolved oxygen directly from the water, as fishes do. But for now the aqualung offers us great gulps of compressed air. Enough to stay down for an hour or so at 20–65 feet—the comfort zone for extended explorations and, fortunately for us, the sea's most colorful and diverse area.

But there are hundreds of creatures which live below the scuba zone. And many which only move about at night, or migrate stealthily through our area. Only a few fishermen or marine biologists dredge the sea's bottom; only a minority of divers are willing to brave its strong currents at night; and only the most fortunate boaters or whale watchers glimpse speedy Harbor porpoises, "transient" orcas, or migrating Gray whales. Our own human size adds another limitation. We can easily appreciate porpoises, seabirds, and salmon since they are within our size range. But what of the hundreds of species of minute plants and animals—some of them bizarre—on which the rest of the marine world depend? It takes plankton nets, microscopes, and special camera lenses to appreciate the smaller creatures, along with a strong dollop of curiosity and imagination.

Gradually, though, we are getting a sense of how this fertile fjord functions. The puzzle has been slowly pieced together over the course of centuries—beginning with the Indians who searched its shores for shellfish and fished its waters from elegantly carved canoes. Then, two hundred years ago, ships from Spain, England, and the newly formed United States arrived to begin systematic explorations of its geography and bathymetry—though more because of territorial ambitions than for the sake of science. Chief among these was the ship *Discovery*, under the remarkable British explorer George Vancouver and the crew's accomplished surgeon/naturalist, Archibald Menzies.

More recently, the University of Washington's Friday Harbor Marine Labs on San Juan Island and Canada's Nanaimo Biological Station on Vancouver Island have revealed many details of the Salish Sea's ecology. The University of British Columbia, University of Victoria, Western Washington State University, Walla Walla College, and The Evergreen State College operate smaller labs. Canadian and U.S. fisheries agencies have plotted life cycles and migrations of important food fishes. The Center for Whale Research on San Juan Island conducts long-term field studies of killer whales. And studies funded by provincial, state, and federal governments are tracing the sources, paths, and effects of human pollution.

This book offers a few glimpses into the Salish Sea, an occasional adventure story, a few snapshots of a dynamic million-ring circus. I hope it arouses curiosity and wonder rather than just adding facts to already overcluttered brains. Better yet, that it inspires personal explorations of our amazing frontyard wilderness. Most of all I hope it adds to our growing awareness of the beautiful, complex realm from which we gather so many riches, material and spiritual. And into which our expanding population now dumps so many toxic wastes.

As a naturalist, I've learned volumes from the inland waters. I've also enjoyed some of my happiest moments—exciting, uplifting, relaxing, aesthetically overwhelming—on and around the shores of the Salish Sea. I can only hope that we of Western Washington and British Columbia will do right by it. For ourselves, and for those who come after us—our children and grandchildren and the growing number of neighbors drawn to the region by the same beauty and rich resources that drew *us* or our ancestors here.

A baby octopus fascinates a scuba diver in Georgia Strait. (Neil G. McDaniel)

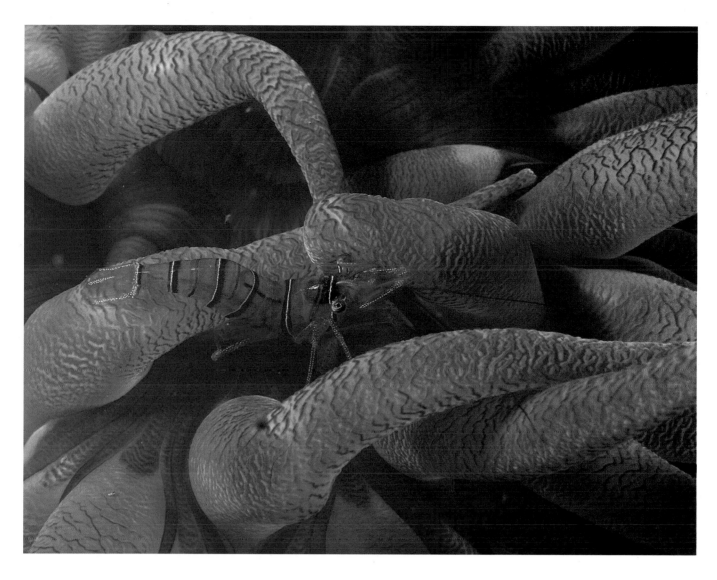

A Candy-striped shrimp finds shelter among stinging tentacles of its host, a deepwater sea anemone. (Neil G. McDaniel)

This delicate basket star is related to sea stars and brittle stars, but its slender arms branch into numerous appendages. (Neil G. McDaniel

Acknowledgements

I'd like to thank all the scientists and naturalists who puzzle over the Salish Sea and share their findings with us; the farsighted environmentalists—past and present—who have struggled to keep our inland waters clear and productive; the businesses that have put corporate citizenship over greed; and the adventurous nature photographers who have brought back the proof of how very rich and beautiful our frontdoor wilderness truly is.

The bizarre headdress of projecting cirri on this Decorated warbonnet help conceal it among seaweeds and sponges. (Doug Wechsler)

A dory floats in front of the Nisqually River's delta in southern Puget Sound, with Mount Rainier in the background. (Peter M. Roberts)

People and groups who helped with this book by sharing information or giving support include Kathy Fletcher/People for Puget Sound; Laurie MacBride/Save Georgia Strait Alliance; Ken Balcomb/Center for Whale Research; and Rich Osborne. Harriet Bullitt and the Bullitt Foundation gave support and encouragement during the early stages of this project.

Photographers who contributed their work for far less than its true value include Ken Balcomb, Kelley Balcomb-Bartok, Terry Domico, Natalie Fobes, Chris Huss, Neil McDaniel, Tim Ransom, Peter Roberts, Ervio Sian, Doug Wechsler, Stuart Westmorland, and Art Wolfe.

Special thanks to David Yates, Jr., for long hours illustrating the book jacket; Terry Domico who helped edit the photos; and Judy Petry who shared her expertise on subjects ranging from jacket design to press checks. To Wendy Pennoyer, who came through in the clutch; Renee Hayes, who listened patiently; Peter Roberts for last-minute advice (as well as for great photographs); and Benardine Jeffrey for help with the final layout.

Thanks also to Brad Bohonus of Digicolor in Seattle; Keith Donally and Kevin Lavergne at CorelDraw in Toronto; the very helpful folks at Far East Offset in Kuala Lumpur and Pica Overseas in Singapore; and Singapore National Printers.

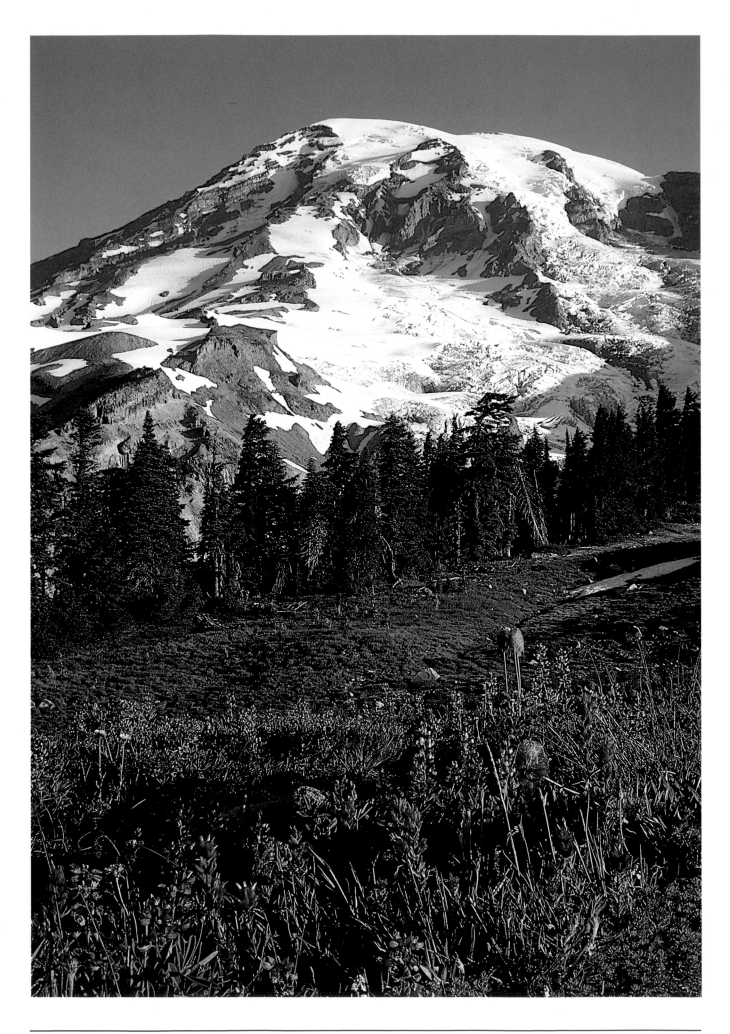

Prologue:

A Sea is Born

Imagine standing on Liberty Cap, a snow-covered ridge near the very top of Mount Rainier. Legs and lungs ache from exertion in the thin air almost three miles above Puget Sound. Behind and just a few hundred feet higher stands the windswept rim of Columbia Crater—at 14,410 feet, the highest point for a thousand miles in any direction.

Surrounding us is a panoramic view that every climber seeks but few have savored. For the sky today is clear of clouds in every direction, and the mountain has not created its own devilish weather. No pinkish-brown smog from freeways, factories, or slash fires blankets the lowland valleys.

On this ideal day we can see for hundreds of miles to the horizon through the clear thin air. Northward, the mile-high sawtoothed backbone of the Cascade Mountains—topped by 10,800-foot Mount Baker and 10,500-foot Glacier Peak—stretches 150 miles to the Canadian border.

To the west, across Puget Sound and the broad Puget Lowlands, the snow-capped Olympic Mountains catch the first morning light. From the lowlands, these 7,000-foot mountains stand impressively against the western horizon, but from this distance and Mount Rainier's imperious height, the range seems a mere roughening of the landscape.

To the south, Mount St. Helens—its top blown off just a dozen years ago—offers a view into its huge, lopsided crater. Even from 50 miles away, and a decade later, the once-symmetrical volcano is an open wound, and the gray moonscape north of it a visible scar—proof that the dormant dragons below our feet sleep fitfully here on the Pacific "Ring of Fire."

Though Mount Rainier's rock seems solid, you might glance back nervously at the double circle of craters that mark its peak. Steam escapes from vents there, as it does along the volcano's flanks. Just 6,000 years ago—a geological eyeblink—an eruption of steam blew a thousand feet off the top of the mountain and sent the massive, heat-induced Osceola mudflow rolling down the Carbon River Valley, covering more than one hundred square miles of land with mud to depths of more than 70 feet. The last eruption of Mount Rainier to leave significant traces of pumice happened about 2,000 years ago, though a number of smaller eruptions have occured since. The latest evidently took place between 1820 and 1854. Rainier, too, could wake at any moment.

The terrain before us sweeps downward at dizzying angles over a jumble of blinding snowfields, glacial fingers, knife-edged ridges, deep valleys, and glittering lakes. Gravity's agent has sculpted these mountains over the millennia since they were thrust high above sea level by the collision of continents and the upwellings of magma and ash. The agent? Water, in all its guises: rain, snow, ice, and glacial meltwater.

Opposite:
Mount Rainier. Looking north toward Nisqually Glacier from a meadow near Paradise. (Peter M. Roberts)

Invisible vapor is lifted from the vast surface of the Pacific Ocean by the sun, swirled into low-pressure whirlpools, and swept inland as dark atmospheric waves to lap up against the mountainsides. As the moisture-laden air rises up the mountain flanks, it contracts and cools; the vapor condenses into water droplets or flakes of snow, and falls—seemingly without letup—from October to June. It is hardly surprising that the desertlands east of the Cascades or the land and waters northeast of the Olympics and the mountains of Vancouver Island are arid, for the western sides of these mountains catch all the rain.

Above the shifting freezing level, precipitation falls as snow. At the highest elevations—as here on the top of Mount Rainier—the snowpack builds up each long, cold winter faster than it can melt in the brief summer warmth. Rainier, in fact, has recorded almost 100 feet of snowfall in one year (1971–2) and averages 53 feet per year; more than any other place in the continental United States.

Freshly-fallen snow is only a tenth as dense as water. But as it piles up, highly compacted granular snow (firn) can become half as dense as water. As the firn is packed further, it recrystallizes, forming larger and larger crystals, squeezing out all the air spaces between. At a depth of 40 feet or more it becomes solid glacial ice, almost as dense as water or rock.

But the solid-seeming ice is not rock-solid. Near melting point, the rounded ice crystals slide over one another, and the ice gradually deforms—like warm plastic or iron in a forge.

The heavy ice mass slips fitfully downhill incorporating the weathered rock beneath it unto its rough underbelly. As it slowly but inexorably rasps the surface, the glacier sculpts the landscape over which it moves.

Sunset Amphitheater, just below a 500-foot sheer rock wall to our left, is a fine example of a cirque—a typical bowl-like form excavated by glacial ice. A glacier cuts most efficiently where it is thickest and flows fastest—midway between the snow accumulating at its head and the wasting at its lower end, or toe. It typically sculpts a series of bowls along its path, similar to the way a stream carves a series of falls and bowls as it flows over solid rock.

Twenty six separate glaciers flow from Rainier's icecap, like some multi-armed albino starfish. Of these, Emmons Glacier behind us, which flows four miles due east, and the Carbon-Russell system to our right, extending six miles north, are the largest glaciers south of Canada.

Yet these impressive glaciers, like those on Mount Olympus and the thousand or so smaller glaciers in the North Cascades and southern Coast Mountains, are only remnants of mightier ice fields in the past. The tall, exposed rock walls of Sunset Amphitheater below us are proof that much larger glaciers once filled these mountain cirques.

For the period from about 22,000 to 18,000 BP (Before Present), world temperatures fell lower than at any time since. And though the average temperature drop was just 10° F (6°C) colder than at present, it was enough to greatly shift the balance of winter snowfall and summer melting.

Why such long-term ups and downs in the world climate? The causes are still poorly understood, but climatologists suspect a combination of reasons. The earth is not always the same distance from the sun, and it cools off at maximum distance. It periodically passes through clouds of cosmic dust, which block the sun's rays, as do major periods of volcanic eruptions. And the sun's energy, as shown by sunspot activity, fluctuates in a cyclic way.

Evidence from nearshore seabottom core samples indicate that at least 17 "ice ages" have occurred during the past two million years. During the most recent one, alpine glaciers much larger than these flowed down from the mountains surrounding the Salish Sea. Moving at a rate of up to a mile every ten years, the glacial fronts advanced far down into the lowlands, widening many of the V-shaped river valleys below us into classic U-shaped glacial valleys. At the lowland ends of these valley glaciers, where melting eventually matched the foreward thrust, the ice front dropped long piles of rock debris (terminal moraines) as evidence of their massive presence.

Ironically, the alpine glaciers were already in full retreat, far back up into the mountains, when a great ice sheet began its invasion from the north...

I magine it is 17,000 BP. Imagine further that time has speeded up like a fast-motion film—each century compressed into a minute, a millennium every ten minutes.

Below us is a large nameless river system, flowing through a deep, broad valley toward an ancestral Fraser River. This proto-Fraser flows westward from a gap between the Cascades and B.C.'s Coast

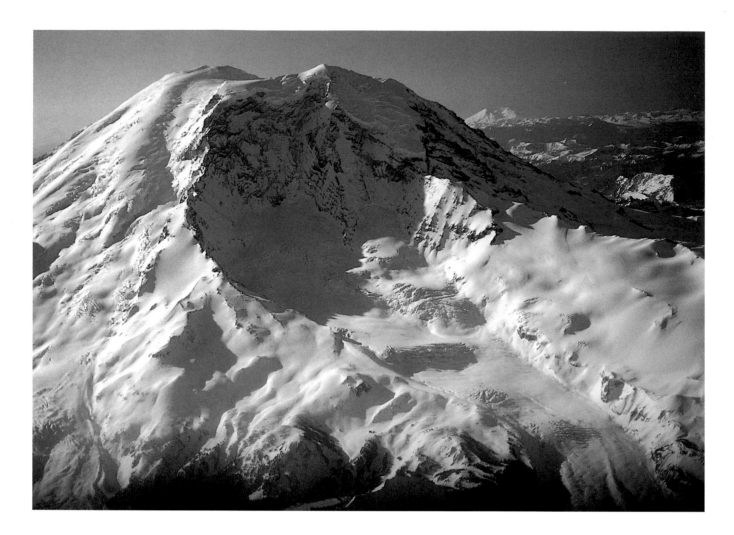

Mount Rainier's Liberty Cap: Sunset Amphitheater, a glacier-carved cirque in foreground. (Steve Yates)

Range. Reaching the lowlands, it gathers the southern valley's river and glacial meltwater rivers from the north. It meanders through the deep, mountainous valley that will later be the Strait of Juan de Fuca, emptying into the lowered ocean about four miles westward of the present-day Pacific coastline.

North of the Fraser, the sun is glinting off a truly stupendous cliff of glacial ice that fills the ancestral Georgia Strait. Yet this is just the southernmost finger of the Cordilleran Ice Sheet, flowing west of the even more immense Laurentide Ice Sheet now covering most of Canada.

Century by century this Puget Lobe has been grinding its way southward, fed by smaller valley glaciers from the the Coast Range to the east and Vancouver Island's Insular Mountains to the west.

Reaching the present international border, the lobe is joined by ice moving eastward along the Fraser River Valley. Ice fills the entire lowlands north of the San Juan Islands.

The ice sheet moves in fits and starts, some years advancing only a few feet forward or even retreating a bit, at other times surging forward several miles in a single year.

Although the climate is warming, the snow supply from the mountains to the north still outweighs the losses in the southern lowlands. More and more ice flows down from the highlands. The lowland ice sheet is pushed over every obstacle by pressure from above, just as the pressure head of an upland reservoir forces water to the top floor of a lowland building.

Opposite:
Looking down the glacier-carved valley of the Nisqually River from the toe of Mount Rainier's Nisqually Glacier. (Steve Yates)

Thousands of feet deep, the ice sheet has become independent of topography. It first flowed through gaps between the peaks that will later form the San Juan archipelago; now it simply smothers them.

The advancing ice sheet, stretching across the entire lowlands, from the Cascades almost out of sight to the Olympics, now dams the Puget Lowlands with a 60-mile-wide wall of ice. The river system draining the entire watershed below us now has no outlet to the sea.

South of the advancing ice sheet, an enormous "proglacial" lake begins to fill the lowlands below us. The lake's level rises higher and higher up into foothill valleys. Finally it finds a new outlet to the south. Overflowing through a gap in the Black Hills—the "Black Lake Spillway"—it drains out the Chehalis River Valley, flowing into the Pacific through what will be Gray's Harbor.

The advancing ice sheet piles up against the steep front of the Olympic Mountains, then splits into two lobes. The Juan de Fuca Lobe moves rapidly westward toward the sea. Joined by more ice from the

Above:
Green shows as red in this false-color infrared satellite image of Puget Sound and surrounding watershed. Developed areas appear bluish.

Taken in summer, the white areas represent permanent glaciers on Mount Rainier (lower right), the North Cascades (upper right), and the Olympic Mountains (left).

These mountains, along with mainland British Columbia's Coastal Range and the Insular Range on Vancouver Island, define an immense basin, with the Salish Sea at the bottom. (EROS Satellite Data Center)

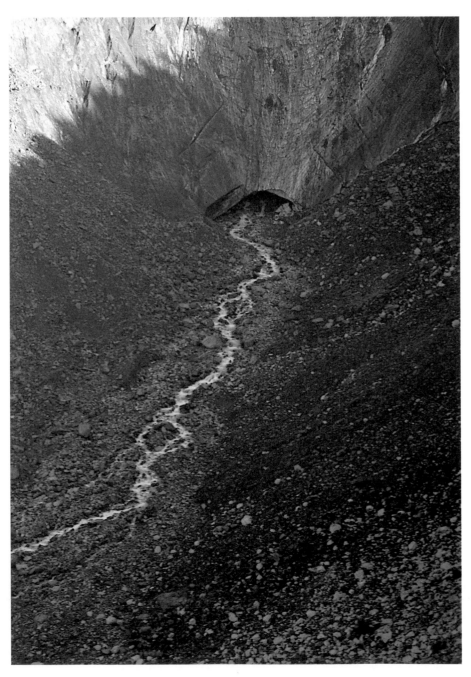

Like many other major rivers emptying into Puget Sound, the Nisqually begins as a small meltwater stream issuing from a glacier. (Steve Yates)

Insular Mountains, it overrides the southeastern end of Vancouver Island.

Ten minutes—one millennium—after we first glimpsed it, the Juan de Fuca Lobe has reached the Pacific Ocean. The ice caps now covering a third of the earth have tied up so much of the planet's water that sea level has been lowered 300 feet. The edge of the Pacific has retreated miles west of the present coastline. Extending onto the exposed continental shelf, the lobe now forms part of a huge tidewater glacier complex along the west coast of Vancouver Island.

As the earth continues to warm, sea level slowly rises. Huge iceburgs calve from the ice sheet into the relatively warm ocean. The rapid melting at the seaward toe of the Juan de Fuca Lobe draws ice westward from the Puget Lobe, grounded to the east.

But soon the Puget Lobe resumes its advance southward. It overrides the huge lake before it, pressing compact glacial "till" over its own outwash gravels, atop the thin layers of fine silt covering the bottom of the proglacial lake.

Along its edges, the glacier snaps off whole groves of forest trees like twigs with every surge; animals living in its path are pressed farther south. Beneath the ice, the landscape is reworked.

With rough boulders frozen into its base, the glacier acts as a giant, flexible sanding block, covered with paper that is much rougher in some places than in others. It presses down with more pressure in some places than others and rubs on rock surfaces of varying hardness. And, since its velocity is greater in some places than others, it stretches.

Like worn sandpaper clumsily used, the ice sheet smooths some surfaces but actually accentuates larger topographic irregularities. The deeper the pre-existing basin, in fact, the thicker and heavier the ice moving through it, exerting more erosive force and further deepening the valley. Large river valleys holding more ice are eroded relatively more than their tributary stream valleys. These are left hanging above the deeper trunk valley, creating spectacular waterfalls.

At the same time, eroded rock and mud are bulldozed up into high moraines on land or plastered onto "drumlins"—long hills lying parallel to the ice flow, such as those Seattle is built upon.

Before the arrival of the ice, rivers had been eroding the bedrock, undermining valley walls, and moving material downstream into the lowlands. Glacial ice now scours out the valley floors and rips away the loose rock from the valley walls.

Abrasive rock plucked from the valleys and embedded in the undersurface of the ice is only a fraction of the massive tonnage of rock carried on and within the ice sheet. Debris rains down from the valley walls against which the glacier is scraping. Rivers from the valleys above its surface carry down eroded material, which, piling against the side of the glacier, will remain as lateral moraines.

As valley glaciers merge together, the lateral moraines on the inner sides merge down the middle of the larger glacial flow, becoming a single "medial moraine." Large rocks fall directly onto the glacier's surface from the mountains above, and eventually all of this material is incorporated into the ice. The power of the glacier to carry huge "erratic" boulders far from their place of origin is amazing—one quartzite erratic carried from the Canadian Rockies and dropped onto the plains of Alberta weighs an estimated 18,000 tons.

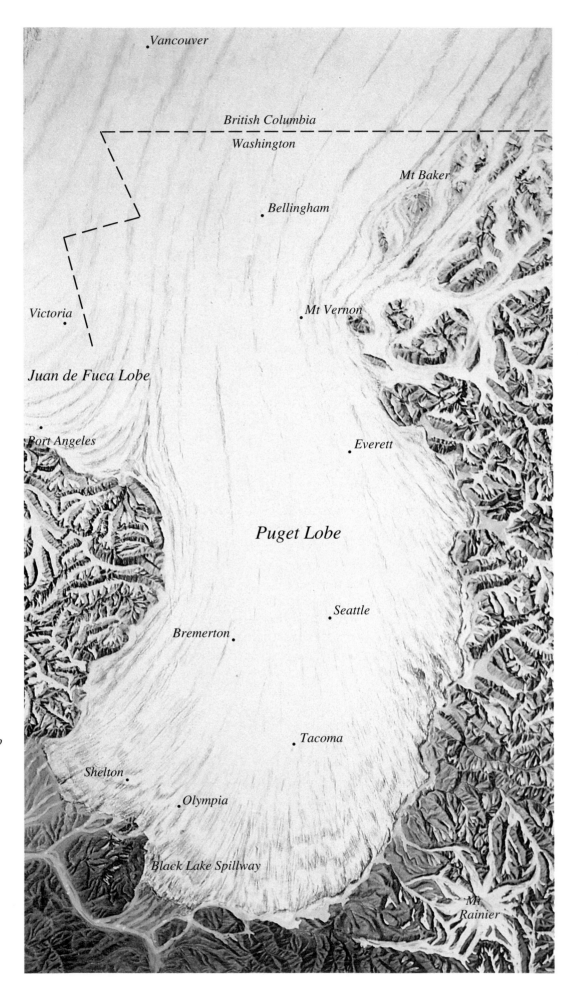

Vancouver

British Columbia

Washington

Mt Baker

Bellingham

Victoria

Mt Vernon

Juan de Fuca Lobe

Port Angeles

Everett

Puget Lobe

Seattle

Bremerton

At its maximum,
the Puget Lobe ice
sheet filled the entire
Puget/Fraser
Lowlands,
 more than a mile deep
near the present
international border.
At its southern
extremity west of
Mount Rainier (lower
right), its meltwater
and ice-margin rivers
emptied through the
Black Lake Spillway
into the ancestral
Chehalis River.
 (Map courtesy D.
Molenaar © 1987)

Tacoma

Shelton

Olympia

Black Lake Spillway

Mt
Rainier

By 15,000 BP, the Puget Lobe has reached the latitude of present-day Seattle and is still moving. Five centuries later, it covers the Tacoma area, 30 miles south.

Meanwhile, the Juan de Fuca Lobe has begun a rapid retreat eastward, as rising seawater moves into the Strait.

The Puget Lobe continues to advance southward for another five centuries or so before finally slowing to a halt against the Black Hills, directly west of our Mount Rainier vantage point.

The size of the ice sheet below is boggling. It forms an immense plateau of hummocky, faulted ice that covers the entire lowlands. Even at its toe, near present-day Shelton and Tenino, the ice rises 800 feet atop a bulldozed moraine of boulders and wasted ice. The future Olympia lies under 1,500 feet of dirty ice; Tacoma under 2,500 feet. At the northeast corner of the Olympics it piles 3,500 feet up the sides of Mount Constance, and where Seattle will stand it is just a few feet lower. Above present-day Vancouver the ice rises to almost 8,000 feet, far above the height of the East Coast's tallest mountains.

The weight of the Puget Lobe's ice south of Vancouver is estimated at 18 trillion tons—sufficient to stretch the earth's crust beneath it like a rubber sheet. At the eastern end of the Strait, the land sinks 400 feet; at the level of Seattle, more than 150 feet; near Tacoma, 75 feet.

The glacier is hardly static. Even as ice is lost by melting and evaporation at its toe, new ice is flowing down from the north to replace it. Sudden increases in the mountains move in bulges down the length of the glacier, like a piglet in a boa constrictor. Everything that happens to the north is amplified at the glacier's southern lobes.

Beneath the ice sheet, rock is being plucked and ground into glacial flour. Unsorted rocks, gravel, and silt—collectively called till—is plastered over the ground beneath. Or bulldozed forward by the moving ice front. Or swept forward by rivers flowing under the ice. Under tremendous pressure from the mile of ice above, wet basal till beneath the ice sheet is squeezed out in all directions.

The action is especially furious during the summer months. Rivers from melting valley glaciers above rush down against the sides of the ice sheet, depositing their gravel and sediments in deltas that may be left as "kame terraces" when the glacier withdraws. The rivers themselves, being warmer than the ice, soon melt their way under the ice. Rain and melting ice on the surface of the ice sheet also works through the ice. Together, they create a network of meltwater caverns and tunnels within the glacier.

Some of these sediment-laden streams reach the bottom of the ice to merge with basal rivers; others exit the ice in spectacular fountains, as from the comparable Malaspina Glacier at the base of Mount St. Elias in southeast Alaska. (Malaspina discharges some four cubic miles of water each year.) Huge terminal moraines of rock, sand, and silt are pushed, squeezed, and washed along the ice front. Everywhere there is gushing water, oozing mud, chunks of melting ice, avalanches of rock.

Around 13,500 BP, after a brief standstill of a few centuries, the glacier front begins to withdraw back north.

And now the amount of liberated water becomes even more stupendous. It rushes through the Black Lake spillway in the Black Hills and southward into the lower Chehalis River, at three times the volume of the present-day Columbia.

The ice sheet's retreat is even more dramatic than its advance; for the rise in temperature is rapid, and it wastes at a much faster rate than it formed. Thousands of cubic miles of ice that took 15 to 30 millennia to create, are destroyed in four. Its accumulated rock and soil drop in place, forming a thick layer of loose till over the compact till that was plastered under its advance.

Surrounded by its own warmer meltwater, the glacier calves icebergs around its margins. Some of these, stranded on higher ground and insulated by rocky debris, will survive for centuries after the main glacier is gone. Some ice-cored moraine deposits will not melt completely for thousands of years, leaving pothole lakes to dot the outwash plains. The disintegrating ice sheet's meltwater becomes a major force in reshaping the land.

Below us, sunlight sparkles on a series of proglacial lakes—long, narrow, ice-free basins now filled with meltwater. On the western side of the lowlands, Lake Skokomish covers lower Hood Canal and the Great Bend; it drains southeastward through Clifton Channel into the complex web of southern basins that geologists call "Lake Russell."

To the northeast, proglacial lakes occupy Sammamish and Snoqualmie valleys. These drain into Lake Puyallup at the glacier's southeast edge.

As the ice front retreats north of what is now Tacoma, Lake Puyallup in turn joins an enlarged Lake Russell which still drains south through Black Lake into the Chehalis Valley.

During the time that the Puget Lobe is retreating 50 miles north, the Juan de Fuca Lobe, calving into the advancing sea, has retreated 120 miles to the east, stalling only when it grounds on the Dallas Banks at the eastern end of the Strait of Juan de Fuca. The sea has penetrated far into the Strait and is now melting its way into Sequim and Discovery bays.

As the ice front of the Puget Lobe retreats farther north, Lake Russell and the separated lakes along the eastern lowland connect up into a single superlake called "Lake Bretz." As land northeast of the Olympics is exposed, Lake Bretz drains northward through a channel running from Hood Canal's Dabob Bay north to Discovery Bay on the now-open Strait.

As the glacier retreats, relieving the land of its enormous weight, the entire basin rebounds; eventually it will rise hundreds of feet. Large areas of the northern Kitsap Peninsula, the Quimper Peninsula, and the Seattle-area lowlands are finally exposed.

From atop Mount Rainier, Lake Bretz looks much like the present-day Puget Sound. But there are striking differences: The water level of the dammed lake is still more than a hundred feet above present sea level. The islands, especially at the northern end of the lake, are smaller, and they are surrounded by much wider channels. Present-day

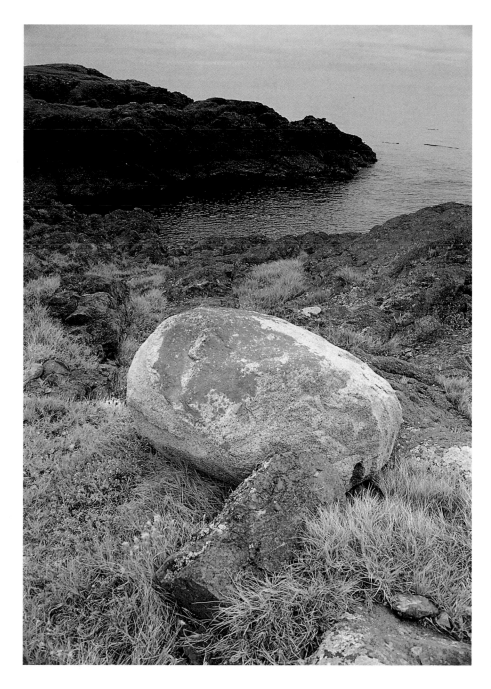

This "erratic" granite boulder on the shore of San Juan Island was transported from the mountains of British Columbia by the most recent Puget Lobe ice sheet. Much larger erratics can be found along Salish Sea shores. (Terry Domico/ Earth Images)

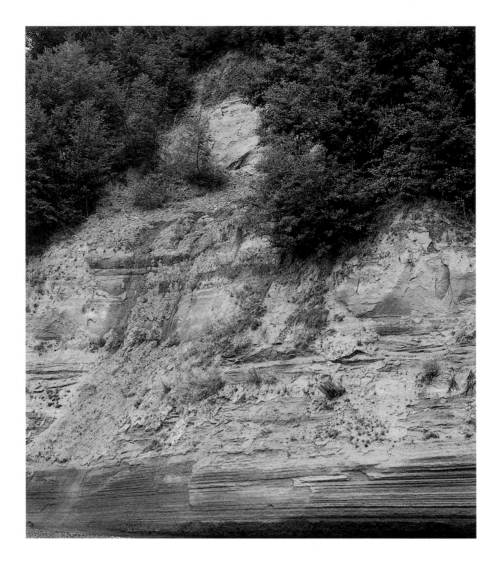

Beach cliffs at Seattle's Discovery Park clearly reveal the area's glacial history. Thin clay strata at the bottom were deposited in a proglacial lake. A thick layer of glacial till (mixed gravel, sand, and clay) was plastered over the clay by the advancing glacier. Atop these is loose till deposited by the retreating ice sheet. (Steve Yates)

Kitsap Peninsula is just a collection of islands dotting the lake, as are the long hills that will someday be central Seattle. The valley arms on the east coast, though, are larger than they will be in the future: Sediment-laden rivers rushing down from nearby mountains have not had the chance to build large rivermouth deltas out into lake's inlets.

The underwater topography (bathymetry), however, has been set. Deep basins—hundreds to nearly a thousand feet deep in places—are separated by shallow "sills," often located at the narrowest passes, such as Admiralty Inlet and The Narrows.

Since it is at the southern tip of the Cordilleran Ice Sheet, the Puget Lowland becomes the final resting place for millions of tons of rock, sand, and silt brought hundreds of miles south from British Columbia's mountains. The entire surface of the basin is covered by hundreds of feet of unsorted glacial till. Flooding rivers cut through the thick blankets of gravelly till dropped in place by the melting glacier, redistributing them over the vast outwash plains.

Though the ice sheet has only been in the Fraser/Puget Lowlands for a few thousand years, its influence has been far out of proportion to its duration, and its effects on the landscape are ten to twenty times as great as normal river erosion and deposition. In tandem with the basin's active rivers, the Puget Lobe has scoured out one of earth's most complex fjords.

Millennia later, its traces will continue to influence our lives—determining where forests grow, or open grasslands, or swampy wetlands; where we farm or build houses; where our roads will slump or hills slide; where septic tanks will or will not percolate; where our harbors will be located; and where the fish will run. The shallow sills left between deep sub-basins will slow the exchange of water between basins, greatly slowing the "flushing" of waterborne pollutants.

As the glacier retreats north of Admiralty Inlet, Lake Bretz rushes out into the strait with the force of a hundred Niagara Falls. The surface of the lake soon drops to sea level. Dense, salty seawater from the Strait sloshes over Admiralty Inlet's rocky sill and slides under Lake Bretz's lighter fresh water.

With every outgoing tide, fresh water flows out atop the inlet's surface. And with every incoming tide the rising sea forces its way further into the southernmost reaches of the doomed lake. The Pacific Ocean enters Puget Sound.

The ice cap does not vanish immediately. Instead, it tarries on Dallas Bank at the eastern end of the Strait of Juan de Fuca before retreating rapidly up the Fraser Valley. Then, a millennium later, it makes a quick counter-assault back down the broad valley to about the level of the present international border.

But its thrust is brief. By 10,000 years ago, the entire Strait of Georgia is free of ice. The three fjords are one.

The Salish Sea is born.

A Reunion of Whales

An Orca goes airborne as it breaches. (Ken Balcomb)

A dozen expectant faces scan the water as the cruise boat *Western Prince* pulls away from the Friday Harbor Marina. Maneuvering the 46-foot converted Coast Guarder around sharp corners between crowded piers, Captain Bob Van Leuven eases into the summer chaos of outboards, inflatables, yachts, and dinghies.

Along the main dock, gulls whirl and cry above returning sportfishing boats. Pleasure-boaters stow their gear and groceries before setting out for the afternoon, while a small group of kayakers, sweating in wetsuits, assemble boats and paddles. Massive purse seiners—masted power winches draped with corked nets, high-powered aluminum skiffs overhanging square sterns—rub shoulders with smaller gill-netters, their nets wound around large drums. Busy crews shout above the blare of boom-boxes, taking on supplies for tomorrow's Sockeye salmon opening.

Beneath the carved orca whales cavorting on the welcome sign above the ferry dock, the superferry *Elwha* disgorges its bellyful of pickup trucks and station wagons. Brightly colored, lycra-clad bicyclists lead a troop of foot passengers up the steep hill of the main street, past the shops, taverns, restaurants, and real estate office windows of the bustling tourist town.

Above the marina, the islands' oldest structure, a former Odd Fellows' Hall circa 1892, stands as lone survivor of times before scheduled ferries, when the San Juans depended more on fishing and farming than on summer visitors and wealthy retirees. The newly refurbished building houses the Friday Harbor Whale Museum.

The Whale Museum was created in the late 1970s from thin air and pure passion by whale researchers and 400 volunteers. "A view into the lives of the world's whales in glass, stone, wood and bone: art, science, and sound." (Where else can you read about whale biology sitting in an easy chair with your head in the ribcage of a Gray whale skeleton suspended from the ceiling—while killer whales, recorded just a few miles away, call around you?) Once considered quixotic, the Whale Museum is now the island's biggest tourist draw.

Heading out of the harbor, we pass the University of Washington's renowned Friday Harbor Marine Labs. In this string of small shoreline buildings students from all over the world pore over sea stars and jellyfishes and microscopic plankton gleaned from the fertile waters surrounding the island. Researchers analyze changes in tidepool communities after catastrophic winter storms or computer models of potential oil spills in Haro Strait. On the dock in front of the labs, a pair of scuba divers wash their salty gear.

Passing Brown Island on our right, we nose out into San Juan Channel. Across the channel, cumulus clouds float over the mountainous spine of Orcas Island and the snow-capped peak of Mount Baker seems to hover, dreamlike, over Lopez Island, though it actually rises from the mainland more than fifty miles to the east. We turn south, into the sun with the wind at our back. Binoculars, telephotos, and videocams prepare for action.

Officially, this Whale Museum-sponsored trip is billed as a wildlife rather than whale-watching cruise. For there is no assurance, even on a fine day like today during peak season, that we will spot such unpredictable creatures as whales. No matter. Seabirds and seals, an eagle or two, and the always spectacular scenery will do.

But there's no doubt about what we *want* to see. Despite the joy of spotting majestic Bald eagles, colorful Tufted puffins, or hauled-out Harbor seals, our lust is for cetaceans—porpoises and whales. And though we will be thrilled to spot a pod of swift, shy Harbor porpoises, catch sight of an elusive Minke whale, or have boisterous Dall's porpoises surf our bow wave, the Holy Grail of every local nature cruise is that certified cetacean superstar, the Michael Jordan of the whale world, *Orcinus orca*—the orca, or killer whale.

Largest of the dolphin family, orcas break the surface (called "porpoising") when traveling at full speed. (Kelley Balcomb-Bartok)

Orcas, largest members of the dolphin family, combine the speed and intelligence of smaller dolphins with the size and power of the great whales. To those of us drawn under their spell, they possess inspiring grace and beauty. Some orca-watchers consider them to have distinctive "personalities," and a unique form of language.

In any case, orcas have acquired a mystique that elevated them to the rank of totemic spirit among Northwest coast Indians; and to the pantheon of beings—wolves, eagles, loons, grizzly bears—that embody the spirit of the wild to outdoorspeople and environmentalists throughout the northern hemisphere.

Orcas, like wolves, travel and hunt in cooperative family groups called pods. Because they were known to attack much larger whales, orcas were originally called "whale killers," and later, killer whales. Like wolves and other successful predators, they were villainized by Europeans for their "bloodthirsty" behavior and were considered competitors by fishermen and whalers. Early Arctic explorers reported them so voracious as to slide up onto ice floes to attack sled dogs (probably mistaking them for baby seals). Only a few decades ago, orca pods were sometimes targeted by Navy fighter planes for practice or sport.

Our attitude toward these so-called killers has shifted remarkably since 1965, when "Namu," the first orca to be observed close-up, was accidently caught in a fishing net. Hauled back to Seattle, Namu was displayed in a waterfront pen to hoards of curious citizens, a tradition now flourishing in dozens of marine amusement parks from California to Florida.

The transformation of the orca's image from thug to culture hero is best voiced by Canadian neurophysiologist Paul Spong, who in 1967, at the Vancouver Aquarium, was one of the first to study orcas in captivity. Spong quickly reached the conclusion that orcas were intelligent and highly social beings. As such, they suffered sensory deprivation by being kept in tiny, concrete pools. He rejected captive studies as inhumane, and also felt that neurotic orcas would give only distorted results. Such research, especially in seaquariums, would become just a thin justification for exploiting the attractive, athletic whales as highly profitable entertainers.

But Spong has continued to observe orcas for the past two decades—in the wild—working out of his residence/lab on Johnstone Strait at the northern end of Vancouver Island. It was Spong who, in the early 1970s, convinced a small group of antinuclear activists in Vancouver called Greenpeace to become active in saving whales.

Spong describes the orca as "an incredibly powerful and capable creature, exquisitely self-controlled and aware of the world around it, a being possessed of a zest for life and a healthy sense of humor, and moreover, a remarkable fondness for and interest in humans."

This last point is not trivial. Orcas, their mouths full of sharp, conical teeth, are larger, smarter, faster—and thus potentially far more dangerous—than Great white sharks. Many pods routinely feed on seals and sea lions, which are about the size of a swimmer or scuba diver. Yet, despite centuries of harassment, no orca has been known to attack a person in the sea.

Orcas use high-frequency sonar to locate prey and avoid obstacles—an ability especially useful in murky water or at night. Sound is generated in the blowhole and focussed by the melon, an oil-filled cavity in the forehead controlled by surrounding muscles, like the lens of an eye. Scientists speculate that orcas and other dolphins can even use ultrasound imaging to "see into" other creatures, the way obstetricians examine expectant mothers.

Orcas also communicate among themselves with unearthly whoops that some people consider eerie, others ethereal. Not only are the sound patterns complex, but each tone is made up of a plethora of overtones; we have no way yet of knowing how much information may be encoded in the calls. "If human speech were likened to a clarinet," notes former Whale Museum Research Director Rich Osborne, "orca vocalization would be more like a full symphony orchestra."

Ever since orca "dialects" were first noted by Canadian researcher John Ford, cetologists have been tantalized by the possibility of cracking the orca's "speech" code and determining whether or not it qualifies as language.

But in order to understand what each call signifies, it needs to be linked to behavior and to responses from podmates. "We really need to be able to tell one individual voice from the other," Osborne cautions. "So far we're just eavesdropping on the party."

Unfortunately, since orcas and other dolphins produce sound from inside the blowhole instead of from vocal cords, there is no way to tell who's talking by reading lips. Osborne dreams of a battery of stationary underwater video cameras and hydrophones to link observed behavior to specific calls; and of supercomputers programmed to identify and analyze those vocalizations in "real time."

Overleaf:
Orcas "spyhop" to scan the surface. Though they use sonar to "see" in the dark, the well-camouflaged eyes are effective above and below the surface. (Kelley Balcomb-Bartok)

"The orca's large brain [four times as large as a human's, though not as densely wrinkled] is not just a reflection of its larger body," Paul Spong explains. "The section of the brain that drives the motor functions of the body is about the same size in most large mammals such as dogs, monkeys, humans, and whales. The extra mass of the orca's brain is made up almost entirely in the cerebral cortex, the section of the brain used for communications, thought, abstraction, creativity, and insight. And whales evolved these large brains thirty or forty million years before big-brained primates emerged on land."

To see in sound and speak in symphonies requires not only a large brain but one with a relatively much greater portion devoted to production and analysis of sound than in human brains.

Orcas may well be the most intelligent of non-human animals, though the demands on their brains and senses are so alien to the conditions faced by terrestrial wolves, elephants, or primates (including ourselves, the testers) that such contentions are pure speculation. Yet whatever else can be said about these "minds in the water," it certainly seems that dolphins are our counterparts in the sea, the brainiest creatures there as we are on land.

What first impresses the casual orca-watcher, however, is not its I.Q. but its awesome physical strength and grace. One can only imagine the power generated to launch an six-ton male or four-ton female airborne as it breaches (leaps out of the water) or cartwheels end over end.

From San Juan's South Beach I once saw an orca leap entirely out of the water and, while suspended in air, slap its tail flukes on the surface with an explosive splash that was visible and audible for miles. It was the most powerful single action I've ever witnessed from a living being.

Renowned whale artist Richard Ellis calls the charismatic orca "a supercetacean...It can do almost everything better and faster than other whales and dolphins, and it has a reputation of almost mythic proportions as the sea's supreme predator. It feeds on anything it can catch— and it can catch almost anything that swims." Few orca researchers ever become blasé about their subject: between the lines of even the most technical report lurks a cosmic WOW!

Of all its names in English—such as "killer whale," "blackfish," "grampus"—orca (derived from *Orcus*, a Roman god of the underworld) seems the most cosmopolitan and non-judgmental. But the name that best fits my own impressions comes from the Ainu people of northern Japan: *repun kamui*, "master of the inland sea."

Off Pear Point, not far south of Friday Harbor, the *Western Prince* slows to cautiously approach a half-exposed reef. Harbor seals haul out here at medium tides to bask in the sun like drift logs. Scanning the rock with binoculars, I can only spot one or two. But as we close in, my disappointment turns to amazement.

In the water on the far side of the rocks, a dozen seals are performing a frenzy of aquatic acrobatics. Some turn in twisting somersaults, singly or in pairs, whapping their rear flippers in resounding splashes. Others zip around in tight circles, like dogs chasing their tails. None of us has ever witnessed such a mad performance by the normally placid seals.

Delighted by the show, we crowd onto the bow deck as Bob maneuvers as close to the rocks as possible without disturbing the seals, while at the same time avoiding the danger zone of submerged reefs clearly marked by patches of Bull kelp. Not an easy task in the powerful tidal currents swirling around the rocks.

The seals seem not even to notice us as they chase and roll.

Only one adult seal and her new-born pup remain on the rocks. Then the mother slides in to join the frey. The anxious pup, evidently wanting no part in the furious action, surprises us by squirming frantically on its belly to the very top of the slippery rock, a good six feet above the water.

Harbor seals rarely venture that far from the water's edge, and they retreat quickly back into the water when disturbed. Seals (family Phocidae) and sea lions (family Otariidae) are members of the same marine mammal order (Pinnipedia, or "finfoots"). But unlike the agile sea lions (especially the female California sea lion, familiar as the trained circus performer capable of balancing a beach ball on her nose and applauding with her foreflippers), seals do not possess long front flippers and cannot pivot their rear flippers beneath them. Despite their grace in the water, on land seals can only hump along awkwardly on their bellies like huge, fat caterpillars, their stubby, nailed foreflippers used only for traction.

Harbor seals are far and away the most numerous of the four pinnipeds encountered in the inland waters. They are easily distinguished from the other species because Harbor seal males resemble the females, whereas males of the three other species may grow to three times the length of the six-foot-long females, and many times their bulk. Harbor seals are generally silent, except for the mewings and whimperings at crowded haul-out spots after the pups are born, whereas the huge sea lion bulls can be heard from miles away—the California sea lions by their loud, hoarse barking and Northern sea lions by their roars. Harbor seals and other "true seals" lack the rolled, pointed external ears (pinnae) that have given sea lions the name "eared seals."

Underwater, seals propel themselves forward with their cupped, elastic hindflippers, using their small foreflippers only to manuever. Sea lions, on the other hand, pull forward with their long foreflippers, using their hindflippers mostly to steer, and they undulate like porpoises when swimming near the surface.

In the water Harbor seals rest vertically, like mermaids, their large, brown eyes above water. When approached, they sink silently beneath the surface without a trace. Seals must haul-out onto land to warm up. Loafing sea lions, on the other hand, float horizontally and lift their long flippers out of the water like solar panels to catch the sun's rays.

Male California sea lions are much larger and more aggressive than Harbor seals. In summer they return south to breed on remote islands off southern California and Baja. There, the formidable bulls battle for favored beach territory and for the "harems" of females who return to these spots to give birth to their pups. Females remain along the California coast year-round, but in winter the far-ranging males spread out, migrating up the west coast as far as Vancouver Island to feed.

As their populations increase under the protection of the federal Marine Mammal Act of 1972, growing numbers of male California sea lions now overwinter in the Salish Sea. During the 1980s local populations grew at an annual rate of 30%. A few thousand now spend their winters here.

A Harbor seal perches precariously on an exposed rock. (Chris Huss)

Like Harbor seals, California sea lions normally feed on hake; but reduced hake populations coupled with easily caught concentrations of steelhead and salmon have turned them into pests. At Edmonds, north of Seattle, aggressive bulls have taken over scuba diving floats at the Underwater Park and often gather on the nearby ferry dock. The large wintering population is spreading. In February, 1992, two sea lions were even found feeding on Steelhead below a diversion dam 26 miles up the Nisqually River in southern Puget Sound.

Off Seattle, a growing group of persistent males—locally infamous under the generic name "Herschel"—feed on dwindling stocks of returning Sockeye salmon and Steelhead trout which gather in front of the Ballard Locks before passing through the Lake Washington Ship Canal into the lake and its feeder streams to breed. Despite experiments with steel nets, underwater noisemakers, and forced deportations, the sea lions have thrwarted all attempts to dislodge them from the area.

Northern (Steller) sea lions—less common and far less visible than their California cousins—breed north of here but also winter in the Salish Sea. Preferring areas of strong currents, they are most apt to be seen along Race Rocks at the southern tip of Vancouver Island or among the Gulf Islands, often in the company of California sea lions. Northern sea lions can be distinguished by their tawny lionlike manes, lionlike roars, and a low forehead crest that is much less prominent than the California's characteristic peak.

Unlike the flourishing Californians, Northern sea lion populations throughout the North Pacific have declined by an estimated 90% over the past three decades—evidently due in part to overfishing of their prey by trawlers. The federal Marine Mammal Commission has supported listing them as Endangered rather than their present Threatened status.

A second seal species is much less apt to be spotted here, though I have seen solitary individuals here and there. The Northern elephant seal, named for the grotesque elephantine snouts sported by the mature males, are much larger than Harbor seals: Bull elephant seals may grow to 20 feet long and weigh 5,000 pounds. Like California sea lions, elephant seals breed in summer along California and Baja California, where populations are rebounding after being hunted to near extinction at the end of the past century. There the huge bulls fight for control of beach areas favored by the pupping females.

Both sexes disperse over the North Pacific after breeding. Some occasionally wander into Puget Sound; I've spotted solitary males in the southern reaches of the Sound, floating upright near the surface like oversized Harbor seals. Elephant seals, which feed on a variety of fishes and squid, are capable of extraordinary dives. Elsewhere, they have been recorded to depths of 2,000 feet, more than enough to reach every nook and cranny of the Salish Sea.

Unlike Elephant seals and the sea lions, the Harbor seals we are watching from the deck of the *Western Prince* do not migrate and were probably born and raised near this very spot. Also unlike their larger cousins who breed on land, Harbor seals court and mate in the water, about now, in mid to late summer—soon after the pups are weaned. So the splashy action we are witnessing is probably connected to rivalries among the males, which are often seen in groups before mating season, whomping their rear flippers on the water in macho displays.

These male California sea lions, with their characteristic high peaked foreheads, are common in winter. Sea lions can be told from seals by their long foreflippers and thin, rolled external ears (pinnae). In the water, they often busk at the surface, their flippers lifted above the waves to catch the sun's rays. (Neil G. McDaniel)

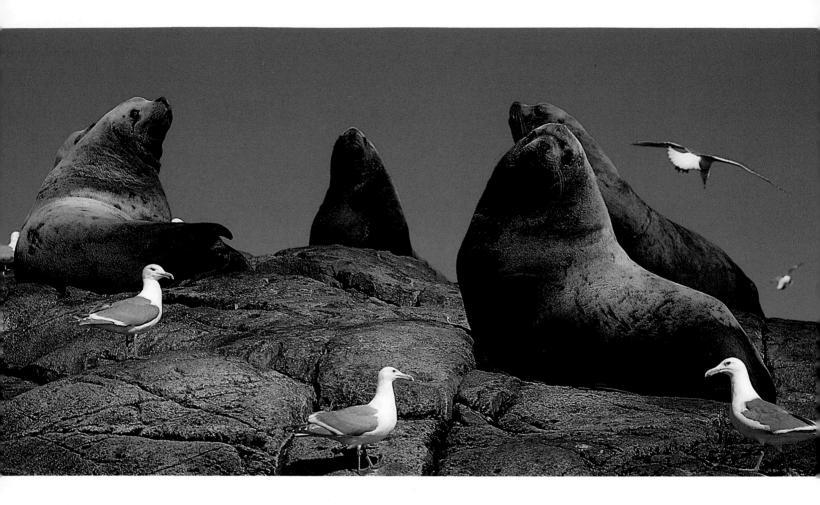

Northern (Steller's) sea lions are common on Race Rocks in the Strait of Juan de Fuca off Vancouver Island. The huge bulls can be told by their tawny manes and roaring calls—unlike the hoarse barking of their California kin. (Neil G. McDaniel)

But why such a frenzied orgy? Perhaps a school of fish have blundered past the rock, drawing the hauled-out seals into the water, stimulating a round of rivalry and courtship. Why? We really don't know. Mysteries riddle our limited understanding of even the most familiar marine animals.

Harbor seals, for instance, were once thought to feed voraciously on salmon. Prodded by fishermen, Washington State paid a bounty on their hides—almost 20,000 were killed between 1947 and 1960. Then, confounding the common wisdom, scientific studies in the 1960s showed that the seals eat mostly hake, eelpouts, and other non-gourmet fishes. Federal protection has given them a great deal more security, though commercial salmon fishermen are still allowed to shoot seals interfering with their nets; and some shoot rather freely.

Harbor seals are just one among hundreds of species of marine wildlife living within sight of our port cities and shoreline homes. Many are secretive or live in deep water, but seals, sea lions, and marine birds are familiar year-round residents. For the persistent wildlife spectator, few days on the Salish Sea are uneventful. And occasionally there are spectacular displays such as this.

Dropping my role as naturalist/interpreter, I go out on deck to enjoy the show, joining the cheers as two seals execute a high-speed roll just off the bow.

Right in the midst of this delightful chaos, comes a call over the marine radio—a cryptically coded message from Captain Terry of the *Rosario Princess* on a Greenpeace-sponsored cruise out of Anacortes. "Terry says he's got 'friends' out past Salmon Bank," Bob mentions with a huge grin. "Maybe the whole crew!"

This, if it pans out, is far more than we could have hoped for.

I mention over the microphone—as casually as possible to avoid possible disappointment—that we have word of an orca sighting out in the Strait of Juan de Fuca and will be leaving soon. Cameras click like sonar as we pull away from the frenetic seals.

Gulls scatter before us, murres and auklets dive to safety as the *Western Prince* steams south down the San Juan Channel. Bonaparte's gulls, some still in their black breeding hood, buzz and fret to either side. A migrant flock of tiny Red-necked phalaropes skitter on the surface, pausing briefly on an annual journey of thousands of miles.

Off our west beam, gnarly madrona trees shine reddish copper along the landward edge of San Juan's shore. Tall gray snags rise from the green forest of hemlock and Douglas-fir; atop one balances a huge, untidy eagle's nest, presently unoccupied.

Our progress is slowed considerably, however, by the incoming flood tide. The suck and glut of tides surging through the narrow channels between these rugged islands cause strong tidal rips. During 15-foot tides like today's, the water resembles a cauldron stirrred by a coven of witches.

Though there is now little wind to stir the water below us, the surface rages. Small whitecaps break against the boat's bow. Broad, circular patches of smooth water are actually the deceptively calm surface of upwellings rising from the depths like massive underwater fountains. Whirlpools dancing along their edges merely swing our oceangoing boat one way then the other; a smaller craft would be turned wildly about, as many a kayaker will discover this afternoon.

Such upwellings and currents stir the sea's planktonic broth, recycling nutrients and bringing single-celled plants called phytoplankton back to the sunlit surface. The rich vegetable soup sustains the billions of minute zooplankton on which schools of silvery fishes feed. These herring and sand lance, in turn, attract the sea's more visible creatures— seals, seabirds, and salmon. Which attract fishing boats. And orcas. And whale watchers like us.

San Juan's shoreline follows the arc of Griffin Bay, curving southwestward, its neck narrowing into the dry fields of American Camp National Historic Park, and finally hooks to the island's southern tip at Cattle Point. Across the channel, the glacial cliffs of Lopez Island diminish southward into a cluster of rock islets across from Goose Island, just off Cattle Point. Beyond the fierce tidal currents at the narrow entrance to the channel lies the eastern end of the Strait of Juan de Fuca.

And—if we can get there in time—the fickle and highly mobile whales.

Pods of Orcas patrol the edges of the entire world ocean. Yet only at the poles are there denser populations, and nowhere are they more accessible to humans than in these waters. About 200 individuals live around the northern tip of Vancouver Island plying Johnstone Strait and the maze of inlets and channels among the cluster of large islands separating Johnstone from Georgia Strait. This "northern resident community" is divided into 16 separate pods, which researchers refer to by letters: from A-Pod to I-Pod, plus R-Pod and W-Pod (though the unwieldy system, originating when little was known about populations or communities, is now being modified).

Another 80 or so orcas inhabit the Salish Sea around the southern end of Vancouver Island. This "southern resident community" is split into three pods: J, K, and L.

J-, K-, and L-pods, like the dozens of purse-seine and gillnet fishing boats that congregate off San Juan's coast during the brief openings of salmon season, are most visible June to September. Both orcas and fishermen are drawn here by Pacific salmon passing through from the ocean to spawn in mainland rivers and streams. Especially alluring are the 10–20 million Sockeye salmon which must run the gauntlet of the San Juan and Gulf Islands on their way back to the Fraser River's tributaries, lakes, and hatcheries.

J-Pod evidently remains in the inland waters through the slack winter months, sustained by rockfishes, resident Coho salmon, and juvenile "blackmouth" Chinook salmon. K- and L-pods range more widely, though little is known of their exact winter movements. L-Pod evidently spends much of the winter foraging along the stormy outer Pacific coasts of Vancouver Island and the Olympic Peninsula.

During the summer, J- and K-pods pass back and forth along the border, through Haro Strait, Boundary Pass, and across southern Georgia Strait to and from the Fraser. They also make periodic forays south into Puget Sound. L-pod spends less time in the island waters; perhaps the food required by its greater population drives it to cover a broader territory.

From June to September, J- and K-pods can be found with some regularity along the west coast of San Juan Island, which lies in the center of their normal hunting route. Growing pods of whale watchers and cetacean researchers follow in their wake.

The frequency of whale sightings along San Juan Island make it a Mecca to researchers and home to three prominent centers of marine mammal research: the Center for Whale Research on San Juan's west coast; the Friday Harbor Whale Museum; and the University of Washington's Friday Harbor Marine Lab, which specializes in marine invertebrates but is utilized by cetacean researchers from as far away as Massachusetts and Britain.

Orcas travel continuously, day and night, though they pause briefly wherever they find a school of fish and slow at irregular intervals to rest in tight formation (scientists speculate that only one half of the brain sleeps at a time), moving just fast enough to neutralize the current.

Traveling, they can easily cover 100 miles in 24 hours, and though J- and K-pods maintain rather regular routes past San Juan Island in summer, the timing of their passage is unpredictable. For days at a time they may remain around the mouth of the Fraser or go south into inner Puget Sound; or simply disappear to parts unknown. To intersect with a moving pod is a gamble at best.

Last week, though, we really lucked out.

At the start of the trip no orcas had been reported in the area during the previous three days. On a hunch we headed north up San Juan Channel, toward Boundary Pass, the wide northeast-southwest trending channel that separates the U.S. San Juans from the Canadian Gulf Islands, hoping that one of the pods might be returning from the Fraser.

Entering the pass, we first spotted a pod of Harbor porpoises (the porpoise family resemble dolphins but their teeth are flattened and spade-shaped rather than conical and pointed; none are as large as orcas). Harbor porpoises are one of the smallest cetaceans. Rolling smoothly at the surface while dining on schools of herring or squid, the sleek, black, five-foot-long Harbor porpoises resemble rotating inner tubes (albeit with triangular fins).

We cut the engines, but they vanished in their usual shy way.

Once common from the western end of the Strait of Juan de Fuca to the southern tip of Puget Sound, Harbor porpoises are now uncommon throughout the inland waters, and are especially rare south of Seattle.

Researchers suspect that Harbor porpoises have declined in part because the fine nylon webbing of modern fishing nets is invisible in the murky water. The porpoise's ultra high-pitched sonar seems poor at discerning it before the speedy cetacean becomes entangled and drowns.

Soon after the Harbor porpoises vanished, we spotted a group of their slightly larger cousins, the Dall's porpoise. Even at a distance Dall's porpoise can be told from the Harbor porpoise by the peculiar way it moves near the surface while feeding. After surfacing for breath, the Dall's dorsal profile shows a ninety-degree bend as it snaps its tail before rolling into a dive. Local Indians called them "broken-backs" or "broken-tails." Predominantly black, a Dall's porpoise can also be identified by whitish trim on dorsal fin and flukes, and, closer up, by the bright white patch covering its lower belly and part of its flanks.

(Like the coastal Harbor porpoise, the more pelagic Dall's is threatened by nets. Tens of thousands drown in deep-sea drift nets, which may be 40 miles long and hang 40 feet down from the surface, forming indiscriminant "curtains of death" throughout the Pacific Ocean. The nets are set at night and left for days at a time, ostensibly for squid but sometimes with a large "incidental" catch of salmon. Some of these huge nets drift away in storms or heavy seas and are never recovered. Such "ghost nets" continue to catch fish, seabirds, sea turtles, and marine mammals until they sink by the accumulated weight of the corpses. Japan and Taiwan have recently agreed to stop using them but enforcement is problematic.)

Speedy Dall's porpoises delight in surfing the bow wave generated by a fast boat. (Chris Huss

An Opalescent squid can change colors with amazing rapidity. Vast schools of this quick mollusk return to the inland waters in late fall to breed in winter. It feeds on shrimps and small fishes and is a favorite of porpoises. (David Denning/Earth Images)

Normally, the six- to seven-foot-long speedsters would have darted over to us at 30 knots, sending up a characteristic "rooster tail" of spray behind them. Zipping ahead of the boat, they ride the invisible underwater wave our bow pushes before it. They puff noisily at the surface as they grab quick breaths, their plump bodies totally visible just below the surface, almost close enough to touch.

Because of their high spirits and the intimacy of such close contact, porpoise-surfing is a spectator sport that rivals orca-watching. But this time the porpoises seemed uninterested in joining us, even when we passed them repeatedly.

Then we realized why. One of the sleek creatures appeared to be no more than three feet long: a recent addition to the pod. Aware that the youngster would be unable to keep up with the high-speed sport, the adults stuck doggedly to their feeding. Like a human couple with a new baby, small sacrifices had been made. We motored on.

The afternoon was passing fast. As a last resort, we cut the engines and lowered a hydrophone—an underwater microphone connected by cables to an amplifier and the boats speakers—into the water just in case we might pick up any of the metallic whoops and hollers with which orcas communicate. Nothing.

But just as we were about to turn back we spotted a tall fin against the cliffs of Saturna Island on the Canadian side of the pass.

Some of the orcas were moving away from us along the shore. But over near Java Islets, another subgroup of eight or nine had corralled a school of fish and were furiously pursuing them. Occasionally one of the orcas would lift its broad flukes from the water and slap it on the surface with the resounding retort of an artillery explosion. Called "lob-tailing," the percussive action is used to drive fish out from their hiding places among the rocks or kelp; it may also serve to stun the fish. At close range, an orca may even be able to stun fish with loud bursts of sonar.

Here was an opportunity I had been waiting for all season. Normally when we encounter orcas they are traveling purposefully between feeding areas or resting quietly, clumped together on the surface. At rest they are silent; and when they are traveling, our engine noise as we follow makes use of the hydrophone impossible. This time we could cut the engines and watch in awed silence as the orcas circled in a broad oval in front of the rocks. We lowered the hydrophone and turned on the amplifier.

It sounded just like the taped symphony of orca voices we had played earlier through the boat's loudspeakers. But now the click-bursts of sonar and high-pitched whoops were live, and we could see before us the furious action that accompanied the sounds. The orcas' unearthly wails and weird metallic glissandos always touch a chord in me; and watching them hunt is awesome even in silence. But this combination of action and sound was truly thrilling. None of the passengers had seen an orca in the wild before, yet everyone was aware that we were experiencing something special. We spent a half-hour with the orcas and left well satisfied.

Transformed by the recent radio message, the *Western Prince* has assumed the intensity of a medieval Quest. Passengers jabber excit-edly on deck, while in the wheelhouse, tension builds. Bob is intent on getting the most speed possible out of the deep-hulled boat and attends every irritating squawk on the ship-band radio, hoping for more informa-tion. Jean Van Leuven, Bob's wife and first mate, scans the sea and fidgets, while I play a tape of orca calls and give a short talk over the microphone about their lives and recent vicissitudes.

J- and K-pods now have about 15 members each. L-Pod—which seems to be in the process of splitting into three separate pods—has almost 50. Populations fluctuate slightly with births and deaths but have remained remarkably stable.

Like humans, female orcas do not mature until at least 13 years of age, and though they may live to a hundred, they evidently stop bearing in middle age. On average, only one in ten females gives birth each year. Orca fertility rates appear to be the lowest of all marine mammals.

This population stability keeps orcas from over-eating their dwindling food supply. But it has slowed the rebound of local pods after a recent crisis—the removal or deaths of one third of their population during chases and captures sponsored by San Diego-based Sea World in the late 1960s and early 1970s.

Ironically, a successful capture effort in the spring of 1976 led to the salvation of local pods. Unfortunately for the whale collectors, who had been chasing orcas up and down Puget Sound for ten years, the capture scene—complete with buzzing aircraft and exploding depth charges—was played out within sight and sound of the state Capitol in Olympia. By a further coincidence, the First International Orca Symposium was being held on adjacent Eld Inlet at The Evergreen State College. Prodded by irate researchers and whale lovers, and a barrage of high-profile national public-ity, the governor's office—led by Secretary of State Ralph Munroe—issued a strong call for the whale's release.

Sea World backed off as graciously as could be expected, promising to release the captured orcas, even the two it had hauled off to the old Seattle Marine Aquarium. More importantly, they would refrain from further captures in Washington waters. (Sea World and other marine amusement parks turned to Icelandic and Norwegian waters for captive performers; more recently they received a controversial federal permit to take ten orcas from Alaskan waters "for educational purposes," but this was later withdrawn after strong opposition by Greenpeace and the Sierra Club.)

Puget Sound's pods would no longer be constantly chased—nor removed or accidently killed during capture, as were more than 50 of their podmates over the previous decade. No more local orcas would experience the brief career that is the usual fate of amusement park whales. (Caught as adolescents with a normal additional life expectancy of 35 to 85 years, most captive orcas die within a few years—often quickly replaced by another one given the same name.)

Despite their size and relative visibility, orcas spend 95% of their lives underwater, coming to the surface only briefly to breathe. So counting them in the wild is about as easy as counting a flock of chickadees in a dark wood. According to Rich Osborne, Sea World capture vessels once thought they had captured 200 orcas in their nets off Whidbey island. Later, after their release and a year of censusing, it turned out there were only 71 in the entire area.

How, then, do we now know the exact number and relationship of every individual orca in the Salish Sea?

"Easy," says Ken Balcomb, co-founder of the Whale Museum and now director of the Center for Whale Research, which he also founded. "Just go out and take their pictures."

In 1976 Balcomb and fellow free-lance cetologists Camille Goebel and Rick Chandler expanded a field study, begun a few years earlier by Canadian researcher Michael Bigg, into the annual Orca Survey. Balcomb and a small staff are joined by groups of Earthwatch volunteers, drawn from all over the world. Using techniques developed by Bigg, Orca Survey participants, working from the deck of the Center's trimaran *High Spirits*, have accumulated and catalogued thousands of black-and-white photos: the side views of the dorsal fin and "saddle patch" of every orca spotted in the inland waters.

By noting peculiarities of fin size, shape, nicks and scars, and the shape of the gray saddle patch behind the dorsal fin, researchers can now refer to each local orca by pod letter, number, and name. (The Whale Museum's *A Guide to Marine Mammals of Greater Puget Sound* includes drawings of dorsal fins and saddle patches and a short biography of each resident orca.) Photographing the whales over time allows Whale Center researchers to tell when a calf appears in a pod and to which mother; which adolescent male is reaching sexual maturity (his dorsal fin begins to grow straight and to a height of six feet); and which individuals tend to swim together in stable subgroups.

Individual orcas evidently remain in the pod of their birth throughout their lives. The enduring "matrilocal" structure of resident pods—from which the males do not emigrate—has not been documented in other large mammals and may be unique to orcas. The pods appear to be led not by males, which are much the larger, but by mature females, which live much longer. What we mean by "lead," however, is not clear. Perhaps individual "personalities" and complex dominance hierarchies ("pecking orders") are more important than age or sex. How these dominance hierarchies affect feeding and breeding is unknown.

It is only in the past decade that researchers have begun to sort out the social complexities of orca pods. There is no accurate way to tell the paternity or lineage of individual orcas because no one has yet taken blood or flesh samples from local pods for genetic analysis. ("Darting" to obtaining small flesh samples for analysis has been proposed; but though a relatively benign technique, it is highly controversial because of its intrusive nature and the precedent it may set, and, so far, has not been permitted.)

After a nursing period of at least two years, during which the mother and calf are inseparable, the rearing of young orcas appears to become cooperative. Female relatives help the mother, and often the juveniles form temporary subgroups with these "aunties" rather than with their mothers. Occasionally, a juvenile male, such as J-Pod's "Ralph," has been known to take on the role of "babysitter" for extended periods. Older juveniles, like human teenagers, become progressively less attached to relatives and form close-knit subgroups among themselves.

Orca communication— though it may or may not be true language— has evolved into separate "dialects."

Rich Osborne offers a rough analogy with American English: The three southern resident pods speak regional dialects, differing about as much as Appalachian speech differs from inner city New Yorkese or California surfer slang. The northern community pods, however, speak not just dialects but separate, related languages: say, German, Swedish, and Dutch.

"Transient" pods—which are based in the same region but roam freely at much greater distances up and down the Pacific coast—use calls as dissimilar from the residents' as English is from Greek or Chinese. Transients presumably cannot communicate with local orcas. These differences in vocalization patterns reinforce the researchers' belief that the three southern resident pods are closely related, but are clearly distinct from the 16 northern resident pods. The transients seem to have been separate, genetically, from the residents for a long time.

A couple weeks ago we responded to an unexpected orca sighting, this one from Limekiln Lighthouse on San Juan's west coast. There the rocky coastline quickly drops off 900 feet as a sheer underwater cliff. The full force of incoming tides drives migrating salmon against the seawall, making it a great place for cetaceans to hunt. And since orcas and porpoises can swim right up to the rocks, it is one of the best spots on earth to observe them from land. The stone lighthouse, built by the Coast Guard in 1919, is now leased by the Whale Museum as laboratory and listening post. In 1983 the nearby coastline was purchased by the state and dedicated as Whale Watching Park.

We caught up with the orcas near the lighthouse. But instead of moving along the shoreline as we had expected, they were swimming westward across Haro Strait toward Victoria on Vancouver Island. The pod kept shifting course, making it difficult for us to run parallel to them. Though we searched through ID photos, we could not identify the half dozen individuals.

We followed the orcas to a group of islets off the southeast tip of Vancouver Island's Saanich Peninsula just a few miles east of Victoria.

There we had to draw back as the whales swam right up to the jagged rocks and nosed through the narrowest of channels.

Suddenly, two Harbor seals flew out of the water onto the rocks as a tall black fin swept ominously past.

A smaller black fin surfaced in front of the seals and circled like a shark's. Perhaps the orca had trapped a seal pup that was too slow, or naive, though we saw no blood or other signs of prey. As the pod passed on, the seals on the rock seemed to have even larger eyes than usual, and all eyes, including ours, were glued on the fins of the foraging whales.

Clearly, these orcas were transients. Composed of 100 or so individuals, which may be members of a loosely organized "superpod," transients travel in small, shifting pods that roam the Pacific coast from Alaska to California. Unlike the fish-eating resident pods, which rarely interact with other marine mammals, transient orcas feed largely on seals and sea lions. Some of them regularly penetrate Puget Sound to the southern end of Hood Canal in summer, when the large colony of Harbor seals near the mouth of the Skokomish River are pupping.

The transient orcas move through these waters in relative silence, either in deference to the resident pods or in order not to alert their pinniped prey. If the former is the case, it does not necessarily imply hostility between the groups—no aggressive acts have been noted even when transients have been seen to pass near resident pods. If the latter is true, it does imply that seals and sea lions may be able to recognize the marked difference in dialect between the benign residents and the threatening visitors.

The whales we were watching near Victoria that day turned out to be the same combination of transient pods Q- and Y- that had been seen a year earlier by Robin Baird and Pam Stacey of Victoria-based Marine Mammal Research Group. As the whales foraged among the rocky islets near shore, report Baird and Stacey, "an adult male was sighted surfacing with a dead, freshly killed Harbor seal in its mouth." Moments later "a seabird was flung approximately 20 feet into the air by a tail lob and was not seen again after hitting the surface."

A few months after that incident, Michael Bigg and Graeme Ellis of the Pacific Biological Station at Nanaimo on Vancouver Island watched a group of transient orcas unsuccessfully ram a Northern sea lion. The massive male "the size of a large black bear with the strength and teeth to match" managed to swim to safety—but just barely. *Killer Whales: A Study of their Identification, Genealogy, and Natural History in British Columbia and Washington State* by Bigg, Ellis, Ken Balcomb, and John Ford also includes a dramatic photo of a Northern sea lion being attacked by a group of transients.

Not surprisingly, much less is known about transient orcas than about the resident pods. They seem not to interbreed with the residents, as indicated by marked dissimilarities in their call patterns and by minor but discernible differences in the shape of the males' dorsal fins. Some researchers even consider the two groups to be separate races, or subspecies.

Individual transients photographed in southern California also have been spotted in Hawaiian waters, proving that they can navigate across half the Pacific Ocean. My own introduction to orcas, in fact, came in Hawaii many years ago, while on a boat sailing between the islands of Oahu and Maui.

Out of nowhere, a lone male suddenly appeared off the starboard beam. His entire body was visible in the clear tropical water; his tall dorsal fin cut the air like a sail. Our boat, running with the wind at a full ten knots, measured 65-feet-long, twice his length; yet our presence diverted his course not a bit. He closed on a collision course. At a hundred feet away, he slowed briefly to regard us. Then, with a few majestic flicks of his flukes, he shot across our bow toward the islands. He gave the impression of having just crossed the ocean, and was easily the most impressive animal I had ever seen.

Today, the half-hour trip down San Juan Channel seems endless. But finally we draw even with Goose Island at the channel's southern end. The dark rock of the small Nature Conservancy-owned island, whitewashed by bird droppings and a drifting snow of downy feathers, is an important seal haul-out and seabird nesting area. Though the nesting season is over, a few juvenile Glaucous-winged gulls still beg from their parents, while crowds of Double-crested cormorants, their nest sites long since abandoned, stand around the shoreline rocks, stretching out their wings to dry. A few sunning Harbor seals, acting more in character than the previous group, open a sleepy eye or slide into the water to float upright, their dog-faced heads above water. We can almost see ourselves reflected in the seals' large, soulful eyes as we pass from the channel.

To our boundless delight, the Strait of Juan de Fuca is gloriously calm. The sky is almost cloudless, and though there is a light haze over the water, the visibility is fine. Rounding Cattle Point, we can see Victoria, British Columbia's picturesque capital, a dozen miles to the west at the southeast tip of Vancouver Island. Far to the southeast we can make out the low profile of the northern end of Whidbey Island; and next to it, Admiralty Inlet, entrance to the complex web of passages and inlets comprising inner Puget Sound.

Bordering the southern edge of the strait the jagged, snowcapped ridgeline of the Olympic Mountains fades out into the light haze blowing in from the west. And beyond the horizon, lost in mist, the vast Pacific Ocean.

We are at the very center of the Salish Sea, and the view alone is worth the effort to get here.

As we pass over shallow Salmon Bank, just south of Cattle Point, a young woman with binoculars runs up to report sighting a fin about a hundred yards off to the left.

"Fin at nine o'clock," I announce as everyone crowds to the port rail. We slow slightly, though nothing is seen. Then, as another shout goes up, I spot a quick glimpse of dark brown fin. "Minke whale at seven o'clock!" Only the long arc of the dark back, with its small, curved, dolphinlike dorsal fin is visible as the whale breaks the surface to exhale a cloud of moist breath and quickly gulp another lungful of air.

Though the top of its long, pointed head is often seen as a Minke (pronounced "minky") rises to breathe, it rarely breaches. The few times this summer that one has leapt partly out of the water in view of the boat I seem always to be looking elsewhere. This time the whale arches its back slightly and "sounds" (dives deep). Even so, its flukes do not break the surface.

A Minke usually will surface two to five times in quick succession, then dive deeper for three to ten minutes. Since its course underwater bears no relation to the direction of its dive, where and when it will rise again is anybody's guess.

At 25–30 feet long, the Minke is the smallest of the rorqual family of baleen whales. Rorquals include Blue and Fin whales as well as the Humpback. Aside from the strange-looking Humpback, the other five rorquals are similar in shape but differ greatly in size, from the orca-length Minke up to the hundred-foot Blue whale—the largest creature ever to exist on earth.

In place of teeth, baleen whales have sheets of tough, fringed cartilage, called baleen. Rorquals also have a grooved, pleated throat that is capable of enormous expansion. When a Minke comes up under a dense school of herring or sand lance, its throat swells like a balloon to engulf huge drafts of water and hundreds of fish. It then sieves the water out between the baleen fringes and swallows the fish.

Until recently, the solitary, elusive Minke was disdained by whaling fleets. But overhunting has driven most of the larger species toward extinction; the Minke has now become the most heavily hunted of all whales. Some 10,000 have been killed each year during the 1970s and 1980s by the combined whaling fleets of Japan, Norway, Iceland, and the USSR. Although the International Whaling Commission called for an end to whaling, Japan, Iceland, Norway, and South Korea continued to hunt thousands of Minke and sperm whales under the guise of "scientific studies," and are presently threatening to resume full-scale commercial harvesting.

In a more genuine spirit of scientific inquiry, Eleanor Dorsey of the Long Term Research Institute in Massachusetts found that individual

A Minke whale, smallest of the rorqual family that includes the similar-shaped but much larger Blue whale, searches for herring and other schooling fishes. (Andy Dalton/Earth Images)

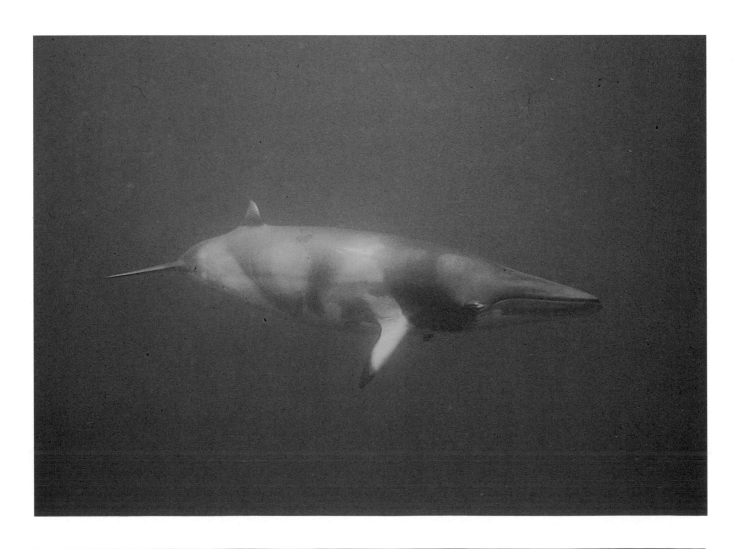

Minkes can be recognized by a combination of dorsal fin shape and small body scars. Following the Orca Survey's lead, she and graduate students Rus Hoelzel and Jon Sterns began a photo identification study of local populations. Since 1982 nearly 30 individual Minke whales have been recorded hereabouts, though no more than 18 have been sighted in any given year. Some return each year to feed over the shallow banks around the San Juans and Strait of Juan de Fuca. Populations peak in summer and fall. No one knows where migrants and summer visitors go during the winter.

A few hundred yards away, a frenzied mob of gulls and seabirds are diving on a school of herring. The Minke suddenly rises up from beneath the herring "ball" as birds scatter in all directions. A shout rises from the crowd on deck, and again the whale is gone.

Normally, we would gladly linger. But today we bid the whale farewell and head south past Salmon Bank into the deeper waters of the strait.

Encouraging the passengers to be extra alert for a glimpse of tall fins, I give another short talk on orcas, with one eye and most of my mind glued to the horizon. Twice, enthusiastic passengers yell out from the foredeck. Both sightings turn out to be the products of feverish expectations. Have the whales moved on since we received the sighting? I'm beginning to fear the worst.

Finally we spot a fin. Three fins. Coming straight at us. "Orcas at twelve o'clock!"

Bob cuts the engines, and we wait as the three whales cross our bow, not more than forty feet away. The explosive "whooosh" as the huge dolphins exhale their moist clouds of steamy breath forcefully reminds us that they breathe the same air we breathe, and that their warm mammalian blood defies the cold sea. We can almost see into the blowhole of the nearest one as the thick black nostril lips open to inhale a huge volume of air, then close tightly as the finned back slides beneath the silken waves.

The three are a young juvenile and two adults. One of the two is obviously the youngster's mother. The other is probably an "auntie," perhaps a sister or older daughter, though it could be an immature male—only a close look at the white pattern on its belly would reveal its sex.

The baby whale sticks close to the mother's right flank. Though the youngster, bobbing higher out of the water and diving at a sharper angle, seems to be swimming faster than the adults just to keep up, it actually is being drafted by its mother—like a car dragged into the continuous vacuum created by a fast-moving 18-wheeler. The baby orca is about eight or nine feet long and must be more than two to three months old; otherwise the white area on its belly and sides would still be tinged with orange. Like those of a human baby, the kidneys of a newborn orca take time to develop, giving it a temporary touch of jaundice.

The three orcas surface close off the stern as two dozen cameras swing into action. The white oval behind the eyes and white patches on the whales' sides are clearly visible.

The orcas ignore us, heading on a straight course north toward San Juan Island. While we debate whether to follow, I spot a movement out of the corner of my eye. As I worm my way onto the crowded foredeck, another shout goes up and arms point to the south.

Out near the buoy at Hein Bank, a shallow seamount in the center of the strait, a large whale is breaching. Repeatedly. We head out at flank speed.

Halfway to the bank we spot a group of whales to the west. And others to the southeast. There is no point in going further. Bob cuts the engines. As our ears adjust, the quiet sounds of wind and seabirds and lapping waves fill the vacuum.

Freed from the cocoon of sound formed by the engines' insistent drone, our minds expand outward over the calm waters. In the silence we can hear blows all around us.

The sea is full of whales.

Off in the distance about a mile south, a large female breaches, leaping almost completely out of the water before she twists onto her side with a great splash. The tall fin of a mature male surfaces about a half mile to the west. And then a group of five or six to the east. And two more larger groups to the south. Everywhere we look in a semi-circle of perhaps a mile, there are small groups of orcas.

The tall, individually-shaped fins of mature males make them by far the easiest to identify. We train our glasses on the nearest bull. Two distinct notches in the straight trailing edge of his six-foot-tall dorsal fin show him to be K-1, otherwise known as "Taku." Farther away, we spot J-6, "Ralph," whose fin has four smaller notches. And J-1, "Ruffles," with his distinctive wavy trailing edge. And what looks to be L-33, "Chinook," with his tall, perfect fin and narrow saddle patch. Amazing! It appears that into this rough circle of a mile radius, centered on this spot, all three local pods have come together at one time. The *Western Prince* sits dead in the water—and we are in whale-watchers' heaven.

We quickly drop the hydrophone. Again, the unmistakable metallic whoops and clicks of the orcas.

As orcas travel, they often divide into subgroups separated by up to a half-mile. Keeping in touch over such distance in rough or murky water demands social cohesion. This, in turn, demands a certain amount of conformity and predictable behavior. Among subgroup members, even breathing is often coordinated.

A baby orca sticks close to its protective mother.
(Kelley Balcomb-Bartok)

An orca expels a lungful of silvery bubbles as it surfaces for a breath. (Kelley Balcomb-Bartok)

Now and then a traveling orca might "spyhop" (lift its head vertically above the surface to look around) or explode in a series of exuberant breaches, or even flip entirely over in a spectacular cartwheel. But normally such play, even if it continues for half an hour, seems no more than a coffee break in the otherwise serious business of the day. The three orcas that just crossed our bow in tight formation, heading on a straight line north toward San Juan Island, embody the orca's weekday deportment.

But this day is obviously not business as usual. The behavior of most of the orcas in sight seems totally spontaneous. Today is a holiday. A family reunion. A time out from the daily demands of making a living in the sea.

As if to emphasize this leisurely freedom, an older adolescent male lazes—belly up—at the surface a couple hundred feet off the boat's bow, playfully slapping his pectoral flippers and tail flukes lightly on the water.

A large female to the south circles furiously, perhaps chasing fish, though it would be hard to imagine fish foolish enough to blunder into this area today.

A mature male surfaces about a quarter-mile away and just floats motionless, his tall dorsal fin like the sail of a becalmed sailboard.

Orcas seem to enjoy playing with Bull kelp. This one stretches a kelp stipe with its fluke. (Kelley Balcomb-Bartok)

Then, as we collectively hold our breaths, a young juvenile, perhaps 15 feet in length swims leisurely over to the boat. Through the calm, clear water we can see its entire body just a few feet underwater and almost within touching distance. The curious youngster circles under the stern of the boat, perhaps checking out the motionless pair of bronze propellers. It surfaces beside us, eyeing us with the same fascination as we have for it.

Were this a captive whale in a viewing tank at a seaquarium, my pleasure would have been tainted by pity for its loss of freedom. But this is not a marine amusement park—these whales are wild and free. And this one chose to approach us without fear. Everyone is silent.

Expelling a whoosh of vaporous breath, the youngster submerges again, turns away from us, and swims back to two nearby playmates, who are casually nosing a small clump of dislodged bull kelp just 50 feet off the boat's port beam. Though orcas sometimes play with the kelp's bulbous stipes, this particular clump holds little interest to the three juveniles. Like children exploring a picnic grounds, the three swim off to look for more exciting fare. But to those of us hanging over the rail of the boat, mouths agape, nothing could be more exciting than this close encounter of the best kind.

Everywhere we look, individual orcas or small groups are chasing around in circles, or leaping from the water in tremendous displays of power. A large whale breaches, and then another. Spectators cheer.

Not far off the stern, three orcas are rolling about in what seems like mating, or at least sensual roughhousing. None of them has the tall dorsal fin characteristic of a fully mature bull, but at least one of the three is a juvenile male. He rolls to the surface sporting a semi-erect penis (termed a "red seasnake" by waggish biologists): slender, tapered toward the tip, an impressive four feet long.

Actual mating among orcas is rarely observed in the wild, but sex-play is not unexpected under the circumstances. Whale biologists believe that orca pods—which are extended families—avoid inbreeding by mating primarily with members of other pods within the same community. This may be especially common after "greeting ceremonies," which occur when two pods or subgroups come together after a separation.

My friend Fred Sharpe had the good fortune to witness such a ceremony.

"J-Pod," Sharpe recalls, "was foraging along the southwest shore of Stuart Island that day, occasionally circling around as they encountered fish, but moving steadily northward. As they rounded Turn Point, the pod heard or sighted another group of orcas coming toward them down Boundary Pass.

"As the two groups approached each other, they seemed to sort themselves out underwater, then reappeared at the surface in two orderly lines that faced each other about 200 feet apart. As they slowly swam toward each other, still at the surface, they began to vocalize. We could hear loud, squeaky sounds through the air." (Sounds recorded during a similar ceremony were likened to rubbing balloons together. When Osborne analyzed them, they turned out to be a common call used by all three resident pods, the lower harmonics not audible through the air.)

At a distance of 50 feet or so, the whales, still in orderly lines, dove underwater and met. Then, for about five minutes, they milled about in smaller subgroups—perhaps individuals of the same age group, or mates from previous encounters.

"At that point," notes Sharpe, "the scene, which began with almost military order, had turned into total chaos. There was lots of breaching, even double or triple breaches by individuals. Also many tail lobs and pectoral fin slaps."

We have arrived too late to witness such a greeting ceremony but are still in time for the aftermath—this spectacular reunion of all three resident pods. And for a magical hour we've felt like members of the family.

The summer sun is still high above the Olympic Mountains, and there is no telling how long the whales will continue to socialize—their schedules being far more flexible than ours. But it will take another hour for us to return to Friday Harbor where many of us have ferries to catch or engagements to keep.

Reluctantly, we leave the frolicking orcas and head back north toward San Juan Channel.

Motoring back to port after such an exhilarating day, it is easy to dream. Someday, researchers will unlock the secrets of the orca's "language." Someday our two species may even swap unimaginable tales and laugh at our earlier clumsy interactions. It will be a great party, and I hope to be around to join the conversation.

I once asked Peter Capen, former director of the Whale Museum, why there seems to be no end to our fascination with whales, especially orcas.

"I think it's because they're extraterrestrials," he ventured. "Like the movie character, E.T., orcas and other cetaceans are intelligent beings from another world. They are the most advanced creatures in their world, as we are in ours, and they may hold the key to our understanding that other world.

"And what could be more exciting than to reach across that gap?"

Meanwhile, we have seen beyond doubt that this scenic inland sea holds treasures and mysteries beyond our terrestrial imaginations. Though few trips will be as eventful as the one just ending, each visit offers revelations. Each time we go out in boats to go fishing, or to look for whales, or just escape the bustling land; each time we walk the shore, exploring tide pools, watching seabirds soar and dive; each time we enter the water to scuba dive, we take one step further into understanding the seaworld—from which ours sprang, and to which we are still intimately connected.

We are all explorers on the Salish Sea.

A mature male orca develops a tall dorsal fin (to 6 feet). Age, heredity, and injuries affect the fin's size and shape, making them easy to identify individually. (Kelley Balcomb-Bartok)

Dungeness Spit, extending four miles out into the Strait of Juan de Fuca, offered Vancouver's ships their first local anchorage. Seen from the Olympics, with Mount Baker in the background. (Doug Wechsler)

Tall Ships Sail In

Dungeness Spit curves out into the Strait of Juan de Fuca like a long, bony finger pointing northeast toward Mount Baker. Its backbone is a jumble of huge gray skeletons—driftlogs of Douglas fir, Western hemlock, and Western red cedar cut from the banks of flooding rivers or escaped from the log booms of Port Angeles a dozen miles to the west. In spring, massive tangles of tough, rubbery 30-foot long bull kelp, ripped from the sea floor by winter storms, rot on the beach. Shells of cockles and Dungeness crabs lie where the waves or gulls have dropped them.

Extending four miles across the path of incoming waves, with only a narrow ridge of sand and drift logs remaining above highest tides, the slender spit seems a fragile barrier against ocean swells rolling into the Strait from storms far out on the North Pacific. Yet it has not only endured for centuries but seems still to be growing.

For the oceanic sailor turning eastward into the Strait of Juan de Fuca after anxious days along the exposed Pacific coast, Dungeness marks the beginning of a sea change. The high, spruce-covered cliffs and surf-lashed sea stacks that stretch from northern California past the Olympic Peninsula up the outer coast of Vancouver Island, end just west of here. East of Dungeness the coast infolds. The relatively strait shoreline transforms into a maze of channels and rocky islets, full of strong, mercurial currents and winds. Though trickier and more hazardous in many ways than the open ocean, the inland waters are at least sheltered from the worst of the Pacific's winter rages.

Seaducks and shorebirds know this too. All winter, huge rafts of American wigeons drift on the shallow bay behind the spit, lifting noisily up and circling low over the water when alarmed. Male Buffleheads bob and splash to gain the attention of the females; Red-breasted mergansers dip and rise in complex mating displays. Stately Western grebes drift with their heads curled back under their wings. Along the spit itself, a lone Willet stands on one leg, while a tight flock of smaller shorebirds—Dunlins and Western sandpipers mostly—line the drift logs, flying up to turn in a synchronized flash of white before alighting further up the beach.

In May, migrants from further south join their relatives here to fuel up on worms and mussels. Soon wintering birds and migrants alike will desert the sheltered bay for the long journey north to Arctic nesting grounds.

"We found the surface of the sea almost covered with aquatic birds of various kinds," wrote George Vancouver on the first of May, 1792. "But all so extremely shy that our sportsmen were unable to reach them with their guns, although they made many attempts."

Yet with his ships safely in from the coast and anchored on the protected east side of the spit, Captain Vancouver had every reason to be pleased. Just 16 months before, in December, 1790, he had been promoted to Commander in the Royal Navy. Six months afterwards he was entrusted with a delicate mission of international significance—to sail from London to the Northwest coast—to the island in fact that would later be named for him—to receive from Spain the port of Nootka and surrounding territories. Even more satisfying to the explorer in him, he had been given orders to chart the entire northern Pacific coast of North America.

At the age of 34, Vancouver had already served in the British Royal Navy for more than two decades. More importantly, he had had the good fortune to sail under James Cook, the greatest of all British explorers. As a young midshipman on Cook's second and third Pacific voyages, Vancouver had been one of the first Europeans to visit the northwest coast. During the intervening dozen years, the Pacific Northwest, though still almost a blank area on the world map, had become a hotspot of international tension.

Since the 16th century Spain had claimed exclusive trading rights from colonial Mexico along the entire coast of North America. Then, in 1741, the great Danish explorer Vitus Bering, sailing under the Russian flag, discovered Alaska. Though Bering died among the Aleutian Islands, his crew had brought back luxuriant furs of Sea otters found in Alaska's coastal kelp beds.

Finding that Chinese merchants were willing to pay a fortune for the pelts, Russian fur traders quickly established outposts along the Alaskan coast. Hastily-built Siberian ships—driving kayak flotillas of skilled Aleut hunters before them—eventually worked their way as far south as the Channel Islands of southern California. In 1774, the Mexican colonial government responded to the threat by sending Juan Perez Hernandez north to explore the coast and to dislodge any Russians he might meet.

Perez sighted Mount Olympus (which he named Santa Rosalia), met with Haida Indians in the Queen Charlotte Islands 500 miles to the north, and founded a tiny settlement in Nootka Sound, about two-thirds of the way up the outer coast of what would prove to be a huge island. A year later, Juan Francisco de la Bodega y Quadra led a second Spanish expedition to Nootka.

The British, meanwhile, had only recently secured eastern Canada from the French. They faced the loss of their American colonies south of Canada and still had only the most tenuous of claims on Canada's west coast. In 1776, Captain Cook was ordered to return to Nootka to search for the elusive Northwest Passage to the Atlantic—and, more importantly, to chart the area to shore up English territorial claims. The next year Cook, with ensign Vancouver aboard, sighted Cape Flattery at the northwestern tip of the Olympic Peninsula; but the ships were driven by a gale past the entrance to the Strait of Juan de Fuca and directly to Nootka.

Trading with the Indians of Nootka, Cook's crew had exchanged pieces of copper for sea otter pelts, and they, too, discovered that the furs were worth a small fortune. Word of the otter fur's value spread like wildfire though the commercial centers of London and Boston.

Between 1785 and 1788, a dozen British merchant ships visited Nootka. Captain John Meares had anchored in the strait to the south—which he named Juan de Fuca after the supposed visit of an earlier Greek sailor who claimed to have sailed that region in the employ of Spain—

and renamed Santa Rosalia "Mount Olympus." But Meares found otters only in the kelp zone of the outer coast, and like the other traders saw no reason to venture farther into the Strait.

In 1789, the friction between the British and Spanish came to a head over the seizing of two British vessels in Nootka by the Spanish as payment for a debt. The ships were soon released, but Captain Meares, who had begun a small trading settlement at Nootka, claimed damages to his ship and territory of over a half-million dollars—a very large fortune in those days.

Though Meares' claims were grossly inflated, his outraged memorial to the British Parliament demanding restitution from the Spanish government coincided with British imperial interests. A formidable English armada was hastily formed. Spain, reluctant to go to war over territory so far north of Mexico, capitulated and signed the Nootka Convention later that year.

Vancouver was ordered to sail to Nootka to receive the port for the Crown and to negotiate final details of the Nootka Convention with the Spanish representative, Bodega y Quadra. He left England in the autumn of 1791.

Under Vancouver's command were two ships: *Discovery*, a newly-commissioned 100-foot, 3-masted sloop-of-war with a crew of one hundred; and *Chatham*, a 60-foot brig with 45 sailors under Lieutenant William Broughton. Sailing around southern Africa's Cape of Good Hope, the party explored Australia's southwest coast and southern New Zealand, overwintered in Hawaii, and in March crossed the Pacific to Cape Mendocino in northern California.

Sailing northward along the rocky, fogbound coast of present-day Oregon and Washington in late April, Vancouver's ships had unwittingly passed the entrance to the Columbia River. A few days later, as they hugged the coast, they spotted Mount Olympus. At Cape Flattery they turned eastward around "Tatooche's Island" and entered the Strait of Juan de Fuca. Lieutenant Joseph Baker sighted a snow-capped volcano rising far to the east. Vancouver named it Mount Baker.

On the second day in, the ships sighted the long spit. Vancouver promptly named it New Dungeness "from its great resemblance to Dungeness in the British Channel," and gratefully dropped anchor in the sheltered shallows.

The commander was buoyant. His two vessels were intact. He and the crews were healthy. Most exhilarating of all, he was at the very edge of the known world.

"Our May-day," wrote Vancouver in his diary, "was ushered in by a morning of the most delightfully pleasant weather, affording us, from the broken appearance of the coast before us, the prospect of soon reaching a safe and commodious harbor..." That very afternoon, exploring the strait's coastline in a small cutter-rigged lifeboat, they reached what Vancouver called "one of the finest harbours in the world." He named it Port Discovery after his ship.

Unknown to him, the bay had already been visited and named by the Spanish. Two years before, two Spanish ships under Lieutenant Eliza and Ensign Manuel Quimper had sailed from Nootka (which Eliza had formally taken under Spanish control) into the Strait of Juan de Fuca. They explored the area around present-day Victoria and named the San Juan Islands.

Attesting to the primacy of the Spanish exploration, Eliza had a wooden cross placed overlooking Discovery Bay, which he had named Port Quadra. Quimper's name is memorialized by the peninsula that separates Discovery Bay from inner Puget Sound.

But for the rest of that May, however, and for the following two summers, Vancouver and his men would be the first Europeans to set eyes on almost every other shore they would visit. More importantly, Vancouver's detailed journal would give his contemporaries—and us— a fascinating glimpse of a regional culture that had been relatively stable for thousands of years, but was already being disrupted by distant events; and which would soon be utterly transformed.

After three months at sea, the landing at Discovery Bay in good weather was a godsend to the British crews. Tents, observatory, chronometers and instruments were set up on shore. Repairs were made and provisions restored. And, for the first time since rounding the Cape of Good Hope, the captain finally allowed a Sunday off.

Vancouver and a small party visited a steep island at the mouth of Discovery Bay, which he named Protection Island. Though he had traveled widely throughout the south Pacific and the Caribbean and was not given to hyperbole, he found the landscape "enchantingly beautiful...The country before us exhibited everything that bounteous nature could be expected to draw into one point of view...A picture so pleasing," he added nostalgically, "could not fail to call to our remembrance certain delightful and beloved situations in Old England."

It being well into the Northwest spring, the Indians of the area had already moved from their riverfront winter villages to food-gathering camps along the shores. Vancouver noted the deserted villages and temporary mat huts.

As evidence of the previous Spanish visits, "The inhabitants seemed to view us with the utmost indifference and unconcern; they continued to fish before their huts regardless of our being present, as if such vessels had been familiar to them, and unworthy of their attention."

One sighting perplexed the captain: "On the low land of New Dungeness were erected perpendicularly, and seemingly with much regularity, a number of very tall straight poles, like flagstaves or beacons, supported from the ground by spurs... They were, undoubtedly, intended to answer some particular purpose; but whether of a religious, civil, or military nature must be left to some future investigation."

Ironically, this description of the beach poles immediately precedes Vancouver's lament that his gunners were unable to procure seaducks for food. Had he been able to communicate with the local Indians, they might have given him a few hints that would have gone far to help feed the British party's 150 sailors.

At dusk or dawn the villagers stretched willow nets between the tall poles. When the ducks flew over the spit, they struck the nets. "It was," notes historian Edmond S. Meany, who edited Vancouver's journal in 1907, "practically a fish net made to work on land." The same seine nets with which the English crews fished "with little success," would have served far better for harvesting sea ducks. And it is not surprising that after seeing the sailors shoot in vain at the shy, speedy guillemots and goldeneyes, word spread among the Indians that the English guns went "Poh! Poh!" but had no power to harm.

Vancouver explored the nearby shore with Archibald Menzies, *Discovery*'s skilled surgeon and naturalist, who had twice visited the Northwest coast on fur-trading vessels in 1786 and 1789. The gnarly, red-barked Madrone (arbutus) tree that thrives along the drier shores of the inland waters would later be named *Arbutus menziesii* in his honor, as would *Pseudotsuga menziesii*, the Douglas fir—later mainstay of the region's economy.

On May 7 Vancouver set out to explore the coast of the Olympic Peninsula in three large rowboats. Around noon, after fighting a strong tidal current, the party rounded the northeast point of the Quimper Peninsula. As the fog lifted, they were given their first view of "a very spacious inlet," to which Vancouver gave the name Admiralty Inlet.

To the southeast stood "a very remarkable high round mountain, covered with snow, apparently at the southern extremity of the distant range of snowy mountains." He named the majestic volcano (called "Tahoma" by local Indians) Mount Rainier, in honor of his good friend, Admiral Peter Rainier.

A day-long survey and depth-sounding of the nearby harbor showed it to be "a very safe and more capacious harbour than Port Discovery and rendered more pleasant by the high land being at a greater distance from the water-side. To this port I gave the name of Port Townshend, in honor of the noble Marquis of that name." Port Townsend (minus the "h") would later become Washington state's first port-of-entry and one of its most elegant and colorful towns.

A longboat styled after those of the Vancouver expedition explores Puget Sound under the auspices of Vashon Island's Pure Sound Society. (Brad Wetmore/Pure Sound Society)

Sailing past Port Townsend, the party encountered a grisly sight: "We found on one of the low points projecting from the eastern shore two upright poles. On the top of each was stuck a human head, recently placed there. The hair and flesh were nearly perfect; and the heads appeared to carry the evidence of fury or revenge, as, in driving the stakes through the throat to the cranium, the sagittal, with part of the scalp, was borne on their points some inches above the rest of the skull." The detached heads most probably belonged to fallen members of a slave-raiding party of the Haida or the Kwakiutl, who periodically swept down from the north in ornate war canoes to prey on Coast Salish tribes.

After a night of torrential rains, the explorers holed up south of the island. Discovering oak trees along the shore, Vancouver named the area Oak Harbor. Here Menzies reports seeing large flocks of migrating Sandhill cranes, a rare species no longer found here.

The following day, May 10, the party moved slowly down Admiralty Inlet against a southwest wind and strong ebb tide. Here, they met with a canoe of local Indians, "who courteously offered such things as they possessed, and cordially accepted some medals, beads, knives, and other trinkets, which I presented to them, and with which they appeared to be highly pleased."

The inlet soon branched into two channels to the south and southeast. The steep land separating them Vancouver named Foulweather Bluff. The three boats headed due south down the narrow, mountainsided waterway which Vancouver named Hood's Channel (Hood Canal), "after the Right Honorable Lord Hood"—the Admiral who had signed the instructions for Vancouver's voyage and after whom he would also later name Oregon's Mount Hood.

"The country hereabouts," he notes, "presented a very different aspect from that which we had been accustomed to see. Instead of the sandy cliffs that form the shores within the straits, these were composed of solid rocks. On them the herbage and shrubs seemed to flourish with less luxuriance, though the trees appeared to form a much greater variety."

Here a group of 17 Indians "approached us with utmost confidence, without being armed, and behaved in the most respectful and orderly manner...In their persons, dress, canoes, etc. they much resembled the Indians of Port Discovery; they had not the most distant knowledge of the Nootka language."

The Indians traded what little they carried, "conducting themselves in a very fair and honest manner." Their village was "situated in a very pleasant cove and built with wood, after the fashion of the deserted ones we had before seen."

After an unsuccessful bout with southwest winds and a strong outgoing tide, the group was finally carried on an incoming flood tide to Hood Head (at the western end of the present Hood Canal Bridge). "Into the bay descended a few small streams of fresh water; with which, so far as we were able to judge, the country did not abound."

Haida and Kwakiutl warriors periodically raided Coast Salish villages from the north. Vancouver's party noted two heads spitted on poles near the entrance to Puget Sound and surmised they were raiders fallen in a skirmish. (Neil G. McDaniel, from a filmed re-enactment)

This lack of streams was, of course, a deception. All of the explorations so far had been within the "rain shadow" cast by the Olympic Mountains. Farther south down Hood Canal the explorers would find a quartet of major rivers issuing from the mountains—the Dosewallips, the Duckabush, the Hamma Hamma, and the Skokomish, as well as a half-dozen smaller streams.

Hood Canal is a classic fjord, without the complexities of Puget Sound's much larger eastern basins. Past deep, narrow Dabob Bay (separated off by the narrow Toandos Peninsula) the channel follows a straight, even-width path to its shallow southern terminus at the mouth of the Skokomish River. The eastern front of the Olympic mountains, forested by huge firs, rise almost directly from its shores to jagged, mile-high peaks. The sun sets early over the peaks, shadowing the canal much of the afternoon. For the explorers, it was an imposing and desolate body of water.

By May 12th, the party's food was about gone. The hunters were unsuccessful, and the western shore of the canal, just a thin strip of forest at the flanks of the imposing wall of mountains to the west, seemed bleak. "The region we had lately passed seemed nearly destitute of human beings. The brute creation also had deserted the shores; the tracks of deer were no longer to be seen; nor was there an aquatic bird on the whole extent of the canal; animated nature seemed nearly exhausted; and her awful silence was only now and then interrupted by the croaking of a raven, the breathing of a seal, or the scream of an eagle."

Unknown to Vancouver, the lack of animal life, like the lack of water, was an artifact of time and place. The wintering seabirds he had seen at Dungeness were in the act of massing to fly north to breed; the Hood Canal flocks had already left. Periods of daytime minus tides, exposing huge areas of clam flats, had just begun. Herring had already spawned. Winter runs of Steelhead trout had ended and the Sockeye salmon run would not begin until July. Summer berries were not yet ripe. Even for the Indians of the area it was a lean time—dried food stored the previous summer and fall was depleted and new stocks had not yet been amassed.

But just below the British ships shrimp and squid schooled in the dark water. Lingcod, halibut and flounder lurked on the bottom. Mussels and barnacles lined the rocky shores. The visiting explorers simply lacked the knowledge of local animals, the edibility of local plants, and appropriate ways of food gathering, preparation, and preservation.

Coast Salish Indians, on the other hand, had woven centuries of experience into a web of technologies passed from generation to generation and spread from tribe to tribe through a common coastal culture. Such skills enabled the Salish bands along this coast to support a population that once reached hundreds of thousands. Living on the excess of food dried in summer and fall, they could even dedicate the dark, cold months of December and January to a pleasant round of inter-tribal visits, ceremonies, and feasting.

Happily for Vancouver's party, Salish Indians were avid traders—a trait essential for distributing tools, clothing, and food among the scattered coastal villages. More importantly, they were hospitable to peaceful strangers.

At the mouth of the Skokomish River at the southern end of Hood Canal, the British boats found an encampment of about 60 people gathering food. The Indians invited them to an impromptu feast. "These good people," reports Vancouver, "conducted themselves in the most friendly manner. They had little to dispose of, yet they bartered away their bows and arrows without the least hesitation, together with some small fish, cockles, and clams; of the latter we purchased a large quantity, a supply of which was very acceptable in the low condition of our stock."

Here, Vancouver noted the prior arrival of a European legacy that had already affected the Indians of the Pacific Northwest far more than introduced copper or steel, and that would continue to influence Indian culture for the next hundred years—more strongly even than the invasion of American settlers. "Some of our gentlemen recognized one man, who had suffered very much from the small pox. This deplorable disease is not only common, but it is very fatal amongst them, as its indelible marks were to be seen on many; and several had lost the sight of one eye owing most likely to the virulent effects of this baneful disorder."

In 1774, the first major outbreak of smallpox, which may have originated from a Russian trading post in Alaska, swept through the Salish villages. Epidemics of tropical malaria and European smallpox would continue to decimate the Indians of the region for the next hundred years. After malaria epidemics in the 1830s the Chinook Indians—once wealthy traders along the lower Columbia River—would be reduced 99% from 50,000 people to 500. Throughout the Northwest, the ravages were similar, if less intense. "It may be somewhat premature to conclude that this delightful country has always been this thinly inhabited," Vancouver realized; "on the contrary, there are reasons to believe it has been infinitely more populous."

Unable to see past Sisters Point up what is now called The Great Bend, and assured by signs from their hosts that there was no other way back to the sea, Vancouver wrongly believed that Hood Canal ended at the mouth of the Skokomish. In reality, it extends 13 miles northeast, almost severing the Kitsap Peninsula from the mainland. It was one of the few mistakes on Vancouver's otherwise accurate chart of the inland waters.

As they rowed back up Hood Canal, another storm blew in from the Pacific. "Our progress homeward was so very slow that it was Monday afternoon, the 14th, before we reached Foulweather Bluff. This promontory is not ill named, for we had scarcely landed, when a heavy rain commenced, which continuing the rest of the day, obliged us to remain stationary." Unable to see into Admiralty Inlet, they left Foulweather on the afternoon of the 15th "attended with heavy squalls and torrents of rain" and returned to the mother ships in Discovery Bay.

Three days later, May 18th, the weather finally cleared. *Discovery* and *Chatham* weighed anchor. Vancouver landed briefly on Protection Island "in order, from its eminence, to take a more accurate view of the surrounding shores." Struck by the "archipelago of islands of various sizes" to the north (the San Juans), he directed Lieutenant Broughton in *Chatham* to sail up there for a closer look.

Vancouver sailed south, past Port Townsend into Admiralty Inlet. From the masthead, the peak of Mount St. Helens was visible for the first time. On the afternoon of May 19th *Discovery* anchored just off the southern tip of present-day Bainbridge Island. South lay two large passages: to the southeast, a continuation of the extensive basin they had been sailing; to the southwest, another passage about half as wide.

"Admiralty Inlet" was proving to be far more complex than Hood Canal. If Port Discovery had been an exciting find, this extensive inland sea must have been thrilling. Vancouver was eager to explore it further. "On my return on board, I directed that a party, under the command of Lieutenant [Peter] Puget and [Ship's Master Joseph] Whidbey, should, in the launch and cutter, proceed, with a supply of provisions for a week, to the examination of that branch of the inlet leading to the south-westward; keeping always to the starboard or continental shore." After almost running out of food on Hood Canal, the captain would take no chances. Who could predict where this amazing maze of passages might lead?

On the 20th, at the usual 4 A.M., Puget and Whidbey set off to the south in their small boats. While *Discovery's* crew replaced two rotted spars and brewed some spruce beer, Vancouver met up with an Indian encampment on Bainbridge Island.

In the mat-covered summer shelters, hung up to be cured by the smoke of the fire they kept constantly burning, [were] clams, mussels, and a few other kinds of fish, seemingly intended for their winter's subsistence. The clams perhaps were not all reserved for

"Fishing Camp—Skokomish." In the early 1900s—half a century after the coming of white settlers—Seattle-based photographer Edward S. Curtis dedicated his career to capturing images of what was seen as a vanishing culture. His idealized portraits attempt to re-create the pre-contact Coast Salish lifestyle. (Edward S. Curtis/University of Washington Special Collections, NA311)

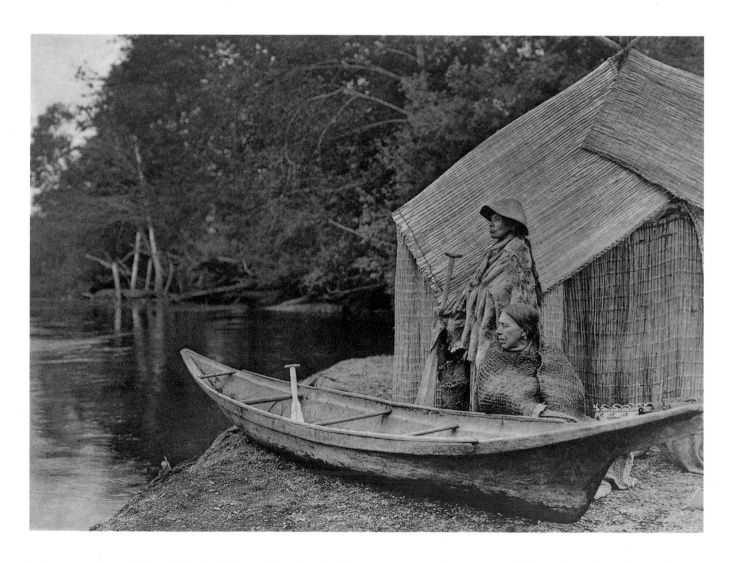

that purpose, for we frequently saw them strung and worn about the neck, which, as inclination directed, were eaten, two, three, or half a dozen at a time.

This station did not appear to have been preferred for fishing, as we saw few of the people so employed. Nearly the whole of the village, which consisted of about eighty or an hundred men, women, and children, were busily engaged like swine, rooting up this beautiful verdant meadow in quest of a species of wild onion, and two other roots. The collecting of these roots was most likely the object of which attached them to this spot; they all seemed to gather them with much avidity, and to preserve them with great care.

A few days later, a small Indian band traded a whole deer, "which cost all these good people nearly a day's labor," for "a small piece of copper not a foot square...such is the esteem and value with which this metal is regarded!" exclaimed the captain, disregarding the lengths to which Europeans would go for an ounce of gold or silver. To the Indians, copper met all the requirements of a precious metal: beautiful, malleable, rustproof, and rare.

Two of the head men of the Indian camp, probably of the Duwamish tribe who lived along the Duwamish River at the southern end of what would become Seattle, visited *Discovery* later that afternoon.

Beside the canoes which brought these two superior people, five others attended, seemingly as an appendage to the consequence of these chiefs, who would not immediately [come] on board, but agreeably to the custom of the Nootka, advanced within about two hundred yards of the ship, and there resting on their paddles a conference was held, followed by a song principally sung by one man, who at stated times was joined in chorus by several others, whilst some in each canoe kept time with the handles of their paddles, by striking them against the gunwhale or side of the canoe, forming a sort of accompanyment, which though expressed by simple notes only, was by no means destitute of an agreeable effect.

This performance took place whilst they were paddling slowly around the ship, and on its being concluded, they came along side with the greatest confidence, and without fear or suspicion immediately entered into a commercial intercourse with our people.

"Their merchandise would have been infinitely more valuable to us," the captain notes wistfully, "had it been comprised of eatables, such as venison, wild fowl or fish, as our sportsmen and fishermen had little success in either of these pursuits."

Two days later, Broughton returned from the San Juans. A large strait "presenting an unbounded horizon," he reported, stretched to the northwest.

Excited by the news, Vancouver made a decision that would increase the crews' labors and would slow the exploration considerably—despite the pressure of fulfilling his diplomatic mission to Nootka; but it would also allow them to chart the new area in unsurpassed accuracy and detail. Henceforth, all the charting would be done from the smaller boats "though the execution of such service in open boats would necessarily be extremely laborous, and expose those so employed to numerous dangers and unpleasant situations..."

The open boats held about ten men. Six would row while others made soundings, measuring water depths with a lead-weighted line marked in fathom (six-foot) intervals. They carried small sails for assistance when the wind was at their backs and no soundings were being made. But most of the time they rowed.

Over the course of the spring and summer and the following ones, these small crews in open rowboats would sound out the entire convoluted coastline of the inland waters, from southern Puget Sound to Alaska—a truly monumental undertaking. Yet the charts were so accurate that they would serve mariners for the next hundred years.

"The main arm of the inlet leading toward Mount Rainier still remained unexplored," notes Vancouver impatiently. "It became evident from the length of time Mr. Puget and Mr. Whidbey had been absent, that the inlet they had been sent to examine had led them to a considerable distance. We had no time to spare, and as it was equally evident none ought to be lost, I directed that Mr. Johnstone, in the *Chatham's* cutter, should accompany me in the morning, in the *Discovery's* yawl, for the purpose of examining the main [southeastern] arm."

Catching a fresh north wind, Vancouver and Johnstone sailed down East Passage in the yawl-rigged rowboat. About ten miles from the ship, the channel turned southwest, and they soon entered an "extensive circular compact bay [Commencement Bay—site of the future Tacoma], whose waters washed the base of mount Rainier...which rose conspicuously above [the Cascades], and seemed as much elevated above them as they were above the level of the sea; the whole producing a most grand, picturesque effect."

Here, Vancouver had an experience that disproved one of the myths circulating in Europe about the Northwest Indians; and evidently, a similar misconception about the Europeans held by the Salish Indians.

> About a dozen of these friendly people had attended at our dinner, one part of which was a venison pasty. Two of them...sat down by us, and ate of the bread and fish that we gave them without the least hesitation; but on being offered some of the venison, though they saw us eat it with great relish, they could not be induced to taste it. They received it from us with great disgust, and presented it round to the rest of the party, by whom it underwent a very strict examination. Their conduct on this occasion left no doubt in our minds that they believed it to be human flesh...and threw it down in the dirt, with gestures of great aversion and displeasure. At length we happily convinced them of their mistake by showing them a haunch [of deer] we had in the boat, by which means they were undeceived, and some of them ate of a remainder of the pye with a good appetite.
>
> These people have been represented not only as accustomed inhumanly to devour the flesh of their conquered enemies; but also to keep certain servants, or rather slaves, of their own nation, for the sole purpose of making the principal part of the banquet, to satisfy the unnatural savage gluttony of the chiefs of this country, on their visits to one another...On the contrary, it is not possible to conceive a greater degree of abhorrence than was manifested by those good people.

When the wind was astern, the British longboats hoisted sail. Otherwise, the exploration demanded arduous rowing, often against strong headwinds and tidal currents. (Jeanne Dickinson/Pure Sound Society)

Passing northwestward from Commencement Bay, Vancouver was able to sight north up a long channel, the same one Puget and Whidbey had traveled down; the land they had skirted was, as suspected, a large island, "the most extensive we had yet met with in our several examinations of this coast." He named it Vashon Island, after his friend Admiral James Vashon.

Rounding Defiance Point, Vancouver decided to follow Puget and company through the southern channel, but to keep to the eastern shore. Sucked into The Narrows by a strong flood tide, "we rapidly passed through a fair navigable channel, [a mile and a quarter] wide, with soundings from 24 to 30 fathoms, free from any appearance of shoals, rocks, or other interruptions. The eastern shore was compact; but on the western, three wide openings were seen [Hale Passage, Carr Inlet, and Balch Passage], whose terminations were not distinguishable; and the strength with which the tide flowed into the two northernmost, induced us to consider them very extensive." At about 8 P.M., they stopped on a small island [Cormorant] about a mile from the eastern shore.

As night fell, "we discovered, coming out of the southwest opening [Dana Passage], two small vessels, which at first, were taken for Indian canoes, but, on using our glasses, they were considered to be our two boats...The evening was cloudy; and, closing in very soon, prevented a positive identification." But after two unanswered musket shots, the captain was left to believe that the boats were Indian canoes after all.

After a rainy night, the British boats were off by 4 A.M.. Three hours later they reached "a low swampy compact shore [Nisqually Delta], forming the southern extremity of the inlet in this direction...The inlet here terminated in an expansive though shallow bay, across which a flat of sand extended upwards of a mile from its shores; on which was lying an immense quantity of drift wood, consisting chiefly of very large trees...The country behind for some distance was low, then rose gradu-

"Mount Rainier from the South part of Admiralty Inlet." (W. Alexander from sketch by J. Sykes/ University of Washington Special Collections, NA3985)

ally to a moderate height..the whole presenting one uninterrupted wilderness."

They then followed Nisqually Reach northwestward between Johnson Point and the Key Peninsula, to "where the inlet was again divided into two other large branches, one leading to the southwestward [Dana Passage], the other towards the north [Case Inlet]. As my plan was to pursue the [lefthand] shore, the south-west branch [Dana Passage] became our first object. This we found divided into two narrow channels, leading to the southward [Budd Inlet, future site of Olympia; and Eld Inlet, site of The Evergreen State College] with the appearance of two small coves [Peale and Squaxin passages] to the northward. Up the westernmost of the former [Eld Inlet], we took our abode for the night, which was serene and pleasant."

The next morning, May 28th, "we again started, and soon found the channel to terminate as the rest had done, in low swampy ground [Mud Bay], with a shallow sandy bank extending to some distance into the channel." Meeting up with some Indians, who greeted them cooly, the explorers rowed out of Eld Inlet, leaving "behind us to the westward the appearance of two or three small islands or points [Hope and Steamboat islands], that might form similar inlets to those we had already examined." These, he felt, "could be of little extent, as scarcely any visible tide was found in the narrowest parts."

Assuming that Puget and Whidbey had already examined the western inlets, Vancouver ran north up Case Inlet, hoping to find a shortcut back to *Discovery*. But "the further we advanced the the more doubtful it became, until...it terminated like all the other channels in a shallow flat before a low swampy bog. Here we dined, and about four in the afternoon set out on our return by the way we had come."

Johnstone, in the cutter, had checked the opening between Hartstene Island and the main shore. He reported that "the opening was very narrow, and could extend but a little way before it joined that which we had quitted this morning." Thus, they missed seeing Hammersley Inlet (leading to Oakland Bay and the present town of Shelton) off to the west of Squaxin Island.

One of Johnstone's crew, however, managed to shoot "a very fine buck" that had come down to the beach, "which provided our people a good fresh meal." On Tuesday, May 29th, the returning boats were whisked on a strong ebb tide up through The Narrows and narrow Colvos Passage west of Vashon Island, arriving back aboard *Discovery* late in the evening.

Puget and Whidbey were there to greet them. It had, in fact, been their boats that passed Vancouver's encampment on Cormorant Island; but though they had seen the campfire, they had not heard the musket shots and had assumed the fire was an Indian camp. They had explored Carr Inlet, and "found the three openings we had left unexamined to be channels dividing that shore into three islands [Fox, McNeil, and Anderson islands]."

Puget's explorations had gone smoothly, except for a single incident. But that one incident, if less skillfully handled, could have led the entire expedition to disaster:

Nine days before, on May 21st, at the head of Carr Inlet, Puget's party had met up with a canoe of unfriendly Indians.

According to Puget's own diary, these were "more Stout than any we have hitherto seen on the Coast. Two of the three in the Canoe had lost the Right Eye & were much pitted with the Small Pox; [they] kept continually pointing to the Eastward, expressive of a Wish that our Departure would be more agreeable than our Visit."

Wishing to show a friendly intent, Puget left some gifts on a floating log as they rowed away. In hindsight, Puget was "of opinion that they had the Ingratitude to impute our Friendship to a fear of their Power, & the Temerity with which they conducted themselves afterwards had near proved fatal to themselves and Companions...To all our Questions they only answered 'Poh Poh' & pointing to Crow Island, alluding as we supposed to the Report [sound] of the Musquets [rifles] at Breakfast."

Ominously, "though they wanted Copper from us they would not part with their Bows or Arrows in Exchange, which were very neat & well constructed & of which they had plenty."

When the British party beached their boats for lunch, six Indian canoes pulled up, holding, according to Puget's own diary, "about Twenty Men, all Armed, among whom I perceived the three Men who had before been to us. They paddled close to the Boats & some immediately landed. On their Approach a Line was drawn to divide the two Parties, the Intent of which the Indians perfectly understood." As another canoe of well-armed Indians arrived, Puget and a few others retired to the top of a low cliff to eat. The crews remained in the boats, armed and on alert.

Looking west toward Key Peninsula and the Olympics from Cutts Island in Carr Inlet, southern Puget Sound. (Steve Yates)

Nearly after our sitting down the Indians quitted the Beach & repaired to their Canoes where an Apparent Consultation was held, about our Party as they frequently pointed to the Boats & us on the Hill; I now began to think they seriously meant to attack us…Three canoes were stealing towards the Boats but on perceiving they were discovered by us on the Hill, immediately retreated to their former Situation.

Another Canoe had now nearly joined the Party and as she Approached, they suddenly jumped on the Beach stringing their Bows & apparently preparing for an Attack. This reduced me to a most awkward predicament, for unwilling to fire on these poor People, who might have been unacquainted with the advantage we had over them & not wishing to run the Risk of having [our] People wounded by the first discharge of their arrows I absolutely felt at a Loss how to Act.

I soon perceived a Young Man ascending the Hill about five Yards from us with his Bow and Arrow ready, however he was not [allowed] to proceed, & unwillingly joined his Companions on the Beach, [along with] the Indians who arrived in the last Canoe. As I now no longer could doubt their hostile Intention we remained on the Hill ready to return their first Salute.

In the Meantime [our] People were removing the things to the Boats to prepare for our Departure. During which time the whole Party remained in deep Consultation on the Beach sharpening their Arrows, & their Bows ready strung for use. The only Circumstance to be dreaded was the Execution they would do in having the Advantage of the first [shots]. Had a single Arrow been discharged…I certainly would have had that Person shot, let the Consequence be what it would.

They by that time appeared irresolute how to act, I therefore thought it a good Opportunity to order a Swivel to be fired with Grape Shot, that they might see we had other resources besides those in our Hands, but contrary to our Expectation they did not express any Astonishment or fear at the Report or the

Effect of the Shot. By this time our Party were united & the Major part under Arms & I believe they then totally relinquished all Idea of an Attack for they now offered their Bows and Arrows for Sale Which had Shortly before been strung for the worst of Purposes & solicited our Friendship by the most abject Submission...but we had the Satisfaction of having convinced them of our Friendship before their Departure.

The care with which Vancouver and his officers interacted with the area's inhabitants and the disciplined response of his naval crews were critical ingredients for the overall success of the voyage. If conflict had developed to the point of injury or death on either side, word quickly would have spread along the coast, poisoning the amicable reception the British explorers met throughout the inland waters.

"Thus by our joint efforts," writes Vancouver, "we had completely explored every turning of this extensive inlet; and to commemorate Mr. Puget's exertions, the south extremity of it I named Puget's Sound."

Little did the captain realize that the honor bestowed on Lieutenant Puget would grow with time to encompass all of "this extensive inlet," which he called Admiralty. Or that Puget Sound would eventually refer to all the inland waters of a state that would, ironically enough, later be named after George Washington—the American general who had just led a successful revolt against the British monarchy, and was just then finishing up his term as the first U.S. President. The cottages and mansions that Vancouver envisioned would overlook Port Townsend and Commencement Bay were just a human lifespan away from reality. But the dwellings would be American, not British.

On May 25, Vancouver named the point to the north of *Discovery's* anchorage "Restoration Point," in celebration of the Restoration of the English monarchy in 1660. On a pleasant Wednesday morning the 30th, the ships weighed anchor, crossing to the eastern shore.

Ignoring Elliott Bay, they headed into the northeast channel toward present-day Everett. As they tried to enter, a strong ebb tide and "a sort of counter-tide, or under tow, that so affected the ship as to render her almost unmanageable" caught the ships. So deep was the channel that they had not been able to reach bottom with 110 fathoms [660ft] of line. It was midnight before *Discovery* could drop anchor near the eastern shore off the present site of Mukilteo.

June first, exactly one month after the arrival at Dungeness Spit, *Discovery* and *Chatham* sailed in a thick fog up the shallow bay. When the fog dispersed in the afternoon, it became clear that there was no through passage. *Discovery* began to retrace its route, but *Chatham* found itself aground at the head of the bay, near the mouth of the Stillaguamish River. Luckily, the shoal on which the ship rested—a submerged extension of the Stillaguamish delta—was almost pure mud, and no damage was done.

Next day the ships sailed back down the inlet, anchoring in Tulalip Bay just north of the future site of Everett. Joseph Whidbey, who had been sent off to explore the channel to the west of Camano Island (Saratoga Passage), reported back to the ships. He had followed the channel for about twenty miles north until it opened into a wider, shallower bay (Skagit Bay) at the mouth of the Skagit River.

Along the eastern shore of the island later named for him (second longest in the contiguous United States), Whidbey was befriended by the headman of a large village. The inhabitants showed by their astonishment at Whidbey's skin color that they had never before seen a European. Vancouver set off to visit the area.

In the center of the island—just south of "a fine harbor which in honor of a particular friend I called Penn's Cove"—was a deserted village; in one of which were found several sepulchers formed exactly like a sentry box. Some of them were open, and contained skeletons of many young children tied up in blankets," perhaps victims of an epidemic.

"The country in the vicinity of this branch of the sea is, according to Mr. Whidbey's representation, the finest we had yet met with, notwithstanding the very pleasing appearance of many others; its natural productions were luxurious in the highest degree, and it was, by no means, ill supplied with streams of fresh water. The number of its inhabitants he estimated at about six hundred, which I suppose would exceed the total of all the natives we had before seen."

Becalmed in Tulalip Bay, the ships' crews finally had a chance for another well-deserved rest. "On Sunday, [June] 3rd, all hands were employed in fishing with tolerably good success, or in taking a little recreation on shore; and on Monday the 4th, they were served as good a dinner as we were able to provide for them, with a double allowance of grog to drink the King's health, it being the anniversary of His Majesty's birth; on which auspicious day, I had long since designated to take formal possession of all the countries we had lately been employed in exploring..."

The commander landed on the shore, accompanied by a royal salute from the ship's guns. There he took possession of the entire coast from northern California to British Columbia—notwithstanding its Salish inhabitants, the earlier Spanish claims, or the discoveries being made to the south by the American Captain Robert Gray.

The entire western margin continent from "north of the 45th degree of north latitude" (about the middle of present day Oregon state) on up to wherever the Russians could lay claim, he named New Georgia, in honor of King George III.

The northern inland waters he named the Gulf of Georgia.

To what is now known as the central basin of Puget Sound, he gave the name Admiralty Inlet.

The branch of Admiralty Inlet in which he took possession of the surrounding region, Vancouver named Possession Sound. He named the bay that would later become the site of the city of Everett, Port Gardner after Sir Alan Gardner, the commander under whom he had served. He called the passage between Camano Island and the mainland, Port Susan, after Gardner's wife.

On June 5th, pushed by a pleasant northwest wind, the two British ships passed down Possession Sound. Turning north, they beat against the wind up Admiralty Inlet on an outgoing tide, finally anchoring for the night off the shore of Oak Harbor. The next morning they sailed out from Admiralty Inlet into the eastern end of the Strait.

Off the the westernmost point of Whidbey Island, just across the island's narrow isthmus from Penn Cove, the ships were becalmed and

Stormclouds darken San Juan Channel. (Timothy W. Ransom)

forced to lay over for three frustrating days. While at anchor, Vancouver, Broughton, Whidbey, and Menzies made a quick trip northwest to tiny, exposed Smith Island. "About the Rocks," reports Menzies, "were a number of black Sea Pies [Oystercatchers] of which we shot several & found them good eating."

Fortunately for the Harbor seals that would be pupping on the shores and the sea birds that would be nesting by the scores just a few weeks later, the hungry explorers arrived too early. On their return to *Discovery*, though, Menzies mentions that "the Vessels had been visited by a few Natives who had nothing to dispose but a few Water Fowls particularly a blackish colourd species of Auk with a hornlike escrescence rising from the ridge of its Bill, & as it appeard to be a new species I named it *Alca Rhinoceros* [now *Cerorhinca monocerata*—the Rhinoceros auklet] & described it."

From Smith Island, Vancouver first noticed "two other very lofty, round, snowy mountains" south of Mount Rainier: Mount St. Helens (which he would name two years later when approaching the Columbia River) and Mount Adams.

Frustrated by the weather, the commander "dispatched Mr. Puget in the launch, and Mr. Whidbey in the cutter, with a week's provisions...in

Part of the San Juan archipelago from its highest point—Mount Constitution on Orcas Island. (Steve Yates)

order to determine the boundaries of the continental shore leading to the north and eastward."

June 8th, *Discovery* reached the San Juan Islands, anchoring off the southeastern shore of Lopez Island. Meanwhile, Puget and Whidbey had entered a narrow inlet. But since the hidden rocks and strong tidal currents "rendered the pasage navigable only for boats or vessels of small burthen," Vancouver named it Deception Passage (Pass). This connected to Skagit Bay— proving that Whidbey Island was indeed an island. Chatham then passed between Fidalgo and Guemes Islands into shallow Padilla Bay, and the smaller Fidalgo Bay, before returning.

On Monday, June 11th, while Whibey explored east of the San Juans, the ships sailed north to explore around what is now the U. S.–Canada border. Vancouver named the peninsula which forms the western side of what is now Boundary Bay, Point Roberts, after his predecessor on the *Discovery*, Henry Roberts. Shared by the two countries, Point Roberts was, and remains, a favorite location for catching Sockeye returning to the Fraser River.

> The broken part of the coast that Mr. Whidbey had been employed in examining, was found to extend but a few miles to the northward of the spot where his former researches had ended; forming altogether an extensive bay, which I have distinguished as Bellingham Bay. It is situated behind a cluster of islands [Lummi, Portage, and Eliza islands], from which a number of channels lead into it. It everywhere affords good and secure anchorage; opposite to its north point of entrance the shores are high and rocky, with some detached rocks lying off it. Here was found a brook of most excellent water [a branch of the Nooksack River]. To the north and south of these rocky cliffs the shores are less elevated, especially to the northward, where some of those beautiful lawns were again presented to our view.

After skirting the shoals of the Fraser River, which Vancouver failed to recognize as such, the ships explored the present site of the future Canadian city that would bear his name. From "Point Gray" (the present site of University of British Columbia) he sailed into "Burrard's Channel" (Burrard Inlet), named after the British Navy's Sir Henry Burrard Neale.

Up the inlet, just past what is now Stanley Park, he met with "about fifty Indians, in their canoes, who conducted themselves with the greatest decorum and civility, presenting us with several fish cooked, and undressed, of the sort...resembling the smelt. These good people, finding we were inclined to make some return for their hospitality, shewed much understanding in preferring iron to copper." That night "our Indian visitors...promised an abundant supply of fish the next day; our seine having been tried in their presence with very little success."

Sailing north the next day along the Gulf in "dark, gloomy weather," Vancouver found the precipitous surroundings dreary:

> The low fertile shores we had been accustomed to see...no longer existed; their place was now occupied by the base of the stupendous snowy barrier, thinly wooded, and rising from the sea abruptly to the clouds; from whose frigid summit, the dissolving snow in foaming torrents rushed down the sides and chasms of its rugged surface, exhibiting altogether a sublime, though gloomy spectacle, which animated nature seemed to have

Looking north over Sechelt Rapids near the mouth of Jervis Inlet on the "Sunshine Coast" north of Vancouver. Tidal currents here are considered the world's fastest; consequently sea life is rich—and scuba diving excellent during the brief periods around slack water. (Neil G. McDaniel)

deserted. Not a bird, nor living creature was to be seen, and the roaring of the falling cataracts in every direction precluded their being heard, had any been in our neighborhood.

On June 16th they left "Howe's Sound" (named after Admiral Richard Howe), sailing northward along what is now called the Sunshine Coast. "This part of the coast is of a moderate height for some distance inland, and it frequently juts out into low sandy projecting points. The country in general produces forest trees in great abundance, of some variety and magnitude." The captain would not have been surprised had he returned little more than a century later to find a thriving forest industry and a trio of huge pulp mills along this coast.

Following the channel between the mainland and long narrow Texada Island (already named, as he would soon discover, by rival Spanish explorers), Vancouver discovered the entrance to Jervis Inlet ("Jervis's Channel"—after Sir John Jervis). "The cataracts here rushed from the rugged snowy mountains with [even] greater number and more impetuosity than in Howe's Sound." Intrigued, he and his crew rowed the full 50 miles up the narrow, twisting channel to its head.

They were now "at least 114 miles" from the mother ships anchored back at Point Gray, and almost out of provisions. On the forth day of rowing—sometimes "with a strong southerly gale against us"—they finally arrived back at Burrard Inlet to find two armed Spanish vessels, a brig and a schooner.

Despite the rivalry beween Britain and Spain, the Spanish captains—Galiano (for whom a major Gulf Island is named) and Valdes (who gave his name to the port in Prince William Sound that is now terminus of the Alaska Pipeline)—greeted Vancouver as a brother. After trading survey charts and information, they gave him a warm letter of introduction to Bodega y Quadra, the Spanish commander at Nootka. They even offered to carry him and his men back to *Discovery*. The captain, driven as ever, "declined their obliging offer, and having partaken with them a very hearty breakfast, bade them farewell..."

While on board the Spanish vessels he discovered that Eliza and Quimper had preceded him to Discovery Bay and that the Spanish had charted the Gulf of Georgia as far north as Texada Island, though hardly to the detail he demanded from his own men. Galiano and Valdes, on the other hand, were surprised to find that the British had not found the major river (later discovered, overland, by Simon Fraser) "said to exist in this region." For some reason, the extensive shoals south of Burrard Inlet never suggested to Vancouver that they were the delta of a large river.

Meanwhile, Whidbey and Broughton in *Discovery* and *Chatham* had been exploring Birch and Bellingham bays. After gathering their descriptions, Vancouver set sail up the Gulf. On the afternoon of the 24th, he again met with the Spanish. Galiano and Valdes joined him on *Discovery* for the afternoon as the four vessels travelled together up Georgia Strait before separating.

The next morning, caught in light, shifting winds, the British ships found themselves—as would the *Western Prince* two centuries later—among a gathering of orcas. "In the course of the forenoon a great number of whales were playing about in every direction; and though we had been frequently visited by these animals in this inland navigation, there seemed more about us now, than the whole of those we had before seen, if collected together." These may have been the ancestors of our J-, K-, and L-pods.

By June 26, the ships reached the northern end of the Gulf and found themselves among a maze of channels "surrounded by a detached and broken country, whose general appearance was very inhospitable. Stupendous rocky mountains rising almost perpendicularly from the sea..." He called the area "Desolation Sound."

At the entrance of "Bute's Channel" (Bute Inlet), friendly Indians invited the British sailors to their village. The unusual village was "situated on the face of a steep rock, containing about one hundred and fifty of the natives...now many came off in a most civil and friendly manner, with a plentiful supply of fresh herrings and other fish, which they bartered in a fair and honest way for nails. These were of greater value amongst them, than any other articles our people had to offer."

A village a few miles away was built atop a cliff, protected by a large platform built out over the cliff. "The whole seemed so skilfully contrived, and so firmly and well executed, as rendered it difficult to be considered the work of the untutored tribes we had been accustomed to meet..."

Eager to see if a route through the islands existed, Johnstone was dispatched with a week's supplies in *Chatham's* cutter. At the end of the week, the cutter hadn't returned, and Vancouver "began to be anxiously solicitous for their welfare."

Early the next morning, though, Johnstone arrived "all well." He had discovered "a passage leading into the Pacific Ocean to the north-westward..." which Vancouver promptly named Johnstone Strait.

In the course of the trip Johnstone had met with Indians who had muskets and were familiar with Europeans. These proved to be "under the authority of Maquinna, the chief of the Nootka..." whose capital village lay on the island's outer coast. The trip had come full circle. Nootka was Vancouver's official destination from the start.

Following the first circumnavigation of the island, Vancouver landed at Nootka at the end of August, to negotiate with Bodega y Quadra. In honor of the meeting, he named the island Vancouver and Quadra's Island.

Failing to arrive at a satisfactory agreement with Quadra, however, Captain Vancouver sent home for further instructions—by ships that would take months to reach their destination. Taking advantage of the opportunity to explore further, he spent the next two summers charting the West Coast, from southern California to Alaska.

In the fall of 1794, Vancouver and his men sailed home, returning to Petersham, England, in September, 1795.

"Upon his arrival home," writes historian Meany, "he gave himself wholly to the work of preparing his journal for publication, but before this was done, on May 10, 1798, he died [at age 39]. His life was evidently shortened by the hardships endured on his great expedition. He never spared himself, and was frequently exposed to rough weather in open boats, short of food, and roughing it like the hardiest of his men."

Vancouver's career had spanned a change of eras in North America. He himself had seen the Salish Sea transformed. Its native peoples—weakened by epidemics of smallpox and malaria—were declining rapidly. The Spanish colonial navy, which had stymied Russian expansion during the past decade, were in turn displaced by British traders backed by the world's most powerful navy. Now it was clearly a struggle between the British and the emerging United States for regional control.

Vancouver's explorations speeded the transformation, even though he had neither conquered territory nor found commercial riches. The publication of his charts and journal alone utterly changed the Pacific Northwest in the mind of the outside world: Puget Sound and Georgia Strait were now on the world map; the frightening unknown had become the comfortably charted. A new picture of the region had been painted, replacing the bleak terrain of treacherous coastlines peopled by cannibalistic savages.

In Vancouver's journal the Salish Sea's scenery was breathtaking, the natives friendly, the harbors deep and sheltered, the soil arable, the trees immense, the climate serene. It was an open invitation to colonize.

Fifty years would pass before another sailing ship entered Puget Sound—American this time—and 60 years before the first real wave of colonists would arrive. But just a century after *Discovery* and *Chatham* sailed back to England, Washington would be a state; railroad trains would be puffing into Tacoma and Seattle; and the ASARCO copper smelter would rise above Commencement Bay like a beacon touting the Industrial Revolution.

For better or worse, these remote inland waters, with their rich natural resources, were now a charted part of the "known world." Just by being on the map, they would never be the same.

Overleaf:
Vancouver's map compares well with modern satellite images.

Eros (above) and Landsat (right) images provide a modern view of the Salish Sea. Green natural areas appear red, developed areas, blue. Some of the white in the upper image is cloud cover, the rest is glaciers.

The Fraser river's influence on the salinity, nutrient balance, and water quality of lower Georgia Strait is highlighted by its immense bluish plume. (Eros Satellite Data Center)

Opposite:
Vancouver's surprisingly accurate map of the Salish Sea. Discovery's path is traced; Chatham and the longboats covered considerably more territory. (University of Washington Special Collections, Negative UW 14343)

In their nest high above Georgia Strait a Bald eagle pair performs a ritual to signal transfer of duties. One takes over the nest, freeing the other to hunt. (Peter M. Roberts)

A Symphony of Seabirds

It was a glorious summer afternoon along the west shore of Discovery Bay, near where Quimper and Vancouver made their first landings two centuries ago. Paddling my kayak around the sheltering cliffs of Diamond Point into the windy Strait of Juan de Fuca, I headed due north toward Protection Island. Absorbed in fighting a stiff chop, I almost missed the eagle, flying just 50 feet above my head.

The adult Bald eagle's distinctive white cowl and yellow, hooked bill contrasted with its dark brown wings and belly, lethal golden talons pressed up against its broad, white tail. It glanced down briefly with piercing yellow eyes as it beat against the same wind, toward our common destination. I felt a surge of energy, and tried to keep up; but the eagle easily pulled away on strong, steady wingbeats.

One of the joys of living along the Salish Sea is the daily possibility of such encounters. I have startled Bald eagles from trees overlooking Olympia's state Capitol, watched them nesting in Seattle's Discovery Park, seen them flying over Victoria. Hundreds of pairs of Bald eagles nest along the shoreline, and hundreds more migrate from inland Canada and coastal Alaska to the Salish Sea and its rivers during winter—both to escape freezing weather and to feast on salmon carcasses along the region's riverbanks and sandbars. In mid-January, up to 300 Bald eagles roost along a single 7-mile stretch of the Skagit River in northwestern Washington.

Eagles are numerous for good reason. Spawning salmon, their favorite prey, return to local rivers June to January. Winter runs of Steelhead on the Skagit and other large rivers offer easy pickings during the otherwise difficult winter season. Flocks of migrant and wintering ducks and other marine birds cover sheltered bays autumn through spring. Eagles pick off sick and crippled ones and will sometimes harass even healthy ones to exhaustion.

Extremely flexible in their diet, Bald eagles are quick to spot carcasses of fish and seabirds washing up onto cobble beaches throughout the year and are not above pirating live fish from Ospreys or dead ones from gulls and crows. On San Juan Island, exploding populations of feral rabbits often end up as roadkill, contributing protein to the feast. Not coincidentally, the San Juans support one of North America's densest congregations of nesting Bald eagles: 40-50 pairs in good years.

During early spring, the eagles build nests near a beach or river, preferably in large snags (standing dead trees) partly obscured by a dense stand of younger trees. Courtship rituals include mutual gifts of nest material and elaborate courtship flights. Mating may take place in the air a mile above the earth!

The huge, untidy nests may contain a ton of sticks; and so, rather than start from scratch, the eagles prefer to refurbish last-year's nests. Over the years a single eagle pair will usually work on two or three in the same general area—good insurance, since it would be difficult to start over from scratch if something goes wrong. The weighty nest may break the limb it's built on. Sooner or later it will be destroyed by winter storms. Eventually, the whole snag will fall from old age. And breeding eagles are quick to desert a nest disturbed by people, logging, or nearby construction.

Once settled in, both parents take turns incubating their one or two large white eggs, though the slightly larger female may spend more time on the nest, while the male does more foraging. After the chicks are hatched, one or the other parent still remains in the nest to protect the nestlings from ravens, crows, and gulls. Food brought to the nest is torn into small strips by the solicitous parent, who feeds it piece by piece to the voracious nestlings.

Dark flight feathers gradually replace the nestling's gray down. As it reaches adult size, the youngster spends more and more time flapping and exercising its wings, moving closer and closer to the edge. Eventually, the fledgling makes its first, tentative flight, landing awkwardly on a lower branch, or even falling clumsily to the ground.

Soon flying with grace, it still spends months accompanying the parents, begging for food while learning to play the tricky summer winds and updrafts. Later it will spar with the hoards of migrant eagles along local rivers for its share of spawned-out fall-run Chinook and the winter Chum salmon returning into small coastal streams. By late winter it will be practiced enough to pick off unwary or injured gulls and ducks and take whatever the sea provides—flounders half-eaten by gulls or washed-up seabirds drowned in fishing nets.

Later it may wander the coast in the company of other juveniles. If energetic and lucky enough it will survive to find a mate and build its own nest, or possibly even reclaim the one of its birth.

A young Bald eagle takes four or five years to assume the distinctive adult plumage. Meanwhile, it resembles its landlubber cousin, the Golden eagle. Where the two are found together—as on San Juan Island—the immature Bald's longer neck and shorter tail is the easiest way to distinguish it (the Golden's wings seem to spread from just behind its head).

Both eagles can be told even from a distance from the Turkey vultures with whom they share the summer thermals: Eagles soar with wings out straight, while vultures hold them in a shallow V. For such a large, fierce-looking bird, the Bald eagle's call is surprisingly weak and reedy; yet it carries well above the low crash of surf or the cacophony of gulls.

Protection Island must be paradise for eagles. The Strait of Juan de Fuca's fish-rich waters surround it. And during a breeding season lasting from February to June, the island hosts 60,000 nesting birds of 30 species. This includes more than half of Washington's entire breeding seabird population.

Named by Vancouver because it acts as a breakwater for Discovery Bay, Protection Island is itself protected from winter storm waves rolling in from the ocean by the long arm of Dungeness Spit, just a dozen miles to the west.

Recently, the island gained even more critical protection.

Previous to the 1970s, Protection had been lightly populated by a few summer visitors. But its future was as clear as its magnificent views of the Olympics and Vancouver Island. Its 370 acres were being subdivided by a developer into more than 800 tiny lots for vacation and retirement homes, along with roads and an airstrip (not to mention the inevitable invasion of cats and dogs). The seabird colonies seemed doomed.

For years Audubon Society members and other environmentalists tried to slow the inevitable. In desperation, they even tried to buy the nesting colony sites lot-by-lot, despite rapidly escalating prices. At the last minute, the island was granted a reprieve. Purchased by the U.S. Fish & Wildlife Service, it was established as Protection Island National Wildlife Refuge in 1988. A handful of long-time residents remain on the island under 15-year grandfather permits, but otherwise only wildlife biologists with special use permits are allowed to step ashore. Even boats are prohibited within 200 yards.

A young Bald eagle exercises its wings at the edge of its nest in preparation for its maiden flight. (Peter M. Roberts)

Adult Glaucous-winged gulls. The Salish Sea's resident gull can be distinguished from closely related Herring and Western gulls by the uniformly gray wings. Large gull species, mottled brown when young, take up to four years to develop adult plumage. (Art Wolfe)

Though Protection Island is buffered from the brunt of southwesterly storms and from direct swells rolling in from the Pacific, its gusty winds, tricky currents, and unpredictable waves add spice to any trip. It was a relief to reach the barely ruffled surface in the lee of the island's tall cliffs, where I could begin a more leisurely paddle.

Above, along the cliff's edge, there were a few houses but no human voices or sounds of activity. The island seemed deserted. Rounding Violet Point at its eastern tip, though, it was wildlife city.

Against the background crash of waves came the low grunts, moans, and sighs of fifty or more hauled-out Harbor seals—adults and fat little pups lining the long sandbar like gray driftlogs. Clumps of cormorants dried their outspread wings in the sun. Flocks of dark, handsome Heermann's gulls stood at the edge of the bar, heads pointing into the wind. A hundred nesting Glaucous-winged gulls, squabbling among themselves with querulous cries, lifted and fell like wind-blown paper.

The Glaucous-winged is the Salish Sea's resident gull—a true seagull, unlike some of the region's migrant species which breed inland. Protection Island hosts the largest Glaucous-winged breeding colony—3,000 or more. A few thousand more can be found on small, uninhabited islets among the Gulf Islands and San Juan archipelago.

Limited to the west coast of North America, the Glaucous-winged gull is closely related to the cosmopolitan Herring gull, lacking only the Herring gull's black wing-tips. It is even closer to the Western gull of the outer Pacific coast, with whom it freely interbreeds; hybrid offspring sport the light gray (glaucous) wings of the former, with the black wing tips of the Western. Some scientists view the Glaucous-winged, Herring, and Western gulls as a single, highly variable, species.

Glaucous-winged gulls lay their two or three eggs in depressions among grass or on bare rock. Fluffy, grayish nestlings elicit food by pecking at the bright red dot near the tip of the parent's lower bill, stimulating the adult to regurgitate scraps of food. Full-grown at about two months of age, youngsters loiter near the nest to beg until they are finally ignored by the parents.

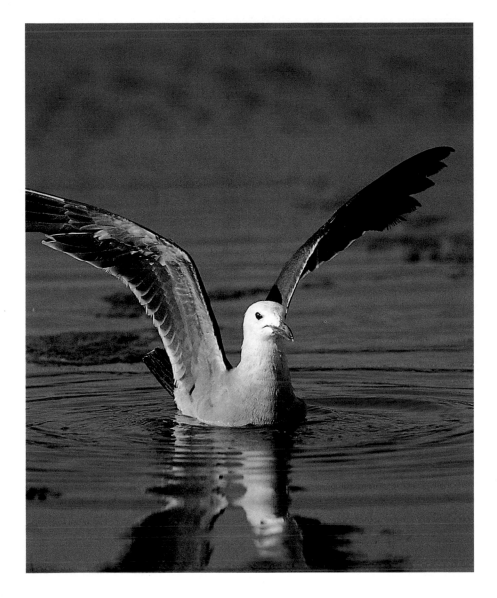

An adult Herrmann's gull sports a bright red-orange bill. Unlike most birds, these summer visitors breed during the winter—from Baja California southward. (John Gerlach/Earth Images)

Even when they are fully independent, the brownish juveniles, still inefficient at finding their own food, will chase and pester adults for scraps of fish or crab, or for the clams dropped onto the beach from above to crack the shell. Like other large gull species, Glaucous-winged juveniles lose their mottled brown feathers over the course of four years, gradually assuming the white body, light gray wings, yellow bill with red spot, and the bright pink feet characteristic of breeding adults.

Avoiding the tumultuous Glaucous-winged colony with its neighborly squabbles and predator alerts, the stately Heermann's gulls remained on the edge of the sandbar.

Heermann's are smaller than the Glaucous-winged but their breeding plumage is more striking. The dark brown tail is edged by a thin, white terminal band; the dark wings contrast with a white neck and head which serve to emphasize the almost Day-glo red of its bill.

Heermann's are not breeders here, as would be expected at this time of year. Unlike most North American birds, they breed in winter. They nest along both coasts of Baja California (winter tourists to Puerto Vallarta or Mazatlan will recognize them as the common large gull species along the coast). Dispersing in fall, most of the Herrmann's gull population remains south of Oregon; but small flocks reach as far north as the Salish Sea. Less versatile feeders than Glaucous-winged or related gulls, they they do not scavange along the beach's edge and are rarely found inland at garbage dumps; they concentrate instead on schools of small fishes in the rip-tide currents.

As I drifted past Violet Point, dozens of Harbor seals floated upright in the water nearby. Some swam out to check out my kayak, and a few followed me rather closely. The most aggressive ones slapped their rear flippers against the water to remind me that it's *their* territory, and I'm a barely tolerated visitor.

Off the seaward side of the island, seabirds rested on the water, including small, wary groups of the one most prized by local birders—the Tufted puffin.

The Tufted puffin's body is an undistinguished dark gray; but in breeding season its stocky neck supports a large, colorful head and massive bill—a work of art rivaling tropical toucans or parrots. The titanium-white face sets off a small dark eye with a bright red circle around it. A long, flaxen plume extends from behind the eye. Except for the yellow rear half of the upper mandible, the swollen bill is a flaming red-orange. The bill's color extends in a thinner line around the back of the mouth, giving the illusion of red lipstick on a clown's face. Gaudiest of the North American puffin species, the Tufted breeds in small, scattered colonies along the entire North Pacific coast. It winters far out at sea.

Once found in small colonies throughout the Gulf and San Juan Islands, Tufted puffin nests are now almost absent from the smaller islands—due perhaps to disturbances from motorized boat traffic. Decades ago a thousand or more nested on Protection Island but the population has fallen precipitously. Recent surveys counted fewer than 70 individuals.

In order to expand the Protection Island puffin colony, U.S. Fish & Wildlife biologist Ulrich Wilson suggests translocating some puffin eggs to Protection Island from the outer coast, where they are more numerous. Raised on the island by the few remaining adults, they might later return here to breed. At the present low numbers, a single predator, disease or oil spill could wipe out the Salish Sea's entire puffin population.

Far more numerous on Protection are the puffin's close relative—the Rhinoceros auklet. The 18,000 Rhinoceros auklet pairs that nest on the island during summer comprise the largest colony south of Alaska, and this colony alone contributes more than half of the Salish Sea's entire seabird population.

Vancouver's surgeon/naturalist Archibald Menzies gave the large grayish auklet its Rhino moniker in honor of the "horn" which rises from the base of its thickened yellow bill during breeding season. Adding dash, a double pair of white plumes extends down the grayish neck from behind the eye and bill. Despite its name, Wilson and seabird biologist David Manuwal consider the seabird more a puffin than an auklet.

Using the sharp nails at the end of their webbed feet, puffins and auklets tunnel into grassy hills at the top of the island or into sandy slopes. The burrows may meander for ten feet or more (Manuwal measured one on nearby Smith Island that wandered 25 feet, including side tunnels). Within these dark burrows, they raise a single chick.

During summer breeding season, the Tufted puffin sports a colorful, inflated bill. The bill and its rough, cornified tongue allow the parent to carry up to a half dozen sand lance, herring, or smelt from distant feeding grounds back to its nestling. Protection Island is the puffin's most important local breeding site.
(Ervio Sian)

Pigeon guillemots are alcids—related to puffins and auklets. In summer they return to local waters to breed in cliff burrows and talus crevices. (R. Wayne Campbell)

Protection Island's Rhinoceros auklets spend much of their days around the San Juan Islands to the north, fishing there in the rip-tide currents. Diving from the surface, they pump their stubby wings to streak through dense fish schools—especially Pacific herring or the slender, eel-like Pacific sand lance.

A rough (cornified) tongue allows auklets and puffins to hold one or more slippery fish against toothlets (denticles) on the upper bill while they continue capturing others. The parent bird can then return over the strait to Protection with up to a half-dozen sand lance dangling from its bill.

The plump chick develops slowly in the burrow, eventually growing even heavier than its parents. One starry night it flutters awkwardly off the cliff and plops onto the sea to begin its oceanic life. Years later, it will return to this same spot to breed.

Puffins and auklets belong to the seabird family called alcids. Most diving birds such as loons, grebes, or cormorants, swim underwater by pushing forward, seal-like, with their webbed feet. But alcids—like penguins of the southern hemisphere—use their stubby wings to "fly" beneath the waves, speedily twisting and turning in a stream of silvery bubbles to chase elusive fishes. Though this unusual action is difficult to observe in the wild, it can be enjoyed behind glass at the Seattle Aquarium's Puget Sound Habitat exhibit.

The bill of each alcid species is modified to capture and hold a different size or type of prey; for most, the preferred prey are small schooling fishes. The Cassin's auklet, however—which breeds on the outer coast but occasionally winters in the San Juans—captures tiny planktonic animals such as euphausiids, copepods, and fish fry with a spoonlike bill, storing the thickened plankton paste in a special throat pouch to bring back for its nestling.

As wintering and migrant seabirds desert the Salish Sea for arctic or inland nesting grounds, our most widespread alcid, the Pigeon guillemot, moves in from Washington's outer coast.

The Pigeon guillemot's summer plumage is black, save for a large white wing patch, used in a courtship "water dance." Males also display their bright red-orange legs and feet in dazzling aerial flights and, on land, to engage in a rather comic swaying courtship dance around potential mates.

Nesting all along the Salish Sea's coastline, Pigeon guillemots are flexible in choosing nest sites. On Protection Island, where dense Rhinoceros auklet colonies monopolize the upper cliffs, the guillemots' eggs are laid in crevices in talus slopes or beneath drift logs on beaches.

Puget Sound's glacial cliffs seem ideal for the guillemot. They can be spotted almost everywhere: Look for the openings of burrows in the sandy soil near the top of a cliff.

The guillemot will dig its own burrow but often time-shares with Belted kingfishers. Kingfishers dig similar nest tunnels early in spring and their young develop quickly, so a late-breeding guillemot can move in after the fledglings leave. Pigeon guillemot parents zip in and out of the burrows throughout the day with slender blennies dangling from their bills. Small flocks occasionally gather in front of the cliffs, talking back and forth in almost continuous soft, squeaky trills.

The three other alcid species which can be spotted hereabouts do not breed locally. The Common murre, a rather large seabird with a long, slender, pointed black bill, is most abundant. In winter the murre's neck is white but in summer its body is dark above the water line and white below—a typical form of seabird countershading that makes it less visible to predatory eagles looking down from above, and to fish prey looking up from below.

Common murres nest in dense colonies on steep, exposed cliffs along the outer Pacific coast (where the fledglings are especially vulnerable to periodic oil spills). Only the shape of the eggs—narrow and pointed on one end so that they will spin in a tight circle—keeps them from rolling off the narrow ledges. By late July or early August large flocks of murres move into the eastern Strait of Juan de Fuca from as far away as Oregon and California to feed in and around the deeper San Juan channels. A strong diver, the murre can stay under for a minute or two at a time chasing larger-sized schooling fishes.

Two species of murrelets—small stocky seabirds about half the size of the Common murre—are scattered about the northern straits but are rare. Ancient murrelets can be occasionally seen in fall and winter in the San Juans and as far south as Seattle. They prefer open water. Small flocks sometimes feed along Dungeness Spit, hunting just off the sandbar in a line, like ducks in a carnival booth. They dive one after the other, in perfect order, then bob back up to rejoin the line.

The more common Marbled murrelet migrates through our region in large flocks; occasionally thousands winter for a while around the San Juans or on Padilla Bay, a popular seabird wintering site south of Bellingham.

In summer, pairs of Marbled murrelets disperse to fish. Mates keep in close contact by whistling back and forth as they poke through kelp beds in front of a rocky shore, and so they are often heard before being seen. Unlike the graphic black and white breeding outfit of the Common murre and Pigeon guillemot, the Marbled murrelet is a mottled brown, perhaps to camouflage it around its varied nest sites.

Its nesting habits, in fact, promise to make this little murrelet the most controversial of alcids, and perhaps of all seabirds.

Nests of the Marbled murrelet have rarely been found—the first one, high in an ancient Douglas fir, in California, was not seen until 1974—though not for lack of looking. One naturalist friend of mine has spent months searching, unsuccessfully, on the Olympic Peninsula, and teams of U.S. Fish & Wildlife biologists have spent futile summers in pursuit.

The reasons are not hard to understand. The dark, wary, speedy little murrelet leaves the well-camouflaged nest before dawn and returns at dusk. And the few nests found so far, mostly by accident, have been inland, mostly in dense old-growth forest.

Even when radio-tagged, the birds have proved elusive—perhaps too elusive for their own good. Marbled murrelet populations have plummeted in recent years, and indications are that the murrelet, like the Spotted owl, may be the victim of rapid deforestation, especially of coastal old-growth. Yet, until more nests are found and populations better estimated, it will be difficult to invoke legislation to protect its habitat.

Ballingal Islet in Georgia Strait. Even the smallest islands, if undisturbed, are crucial breeding sites for Double-crested cormorants and other marine birds. Boaters should stay well offshore during the spring and summer nesting season. (R. Wayne Campbell)

W henever I approached Protection Island's cliffs, cormorants leapt from their narrow ledges. Cormorants are the most obvious of all local seabirds due to their habit of standing on piers and pilings while holding out their large wings to dry (they lack the water-proof surfacing of most aquatic birds). But they are not particularly tame. Since they are heavy-bodied and have difficulty getting airborne, they often spook before other seabirds, leaping from land or diving beneath the waves.

With their dense bodies, wettable feathers, and large, webbed feet set far back on the body, cormorants are able to dive to more than 100-foot depths in pursuit of fish. In shallower water, their maneuverability and long, flexible neck allows them to slither through the kelp or eelgrass after the quickest fish, which they grasp with a long, hooked, serrated bill. Double-crested cormorants prefer small schooling fish, while the smaller Pelagic cormorants search rocky reefs for sculpins, shrimps, and octopus. Cormorants gather from their feeding areas at dusk, returning in tight V-formation to colonial roosting spots to settle in for the night.

Brandt's cormorant, the largest of the three local species, breeds mostly on the outer coast, sometimes moving into more sheltered water for the winter (though a small breeding colony has recently been noted on Protection Island). The familiar Double-crested and and the smaller, glossy Pelagic cormorant breed on Protection Island, as well as on the isolated Gulf and San Juan islands and other locations scattered throughout the Salish Sea.

Surprisingly, cormorants are related to pelicans—most apparent in the expandable gular (throat) pouch. The Double-crested's is bright yellow-orange, the Brandt's a vivid turquoise blue. Like the pelican's larger one, the cormorant's elastic pouch also stretches to swallow a large fish or to store food for the nestlings. Cormorants also pant by fluttering the bare skin of the gular pouch to cool themselves while incubating their eggs or shading the nestlings during warm afternoons on the open nest. The brightly colored throat patch is also important for courtship rituals, which include crouched poses with tail spread and bill held skyward, and in the pair's sensuous intertwinings of the snakelike neck.

The mature Double-crested's flaxen crests may be difficult to see but its large size and orange throat patch are diagnostic. It lays three or four eggs in a platform of sticks lined with seaweed and feathers—in trees but more often on grassy knolls or bare rock—often in dense concentrations.

The less sociable Pelagic prefers isolated ledges on the cliff-face. It builds a minimal nest (if any) of seaweeds or grasses cemented together with its own excrement. Its pointed eggs, like those of the Common murre, are designed to revolve in place so that they won't roll off the narrow ledge. The adult Pelagic has a bright white rump-patch and in flight can easily be distinguished by its straight slender neck (the Double-crested's thicker one is held kinked) and a tail that is almost as long as its neck.

Juveniles of both species are brown, but the young Double-crested is pale-breasted and has a yellowish throat patch.

We think of the ubiquitous Double-crested cormorant as abundant because it is so visible. Yet one seabird expert estimates that there are fewer than 10,000 breeding pairs on the entire west coast of North America. Nest disturbance, fishing nets, pesticides, and oil spills are serious threats to the species.

Two resident shorebirds also nest along Protection Island's beaches. The ubiquitous Killdeer, with its white, double-collared neck can be found on every beach along the Salish Sea, as well as sites farther inland. The Killdeer lays its clutch of three or four eggs behind drift logs or even out in the open above the high-tide line and depends upon

The Black oystercatcher uses its bright red bill as a bar to pry limpets from rocks and as a knife to slice open mussels. During breeding season along rocky shores, pairs can be heard "piping" and be observed bowing ritually to each other. (David Denning/Earth Images)

its aggressive energy alone to protect them. It flies noisily out at every intruder, cheeping and complaining, flying off down the beach to divert attention from the nest. If it feels seriously threatened, it fans its rust-colored tail and walks unsteadily away, dragging a wing as if injured, leading a naive predator away from the nest.

The more specialized Black oystercatcher is adapted to feeding on rocky, waveswept shores. Its pattern is striking. The chunky body is all black, but is elevated on slender pink legs. Its bright yellow eye is encircled in red. Its long, slender bill is bright red-orange. The oyster-catcher uses its colorful, laterally compressed bill as a multi-purpose tool. It can pry limpets and chitons off intertidal rocks; it opens clams and mussels by sliding between the valves of the shell to slice the adductor muscle holding them together, then serves as a slender forceps to extract the meat.

Black oystercatchers are most visible during spring, when contrasting colors are brightest. Often first noticed as the pair pipes shrilly back and forth to keep in contact, they can be seen piping and bowing stiffly to each other, over and over, in courtship.

As I slowly round the island, the late afternoon sun turns the massive, wind- and wave-carved glacial cliffs a golden yellow. At intervals, the slender, glossy-green forms of Pelagic cormorants stand like statues in niches in the cliffs, above a patina of white birdwash. The whole island resembles a temple designed by a master architect from another age. Thankfully, it is not a ruins but a living testament. I can only offer a moment of meditative thanks to those who fought to preserve it.

On a time-lapse video from a stationary satellite, the Salish Sea would resemble a large-scale version of Seattle or Vancouver international airports at Christmas rush. It is a busy hub of North America's major west coast flyways.

Winter descends early on the Arctic tundra, and not much later on breeding lakes dotting the high plains of Canada. By late fall, storms begin to lash the exposed Pacific coast. In response, vast hoards of waterbirds move into the Fraser/Puget lowlands from three directions: south from northern breeding grounds; westward from interior lakes and forests; inland from the exposed outer coast.

We see these migrating birds mostly when they're feeding and resting. It takes a stretch of the imagination to realize that the rest is well deserved.

Many ducks, geese, and shorebirds are midway on strenuous migrations up or down the entire west coasts of North and South America. Tiny Dunlins and Western Sandpipers have no hospitable "fueling stops" between the Frazer River Delta and Alaska's Copper River Delta, a thousand miles to the north. Some Arctic terns and Sanderlings hardly rest between the high Arctic and Tierra del Fuego at the tip of South America. Every stop is crucial if they are to balance calories in with the energy needed to fly, stay warm, and feed on the move.

Even those birds which winter no farther south than our shores have to build up tremendous energy stores for the annual bouts of moulting, courtship (due to the added weight, testes and ovaries develop only during this period, then wither until the following year), nest-building, egg-laying, and the protection and feeding of their young. And they often arrive in the far north or inland prairies while the spring climate is still harsh and food still scarce.

Just inland from a coastline that is almost entirely rocky and mountainous for hundreds of miles in either direction, the Salish Sea and surrounding lowlands offer something for everyone—a sheltered arm of the Pacific, large estuarine bays, freshwater lakes and rivers, and

Long-billed dowitchers extract worms and crabs from the intertidal mud as they pause on muddy beaches and salt marshes along their migration routes to and from Arctic nesting grounds.
(John Gerlach/Earth Images)

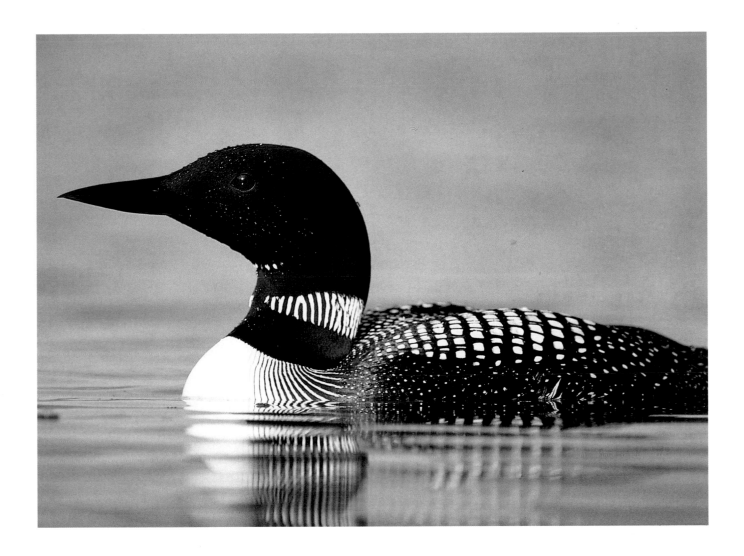

remnants of once-extensive wetlands. The area is invaluable, both as a fuel-rich stopover for migrants and as a relatively mild winter refuge for those that remain until spring.

Populations swell at the height of fall migration, stabilize at high levels during winter, swell again as migrant flocks join the wintering birds, then plummet in May as all but the few local nesting species leave for the far north's brief, intense summer.

Not all migrating birds take the same route south as they do north. Common terns and Red-necked phalaropes, for example, are much more common here in fall than in spring. Tundra swans, Brandt geese, Black scoters, and Red-breasted mergansers are more common in spring. But almost every West Coast species uses the area at some time. And many, finding conditions ideal, go no farther.

One day in August, a walk along the inland waters might yield only Glaucous-winged gulls, Mallard ducks, Great blue herons, a kingfisher or two, or early flocks of migrant Bonaparte's gulls and Common terns. The next week flocks of Dunlin rise from drift logs, Mew gulls pick through the muddy sand along the shore; a half-dozen species of sea ducks cover the bays; Horned grebes and a Common loon dive from the surface.

The Common loon, usually solitary, hunts for fish just off shore—its head almost below water as it searches for fish. Able to squeeze the insulating air from between its feathers, the loon rides low in the water,

A Common loon in breeding plumage. This handsome bird was revered by some Salish tribes and has achieved modern cult status on nesting lakes in the midwest and New England. (Peter M. Roberts)

like a cormorant; but its shorter, thicker neck is white, its bill spear-shaped rather than hooked.

The Common loon breeds on inland lakes throughout Alaska and Canada, and on scattered ones from Minnesota to Vermont—where it has become something of a media star, especially since the Broadway play and hit movie "On Golden Pond." In the northeastern U.S. there are now societies formed exclusively to protect and celebrate the loon. Recent years have seen it the subject of innumerable books, television specials, and home videos (some of the best by Seattle-based Peter Roberts Productions).

It is not hard to sense the loon's appeal. It's one of our larger waterbirds (equal in size to a Double-crested cormorant). It's a powerful diving bird (in fact "diver" is its name in Britain), with a formidable sharp bill. Its costume is striking: green head with black bill and red eye, complemented by a handsome body pattern of white and black collar, stripes, dots, and reticulations. And its "crazed yodeling" on breeding lakes rivals the wolf's howl as voice of the northern wilderness.

Loon yodeling is rare on the Salish Sea, and its summer finery quickly fades to undistinguished winter gray. Even so, the loon was revered by some Salish groups as embodying *swo-kwad*, a powerful war spirit.

Three other loons spend the winter here. The largest, the Yellow-billed, is not easy to spot. It closely resembles the Common loon but is slightly larger; and its longer, sharper bill is yellowish rather than black. Though not often noticed here among the more numerous Common loons, the San Juan and Gulf islands are, according to Mark Lewis and Fred Sharpe's *Birding in the San Juan Islands*, center of one of the Yellow-billed's most important wintering areas south of Alaska.

Flocks of swan-necked Western grebes winter in sheltered bays. The spearlike bill is designed to stab fishes. (Peter M. Roberts)

The Red-throated loon can be told in winter plumage by its small size and its thin, slightly uptilted bill. Its gray crown and back of neck contrast sharply with its white cheeks. Red-throateds feed in small groups in shallow bays. Fairly common hereabouts, it is most often overlooked among large flocks of the far more abundant Pacific loon.

Formerly lumped with the Eurasian Arctic loon but now separated into its own species, the Pacific loon makes up in numbers what it lacks in size or mystique. Flocks from the tundra pass through late in the summer; by October they comprise large rafts, most often in the eastern Strait of Juan de Fuca or off the San Juan and Gulf islands, where they feed in tidal rips. Wintering populations here are said to be the greatest in North America.

Grebes are another family of birds well-adapted for diving but poorly designed for land. Like loons and cormorants, their legs are set far back on the body. Instead of the webbing between toes possessed by most diving birds, grebes have lobes of flesh, resembling willow leaves, alongside each long, slender toe. When pulled forward, they close up to offer little resistance but when pushed against the water, they open to create a weblike surface.

Like loons and cormorants, large grebes dive for fish. Smaller species take shrimp, amphipods, and other small crustaceans as well. Even though all three of our common saltwater grebes have light necks with dark cap and back, the three can easily be told apart by their size and by the relative lengths of their necks.

The ubiquitous Horned grebe is found in twos and threes off every rocky beach, seawall, and marina along the Salish Sea through all but the summer months. Smallest and most active of the three North American saltwater grebe species, it gives a characteristic little leap up

Western grebes perform dazzling courtship runs along the water. Fully developed only on inland breeding lakes, this behavior can be glimpsed here during spring migration. (Peter M. Roberts)

A Bonaparte's gull lands on an evergreen. The black head of breeding plumage will lighten to a single dark spot behind the eye soon after the birds arrive from the north in late summer. (Art Wolfe)

from the surface at the beginning of its dive as it goes down to search for blennies or shrimp. Like other grebes, it can also sink slowly beneath the surface.

The occasional Horned grebe still sporting its colorful breeding plumage when it arrives here might be thought another species from the drab bird of winter: its sides and neck are a bright rust color, its cheeks and head are puffed out by dark feathers and topped by long, golden "horns" running from the sharp black bill and over the bright red eye.

The Red-necked grebe has a much less spectacular breeding costume—its neck turns rusty gold and its gray cheeks are bordered by a white crescent—but in winter it stands out from the Horned grebes. Its longer, yellowish bill and white ear stripe distinguish it; but its sillhouette is a more useful field mark. Fifty percent larger than the Horned, it is much more stately, holding its longer, more slender neck straight up most of the time.

The Western grebe, our largest species, takes elegance a step further. Its long, slender neck gives it the nickname "swan-grebe." Even with its distinctive profile, the Western grebe would be hard to confuse with other local aquatic birds. Its bright white cheeks and throat contrast strongly with its dark crown and back of neck. Its eye is red. Its long, bright yellow bill is slender and sharp (the apt generic name, *Aechmomophorus*, is Greek for "spear-bearing"). With it, the long-necked grebe stabs small fishes and crabs.

Late in fall a large flock of Western grebes regularly appears off Seattle's Discovery Park near the Lake Union Ship Canal. It is not unusual for 250 or more to be found out beyond the kelp beds day after day, resting with their heads laid on their backs or calling back and forth in loud, creaking voices. Even larger aggregations may be seen farther north on Padilla Bay. In May, the flocks suddenly vanish for inland breeding lakes throughout the American west and Canadian prairie provinces.

Even before leaving, Western grebes begin to practice their spectacular courtship dance. Here, on salt water in spring, the dance usually peters out half-heartedly. But on breeding lakes potential pairs culminate face-to-face head-bobs with long side-by-side upright runs on the water surface. Necks extend upward, with the spear-billed head curved forward at a 90-degree angle, folded wings held stiffly out behind.

As summer wanes, migrant gulls, seabirds, and shorebirds return to the Salish Sea from distant nesting grounds. Three of the earliest represent three different sub-families of gull-like birds.

Bonaparte's gulls arrive from the northern tundra as early as July, some adults still wearing the black hood of breeding. But eventually they are all capped in winter white, with only a dark spot behind the eye remaining. Bonaparte's are handsome little gulls (half the size of Glaucous-winged) with thin black bill, black eyes and black-tipped wings. The pure white fore-edging to the the gray wings adds a touch of high fashion, and the orange feet a touch of color. Most pass through Puget Sound on their way south, but large flocks remain through the winter.

When feeding, Bonaparte's are more gregarious and aerial than larger gulls. They gather in large rafts, held together by a continuous conversation of "zhwee, zhwee, zhwee." When a school of herring or Sand lance are spotted, Bonaparte's wheel above, diving headfirst from about six to twenty feet at a steep angle into the school. I've also seen them hawking insects, like swallows, over beaches on San Juan Island at dusk.

The true "sea swallows," though, are the terns. A single colony of Arctic terns breed locally near Everett, Washington; large, gull-like Caspian terns can be spotted at Nisqually Wildlife Refuge near Olympia, and on other large river deltas. But by far the most prevalent tern here is the Common tern, whose sleek black cap and forceps-like orange bill of breeding season have faded to gray and black by late summer. Flocks of these aerialists arrive in July or August, about the same time as the Bonaparte's, almost as if to put the latter to shame.

Terns have taken flight to one of its logical, and most pleasing, conclusions. The Common tern's elegant, slender, pointed wings and slender V of a tail allow it to cut through the air like a swallow, hover like a Kestrel, and dive like a falcon. They fly back and forth, heads pointed downward in their search for fish. Spotting a school, they plummet headfirst from 20 or 30-feet straight down into the water, pulling buoyantly up with a silver fish wriggling from the delicate bill.

Watching terns fish out past the kelp bed in August, the sky washed with subtle pastels as the sun sets over sawtoothed mountains, is one of this frenzied earth's most aesthetic moments.

One of its most dramatic often follows.

Shadowing the terns is a merciless pirate of the air—the Parasitic jaeger. Jaegers (the German for hunter) are stocky, gull-like birds with pointed, ternlike wings. The Parasitic has a triangular tail trailing a pair of long central feathers. In summer it preys on eggs and nestlings of gulls and shorebirds breeding on the arctic tundra; for the rest of the year it dogs migrating flocks of Common terns and Bonaparte's gulls.

Spotting a successful tern from above, the jaeger swoops down. The tern zigs and zags, twists and turns, but the jaeger matches it move for move in one of the most impressive shows of aerial acrobatics in the bird world. Inevitably, the tern drops its hard-earned fish. The jaeger dives low to snatch it out of the air as the defeated bird flies off with empty bill.

This parasitic strategy would seem to take more energy than simply catching its own fish, but it seems to work for the jaeger—and it certainly provides the sharp-eyed observer a moment of awe.

Another early migrant, the Red-necked phalarope can sometimes be seen from boats in such areas as the San Juan Channel, as flocks briefly alight on the water surface. Phalaropes swim in tight circles, stirring up tiny fishes and planktonic crustaceans, which they pick off with needle-like bills.

The Red-necked phalarope breeds inland on the tundra. But with a twist. Its sex roles reverse the norm: the aggressive female is the larger and more colorful. She is also promiscuous. After courting a male and laying one clutch of eggs, she moves on to find another mate, leaving the first male to guard the eggs and feed the chicks.

Though it is technically a shorebird, like plovers and sandpipers, the Red-necked phalarope is, for ten months out of the year, a true creature of the sea. Its feet have even evolved fleshy lobes on the toes to help it swim. and despite its small size and dainty appearance, it usually migrates and winters well offshore. Some populations travel back and forth from the Arctic to near the Antarctic each year, barely stopping to rest. If offshore conditions are stormy, large flocks pass through the northern Salish Sea July through September. As they continue south, their lives and distribution are largely a mystery.

During spring and fall, vast flocks of sandpipers converge on the region's estuaries (the most famous being Gray's Harbor's Bowerman Basin on the Olympic Peninsula's Pacific shore, but closely followed by the Fraser River Delta). Sanderlings run along the wave's edge on quick little legs. Lanky yellowlegs and short-legged, plump dowitchers probe the intertidal mud with long, slender bills. Plovers and turnstones pick through the wrack above the tideline. Solitary Spotted sandpipers and Wandering tattlers pick small creatures off rocky shores.

The shorebirds most apt to be noticed, though, are Western sandpipers and dunlins (often seen together). Westerns because they're so numerous, dunlins because of their flight.

On the ground, dunlins are distinguished from other shorebirds by their fairly long, drooping bill which allows them to probe deeper than the Western sandpiper. In the air, dunlins flock tightly. When disturbed, they rise as one and zip around like a school of small fishes, delightfully described by Seattle artist/educator Tony Angell in his and Ken Balcomb's *Marine Birds and Mammals of Puget Sound*:

> Along the tideflats of Hat Slough, a vaporous ribbon of sandpipers stretches out for nearly a mile. These are dunlin, thousands of them forming a huge flock that tapers, then swells, as other birds join the relentless movement of the line. When they

turn, the flock suddenly reverses itself in a soundless explosion of flight as their white breasts are caught in the sun's glow....

What subtle cue causes the flock to turn with such synchrony, and then signals them so suddenly to a halt that they settle over the shore like a veil? Part of the pleasure of watching such a spectacle is knowing that there are no simple explanations and one can simply enjoy being set adrift in fantasies of flight.

A Ruddy duck in breeding plumage. The bright blue bill of our only "stiff-tailed" duck will turn black while wintering here on shallow bays, but its profile is always distinctive. (Peter M. Roberts)

The most common large wintering birds on and around the inland waters, both in numbers and in species, are ducks and geese. Which is not surprising considering the variety of habitats, the expanse of sheltered bays, and the lack of winter freeze. One can only imagine the numbers of waterfowl that congregated here before so many of our wetlands were drained and filled for development, our deltas diked for farms, and rich mudflats dredged for ports.

Along the Salish Sea's landward edges, a dozen species of "dabbling ducks" (which characteristically tilt their heads down and tails up when feeding) are seen in shallow water. The Fraser River Delta, the Skagit River Delta, the Nisqually National Wildlife Refuge, along with Padilla and other sheltered bays, host thousands of Mallards, Pintails, and American wigeons. All three have wintering populations which still average 30,000 to 40,000.

Bay ducks, also called "pochards," are diving ducks restricted to shallow waters. More adapted to aquatic life than are Mallards and Pintails, the legs of bay ducks are placed further back on their bodies; and so they have more trouble getting airborne. They also feed less on vegetation than do dabbling ducks, concentrating more on the small aquatic animals found among the Eelgrass or in the mud.

Scaups, both Greater and Lesser, are the most numerous of our wintering pochards, rivalling the more common species of dabblers. They are also more at home on salt water than are other bay ducks such as the familiar Canvasbacks and Redheads of river and slough.

Our only "stiff-tailed duck," the Ruddy duck, is small and chunky with a large, broad bill. The cocky, active male's bill turns bright blue during breeding season on inland prairie lakes. West of the Cascade and Coastal mountains it prefers freshwater but can be found on protected bays around the San Juans.

The sub-family is so-named because they often carry their tail stiffly upwards and spread like a fan. Lewis and Sharpe consider them

the best divers in the entire [waterfowl] family and share many behavioral traits with grebes. These include the ability to sink below the water's surface without a ripple, night migrations, weak flight low over the water, and an inclination to dive when escaping danger. Supremely adapted to a waterbound existence, their big feet are nearly useless on land and their long tails, providing underwater steerage, are often held erect. Stiff-tailed ducks also differ from other ducks by wearing a dull winter plumage and having male assistance during the raising of the young. Ruddy duck courtship is a weird ritual of piglike grunting accompanied by the slapping of the male's large blue bill against his breast, forcing large quantities of bubbles into the water.

Sporty male Harlequin ducks gather along the rocky seashore after a brief visit to mountain lakes to breed. Females and ducklings make a more leisurely return trip downriver. (Art Wolfe)

The Salish Sea is winter home to every North American sea duck: three species of scoters, two goldeneyes, and three mergansers, along with Bufflehead, Oldsquaw, and Harlequin. These tend to be stocky with short necks; perhaps not quite as good divers as the Ruddy duck but better than bay ducks and better adapted to salt water.

Sea ducks can be found off every seawall and cobble beach, diving for small mussels, crabs, amphipods, shrimps, and fish or jockeying for mates. In Puget Sound, they seem to be most common at the northern and southern ends, perhaps because human populations are less dense than in central Puget Sound; I've noticed, for example, that on sunny spring weekends they mysteriously disappear from the shoreline of Seattle's Discovery Park.

Most sea ducks breed on northern lakes, returning here in fall. But small groups of Harlequin ducks can be seen around Protection Island even in summer as they feed and rest along rocky coasts. Birders soon notice that these summering flocks are composed almost entirely of males, who sport a clownlike costume of white, gray, and rust.

Harlequins breed inland, along the headwaters of mountain streams. The first Harlequin I ever saw was a male floating down the Skokomish River above Hood Canal. It held itself immobile as a bobbing rubber ducky as it hurtled passively through a rapids, tilted left and right by the whirling current; I was sure that someone had released a painted decoy upstream—until its eye turned to regard me as it passed. The Harlequin's complex pattern serves to camouflage it against the surf-splashed seacoast on an overcast day. But on this sunny day on the river the male Harlequin stood out like a puffin in a pinetree.

Though the males waste no time returning to sea, Harlequin mothers and chicks spend the summer floating down the rivers at a more leisurely pace, feeding on aquatic insects as they go. The ability of the very young ducklings to scoot and scramble through rapids behind their mother is boggling. By late fall, Harlequin families are united along the coast, where they winter.

Goldeneyes are handsome sea ducks whose whirring wings have given them the nickname "whistlers." Males of both species—Common and Barrow's—have bright golden eyes on iridescent heads, sharply contrasting white breast, and white "windows" on their dark, folded wings. They can easily be told apart: the Common goldeneye has a large round white patch between its eye and bill, while the Barrow's has a crescent-shaped patch. Common goldeneyes winter throughout the continental U.S., while Barrow's are restricted to northern seacoasts. Both are locally common on the inland waters from late fall to early spring.

Our most common sea ducks are three species of scoter—Surf, White-winged, and Black. The first two rival the dabbling ducks and scaups in number. They are common near seawalls and near the kelp line off rocky shores, where they dive for mussels clinging to the rocks.

Like goldeneyes, scoters draw attention by the whistling whirr of their wings. They lack the iridescent colors and bright wing patches of many duck species, and the females are drab. Male White-winged scoters sport only a small white horizontal crescent behind the yellow eye; a barely visible white wing patch is common to both sexes.

The face of the male Surf scoter, however, is outlandish. Circular white patches cover the back of the neck, the forehead, and behind the thick, bright orange bill (the last patch with a smaller dark patch within).

The much less abundant Black scoter is seen mostly in late winter or during spring migration. The male is all-black except for a bright orange knob at the base of its bill. In spring, he vies for the attention of females by swimming forward, "butterball" bill pointing upward, uttering a plaintive "wheee." He then lowers his bill to his breast, at the

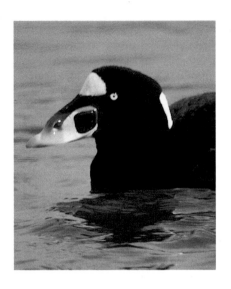

Surf scoters winter in small groups just offshore, feeding on mussel beds. The male's bill and neck contrast strikingly with its chunky black body. (Ervio Sian)

same time raising the tail stiffly up. After a series of these, he ends with a mad dash along the water, skidding to a stop on his breast. The dance is not the epitome of grace but it certainly works as an attention-grabber and, like the more spectacular Western grebe's dance, compensates for simple breeding plumage.

Oldsquaw sea ducks sometimes join the larger flocks of scoters. Most remain north of Admiralty Inlet. Though uncommon, Oldsquaws are quite noticeable, due to their noisy, yodel-like whistles and distinctive plumage. Most duck species have two basic plumage patterns: the colorful one of mature males and the drabber one that helps camouflage females, juveniles, and moulting males ("eclipse"plumage). Oldsquaws, though less brightly colored, add distinct winter and summer patterns. The result is a varied wardrobe of browns and whites, culminating in the breeding male's dark brown breast, neck, and head with large tan eyepatch; brown wing feathers edged with tan; and white flanks. For accessory, adults of both sexes sport a long, slender, up-wardly-curved tail plume.

The smallest of the sea ducks—but hardly the most reticent—is the engaging little Bufflehead, which makes up with enthusiasm what it lacks in size, color, or style. Males spend much of their time bobbing their heads—which resemble a dark pie with a huge white piece re-moved—or scooting around, interacting with other males or prospective mates. Females are not much less frenetic. In late winter every bay seems to have its own small flock of Buffleheads, too involved in their own affairs to pay much attention to other birds, boaters, or birders.

The most fish-oriented of the sea ducks are the Mergansers, whose thin, serrated bills are well adapted for holding on to slippery fishes. Consequently, they are not particularly popular among salmon hatchery and pen-fish personnel. The Red-breasted merganser is the one most apt to be seen on salt water, while Common mergansers prefer to winter on rivers, and Hooded mergansers on lakes or marshes.

All three species are attractive, but the male Red-breasted is surely the most handsome, with his bright green head, double-crested punk hairdo, white collar, speckled red vest, and graphic black-and-white wings. He and the shaggily red-headed females can be seen nearshore alone or in small groups in spring. The male performs an endless series of neck thrusts to entice a mate—as if the spiffy outfit alone were not enough.

Brant geese are another harbinger of spring. Off Seattle's Discovery Park, flocks of these small dark geese with white necklaces appear, fuel-up on eelgrass and sea lettuce for a day or two, then fly north. Almost 10,000 winter in Padilla and neighboring shallow, sheltered bays, though their numbers are a shadow of former days. In spring, counts triple to 30,000 or more, before the Brant take off for the far Arctic to breed.

In spring, the male Red-breasted merganser dresses nattily in checkered red vest to dazzle a potential mate. Its long, serrated bill is designed to catch small fishes. (Art Wolfe)

Of all the rich and varied wildlife in and around the Salish Sea, marine birds are by far the most visible. Yet they are commonest in the cooler, wetter months, when boating is iffy and beachwalks are often wet and dreary. They tend to avoid large cities and groups of people. And though their patterns may be graphically striking, their occasional bright colors need to be seen close-up or with binoculars to be appreciated. To fully enjoy their presence takes patience and a certain amount of skill.

But getting to know them has immense rewards. They enliven the sea and shore in every season; once you know who's who and where to look, even the dreariest winter day dances with wings.

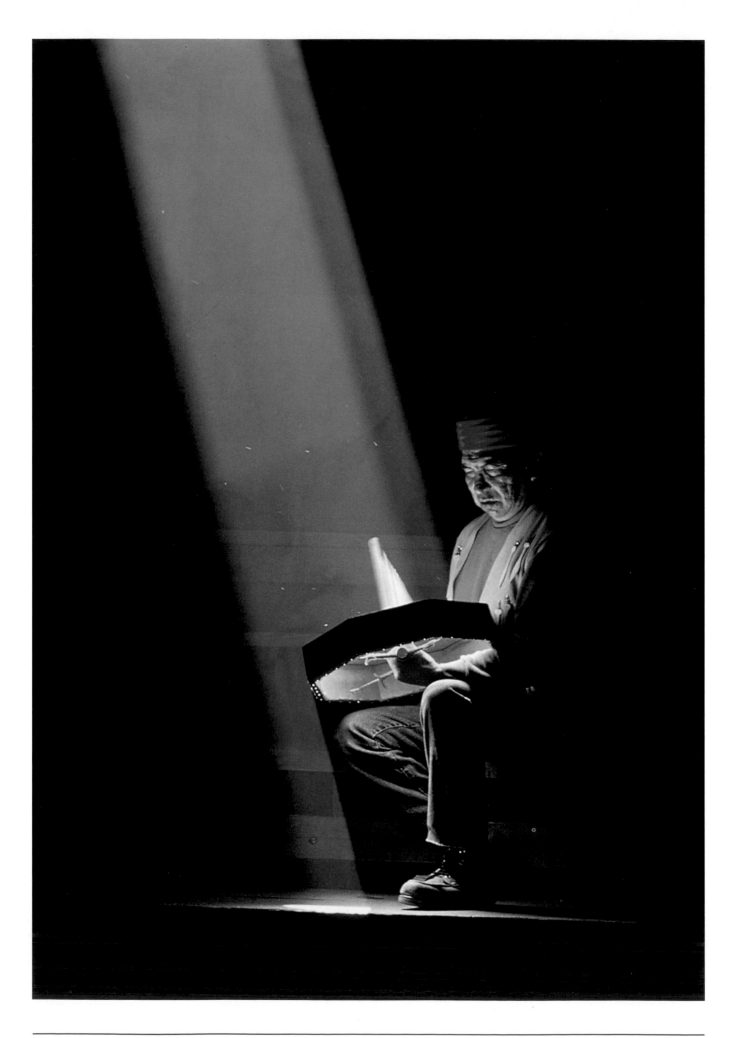

The Salmon People

The Lummi Indian Reservation covers most of a five-mile-long by two-mile wide peninsula that forms the western boundary of Bellingham Bay, just south of the Canadian border. As I drove the shoreline road past the southern tip of the peninsula, the long, gravel bar curving out to Portage Island was exposed by a minus tide. I'd never been on the 1200-acre island; on impulse I decided to take a quick hike out and back before the tide could cover the bar.

The narrow, sandy outer edge of the bar stood far above the waterline. The wide, low inner side of the curve was flat and cobbly, dotted with shallow tidepools, green sea lettuce, patches of Blue mussels, and barnacle-covered rocks. A dozen Great blue herons stalked the pools on stilt legs, searching for stranded fish.

On the wooded island, cattle grazed a narrow, marshy meadow between the woods and the western shoreline, while a flock of more than a hundred crows moved in a ragged, noisy mob before me on the beach. A Red-tailed hawk soared over the meadow behind the beach, looking for rodents, then followed the thermals eastward over the forest, and out of sight.

I soon covered the two miles of beach to the southern end of the island and around the tall, sheer cliffs of Point Francis to where I could see west across the bay. A Bald eagle perched on a snag above the glacial cliff as I ate my snack below. Off toward Bellingham, sportfishing boats buzzed in and out, while large purse seiners attempted to enclose entire schools of Sockeye in long, circling nets anchored by hefty aluminum power skiffs. Stripped of its industrial details by the distance, the bustling port seemed picturesque against the spectacular backdrop of Mount Baker and the North Cascades.

After a long rest in the lulling sun, I spotted a pair of River otters swimming sinuously through the rocks just offshore, busily hunting crabs and small fish in the shallows. Eventually, the two climbed out on a small rock, only a few feet off shore, almost too close for my binoculars to focus. The otters seemed not to see me as they stretched contentedly in the sun, twisting bonelessly to clean their dark fur coats. I watched, enchanted, until one of them looked up—they slid quickly into the water, scolded me for a moment, and were gone.

I headed back; but when I arrived at the bar, most of it was underwater. Waves were rolling over its center, and the tide was rising fast. With no choice but to wait for the next low tide, I lay in the windshadow of a huge drift log, and drifted off to sleep.

When I awoke, the sun had dropped behind Lummi Island, and an enormous, lopsided moon was rising above Mount Baker. Along Hale Passage lights on the masts of a dozen commercial fishing boats rocked back and forth gently above the waves. The boats had spaced them-

Opposite:
Raymond Moses tunes his drum for a traditional First Salmon ceremony.
(Natalie B. Fobes)

selves evenly every few hundred yards, and were calling back and forth to each other while waiting to set their nets.

As the sunset faded into chilly moonlight, the truth sank in. The second low tide, which was much the higher of the day's two low tides, would not be low enough to uncover the gravel bar. I considered trying to wade across, but I was not feeling all that daring at the edge of the cold, dark water sweeping over the bar and remembered that its center was a few feet lower than its ends.

Then I noticed a flickering light a half mile or so down the island's inner shore. Feeling a little foolish, I walked the beach to the campfire.

Two young Lummi women were sitting close to a small driftwood blaze. When I explained my situation they kindly offered me a place by the fire.

Sisters Ann and Rolanda had been out on the island for three straight days and nights, mostly without sleep. A male friend, who had taken the day shift, was sleeping in the small housetrailer behind the dunes. Ann's children, who had been staying with their grandmother on the mainland while their mother worked the fishing net, had just arrived for a night's camp-out.

We sat around the fire for a while, sharing steamy coffee and stories of strandings and other misadventures. And of fishing. Though Portage Island belongs to the Lummi tribe in general, this particular fishing spot had been in the sisters' family for many generations, and was now controlled by their mother. Their great grandfather was the first to run cattle out here. He and his sons and grandsons also fished of course. "Scratch a Lummi," it was said, "and you'll find a fisherman." Most of the Lummi men, in fact, were off purse-seining up near Point Roberts.

Three days earlier, the two women had set poles into the shallows, in a line perpendicular to the shore, and had strung nets between the poles. As Sockeye, Coho, or Chinook salmon returned to the Nooksack River or wandered into Bellingham Bay on their way north to the Fraser, some passed along the shoreline. Guided by the sweep of the gravel bar into the shallow curve at the north end of Portage Island, they ran into the invisible net. Unable to swim in reverse, the powerful fish wedged deeper into the net's just-large-enough hole until caught by the gills. The salmon—up to three feet long, always powerful, always slippery—sometimes managed to thrash and wriggle away in the dark. Most times it was gaffed and pulled into a boat.

A bell jangled. Rolanda and Ann ran down to the dark water, pushed the dory off the cobble beach, and paddled out along the net. After some moments of muffled calls and distant splashings, the two returned, smiling broadly, with one of the biggest salmon I had ever seen. It must have weighed 35 pounds.

Glistening in the firelight, the iridescent body was deep-chested but sleek, the ultimate combination of power and endurance—a true Olympian of the fish world. Its black gums and small dark spots on both lobes of the tail identified it; but size alone was enough. Though a very large Coho (silver) might be this long, it could not match this one in sheer bulk: a mature Chinook— "Tyee" (great one)—or King (or, across the border) Spring salmon.

Earlier that summer (which one journalist called "the summer of the big Kings") three 55-pounders had been landed by sports anglers, two near Port Angeles and one off Whidbey Island, followed a week later by a 65-pounder taken just inside the entrance to the Strait of Juan de Fuca (near where a 70-pounder, the largest caught in Washington memory, was landed in 1974). Even larger ones, up to five feet long and 125 pounds, have been caught off Alaska.

Immature "blackmouth" Chinooks can be found in the Salish Sea year round in deep water near ledges and jutting points of land, where they prey on smaller fishes and large planktonic animals—copepods, crab larvae, and amphipods. Many that remain in the inland waters are hatchery fish, held in check until their urge to roam has faded. Wild Chinook, however, spend most of their adult lives far out to sea.

After two or more years in the ocean, circling the Gulf of Alaska, chasing schools of herring along the Aleutian Islands and down through the eastern North Pacific—the urge to breed pulls them back to the shores near their river of origin. Mature Kings return from the Pacific to the Strait of Juan de Fuca in two major runs—the "spring-run" in late April and May, the "fall-run" in July and August. With smaller sub-runs, there are returning Chinook from April to November. A few, like this one, follow the great ocean circle many times before turning landward to breed. These five- to nine-year-olds grow to 50 pounds or more.

Even in death, the King that Rolanda struggled to hold up for us to admire exuded Power. With the campfire dancing on one side and moonlight shimmering on the other, its silvery scales still rippled with life, as if starting a final run up the starry stream of the Milky Way toward the beckoning moon.

A powerful King (Chinook) salmon develops a hooked jaw as it enters the river of its birth, spawning, and death. (Chris Huss)

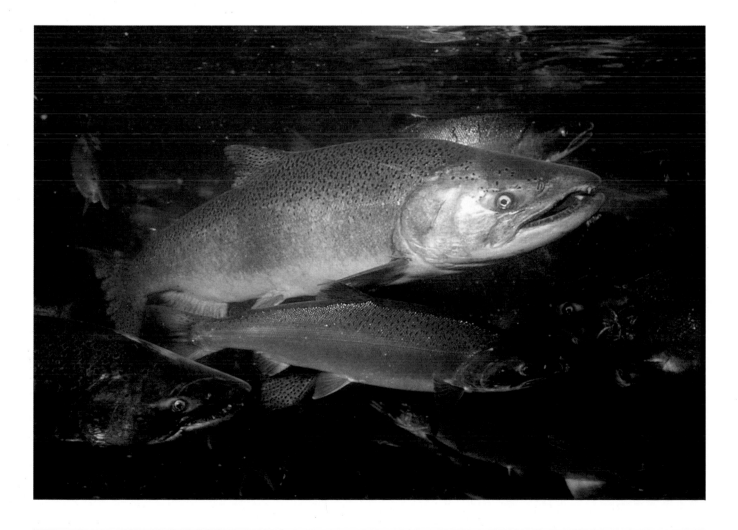

It was not hard to see why the salmon was the central motif for Northwest Indian art and ceremony. Here was an animal that was singularly beautiful and emanated undeniable spirit power. It moved in numberless schools, providing more high-protein food than people could eat. It came and went with great mystery but amazing regularity. It was the source of wealth and strength—of life itself.

Mystic "Salmon-people" lived in great longhouses far at sea; they must be treated with gratitude and reverence, and placated with ritual, to ensure their annual return.

The first salmon catch of the season's major run was celebrated with the First Salmon Ceremony—a rite common to coastal Indians from northern California to Alaska.

Many taboos guided all that followed. Among the Lummi and other Straits Salish tribes, netted Sockeye were not clubbed as were other fish, but allowed to die in the canoe. Never addressed by their species name, Sockeye were called by the term for elder brother or sister. They were always cut longitudinally, never crosswise. Children must never play with the caught salmon.

An elder of the Clallam tribe told anthropologist Erna Gunther that a girl "was swimming in the Dungeness River and made fun of an old salmon. Soon after, she became ill. Her eyes began to look like salmon eyes and her actions were just like the movements of the fish as they swam. Her people asked her if she had played with a salmon. She admitted that she had. The shaman could do nothing for her and she soon died." Some young men who mocked a very old salmon became ill, and the shaman could not help them, either. When they were dying, they acted like expiring salmon.

The alternative to this harsh punishment could have have been far worse. The mistreated Salmon-person, returning to the sea to guide his relatives back next year, might report that the Human people were unworthy of the Salmon tribe's generous sacrifice. The salmon might not return.

Salmon runs were the pivot points around which the Coast Salish's yearly tasks revolved. The Clallam, who lived along the eastern Strait of Juan de Fuca from Port Angeles to Discovery Bay, were especially dependent on spring-run Chinook entering Discovery Bay and the Dungeness River. The Skokomish, at the southern end of Hood Canal, were blessed with heavy runs of Chum salmon in late fall. The upriver Nisqually in southern Puget Sound feasted into April on late runs of Steelhead.

Then, as now, the food gathering cycle of the Lummi was geared to the late summer Sockeye runs.

Sockeye salmon (called Red salmon in Alaska) can reach 33 inches long and 15 pounds, averaging about 8 pounds. In the sea they are slender and silvery-sided, blending to greenish blue on their finely speckled backs. They can be distinguished from Kings or Silvers by their small eye pupils and lack of large spots on body or tail.

In July and August, adult Sockeye return to the inland waters after three or four years at sea. Numbering up to 20 million in a good year, they move rapidly through the Strait of Juan de Fuca. A few head south into Puget Sound toward Lake Washington and its feeder streams. But most are destined for the huge Fraser River system. And these must pass through the San Juan Islands or up past Point Roberts Peninsula to reach the mouth of the Fraser.

Sockeye salmon assume bright red sides, green heads, and grotesquely hooked jaws for their spawning journey to the Fraser River and Seattle's Lake Washington. (Natalie B. Fobes)

Below: A First Salmon ceremony performed on the Tulalip reservation, north of Everett, Washington. All along the northern Pacific coast, the symbolic first salmon of the season was celebrated to show gratitude for its gift of food and to insure its return the following year. Here, the Sockeye is carried to the ceremonial long-house on a litter, covered with ferns and accompanied by drummers. (Natalie B. Fobes)

Since the Sockeye herds feed on plankton (if at all, during their spawning run, they can only be netted. The first were taken by the Soongish—relatives of the Lummi living near present-day Victoria. All along the route through the San Juans and into the Strait of Georgia, the schools of silvery Sockeye crossed shallow, kelp-covered reefs. And at those spots, the Lummi set their nets.

The Lummi tribe seems to have once been centered on San Juan Island, spreading east to the mainland only in the early 1700s. They eventually controlled the shore from Bellingham Bay to Birch Bay, along with Lummi Island at the mouth of Bellingham Bay, and much of the San Juans. Above Bellingham, they shared the Point Roberts fishing grounds with their Semiahmoo and Tsawwassen neighbors to the north.

Aggressive, adaptable, and relatively isolated from the main thrust of white settlement, traditional Lummi society survived culturally intact for longer than most other tribes. The famous Seattle photographer and amateur ethnologist Edward Curtis visited the Lummi in the early 1900s. Anthropologist Bernard Stern spent two years with them in the late 1920s, talking to the elders about the old ways. Twenty-five years later, Wayne Suttles did his doctoral research among the Lummi and neighboring Straits Salish tribes—the Samish just to the south (and southern San Juans); the Songish to the west; the Saanich of the Canadian Gulf Islands; and the Semiahmoo of Birch Bay. The Lummi intermarried with and differed little from the related saltwater tribes of Puget Sound and Georgia Strait.

The Lummi of the 1800s lived in six major winter villages of 100 to 200 people each. Each permanent village consisted of five to twenty longhouses that faced the sea, fronted by rows of beached canoes. Longhouses measured 30- to 50-feet wide by 200-feet long. Each consisted of a permanent framework of large posts, cross-beams, and roof stringers covered with a removable sheathing of horizontal cedar planks. The roof of interlocking cedar boards was single-pitched, higher in front than back. The overlapping horizontal wall planks, also of split cedar, were tied not to the main house posts but to thinner, outer posts.

The skeleton of the ceremonial salmon is returned to the sea. (Natalie B. Fobes)

Opposite:
Drumming and singing honor the First Salmon around a fire in the ceremonial longhouse. (Natalie B. Fobes)

Large support-posts, spaced along the wall every 50 feet or so, defined living areas for separate families. Sometimes these subunits were walled off by planks or mat partitions. A family—parents with children and sometimes the father's parents or an unmarried relative—lived between the posts along one wall of the large structure, sleeping on wide shelves built out from the wall. Under the shelves, up along the matted walls, and in the rafters above was storage space for the family's dried food, tools, clothing, and excess blankets. Each family had its own fire.

Since marriage was the main institution for cementing friendships and alliances with neighboring villages and nearby tribes, it was ideally forged between families of different villages. This gave the family access to resources controlled by in-laws living in another village. Wives usually moved to the husband's village; and so households often consisted of adult males who were mostly Lummi and adult females who were often from other villages, tribes, or even different language groups. Two or three languages might be spoken within the household.

The advantages of living in such a large house through the dark, wet winter were manyfold. Aside from sleeping area, the spacious structure served as a lighted, sheltered workspace for manufacturing tools, clothing, and nets, and for drying the fish caught in late fall. Since a number of families often cooked together and shared excess food, perishables were distributed beyond the nuclear family. Strong bonds were created between families in the otherwise competitive social environment. Work specialists like canoe builder, hunter, or expert weaver might complement each other to create a large, stable economic unit.

Coast Salish social classes consisted of the *siems* or nobles, a larger group of regular citizens, and a large class of underlings—slaves, descendants of slaves, and orphans.

Siems had "class": They were well-mannered and were well advised by successful elders; they knew their lineage for many generations; they owned the best fishing and clamming spots, as well as powerful names, spirit songs, and dances.

The Coast Salish developed basketry to a high craft. Mats were used for summer shelters; baskets for cooking, carrying, and storage. (Hand colored print by Edward S. Curtis/University of Washington Special Collections, NA256)

Less fortunate families also had the marks of free people—flattened foreheads and long hair—but they could lay no claim to special fishing or clamming places. They had not acquired important names and ceremonies, and they put less emphasis on proper upbringing. Though the entry to the upper class was not fixed, those born into poorer families faced a number of obstacles to accumulating wealth and prestige.

Slaves—women and children captured in raids—were destined for a life of hard work and few rewards. They were not usually mistreated, but they worked at tasks that could bring no status and their descendants were forever without "class." Among the Clallam, the descendants of slaves lived in slums along the beach, where they bore the brunt of attacks from raiders from the north.

The scattered Lummi villages were united by intermarriage and shared customs rather than by formal political organization or central political control. Village "rulers" were older men of the *siem* class who had gained their authority by accumulation (and canny ceremonial distribution of) inherited and garnered wealth; by their spotless lineage; and by displaying the important traits that allowed ambitious men to accumulate wealth—wisdom, fishing skills, bravery, luck in gambling, and the acquired spirit powers that underlay all success.

Lummi society was largely capitalistic: Wealth and the means for accumulating it were individually held and inherited. Property rights extended to names, ceremonial objects and dances. Land itself was not privately owned, but good fishing spots, such as the one I found myself visiting, often were. Large property—substantial houses and ceremonial buildings, as well as houses canoes, and fishing spots—might be held in common by a group of wealthy men, while smaller items were usually owned by individuals.

Lummi women gathered bulbs and berries; spun wool and twine; tanned hides; and wove fishnets, wicker baskets, wool blankets, cattail mats, and clothing textiles. They made a variety of clothing; the most important types were made of woven textiles. Wool from the shorn hair of the specially-bred dogs was mixed with fine white clay and beaten, then mixed with fireweed down or duck down and then woven. Duck down was also entwined with nettle fibers and woven into cloth. (In the chilly wet of the Pacific Northwest, both of these easily-dried, open-weave fabrics were much superior to the cotten clothing later brought in by the white settlers; many Indians were to sicken and die in brightly colored cotten that stayed damp.) Women also did most of the cooking, though men also cooked, especially during the large winter ceremonial feasts. Both sexes gathered shellfish.

Men hunted and fished. They made rope, halibut hooks, and net sinkers. They also worked with wood—building houses, canoes, and wooden chests of soft, straight-grained, water-resistant cedar.

The spread of Western red cedar throughout the region about four thousand years ago was an important milestone in the development of Northwest Indian culture. Not only was the wood of cedar used for houses, canoes, and boxes, but for a hundred lesser items: cradles, arrowshafts, fire hearths, spindles, plates, mat creasers, and canoe bailers, as well as medicinal and ceremonial uses. Cedar bark, too, had a hundred uses. "In fact," writes Erna Gunther in her *Ethnobotany of Western Washington*, "there is no single item so ubiquitous in the

Indian household. The shredding of bark is a constant bit of busy work for women...It is shredded fine enough to be used as padding for infants' cradles, as sanitary pads, as towels. A coarser grade is plaited into skirts and capes, later into complete dresses for women."

"Large cedars were felled by making two cuts with the antler wedge, driving it with the stone maul, and knocking out the wood between them," writes Suttles. "Perhaps fire was used in the process. Logs were split in half for canoes or split several times for house-posts or house-planks. This was done by driving the antler wedge to make the cut, then holding it with several wooden wedges while prying. Wood was cut across the grain with the adze or chisel. In making a canoe, fire was also used to burn out part of the center. The wood was bent after softening it with steam...and joined by drilling holes and driving hemlock knot pegs or sewing with cedar-withe rope." Every man was expected to be able to do rough woodworking, though the making of canoes, house posts, and fine wooden storage boxes was usually the job of specialists.

The graceful canoes were of three kinds. Most common was the widespread Coast Salish saltwater canoe: 20- to 30-feet-long, pointed at both ends with a cutwater in the bow. Both bow and stern rose with a graceful point far above the water. These canoes were employed for trolling and for duck hunting as well as general transport. For moving camp, and probably for raids, a larger version with more elevated bow

"Large Lummi canoe and paddle." Such graceful canoes—the body laboriously carved from a single tree—were the acme of Coast Salish art. (Eugene Field/University of Washington Special Collections, NA1806)

was used; these were imported from more northern tribes or from the Squamish of central Puget Sound. The third type, used exclusively for reef-netting salmon, had a wide, flat bow and square stern.

The Lummi bartered with neighboring Straits Salish tribes and southward with the Swinomish, Skagit, Snohomish, Suquamish, and Duwamish. Much of the trading occured as an integral part of pot-latches, feasts, and marriage protocol.

During the short, cold, wet days of December and January, people were confined to the longhouses. To liven up the time, whenever proper occasions arose a family would give a feast for its household, or a house-hold for the village. Feasts were celebrations to mark changes of status or milestones of life: birth, puberty, namings, weddings, recovery from sickness, and funerals. They were also times for spirit songs and spirit dancing—for in winter the guardian spirits, gone wandering during summer, returned in force to "fill" their hosts, demanding to be sung. To deny them could bring sickness or misfortune.

The host and others, one after the other, would sing his or her guardian spirit song and spirit dance. Accompanied by drums, everyone present would learn the dance and song from the originator (though its meaning might be enigmatic) and accompany him or her.

Songs were also sung to demonstrate ceremonial powers; a man might cut himself with knives or handle hot coals, without pain; the 10-foot-tall drumming sticks used to pound against the roof might pull someone around the room or beat on their own accord. Mythic stories, some of them ribald, would be danced and acted out with elaborate masks and costumes, impressively dramatic in the fish-oil-enhanced firelight of the cavernous longhouses.

Potlatches—larger, more formal feasts— were often held in summer or fall when distant travel was easier and more food available. Though given by a single wealthy family, the success of the potlatch reflected on the entire village, and resources for it were usually pooled. It was at once a conspicuous demonstration of social status, repayment of past social events, and guarantee of future invitations. The host made sure to invite people of the highest class from many far-flung villages within his circle of allies and in-laws.

As with the smaller winter feasts, the potlatch was given to celebrate major family or personal events—a birth, a successful spirit quest, or recovery from an illness. But for most families, a potlatch was a rare and taxing event. Goods such as blankets, pieces of copper, robes, and canoes, sometimes contributed by the entire village, would be given away to the guests. The best goods were distributed formally, in strict order of the guest's status; remaining cloth and blankets might be cut up and given piecemeal to poorer guests.

A truly spectacular potlatch could bring even the wealthiest host to temporary poverty. As in a modern wedding, however, accounts were kept of who was given what, and return in kind would be expected. The wealthier you and your family were, the more you could give away, the more prestige you would gain by doing so, and the more you would ultimately receive. In the process, some of the wealth was redistributed to less fortunate families and relations.

Aside from gift-giving, there were performances demonstrating inherited ceremonies and privilages; games, singing, and masked enter-tainments; gambling and trade. The dancing, singing, feasting, and

"Carved Figure—Cowichan." The Cowichan live near the river of the same name in southeastern Vancouver Island. Their art is particularly imaginative. (Edward S. Curtis/University of Washington Special Collections, NA279)

gambling might go on for days, during which time family alliances were strengthened, status was reinforced or sometimes downgraded, romances and intrigues were initiated. For the wealthy, the potlatch was a status symbol; for the lower classes a carnival, for the village a reaffirmation of its place in the larger world. In general, villages did not have to fear raids or warfare from tribes within the large circle of potlatch and intermarriage.

From March through October, the Lummi, like other Northwest groups, left their winter houses, moving back and forth to wherever the fish were running, the clam flats exposed, or the berries ripe. During this time they often lived in temporary fishing and food-gathering camps like those described by Vancouver. Shelters were made of light, durable cattail mats, but at major fishing spots permanent house frames might stand.

March and April were months for hunting seabirds. Three types of net were used: long willow nets raised on poles, such as the ones that mystified Captain Vancouver; smaller nets held by men in canoes, who lured the ducks at night with a small fire; and submerged nets in which diving ducks tangled and drowned. Ducks were also taken at night with multi-pronged spears. At least 27 different species of loons, mergansers, grebes, cormorants, swans, geese, sea ducks and bay ducks were hunted. So many seabirds wintered on the Padilla, Bellingham, and Birch bays that people of the mainland Samish, Lummi, and Semiahmoo villages, clothed and blanketed in thick duck-down wool, were considered to be better dressed than villagers elsewhere.

During March, schools of Pacific herring returned from the ocean to spawn in the sheltered bays. The coastal Indians would follow flocks of gulls out to the dense schools and would sweep the water with long-handled, sharp-tined "rakes," which could spike dozens of herring at a time. Herring eggs were also harvested—by collecting the egg-covered

In spring, Pacific herring deposit their eggs on kelp. Local Indians increased the natural harvest by setting weighted evergreen boughs into spawning bays. (Terry Domico/ Earth Images)

kelp or Eelgrass after spawning, or by placing weighted fir boughs or small hemlock or cedar trees underwater in spawning bays just before the herring arrived. After the herring had cemented their eggs to the branches, the boughs were pulled up. A submerged net—4 to 5 feet wide by 50 to 75 feet long—was sometimes laid over the Eelgrass in bays where herring were known to spawn; when ducks dove to feed on the spawn, they got caught in the nets.

In April the Lummi caught flounders in the shallows, mainly with spears. In deeper water they used long lines of slender Bull kelp stipes to which were attached ingenious bone hooks to catch large Ling cod and Pacific halibut.

In May the mainland villages went to Matia, Barnes, Spieden, and Clark Islands in the northern San Juans to dig the starchy bulbs of a blue lily, the camas—just as Vancouver had seen the Duwamish do on Bainbridge Island. While the women and children gathered bulbs, the men trolled for spring-run Chinook salmon from their canoes. The trolling line was held with the paddle, causing the line to jerk forward with each stroke; far behind, a sinker stone trailed the bone hook baited with fresh fish. A few men continued to troll for Chinook while the majority switched to the mainstay of the fishery—netting Sockeye.

In June, Sockeye fishing crews of a dozen or so men were organized by owners of the fishing spots. The owners, crews, and their families moved to the fishing camps on Lummi, Orcas, Lopez and Waldron islands, or up to Point Roberts near the Canadian border.

There, they refurbished the frameworks of the fishing camp shelters, roofing them with planks brought from the winter longhouses and walling the frames with mats. Since exposure to sun and wind were needed for drying the Sockeye, most sites were built on south-facing points of land. The women of the crew families gathered the bark of willow saplings to make the reef nets.

Reef nets were rectangular, about 30 feet wide by 40 feet long. They were designed to be supported between two large, specially designed canoes that held crews of from six to more than a dozen men. The reef-net canoes were firmly anchored on both sides and were built low at the stern so that the watchman could see the sockeye swimming over the net. The net was hung above the reef at mid water levels, with a "ladder" of ropes leading gradually up from the reef to the net. The ladder and its side ropes, held up by floats, defined a chute through a channel cut through the kelp. The salmon could swim out between the ropes of course, but they tended to follow the clear channel to the net. The sides of the flat net had pull-ropes leading up to the canoes, and the front section, billowed out by the current, reached toward the surface.

The net, according to Suttle's informants was considered female. A hole, left betwen the sections of the net, was considered the vulva. "When you lift, the salmon they never go through this hole," said one informant. "It's forbidden for them to go through. Xelas the Transformer, showed the first people how to make this. The reef net's a lady, that's why that hole." The men, for their part, gathered boughs of cedar saplings to make the lines for anchoring and hauling the heavy nets.

"The Sockeye salmon fishing season is waited with keen anticipation by the people," writes Stern. "For the Sockeye is the *siem* or rich man of all the fishes and no fish is as highly esteemed or is surrounded with as much veneration. If treated with proper respect, the Sockeye leaves his long-house [far at sea], the smoke of which is like a rainbow, and makes pilgrimages to the fishing sites to be food for the people."

When word came that the first Sockeye have been caught at Beecher Bay, across the Strait from Port Angeles, the Lummi knew that the salmon would soon arrive at their fishing sites. According to Stern: Every man stands tense at his post, firmly gripping the net, and as the fish reach the center of the net, the captain cries "Lift, Lift, Lift." Every man pulls with all his strength to raise the net to the surface of the water. If the men at the rear of the canoe are a little slow, the captain shouts at them to lift the head of the net because there is danger of the fish passing over it. When the net is brought to the surface, the captain calls, "Release lines" and the canoes are brought together as the men pull in the net, shouting as they pull. As the fish struggle at the surface of the water, a spray goes up and a rainbow can be seen extending from one end of the canoes to the other.

This is the first catch of the sockeye salmon and everybody is happy although constrained by veneration for the fish...
Winter fern, duck-down, red paint, cedar bark and spice plants have been gathered by the women who are ready to perform the first salmon ceremony. The children with their backs painted and with duck-down in their hair are waiting to honor the fish. As canoes land facing the west each child goes to receive a fish, which is placed with its head resting on the child's left arm and its tail on his right arm. He steadies the fish by holding the back fin with his teeth, and carrying it like a baby in his arms as he turns to the left and sidesteps up the beach to the place where the women are preparing to cook it. The fish are gently placed with their heads toward the water, on the winter fern which has been laid out for this purpose. All the children take part in this performance. When all the fish are ashore and are placed on the winter fern, old people put kernels of the spice-plant and duck-down and red paint in front of the fish. This is the fishes' first meal to show the good will of the people at their arrival. A bunch of shredded bark is lighted, and the food placed before the salmon is burnt.

The women, with red paint on their arms and faces and with down in their hair, split the fish, laying each one open. A long trench is dug and a fire of hot coals is built in the trench. Then pieces of green ironwood are set across the trench from one end to the other, side by side about two inches apart. The cleaned fish [cut only with ancient mussel blades] are set on these sticks and roasted over the burning coals, and places are prepared on both sides of the trench to lay the fish after they are cooked. Great care is taken in all this work.

While these preparations are being made, some old man or woman who knows the traditions of the fish and who has been careful to learn all the details of the ceremony sings a spirit song. At the end of each strain, the names of the various places are mentioned where fish of different kinds are caught, and a gift is cast into the water for the fish of that particular place.

When the song and naming of the fish is ended, and the baked salmon set in two rows on either side of the fire, the women call to the children who carried the fish, "Come, children, eat." The children sit before the baked salmon as though they were going to eat it all, but do not touch it. Meanwhile the old men pass behind them and the children are permitted to eat as much as they desire. The fish is then given to the people, family by family, in as large quantities as they need for a meal. Those remaining are hung up to dry. The bones and sticks of iron wood are gathered and thrown into the water, symbolizing the breaking up of canoes, as though the occupants, the fish, did not intend to leave...

All the requirements have been carried out and there is now freedom in the use of the salmon and confidence that the salmon will come again next year.

O f all the fishing spots, Point Roberts, near the Canadian border, was the largest and most important. "The stream of sockeye that come northward through Rosario Straits" writes Suttles, "follows the mainland shore into Boundary Bay, then wheels to the left across the shallow flats and pours over the reef and around Point Roberts to the Fraser. Along it fishermen wet their gears to form a great arc. There was room for at least 14 gears side-by-side...Beyond this arc in deeper water there was room for an indefinite number of more scattered gears."

Vancouver noted the house frames on the Point Roberts peninsula in June, 1792, on his way north, and thought them remnants of a deserted village. But just a month later, during July and August, the peninsula must have seethed with activity—many fishing camps, many feasts and social events.

Then, in the early 1880s, a white squatter named John Waller cut down the drying racks and house posts and fenced his homesite with them; he refused to let Indians camp. The Lummi fishermen moved north to Goodfellow's Point and continued to fish. "The end came for most reef-netters in 1894," writes Suttles, "when the Alaska Packers completed a continuous line of traps which cut off most of the reef." The United States Attorney General filed a brief for the Indians in 1897, but the court decided in favor of the trapmen. From then until fishing traps were outlawed in 1934, netting was abandoned. In 1950, Suttles concludes, "a few whites [were] operating reef nets at Point Roberts."

Lummi living on the mainland also paddled across Rosario Strait to East Sound and West Sound on Orcas Island to gather large quantities of shellfish from the tideflats during the week-long periods of very low tides that occur with full and new moons throughout the summer.

Four species of clams made up the bulk of the harvest: Littleneck clams, found near the surface, were eaten fresh, either raw or steamed; Butter clams were eaten fresh or were dried and carried in strings around the neck for working snacks; the large Horse clams, deep in the muddy sand at the lowest tide levels, were always dried for winter; Heart cockles, which sometimes grew right on the surface of the beach, were usually dried.

Crabs were caught along the shore. Giant sea cucumbers, called "sea sausages," were taken for the strips of muscle. Limpets, chitons, whelks, and barnacles were collected. Sea urchins, called "sea eggs," were gathered for their yellow gonads.

Overleaf;
"Lelehalt—Quilcene." This series of Salish portraits was taken in the early 1900s and published in Curtis's monumental set of texts and oversize portfolios, The North American Indian. *(Edward S. Curtis/University of Washington Special Collections,*

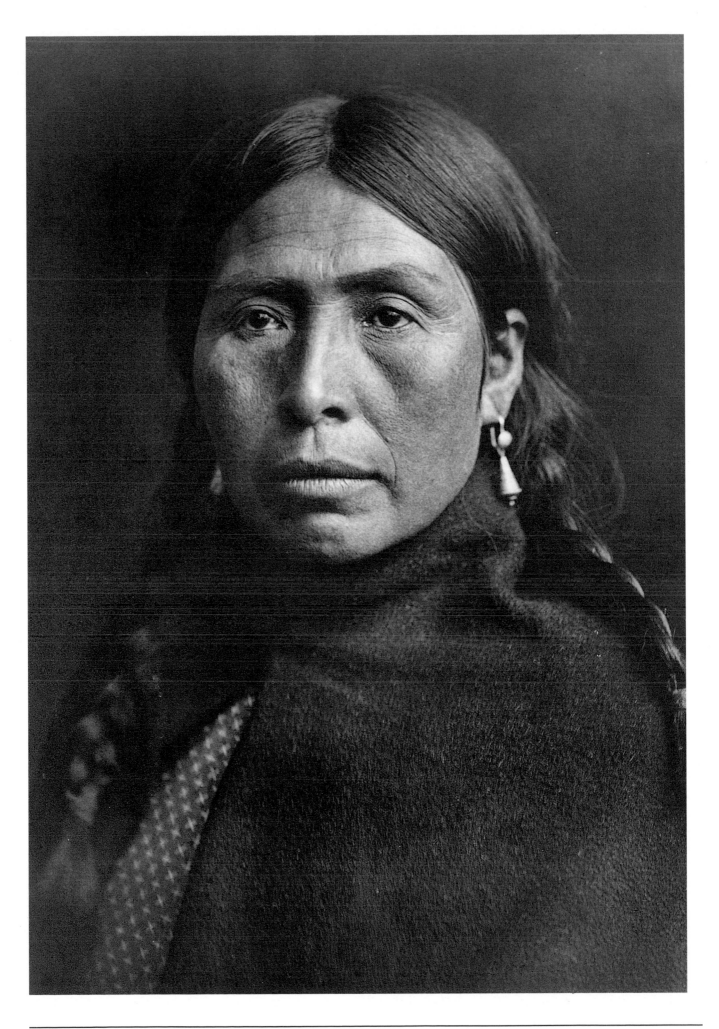

Men hunted deer on the islands, driving them into snares or pits; the hides were cured for clothing and the hooves saved for ceremonial purposes. At the end of October, as they traveled back to Lawrence Point (across from Lummi Island on Orcas's eastern tip), the men speared codfish; the fish were dried, the oil saved for pouring onto ceremonial fires later that winter. Meanwhile, back at Portage Island's gravel bar, stay-at-homes netted Surf smelt along the beach from June through September.

In November, Chum and Silver (and in odd-numbered years, the Pink) salmon return to the rivers, along with Steelhead. These were caught in the estuaries with an elaborate variety of weirs, nets, spears, and hooks. Bears were hunted; beaver, otter, and mink trapped. When the surplus food was safely stored in baskets in the villages houses, the yearly round of food gathering ended and the season of the feast and the spirit dance returned.

Previous page:
A Lummi woman. (Edward S. Curtis/ University of Washington Special Collections, NA313)

"Hleastnuh—Skokomish." (Edward S. Curtis/University of Washington Special Collections, NA307)

Here on Portage Island, the fishing season was still in full swing. Long past midnight, lights from the mainland suddenly beamed over the dark water as cars and pickup trucks rolled down to the parking lot at the far end of the gravel bar. The older fishermen were probably at home with their families, fast asleep. But from the sound of the music and loud voices, the younger crew members, used to fishing on an all-night schedule for the past week, were in a mood to celebrate after a week of heavy work.

I had read the day before in Bellingham's newspaper that there was a humongous Fraser River Sockeye run, now estimated to be 20 million fish—50% greater than earlier predicted. As a result, the U.S. catch quota for the latest three-day opening would almost double—to over 800,000 Sockeye, an added windfall of almost $3 million. And half of that would go to Indian boats. Three days ago, 450,000 Sockeye were landed. According to one seafood processor in Bellingham, some boats were making $5,000–10,000 per day during the short season.

For the Lummi, it has been an amazing turnaround. From 1897—when the Point Roberts reef netting ended—until 1973, the Indian fishery in Puget Sound had fallen on hard times. First the huge, cannery-operated fish traps had taken the lion's share of the fish. Then when a 1934 state initiative banned fish traps, it also banned net fishing for Steelhead, except on the small reservations themselves.

Raising the capital to buy and operate new fishing boats, especially the large, mechanized purse-seine boats that became dominant after the 1950s, was not easy for those few families who kept at the trade. Aside from a few diehards who continued to gillnet with small boats, the Indian fishery was moribund. Although fishing was still the main occupation, tribal fishermen landed only about 5% of Washington State's total salmon catch; and less than a fourth of the Steelhead.

Then, in 1973, the Puget Sound fishery was hit by a "lightning Boldt." For a dozen years, the Nisqually Indians had openly defied Washington State Department of Game regulations by netting fish, including steelhead, off the reservation on the Nisqually River south of Tacoma. Nisqually leader Bill Frank, Jr., and other tribal leaders argued that the federal Treaty of 1855 guaranteed Indian rights to fish, not just on the reservations but at "all the usual and accustomed places." A dozen years of bloody confrontations on the banks of the Nisqually River culminated in a ruling on the issue by U.S. District Judge George H. Boldt.

Boldt, a politically conservative judge nearing retirement, ruled for the Indians. The State had argued that the treaty gave the Indians fishing rights "in common with" other citizens of the state. Judge Boldt ruled that—according to the legal dictionaries of the 1850s—"in common with" meant "shared equally."

Within a decade, the "Boldt area" tribes' share of the salmon catch soared from 5% to about 50%. And of the Indian harvest, the Lummi take almost half.

As the music faded, the cars pulled away, and the moon sank behind Lummi Island. Fish weren't hitting the net much anymore. Rolanda was curled up beside the fire. Ann crawled under a blanket with her children and dozed. Buzzing with strong coffee, I offered to stay awake to listen for the bell.

"Quilcene Boy" (Edward S. Curtis/ University of Washington Special Collections, NA312)

Sitting by the predawn fire, I tried to imagine this spot a century ago. People had sat around similar driftwood fires on this beach for hundreds, perhaps thousands, of years. Yet, little is certain of the origins of the Coast Salish tribes.

Did they move through the Fraser and Columbia river valleys from the interior plains, following the salmon runs down to their salt source? Or were their ancestors people who skipped by boat along the north Pacific coastline—from Siberia through Alaska and British Columbia to Puget Sound? Did saltwater people replace the earlier land-based hunters? Or did land-based hunters gradually acquire coastal skills?

Or did many different waves of people blend many distinct coastal and plains cultures?

We may never know. "Good 'hard' convincing evidence is going to be difficult to get," lamented archaeologist Richard MacNeish at a recent conference on the history of the first peoples to reach North America. "The earliest inhabitants were very limited in number. Their sites are likely to be buried deeply, and often are destroyed or disturbed. The earliest crude artifacts are difficult to recognize and hard to interpret, and the accurate dating of these remains may be almost impossible."

Other than controversial evidence of the presence of very early people from the Manis Mastodon site (about 12,000 years Before Present) near Dungeness Spit, and later Clovis sites on Whidbey Island, very little or nothing is known about humans along the inland waters before about 5,000 years ago. The earliest significant sites excavated on the Gulf of Georgia date to the period from about 10,000–5,000 BP—termed the Old Cordilleran Tradition.

The tools of that time were made of chipped stone, and probably also of bone, which is rarely preserved for that long. The bones of elk, deer, bear, and beaver have been preserved, and so we know the Old Cordilleran people hunted game. Whether they caught fish is probable, but unknown. Delicate fish bones preserve far less well than heavy mammal bones. Interestingly, no early shell middens have been found. Not until about 5,000 BP (3,000 B.C.) are the first shell collections seen.

People of the St. Mungo and Locarno Beach periods (about 5,000–2,500 BP) relied heavily on shellfish, as well as on fish, seals, ducks, and terrestrial animals. Their tools were of bone and ground slate. They used stone spear points for weapons and wore stone lip plugs, called "labrets." During this period, Western red cedar had recently spread throughout the area, and the tools for felling and working with the valuable wood were being developed.

The Marpole period, from about 500 B.C. to 500 A.D., saw the blossoming of the Indian lifestyle described by early anthropologists—a culture that would endure, virtually intact, until Vancouver's time.

The gravel bar that connected Portage Island to the peninsula had once been a broader link to the mainland, and there had been a Lummi village on this very spot. Near the small marina on the mainland, a wealthy *siem* named Chowitsut had organized the construction of a 400-foot-long ceremonial house. Chowitsut, the best-known Lummi potlatcher of the mid-1800s and a signer of the Treaty of 1855, had a rare combination of shaman's power, wealth power, and gambler's power. His gambling power—a black duck—told him to give many potlatches, and he did: Perhaps one too many, say Suttles' informants, implying that he overreached himself and brought on an untimely death.

I finally dozed off as the rose-colored dawn tinted Bellingham Bay, dreamily imagining an evening at one of Chowitsut's grand potlatches. The costumed, masked dancers in the ghostly light of oil fires flaring in the huge hall. The hypnotic singing. The beat of drumming sticks against the rafters.

I woke to the sun glinting fiercely over Mount Baker and the North Cascades. Ann was making coffee as the kids gathered driftwood. The sea had withdrawn again, exposing the gravel bar.

We said our groggy goodbyes, and I headed across the curving bar, past the herons stalking the tidepools, toward my car. Looking back, the fishing camp, with its tiny fire, seemed to disappear against the island background, like a fading dream. But it was not a dream—it was, in reality, the enduring kernel of life on the Salish Sea.

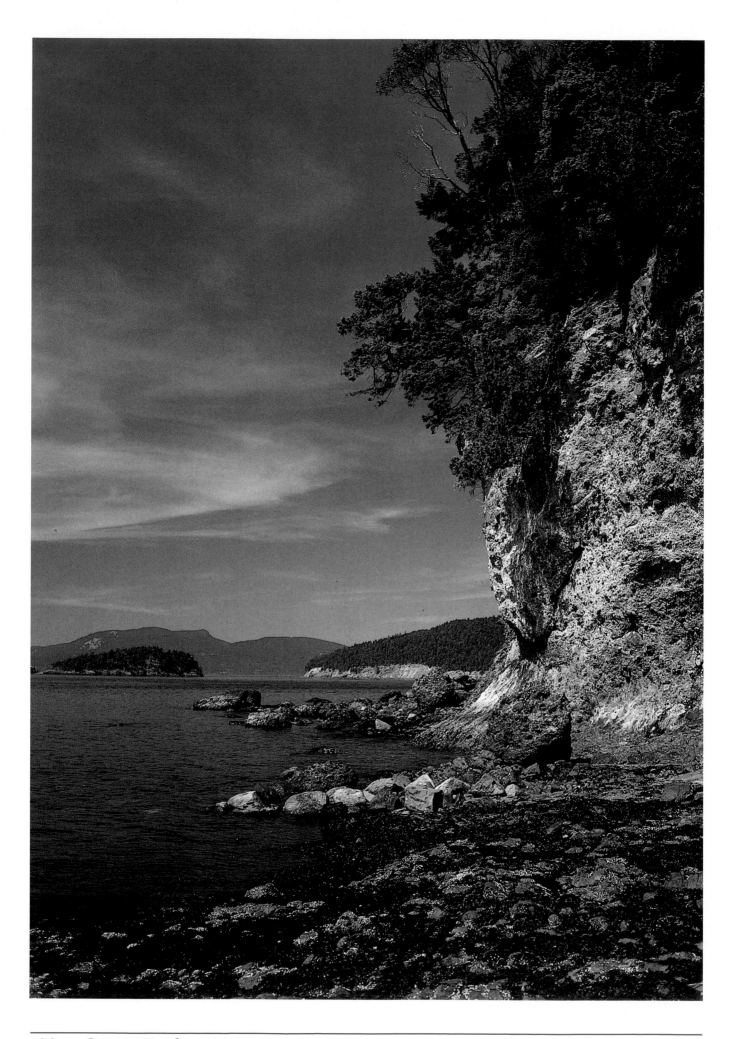

Tug of the Moon

As we emerge onto the barnacle-covered rocks, the cobble beach remains in shadow, the sun not yet over the tall cliffs. Wisps of morning haze drift into the azure sky. Across Puget Sound's central basin, the ragged Olympic peaks, still spotted with bright patches of snow, loom over suburban Bainbridge Island and the sunlit cliffs of the northern Kitsap Peninsula. To the north, a weekend armada of sailboats and powerboats fan out into the Sound from Shilshole Marina and the Lake Washington Ship Canal.

This glorious mid-June day will be one of the longest of the year. Last night, on the other hand, was almost too brief for sleep: The dimmest stars appeared just an hour before midnight and faded by 3 A.M.. It was also one of the darkest nights, as the moon joined the sun on the far side of the earth. Though it is now high above the Cascades, this "new" moon is still invisible—a shadowed rock obscured by the dazzle of the adjacent sun.

But despite its being hidden from us, the moon's presence is strikingly visible throughout the Salish Sea. Rip-tides boil furiously through Sechelt Rapids, Deception Pass, Admiralty Inlet, and The Narrows. Stiff chops arise without wind or warning between hundreds of isles and islets in the Gulf Islands and San Juan archipelago. Along the Strait of Juan de Fuca, Bull kelp flattens in the current as the outgoing tide rushes toward the receding Pacific like a river in flood.

As the tide ebbs, wide expanses of exposed beach reach far out from land. By noon, a tenth of Puget Sound's entire surface area will be laid bare. Boat-launch ramps will hang uselessly above the mud. Seaweeds and attached animals living four feet below zero tide will be exposed, limp and drying in the midday sun. Families carrying rakes, shovels, and buckets will join flocks of gulls and crows, turning the mud and seaweed-covered rocks into a vast fleamarket of crabs and clams and sea stars.

Yet, just eight hours later, sea water will cover the beaches completely, and waves rise to levels matched only by occasional winter storms. At the mouths of large rivers, drift logs and mats of detached seaweed will float upstream, and meandering sloughs overflow to cover marshy fields of pickleweed and saltbush.

As we rotate beneath the moon and sun, both tug at the ocean's surface. Though the moon is very much smaller than the sun, it is also very much closer (thus the two appear equal-size in the sky). And since it is twice as dense as the sun, its pull on the ocean is about double the sun's. Both attract the water nearest them, and also pull the earth

Opposite:
A cliff of glacial till stands above a cobble beach in southern Puget Sound. (Steve Yates)

away from the sea on the far side of the planet, forming two low bulges on the ocean's surface, one directly below and one on the opposite side of the earth.

Because the plane of the moon's path usually lies north or south of earth's equator, one tidal bulge is normally centered in the northern hemisphere while the other maximum is opposite it in the southern hemisphere. Thus, the bulges sweeping across the North Pacific at 12-hour intervals are of unequal size, and this gives us two daily tides of unequal range.

Our two high tides reach about the same height; but one low tide is generally much lower than the other. The average of the lower of the two daily low tides, termed Mean Lower Low Water (MLLW), is designated as the zero level from which all ocean depths and terrestrial altitudes are measured.

As the incoming tide presses through the Strait of Juan de Fuca (and, to a lesser extent, Johnstone Strait) into the Salish Sea's deep channels, narrow inlets, and shallow bays, its actual height and timing are also determined by the sea's bathymetry (underwater topography). Since this is one of earth's longest and most intricate seas, the tides and currents here are bogglingly complex.

Yet oceanographers can predict the approximate height and timing of the tides years in advance because the movements of moon and sun are predictable, and the bathymetry is constant. Actual tides are modified by prevailing winds, barometric pressure, and discharges of nearby rivers, especially when these combine during regional storm systems.

As the moon revolves around us during each 28-day period, the angle of moon, sun, and earth varies from perpendicular to directly in-line. In-line happens twice a month: at full moon (when the moon is opposite the earth from the sun—rising at sunset and fully mirroring the sun's reflection) and at new moon (when it passes between us and the sun).

Lined up, sun and moon reinforce each other's influence, causing the tidal range (rise and fall) of spring tides to be 20% greater than average. The term "spring" tides comes not from the season but from the Anglo-Saxon *springan*—rising. When sun and moon are at odds, they tend to cancel each other's influence, giving a tidal range 20% less than average. We call these "neap" tides, from *neafte*, scarce.

As further variables, our path around the sun is not a perfect circle—we are closest in June and December. The moon's path around the earth is also elliptical: At minimum distance (perigee) the moon is 15,000 miles closer than average; at apogee, the same distance farther away. These varying distances add or subtract another 20% to the tidal range.

This week the sun and invisible new moon are in line; and both are near perigee, closest to the earth. Today's spring tides will be the most extreme of the entire year. The Salish Sea is being sucked out of its maze of deep inlets and shallow bays, and swirls over the shallow sills (underwater ridges) defining its sub-basins.

Places nearest the ocean emptied first. Neah Bay, at the entrance to the Strait of Juan de Fuca, was low this morning at 8:30 A.M.. At the eastern end of the Strait, Dungeness Spit and Victoria will soon be low, at 11 A.M.. Delayed by the narrow passes between San Juan and Gulf islands, Vancouver's Burrard Inlet won't empty until three hours later.

Port Townsend, just inside the sill at the entrance to Admiralty Inlet, will be low at noon. Friday Harbor and Bellingham to the north of Port Townsend, Everett to the east, and Seattle to the south, will be low at about 12:30. Farther south, Tacoma will be lowest 15 minutes after Seattle—the same time as Union, at the southern end of Hood Canal.

Since the shallow, pinched Tacoma Narrows greatly impedes the outward flow, Olympia, at the head of Budd Inlet will not empty until almost 1:30 P.M.. Shelton, inside long, narrow Hammersley Inlet at the southwestern end of the Sound will not reach its lowest level until an hour later.

The tide's rebound will be equally extreme. Hammersley Inlet will barely have drained before the massive wave of the flood tide will begin filling the Strait of Juan de Fuca. By 3:30 P.M.—just an hour after Hammersley has been laid bare—Neah Bay will see its highest levels.

Within the Strait, however, the momentum of the immense tidal outflow will impede the incoming flood. Port Townsend will not see highest levels until 8:15 in the evening. Seattle's Elliot Bay and Tacoma's Commencement Bay will be high around 8:30 P.M.; Olympia not until 9. North of the Strait, Vancouver's Burrard inlet will not fill completely until 9:30.

As the peak of the flood wave moves down the Sound, the high-tide level increases. Port Townsend's maximum is only 9.5 feet above MLLW, but Seattle's and Tacoma's will reach 13 feet. At Olympia and Shelton, on shallow bays at the southernmost end, the flood tide will pile up to more than 15 feet: a 19-foot vertical rise in just eight hours.

Massive spring tides flowing in and out of the Salish Sea generate awesome currents, especially through narrow channels with shallow sills. At the entrance to Admiralty Inlet, maximum currents will reach four knots (nautical miles per hour); at the entrance to the San Juan Channel, five knots; at the Tacoma narrows, six; and in Deception Pass,

A night walk at low tide reveals a magic world on Strait of Juan de Fuca. (Doug Wechsler)

more than seven. Even the broad Strait of Juan de Fuca will experience three-knot currents near Race Rocks at the southern tip of Vancouver Island.

The wind blowing against such currents—as the prevailing westerlies on the Strait of Juan de Fuca are now doing against the outgoing tide—create an especially stiff chop. Naive pleasure-boaters, deceived by the balmy summer weather, will find more adventure than relaxation on the Strait today.

Behind us, at the beach's uppermost level, last night's high tide has cut small chunks of sand and rock from the base of the glacial cliff. Most of the cliff is vertical, but huge slumps moderate its steepness; and during the wet winter, whole saturated sections slipped downward toward the beach. Red alders tilt progressively toward the water, the foremost ones toppled onto the upper beach, some still leafed in green, others completely dead, their rootwads cleansed by the surf.

Up near the sheer top of the cliff, in the layer of sandy glacial outwash that blankets the uplands, tunnels have been excavated by Belted kingfishers and Pigeon guillemots. Lower down, a trio of rusty pipes drainpipes protrude from the cliff, offering convenient perches for the kingfishers to survey the beach. And to use as launching pads for high-speed territorial chases, complete with machinegun-like rattling. On the slopes and eroded gulleys of the cliff's lower half, flocks of Purple and Rosy finches flit and twitter among weedy Himalayan blackberry, pink-flowered Fireweed, and hardy horsetails, while Rough-winged swallows whizz back and forth, hawking insects above the beach.

It is not difficult to tell the origins of the beach material: Chunks of slumped or fallen cliff appear to be melting in place. Both cliff and beach display the same patchwork of cobble stones and quartsite sand, flat gray beds of hard clay, and scattered clusters of small boulders. The variety of colors, lines, and swirls in the beach stones—gray slates and peppered granites, green olivines and diamondlike quartz crystals—show they come from many widely scattered sources. Only a massive ice sheet could have brought them here from far-away mountains.

The only feature that has no apparent counterpart in the cliffs are the three huge erratics along the water's edge. One, the size of a room, is now fully exposed; another of similar size is half out of water, its lower portions covered with barnacles and mussels and dripping rockweed. A kingfisher stands on its outer edge, peering intently down into the water. On another, gulls and cormorants preen. In spring, before the breeeding season called them away, it served as a haul-out for a California sea lion, his huge bulk propped up by strong foreflippers, his nose to the sky, eyes closed contentedly in the warming sun.

At the foot of the cliff, the beach cobble is covered by a layer of smooth sand and broken shell washed up at high tides by the leading edge of the waves—the swash. Most wave energy merely lifts particles of sand or water into a circling motion, moving slightly forward on the upper part of the wave then sinking backwards to their original position. The swash, though, actually pushes particles up the beach slope then drops them, as the seawater retreats down the beach or sinks into the sand.

As the swash moves up the beach on the incoming tide, it carries dislodged seaweed (along with beer bottles, plastic baggies, and styrofoam jetsam). As the tide ebbs, Sea lettuce, Turkish towel, Sargassum, and

Feather boa, along with narrow, straplike leaves of Eelgrass and rubbery tangles of Bull kelp, are stranded in a narrow windrow along the limit of the highest tide.

Most of the wrack here is Sea lettuce. The thin, green, translucent sheets appear fragile, easily ripped by waves from the rocks on which they grow. But the fragility is misleading: Detached Sea lettuce continues to photosynthesize while floating on the water, and whole quiet bays are sometimes covered with it through the summer. Meanwhile, new growth can occur on the vacated substrate. Eventually the floating lettuce is stranded, and the fronds bleach white in the sun.

The surface of the wrack has become black and crispy in the heat. Small fruit flies, the only insect adapted to this beach environment in harsh sunlight, gather on it in droves. They seem to spend most of their time and energy standing on high spots, fanning either one or both wings. Is this a mating dance displaying sexy body shape or virtuosity with the wing? or to disperse a perfumed attractant pheremone? A male-to-male challenge?

The tiny flies guarantee that spider webs will fill the branches of the nearby fallen alder trees. The flies also provide food for the only animal which seems at home on the uppermost beach sand even at midday (or, on rockier shores, high above the tideline on lichen-covered granite or sandstone). The bright red mite *Neomolgus* is hardly larger than a large grain of sand, but it stands out clearly. The little mites, too small to see in detail as they scoot across the sand, are closer to spiders than insects. Though they add a touch of color to the beach, it is hard to empathize

Beach still-life: Kelp crab exoskeleton and scallop shell. Few creatures can survive on the upper beach, but Acorn barnacles contend with Small acorns for space on the stones and driftwood. (Steve Yates)

with their food habits: They suck out the innards of the wrack-flies. I assume they scavenge fallen flies since I can't imagine them able to ambush the sprightly live ones.

Below the wrack's crispy crust, the Sea lettuce remains moist as fresh spinach even in the hottest sun. Expose the soft interior and countless little "sandfleas" jump out in every direction. These beachhoppers are actually amphipods: half-inch-long crustaceans resembling shrimp but flattened side-to-side. Though quite capable of crawling over the sand, they prefer to hop about, propelled by strong rear legs. This random movement not only keeps them off the hot sand but makes them difficult prey for predators—mainly Sanderlings and other shorebirds, which pick among the wrack at high tide while the lower beach is flooded and unavailable for foraging.

The Sanderlings themselves are a remarkable story. These small sandpipers breed in the high Arctic. In autumn, some return south as far as the tip of South America, their annual migration equal to a flight spanning the globe. Some flocks overwinter in this hemisphere, on sandy beaches between here and California. Every winter I spot what seems to be the same flock of about 50 birds along the beach near Seattle's West Point lighthouse. Others move on to parts unknown. Seeing such small, fragile creatures running in front of the waves, it's amazing to realize they might be on a journey of 10,000 miles.

Another interesting animal—the Surf smelt—also uses the upper beach, though just briefly once a year. Smelts are slender schooling fishes with a small adipose fin, like salmonids; and some, like salmon, are anadromous, returning to rivers to spawn. The Surf smelt, though, spawns on beaches, at twilight, on a summer night before a high spring tide. The sticky fertilized eggs adhere to cobbles and sand. They hatch at the next high tide and the larvae, still bearing their yolk sacs, escape directly from the gravel into the plankton.

Unfortunately, most of our beaches have been modified by bulwarks protecting shoreline houses; and so the wriggling spawners once welcomed and harvested by Salish Indians are now increasingly scarce.

Though the upper beach has few live residents, it is a treasure trove of momentos from beyond the tides. A multi-colored collection of seaweeds deposited in the wrack. Driftwood, some of it tunneled by shipworms or festooned with colorful Goose barnacles or clumps of long, leathery tubes of Feather duster worms. Empty crab shells shed by moulting crabs, and dead ones still containing tissue left half-eaten by gulls. Large, rectangular shells of Geoducks and Horse clams washed in by storms. A Bent-nosed clam shell with a circular hole drilled by a predatory Moon snail (along with large, fragile "sand collars" containing the huge snail's eggs). Shards of brittle Heart cockles or Butter clams dropped onto stones by gulls. Other bleached clamshells pitted or turned to lacy filigree by Boring sponges. The brown, rectangular egg cases of Big or Longnose skates.

The upper beach has more empty shells than living creatures for good reason: it is one of earth's most stressful habitats. Even creatures living at a beach's lower margins must be able to withstand pounding waves of exposed shores and survive in hard clays; or sterile, shifting sands; or the thick, anoxic mud of protected bays. When the tide recedes, anchored residents are exposed to the burning sun and drying wind of a midsummer afternoon, or the freezing air of a midwinter night. Rain covers the beach with pools of highly diluted water which may quickly evaporate in the noon sun or turn to ice at midnight. Immobile filter feeders such as mussels and barnacles must go without food for hours, or even days. In the meantime, they are exposed to gulls and Oystercatchers.

Aside from the beachhoppers hiding in damp wrack, few marine animals can survive at the upper levels. But even above the lower of the two high tides, the surface of driftwood and rocks is covered by tiny barnacles. The Small acorn barnacle—the most diminutive of our three intertidal barnacles—grows at levels reached only by spring tides, forming a distinctive swath above the slightly larger Acorn barnacles that dominate the mid-beach.

Barnacles have evolved a simple but highly efficient structure for coping with intertidal extremes. An armor of six interlocking calcified plates protect the strange crustacean from predators; four inner plates shut to enclose it in a water-tight container during exposure. The pattern of interlocking inner plates differs from species to species: The Acorn barnacle's plates make a distinctive cursive pattern; the Small acorn can be told by its Christianlike cross. (The unusual Goose barnacle, limited to exposed shores and rarely found above the splash zone, has only five outer plates and lacks inner ones entirely.)

But a barnacles' armor is a prison as well as fortress. To disperse their progeny, the immobile adults must release them into the waves. This is particularly tricky for the Small acorn barnacle, which must perfectly time its spawn to match the peak of spring tides.

Goose barnacles prefer areas of heavy surf but can sometimes be found attached to floating driftwood. They grow on flexible stalks, but like other barnacles, they kick out modified legs to strain plankton from the water. (Neil G. McDaniel)

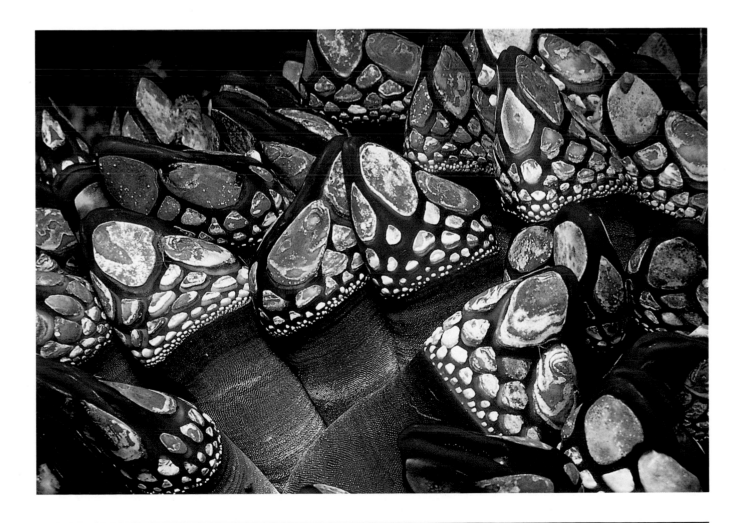

Getting together in the first place would seem to be an even greater obstacle to barnacle reproduction. Surprisingly, though, barnacles don't just pour eggs and sperm into the sea as many sea creatures do. Each individual is hermaphroditic, possessing both female and male sex organs, including a long, slender penis—the Giant barnacle's may be 8 inches long!—which can reach into the cavities of all its bisexual neighbors.

The early larvae are brooded in a special sac within the parent's shell. The first independent stage (nauplius) is released in sync with the spring bloom (population explosion) of planktonic diatoms on which it feeds. Eventually the larval barnacle settles on a hard surface, where it wanders around searching for a congenial spot. If satisfied, it secretes an adhesive—one of the most powerful known—from a gland in its antenna and attaches, head-first, to the rock or shell or log. Once attached, it processes calcium from seawater to secrete it's armoring plates.

Since barnacles are limited to hard surfaces, living space is at a premium. Larger species tend to squeeze out smaller ones. The Acorn barnacle prefers the company of others of its species, perhaps drawn by chemicals released by its fellows. If many larvae settle on a freshly cleared area, they squeeze together into hummocks, growing tall rather than broad.

Within the protective shell, the larva metamorphoses into an adult. Its six legs become feathery appendages called cirri, with which it filters plankton and detritus from the water. The transformed adult can rotate its body 180 degrees within the shell, so that its net of cirri can face directly into the current as the tide changes. To expand its hard plates as it grows, the barnacle dissolves the interior layers and secretes material onto the outside.

The two acorn barnacles dominate the upper beach, but on the lower beach they are more than matched by the larger Thatched barnacles, whose ropy shells make them look like candle-holders with wax dripping down the sides. Just below the lowest tides, the beautiful Giant barnacle lives in a three-inch-tall volcano, the inner plates of which are lined with golden yellow. Its long, feathery magenta legs form a formidable lacy net.

About the only other creatures that can survive in the upper zone of rocky beaches are the common little globular snails called periwinkles. Periwinkles are sea snails but are so well adapted to long periods of exposure that they are thought to be the ancestors of all land snails. Like land snails, they exude slime to help them glide over rough surfaces, so they can function even when the tide is out. Though our two local species are often found together, the Checkered periwinkle is the more marine of the two: It better withstands heavy surf, and it releases its eggs directly into the sea. The Sitka periwinkle, on the other hand, prefers sheltered crevices or quiet water, even salt marshes, and it lays its gelatinous eggs out of water. Periwinkles scrape food particles off the rocks with their radula—a rough ribbon covered with up to 300 rows of tiny denticles (toothlets) that functions like a flexible belt of sandpaper.

As the tide recedes halfway down the beach, it exposes a much more diverse community. Only the lower of the two low tides ebbs below this level (about 5 feet above MLLW), and so exposure lasts for only few hours each day. The animals and seaweeds here must be adapted to short periods of drought and fasting, but they needn't be as specialized as the upper beach creatures.

Here, the Thatched barnacle takes over from the smaller Acorn barnacles, jostling for space with mussels, the only other sessile (attached) animal that can compete with barnacles on intertidal rocks and wood. Mussels are essentially clams that live in the open rather than burrowing into the beach. Instead of the barnacles' superglue, mussels attach with masses of slender but very strong "byssal threads." The Salish Sea's most common intertidal species, by far, is the Blue, or Edible, mussel, but the much larger California mussel lives on exposed beaches such as those of western San Juan Island. A third species, the Horse mussel, can be found in quiet bays, but is abundant only in deeper water.

Mussels, like other bivalve mollusks, have an incurrent siphon to suck water in, and an excurrent one for expelling water and wastes. Along with the inflow comes dissolved oxygen and millions of tiny planktonic plants and animals that the mussel filters out on its gills. Though the food is microscopic, a mussel pumps so much water during its time underwater that it can store up enough to survive long periods of exposure. It's feeding also affects the entire intertidal community: One medium-sized Blue mussel can remove an estimated 100,000 clam larvae each day during the several weeks at height of clam breeding season, and I assume it takes equal numbers of other larvae, along with billions of single-celled planktonic animals and plants.

This Red rock crab—a close relative of the Dungeness crab—was hiding under a blanket of Turkish towel seaweed at low tide. The crack on its carapace tells of a close encounter with a crow or gull. (Steve Yates)

The dominant seaweed here is rockweed—sometimes called "popping wrack" because of its swollen tips, which kids love to pop. These are actually receptacles that produce and store the gametes (sex cells). Rockweeds cover the mid to upper levels of rocky beaches worldwide, held securely to rocks or pilings or barnacles by a tough little button called a holdfast.

Wherever we look carefully among the rockweed or on top of rocks or in crevices, we find limpets. Like periwinkles and mussels, limpets are mollusks—the most varied and successful of all marine invertebrate phyla. Limpets employ a unique strategy, different than the mussels' byssal threads or the barnacles' glue, to hold them in place. When crashed by surf or disturbed by predators, a limpet's large "foot," the same oval shape and size as the cap-shaped shell, suctions to rocks like a rubber-tipped arrow as it squeezes water from the mantle. About the only predators that can remove a clamped-down limpet are Oystercatchers, which pry it off the rock with a chisel-like bill, and sea stars, which patiently pull until the suction releases. Coast Salish Indians harvested them, and many Pacific peoples consider the larger species (especially the Hawaiian *opihi*) a delicacy.

When the tide returns, a limpet glides slowly away on the large, mobile, muscular foot to find patches of surface diatoms or algae, which it, like the periwinkles, scrapes off the rocks with its radula. Later it will return to the same spot, clearly marked by its well-scraped outline. The

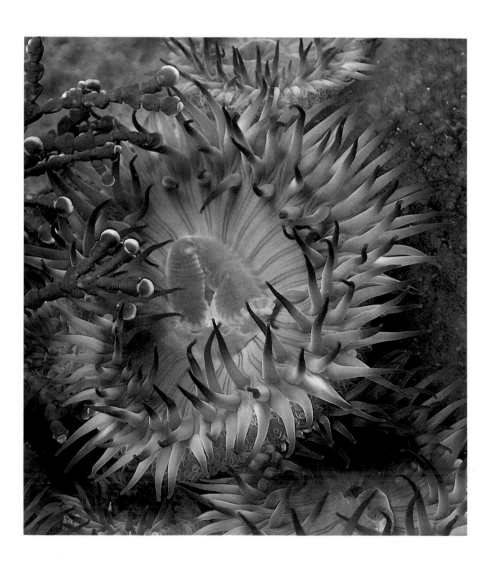

Aggregating (Elegant) sea anemones live in cloned colonies on rocks or in the sand. Individuals of the same colony tolerate dense packing but not the presence of rival colonies. (F. Stuart Westmorland)

A tiny Tidepool sculpin captures an even smaller shrimp. (Chris Huss)

Salish Sea hosts six types, ranging from the conical Whitecap limpet and the strongly-ribbed but somewhat misshapen Finger limpet to the smooth, flattened Plate limpet. They vary in size, shape, and brown-and-white pattern but there is a lot of variation within each, and some are notoriously difficult to tell apart. Another type, the Keyhole limpet—volcanic in shape, with a hole in the top—is not closely related to these "true" limpets, and lives below the tides.

Primitive mollusks called chitons also scrape algae, diatoms, and bacteria off hard surfaces with a radula; like limpets, they use the suction strategy to cling to hard surfaces. But instead of a single, conical shell, chitons are protected by an interlocking series of eight butterfly-shaped plates. These, like all mollusk shells (valves), are secreted by glands in the mantle—a tissue that covers the inner organs. A leathery outcrop of the mantle called the girdle holds the chiton's plates firmly together.

The girdle of Mossy and Hairy chitons is covered with fuzzy projections; the "Black Katy" of exposed shores has a smooth, tough, dark girdle that covers all but the center of the valves. Down below the tides, the world's largest species, the Giant Pacific, or Gumboot chiton, is completely covered by a leathery, monochromatic orange-brown girdle,

The long, slender white threads seen snaking over intertidal beaches belong to the aptly named Spaghetti worm. The worm itself lives in a fragile tube under a rock. Cilia on the sticky threads, which may extend two feet, transfer food to the mouth. (David Denning/Earth Images)

while at the opposite extreme, the colorful Lined chiton is small and its exposed valves exquisitely etched.

Cobbly or muddy beaches appear to be far less populated than rocky shores. But this is only because on rock the creatures all live on the surface or in crevices. The muddy substrate, though it may look almost deserted, has a third, invisible, dimension that is surprisingly lively. If we dig down into the wet, muddy sand, we invade the kingdom of the clams.

As a child, vacationing on the Maine coast, we used to spend summer afternoons using beach shells or just our scratched-up fingers digging in the mud for tasty Soft-shelled clams (introduced, inadvertently, to Pacific Northwest beaches in the 1920s). The faster we'd dig, the faster the clam retreated, and we were convinced that it could burrow downward at an amazing speed. Only later did it finally dawn on me that just the clam's neck withdraws, not the whole clam.

Clams, like mussels, are bivalves. Their soft internal organs—gills, nerve nodules, heart, stomach, and gonads—are protected by two calcareous shells held together at an interlocking hinge by tough cartilage and closed by a strong adductor muscle. When the shell is open, a clam can extend both its "foot" and, sometimes, a tough, fleshy neck. The muscular foot is used for digging into the substrate. The neck contains the siphons—one for drawing in water and food, one for expelling water and wastes.

Not all clams have necks. Heart cockles, which live on or very close to the surface, need only the shortest of siphons. Sand clams and the oddly shaped Bent-nosed macoma abundant in muddy beaches both have long, slender, flexible siphons, separate and unenclosed in a neck—the incurrent one capable of sweeping the surface for detritus.

In general, the length of a clam's neck, or its naked siphons, determines how deep below the surface it lives. And the size of the shell generally indicates how far down the beach it is found. Native little-necks and related Manilla clams, with short siphons and three-inch shells, live near the surface. Six-inch Butter clams live a foot below the surface and their range begins at lower tide levels. Eight-inch Horse clams burrow to 20 inches below the surface and can only be only be dug up during minus-tides on days like today. The huge Geoduck, its neck extending two to three feet, is subtidal.

Bivalve mollusks have managed to exploit every type of substrate. Even patches of rock-hard clay at lowest tide levels are populated by an unusual clam, the Rough piddock. The siphon end of the piddock's shell is typically clamlike, but the anterior half near the foot is roughened like a wood rasp. The muscular foot rotates the shell back and forth to make a permanent burrow in the clay. The tip of the neck branches into two siphons, the openings of which are impressively large.

Another, even more specialized boring clam is the "shipworm" whose tunnels are seen in driftwood and pilings. Its wormlike body extends from a tiny shell that has become little more than a pair of rasping "wings" rotated like the Rough piddock's shell.

This cobble beach has no solid rock basins to form upper-level tidepools, but there are spots at mid to lower levels that hold water long enough to act as tidepools. The largest lies shadowed at the base of a giant erratic boulder beneath a dripping wall of barnacles, mussels, and rockweed; large Red-and-green sea anemones, their tentacles retracted, hang saclike over it. The pool's bottom is carpeted with a thick rug of Aggregating, or Elegant, sea anemone.

Both names are apt. The small anemones' olive-green bodies appear drab when retracted, especially when growing almost covered in sand. But extended, the delicate violet-and-green tentacles are truly elegant (despite which, they are deadly to small amphipods, fish larvae, and other tiny creatures). The plantlike animals commonly reproduce by fission, cloning themselves in vast numbers. The clones pack tightly together but do not tolerate other clones. When two expanding groups come in contact, they battle along their borders with special chemicals in their stinging nematocysts, creating a "no-man's-land" between.

Two very engaging creatures also live in Salish Sea tidepools. By far the most common in this one are dozens of tiny Tidepool sculpins. As the name suggests, these small fish are specialists: able to tolerate radical swings in temperature, salinity, organic wastes, and dissolved oxygen— in pools containing no more water than a small aquarium but without filters, bubblers, or coolers.

Broken-back shrimp, named after the sharp bend in the abdomen, can be found darting backwards among tidepool seaweeds as they feed on tiny amphipods and copepods. (Doug Wechsler)

Actually, there are three fairly similar tidepool species. These under the erratic may in fact be Fluffy sculpin, but I haven't had the desire to check them out that carefully—they're too damn cute. When I lie on my belly to get a close look into the shadowy pool and stay really still, up to a half-dozen come to the edge of the pool to check *me* out. Some even inch half-way out of the pool, for minutes at a time, evidently able to absorb oxygen from the air until the film of water covering them dries out. I've never seen this behavior elsewhere. Maybe because rocky tidepools are usually exposed to the drying sun rather than well-shadowed like this one. Maybe these sculpin are special. They are to me, anyway.

The other main player in tidepools is the Hairy hermit crab. This hermit, like most, uses abandoned snail shells as protection for its soft, coiled body. Like the Tidepool sculpin, hermit crabs are pugnacious, fighting among their peers and with the sculpins for scraps of food that wash or fall into the pool. A hermit crab must also continuously find larger shells to move to as it grows, and so there is also a constant struggle between neighbors for new shells. The Hairy hermit tends to utilize shells that seem to small; thus its attractive banded legs and green, spotted antennae cannot retract into the shell.

Also common in pools filled with Sea lettuce is the strangely shaped Broken-back shrimp—colored the same green as the algae. But easily the strangest-looking creature here is the bizarre caprellid, or Skeleton shrimp. Resembling a cross between a preying mantis and Captain Hook, this small, slender crustacean is all legs and antennae. Despite its gaunt, predatory look, it is mostly vegetarian, feeding on the detritus and diatoms that coat the seaweed, though it also captures protozoans and small crustaceans. It lives among Eeelgrass beds, but at low tides can be seen squirming from pool to pool or drifting in droves along the water's edge.

As the tide ebbs to the zero-foot level, there is a gentle cacophony of noises: squishings, cracklings, lappings, and whooshings—the last when clams necks, hidden under a damp blanket of seaweeds, squirt water in slender fountains three feet into the air (or up your pantleg). Gulls cry; crows squabble; herons squawk.

Here, the intertidal and subtidal communities blend, offering the curious tidepooler a brief feast of diverse and colorful creatures. Few animals can be seen immediately, aside from the occasional stranded seastar or flounder. But Clumps of dripping mussels bulge from barnacle-covered rocks; Green sea anemones retract into tight balls; Orange sea cucumbers withdraw into crevices. Large Red rock crabs hide under colorful seaweeds, and under every rock there are smaller creatures waiting out the ebb.

Lift up a flat-bottomed rock, and there is sure to be either small Green or Purple shore crabs or graceful brittle stars or a wriggling "blenny eel."

Blennies are the popular name for our 16 or so species belonging to two fairly advanced fish families—gunnels and pricklebacks. Both have slender, eel-like bodies with a long, continuous dorsal fin extending from head to tail. Seven or eight types are common in shallow rocky areas and seaweed tidepools, where they feed on amphipods and other small crustaceans. In spring, breeding males become highly territorial, and the females (and sometimes the males) protect the clumps of tiny eggs by coiling around them.

The Penpoint gunnel's body color varies from green or yellow to red but the row of small dots along the lateral line, the thin black line pointing diagonally backwards from above the eye, and the "penpoint" spine at the front of the anal fin are all diagnostic. The Crescent gunnel is mostly mottled yellowish green, with a small line running forward from the eye; white or golden spots along the base of the dorsal fin are partially enclosed by opposing crescents, resembling a row of bold parentheses. The Saddleback gunnel has two lines converging at the eye and dusky vertical bars along its sides; the name derives from the rows of U-shaped marks along the base of the dorsal fin.

Pricklebacks are similar to gunnels, with eel-like bodies, body-length dorsal fins, and long anal fins. The dorsal fin, though, is prickly rather than smooth; and some species have fleshy crests or projecting "cirri" above the head. Three common intertidal species—Snake, Rock, and Black pricklebacks—strongly resemble the gunnels.

Three others are decidedly stranger-looking. The High cockscomb, common under rocks in the northern portions of the Salish Sea, can be easily told by the fleshy crest atop its head. The far less common, deep-bodied Mosshead warbonnet, which hides in holes and crevices rather than under rocks, sports a mossy growth of cirri, like a badly trimmed crew-cut. The most bizarre member of the family, though, is subtidal. The aptly named Decorated warbonnet wears a tall headdress of branching cirri that makes it stand out in an aquarium but, in the wild, evidently camouflages it among hydroids and seaweeds.

Another strange little fish commonly encountered under rocks is the Northern clingfish. From above, it resembles a tadpole, with large, compressed head and very narrow tail. When removed from the rock or kelp to which it clings, it can be seen to have a large suction disk

Overleaf:
Bull kelp, Blood star, and Iridescent seaweed stranded at a minus tide. Note the kelp's tenacious holdfast and bulbous stipe. (Steve Yates)

The Skeleton shrimp, a bizarre amphipod, attaches itself to seaweeds with a hooked posterior segment to feed on diatoms and detritus. Hordes of these tiny creatures are sometimes seen at the water's edge at low tides. (Doug Wechsler)

under the chest, formed by the fusion of its pectoral fins. The clingfish feeds on small molusks and crustaceans. In spring, the female attaches concentric rings of tiny yellow eggs to the undersides of rocks, which the male guards until hatching.

The undersides of lower level rocks is also populated by a community of permanent residents. Thin, flat Rock oysters, or "jingle shells," open to reveal bright red insides. Purple-hinged rock scallops, free-swimming when young, later attach to rocks, the upper valve soon growing thick and misshapen. Calcareous tubeworms grow in hard, meandering tubes. They and the much smaller, tightly coiled Tiny tubeworms extend bright red plumes when covered by the tides. Exposed or threatened, they retract into the tube, perfectly sealed by a red, golf-tee-shaped operculum.

Another tubeworm is probably the most unusual creature found under rocks. Called the Hairy-gilled or, more aptly, Spaghetti worm, the thick reddish creature lives in a fragile tube of sand cemented to the rock's underside. It extends it long strands of thin spaghetti-like feeding tentacles—many times longer than the six-inch body—outward over the rocks. Thousands of pulsating hairlike cilia on the tentacles propel small food particles back toward the mouth. A similar, greenish species lives on muddy sand beaches.

Under most rocks, or in rock crevices, you can usually find an Orange sea cucumber, whose body, when contracted, is dull reddish-orange, lined with five dark muscle bands. But when extended into the sea or a tidepool, the finely divided tentacles can be seen as brilliant red.

All of these creatures—blennies, shore crabs, jingle shells, tubeworms, and sea cucumbers—survive the low tides because they are sheltered and shaded by the rock under which they live. All of them will die if the curious beachcomber fails to replace the rock, slowly and carefully, back into its original position.

As the tide ebbs to its lowest point of the year, about four feet below Mean Lower Low Water, the rocks are draped with a thick blanket of seaweeds; patches of Eelgrass are exposed; Bull kelp stipes and fronds drape limply on the water. Herons wade in the shallows, stabbing at flounders and crabs.

Most of the creatures found here at minus tides are subtidal organisms—seaweeds, sea stars, sea anemones, and the like—that must ride out the hour-long exposure without any adaptations to the heat or drying wind. It's a rare opportunity to meet true sea creatures that are usually available only to the scuba diver.

Probably the most unusual, and exciting, encounter—one I've experienced only once, on a walk along Dungeness Spit—is meeting up with a Gray whale right near shore.

Gray whales are medium-sized baleen whales with narrow heads and bodies covered with white patches and barnacles. They spend much of the year commuting between breeding lagoons in Baja California and feeding grounds in the North Pacific. Driven almost to extinction by land-based whaling stations earlier in this century, populations have rebounded under multi-national protection afforded them since 1946. During northward in spring, a dozen or two wander into the Salish Sea and a few hang out here through the summer.

The Gray whale's diet is eclectic: mollusks, worms, mysids, fish larvae, and small schooling fishes—all of which live just above or buried in the mud or sand. Its method of gleaning them, though, is unique: The whale swims just above the bottom, tilts to the side, and squirts a jet of water into the sediment (similar to the way human divers harvest geoducks). This loosens the bottom material and drives up small creatures, which can then be sifted through the whale's baleen.

Though the oval feeding pits in sand or soft mud are naturally filled in fairly soon afterwards, they can been found where the sediment is firm and the wave action weak. Some 3,000 pits, measuring about ten feet long by four feet wide, and about 4 inches deep, were found recently along a single 12-mile strip of sandy beach in Puget Sound's Sarasota Passage—attesting to an extended feeding bout, perhaps by many whales, probably at evening high tide. It would have been something to have been there when the feast was on.

There's no telling what you might meet on a beach walk when the tide's out, under the moon's magnetic spell.

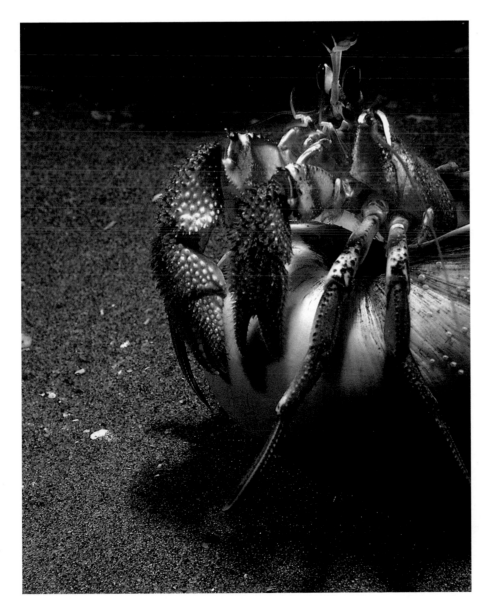

Though the Hairy hermit crab, common in tidepools, tends to pick shells that are too small to withdraw into, this Granular hermit has chosen an abandoned Moon snail shell that is more than adequate. (F. Stuart Westmorland)

Beneath the Tides

Icy water numbs my lips, the only skin exposed between the glassy mask and thick wetsuit hood. The sharp cries of gulls and the buzzing of outboards muffle, then disappear, as we abandon the breezy world of clouds and waves to slip below the Salish Sea's bright, mercurial underside. The only sounds now are the loud, comforting inhales from my regulator mouthpiece and the outgoing flock of shimmering, silvery bubbles escaping back up to the surface.

I swallow to clear my ears as the pressure begins its relentless squeeze, then consciously slow my breathing as the thin layer of water leaking into the wetsuit warms against my skin. Then with a few kicks of my fins I'm gliding just inches above the sand and rocks, down the sloping, tide-flooded beach, all attention focussed on the liquid world before my mask.

Blobs of light play over the shadowy cobbles. Tiny ivory volcanos that seemed gray and dead when the beach was exposed at low tide—barnacles by the thousands—now dance on the rocks, their reddish, feathery scoops of modified legs kicking rhythmically out and back to glean invisible plankton from the tide. Clumps of edible Blue mussels, held to the rock by strong byssal threads, compete with the barnacles for space. Both are partly covered by swaying greenish-brown Rock-weed and delicate sprigs of iridescent blue *Iridea*.

Hermit crabs scurry for shelter, their sharp, colorful legs projecting from recycled snail shell houses covered with encrusting pink algae. Slender, eel-like blennies slither through the slippery seaweeds. Small Green and Purple shore crabs slip into crevices or under seaweeds to peer up at me.

I follow a double line of pilings from an old pier out towards the beach's hidden lip. The bottom 15 feet of the poles are covered with a thick, rough overlay of intertidal mussels and colorful fan worms reaching out from leathery tubes. As we go deeper, masses of Giant (Frilled) sea anemones extending up to two feet from their bases transform them into a fantasy world of Roman columns and ghostly apparitions. Most of the anemones are white; some are delicate shades of pink or yellow. At their tips, hundreds of feathery tentacles filter plankton from the murky green water.

Schools of seaperches—Pile perch, Shiner perch, and Striped seaperch—drift among the pilings, nipping at baby mussels and small crabs and worms. All three have highly compressed, oval bodies and so seem rather large from side-view, then almost disappear when seen head-on. Abundant in shallow water during the warmer months, they move deeper in winter.

Unusual among fishes, the seaperch (or surfperch) family breed almost like mammals. Fertilization is internal, and the female nourishes the larvae within her body during the year-long gestation before

Opposite:
Giant (Frilled) sea anemones transform pilings into exotic columns. The plantlike animals trap planktonic creatures with hundreds of finely divided tentacles. (Neil G. McDaniel)

A Giant barnacle extends its feathery modified legs as an efficient plankton net. Found on beaches on the outer coast, this species is subtidal in the Salish Sea. (F. Stuart Westmorland)

releasing up to 40 tiny replicas into the sea. Shiner perch never grow longer than six inches or so, but the others reach a foot or more. All three are favorite catches for pierside anglers, the smaller ones for bait. (Pregnant females should be released.)

Near one of the pilings is a Painted greenling. A smaller relative of the Kelp greenling and Lingcod, its five to seven dark stripes are a deep red. Painted greenlings are tame and slow moving, but during summer breeding season, they engage in elaborate courtship activities. The male actively guards the egg mass (often of two or more females) against other fishes, especially other males of the same species.

Two other engaging fishes, usually found over rocks and seaweed but just as common around piers and wrecks, are much less visible. The tiny Grunt sculpin hides in crevices or even in discarded cans and bottles. It swims slowly, holding its fanned tail below its round, yellow body, crawling and hopping over the seaweed on the tail and enlarged lower rays of its pectoral fins.

Its cousin, the Sailfin sculpin, has an elongated first dorsal fin (the sailfin) and a broad diagonal stripe through its eye and cheek. A favorite in aquariums, it hides in crevices and under seaweeds during the day but can be seen on night dives, along with scores of colorful crawling Coon-stripe shrimps.

At the end of the old pier are the remains of a wrecked fishing boat, partly buried in the soft seabed, its ribs and rusted iron covered with

A small Painted greenling finds shelter among a sea anemone's stinging tentacles. (F. Stuart Westmorland)

seaweeds and diatomaceous algae. Exploring it is like moving through the carcass of a whale. We move gingerly, careful not to rip our wetsuits or catch air hoses on protruding fingers of rusted metal or splintered wood. Visibility is particularly poor in the hull's shadows, and the murky water becomes even more so when anything is disturbed. Such as when an unnoticed three-foot-long Cabezon (largest member of the sculpin family) slithers away from us in a cloud.

Like the pier pilings, the wreck offers a solid habitat on the otherwise soft sediments of the bay, and within the wreck we encounter large rockfishes and sculpins normally found only near reefs. Rounding a rotted bulkhead, I come come face-to-face with the bulging eyes of a colorful Red Irish lord. In this murky brownish world it is rather drab, but ones that live near more colorful reefs assume almost tropical coloration.

Outside the wreck, I'm greeted by two apparently disembodied eyeballs hovering over the sediment. The C-O sole streaks away in a plume of mud. Named for the distinct markings on its body, the C-O is particularly bug-eyed; but most flounders and sole (including the huge, tasty Pacific halibut) have protrusive eyes also.

Flatfish are unique in that they develop from normal-looking larvae into adults with both eyes on one side of the body. During the course of development, one eye migrates to the other side (the right side in most local flounders and soles); and the skull gradually twists to accommodate the eyes. As strange as this may seem, it works well for fishes that spend most of their time on or buried in the seabed, where they feed on worms and small crustaceans in the mud (or suck in small fishes, as do the larger halibut).

But the strangest-looking fish around here is one I watched recently near a salmon aquaculture pen, where a large school of Ratfish were vacuuming up feed pellets that had escaped the net-bound salmon.

Most of the chimaerid familiy—ratfish, rabbitfish, and ghost sharks—according to Andy Lamb and Phil Edgell's excellent *Coastal Fishes of the Pacific Northwest,* "inhabit deep and dark offshore haunts...becoming more grotesque as the depth increases: long-nosed, ghostly forms abound at abyssal reaches."

Our single local species, bizarre as it may be, is rather attractive in an off-beat way. Its face resembles a rabbit far more than a rat. Its long, tapering body is iridescent pinkish-brown with bluish spots, with a tall, sharklike dorsal fin fronted by a sharp spine. It ends in a sharp-pointed tapering tail which seems not to match its head.

Normally nocturnal, Ratfish pick small creatures off pilings and the bottom, and can be attracted by strong lights. The ones moving beneath the salmon pen in daylight ignored me, and up close I could see the complex "claspers" under the body that males use in copulation. Like its distant cousin the Dogfish shark, Ratfish were once harvested locally to extract a fine machine oil.

The Spotted ratfish's face looks more like a rabbit's. Distantly related to sharks, its thick body tapers to a pointed tail. (Doug Wechsler)

Reaching above the mud of the silty area around the wreck are stout clam necks with a pair of rectangular, valved siphons. The "gooeyduck" (geoduck) is our largest clam, second in size worldwide only to the Giant clam of tropical waters. Weighing up to 20 pounds at maturity, geoducks soon outgrow the small, squared-off shell, leaving some of the body and all of the neck unable to retract into the shell. They don't have much need of protection though, except from human divers. Living two or three feet below the seafloor surface, the animal sucks in oxygen-rich, plankton-laden water with one siphon and expels waste products through the other. Geoducks are found from just below normal low tides to water depths of 200 feet.

With its three-foot-long neck (5 inches when out of water), the geoduck has been the butt of ribald jokes since settler times—and probably for millennia among Salish Indians. It has even been adopted as the official student mascot at The Evergreen State College in Olympia. TESC pennants and sweatshirts carry the image of a large geoduck wearing a mortarboard on its siphon, with the Latin motto *Omnia Extares* (roughly, "Let it all hang out").

But geoducks are also serious business. Beds containing an estimated five million pounds of geoduck are leased out by the state's Department of Natural Resources. Commercial hardhat divers, supplied from boats, descend to the seafloor armed with powerful hydraulic jets. Squirting away the mud around the body of the clam—much like the feeding technique of the Gray whale—divers remove the clams, placing them in baskets to be hauled up to the boat. The meat of the neck and valve muscles is used mostly for clam chowder.

Among the geoduck siphons, fields of flowery Sea pens rise from the mud. Resembling artistic orange feathers with swollen quills, Sea pens are related to the sea anemones lining the piers but are actually colonies of smaller animals working together to filter plankton from the water. The "plumes" are made of 20 or so pairs of branches, each bearing hundreds of feeding polyps. The polyps composing the shaft force water currents through the colony to distribute food and remove wastes. When disturbed they contract down into the mud and will luminesce in the dark. Vast numbers are sometimes washed onto beaches, where their stiff internal structure can be felt within the shrunken skin.

Sea pens feed a community of animals. The polyps are munched on by the specialized Brown-striped nudibranch and by one of the world's largest nudibranchs, the handsome Orange-peel. Three colorful sea stars—the Vermilion, the Spiny red, and the Leather—also feed on it.

Here and there Giant sea cucumbers, a foot or more long, vacuum the surface of the seafloor, gleaning tiny creatures and detritus from the silt passed through their gut. Their warty, sausagelike bodies look primitive, but Giant sea cucumbers (like their smaller orange and white intertidal cousins) are echinoderms, the same relatively advanced phylum containing sea stars and sea urchins. The relationship is most apparent in the five groups of frilly tentacles surrounding the mouth and the five thin bands of muscle (considered a delicacy by many Pacific cultures) along the body. Like the sea stars, sea cucumbers move along on thousands of tiny tube feet. When disturbed, the Giant cucumber can "eviscerate" (extrude and discard the gut) to distract a predator. Taken out of water, its body is flabby, but in the sea it can rear up and can even undulate to swim away from predatory Sunflower stars.

A green meadow of Eelgrass stretches away from one side of the wreck.

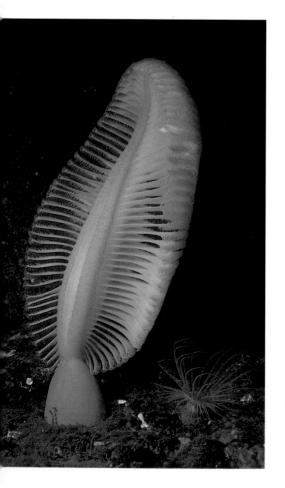

Resembling a large orange feather with swollen quill, the Sea pen is actually a colony of tiny polyps related to sea anemones. Dense aggregations cover muddy or sandy bottom. (Neil G. McDaniel)

Eelgrass is not really a grass. Unlike algal seaweeds it is a flowering, seed-producing plant, one of the few fully adapted to marine existence. Its half-inch-wide straplike leaves arise from rhizomes—spreading underground stems that anchor it in the soft silt. Clusters of tiny flowers are hidden within the curling leaves.

Now, in late summer, the three-foot-long leaves are at maximum length, their rich green surfaces covered with luxurient growths of small red seaweeds, fuzzy white hydroids, and a thick brown beard of single-celled algae called diatoms.

Two flowerlike creatures are common on the Eelgrass leaves: a small sea star and an even smaller sea anemone.

Since typical sea stars have five rays the tiny, Six-rayed sea star is unusual even on first sight. At low tides it is hard to spot, but at high tide, as now, it crawls up to the tops of the Eelgrass blades. There it feeds on the abundant *Lacuna* snails, whose egg cases form the conspicuous little white lifesavers that are visible all over the blades.

The little Brooding sea anemone, merely an inch or so wide and tall, has a striped column, from the top of which dozens of slender, sticky tentacles encircle its mouth. With tentacles expanded, sea anemones resemble colorful blossoms, but they are actually predatory animals. The tentacles contain miniscule coiled harpoons containing neurotoxins which sting and paralyze larval fishes and other small animals. Like the sea star, this sea anemone is also found in crevices of rocky beaches at lowest tide levels but is far more conspicuous on the Eelgrass.

The Brooding anemone is a cnidarian (or coelenterate)—a primitive invertebrate phylum containing jellyfishes and corals, while the Six-rayed sea star is an echinoderm—considered the most advanced invertebrate phylum. Yet these two very different organisms share an unusual trait. Most aquatic invertebrates simply release their countless eggs and sperm into the sea or set their larvae free to join the plankton. These two doggedly protect their offspring, despite the cost to the parent.

In early spring, the mobile female Six-rayed sea star humps protectively over her fertilized eggs and the developing larvae—barely moving for two full months and going without food in the meantime. Growing from each Brooding anemone's column are a half dozen or so skinny little replicas. As eggs, they were held unharmed inside the parent's digestive cavity, where they were randomly fertilized by sperm from other individuals. The half-grown larvae eventually escape through the mouth in the center of the anemone's tentacled top, slide down the parent's side, and embed themselves in the broad, circular "pedal disk" which holds the adult to the Eelgrass blade. There the juvenile Brooding anemones remain, protected by the parent's tentacles, until they grow large enough to move off on their own.

Among the upper ends of the Eelgrass leaves is a small crab that is common but easy to miss in the brown fuzz of diatoms. The spidery-legged Graceful crab is a decorator. It glues tufts of seaweeds, hydroids, and diatoms to its rough carapace—a perfect camouflage, and one which can be changed to fit the place and season—while it busily works its way among similar plants, feeding on algae and detritus (decaying plant matter mixed with fungi, bacteria and other delectables).

Parting the Eelgrass leaves, I spot a much larger crustacean—a species familiar to gourmands everywhere.

This Dungeness crab measures about four inches across its broad carapace, but it might eventually reach eight inches. Picking it up with my clumsy glove, I turn it over to check its sex. The male's triangular abdominal flap—the vestigial equivalent of a lobsterlike tail—is narrow. The female's is much wider. When she is "gravid," or "in berry," her large, frothy mass of pinkish eggs is held tightly by this curled-under abdominal flap until she attaches the eggs to the Eelgrass.

This single species is the basis of Washington state's entire crab fishery. Five to twenty million pounds of Dungeness are harvested throughout state waters, both from Puget Sound and from shallow bays along the outer Pacific coast. Legal-sized males are taken in lines of circular traps set at 30 to 120 feet deep; gravid females have been found to congregate at these lower depths.

Most of the Dungeness crab's adult life, however, takes place in the shallows among the Eelgrass meadows. As the female "moults" (sheds her old shell while secreting a larger one) a larger male clings to her, sometimes carrying her around for days as she produces her eggs and gathers the fertilized eggs into a clump under her carapace.

One spring day I assisted researchers Si Simensted, Ron Thom, and Jeff Cordell of the University of Washington's Fisheries Research Institute as they sampled Eelgrass habitat with a huge beach seine. A single haul netted half a dozen pairs of Dungies, caught in the mating act, clinging belly-to-belly.

The same hauls also revealed hundreds of one of the most bizarre-looking of Puget Sound's denizens—Hooded nudibranchs.

Nudibranchs are called sea slugs because they, like land slugs, are closely related to snails yet lack the snail's shell. Many nudibranchs are wildly colorful, even beautiful in an other-worldly way. Most of them look weird because they have warty extensions on the body called cerata that increase the body surface area to help absorb dissolved oxygen from the water; sometimes they also provide more space for extensions of the digestive system. Most nudibranchs also have organs of smell organs (rhinophores) projecting from the head end; and some species have a second set of tentacles.

An Alabaster nudibranch. The bodies of "sea slugs" are decorated by projections called cerata, which help increase the surface for absorbing oxygen. Many nudibranchs are extremely colorful and lay ribbons of egg masses in flowerlike patterns. (Neil G. McDaniel)

Some of the more colorful nudibranchs have sharp spicules that irritate the mouths of potential predators. Or they exude acids or poisons. *Aeolidia papillosa* is immune to the nematocysts in the small Aggregating anemones on which it feeds. In fact, it stores them in special sacs in the tips of its dorsal appendages and uses them to ward off other predators. *Diadora aspera*'s mantle repels Pisaster sea stars and, temporarily at least, the large, multi-armed Sunflower star.

Other nudibranchs, though, are well camouflaged. The Green sea slug's color and thin dark lines make it almost invisible on Eelgrass blades, to which it is entirely adapted. Also common on the Eelgrass is the greenish, fuzzy-looking Sea mouse, which dines almost exclusively on the living tentacles of the Brooding anemone. Its much showier relative, the flame-tipped Opalescent nudibranch is omnivorous.

The Hooded nudibranch is rarely noticed, but its body shape and behavior make it one of the strangest of all. Four to six pairs of large, leafy cerata project from the sluglike rear portion of a transparent body which may total three to four inches. Its front end consists of a transparent, inflated oral hood. Bordered by long, stiff, inward-pointing "hairs," the hood resembles the business end of a carnivorous Venus flytrap. It waves in the current, almost invisible, then snaps closed to trap small amphipods and other zooplankton.

The oversized hood also serves as a means of transport. It can close tightly to trap gasses expelled by the animal. Using it as a float, the writhing nudibranch can swim to a more favorable location in the Eelgrass.

The meadow is also full of fish. Below my mask, a foot-long Whitespotted greenling, a relative of the much larger Lingcod, waits patiently for juvenile fishes. Like the Lingcod, its predatory lunge is lethal. Otherwise, it swims slowly though the meadow, searching for amphipods and tiny crabs.

A Bay pipefish—incredibly elongated and skinny as a pipe-cleaner—also twists sinuously among the Eelgrass leaves. It oftens assumes an upright position like its close relative, the seahorse, which it closely resembles. There are probably dozens more lurking upright in the

The bizarre Hooded nudibranch attaches itself to Eelgrass and kelp. The inflated oral hood snaps shut to trap plankton and also closes up as a float to help this sea slug move to more favorable locations. (F. Stuart Westmorland)

The slender, flexible Bay pipefish swims jerkily through Eelgrass. Related to seahorses, the male pipefish also broods the eggs in a special abdominal pouch. (F. Stuart Westmorland)

meadow, but they are so well-camouflaged that detection is impossible. The female pipefish, like the familiar aquarium seahorse, transfers fertilized eggs to a pouch on the male's armored body. He then broods them in the pouch until they swim off on their own.

Hovering over the edge of the Eelgrass meadow is a large school of Tube-snouts. Just a bit stouter and more rigid than pipefish, Tube-snouts stay horizontal, darting forward to suck in copepods and fish larvae from the plankton. The Tube-snouts themselves serve as food for greenlings, rockfishes, and flounders.

The larvae of many commercial and sport fishes also hide among the dense Eelgrass. The most directly valuable, to us at least, are the parr (striped juveniles) of outmigrating salmon. For weeks or months after moving down their natal streams the developing juveniles adjust to marine life here in the sheltering Eelgrass, hidden from larger predators.

The Lingcod, which ranks with salmon and Pacific halibut as Puget Sound's tastiest gamefishes, also spends its youth in the meadows. Eventually growing into a five-foot long voracious predator with distinctive large, pointed mouth and clusters of dark spots, it moves deeper as it grows. The mature male eventually returns to the shallows to mate. Here, it protects the female's eggs and broods the young until the juveniles are large and quick enough to themselves take refuge in the Eelgrass.

As valuable as the living Eelgrass is as substrate, meadow, and nursery, its dead blades are equally valuable. Decomposed Eelgrass leaves are one of the principal components of detritus, the mix of decaying organic material, fungus, and bacteria that covers the nearshore seafloor.

Though decidedly unappetizing to our tastes, detritus is very nutritious and easily assimilated by the many creatures that feed on it—worms, burrowing shrimp, sea cucumbers and sea stars, and a number of small crustaceans. These in turn, provide food for tiny Pink, Chum,

The Lingcod is a greenling that grows to 5 feet. A voracious predator with large mouth and canine teeth, it is prized by human anglers. In winter, the male returns to the shallows to guard the pink egg mass for up to six months. (Neil G. McDaniel)

and Sockeye salmon in the estuaries before they migrate to the ocean; and for Coho and Chinook salmon until they grow large enough to prey on small fishes.

At low tide, when the Eelgrass is closer to the surface, it will also provide food for huge flocks of migrating Brant geese. As Ron Thom was quick to point out, even the seemingly barren mud flats above the Eelgrass are valuable. The scummy layer of sediment-related diatoms on the surface of the mud, exposed directly to the sun at low tides, is another major food source for the copepods on which salmon smolts feed.

Unfortunately, over the past century the Eelgrass beds of Puget Sound and the Fraser River Delta have been destroyed or degraded by harbor developments, private piers, and seawalls. The harbor that the Fisheries Research Institute scientists seined that day, for example, was to be dredged for a marina expansion.

Not many years ago, the Army Corps of Engineers and state fisheries would have automatically approved such developments. Now, before permits are granted—even for private piers—Washington's Department of Fisheries requires biological surveys to determine if the project will impact Eelgrass beds. As "mitigation" (the softening of a project's environmental impacts), some Eelgrass beds destroyed by siltation and toxic wastes have even been replanted—a recent FRI project in Tacoma's Commencement Bay is one of the best examples. But this is a labor-intensive, chancy alternative to protecting our existing Eelgrass beds before they vanish.

At the far edge of the Eelgrass meadow, I find myself amid a shimmering school of Pacific sand lance. These slender, silvery fish resemble eels, and they swim sinuously with their entire bodies (the dorsal fin stretches from behind the head all the way to the forked tail). Adults may reach ten inches, but these juveniles are only two to three inches long. The fish's pointed lower lip characteristically sticks out beyond the upper, perhaps helpful in catching plantktonic creatures.

Sand lance get their name from their habit of burying themselves, tail first, in fine sand in the shallows to escape the notice of predators. They are certainly in need of some refuge: when feeding near the surface in large schools, they are a favorite prey for seabirds, large inshore fishes, and porpoises.

Among the school of sand lance are smaller groups of juvenile Pacific herring—shorter, stouter, and more conventionally shaped than the sand lance. Herring, which often form their own massive schools (called shoals when spread out and "herring balls" when concentrated) are equally popular prey for seabirds and fishes, and prized by humans.

For centuries, local Indians harvested dense herring runs from canoes, using wooden "rakes," as the adults moved toward shallow bays to spawn. The eggs were also harvested after being laid on seaweed—or on weighted cedar branches placed in the water as an artificial substrate to be pulled up covered with eggs.

Herring and sand lance may well be the Salish Sea's most important fishes. They form a critical link between the plankton's microscopic organisms and such large, visible animals as King salmon, Lingcod, Tufted puffins, Dall's porpoises and Minke whales.

Surrounded by hundreds of silvery fish, I drift in a timeless, three-dimensional dream world as the school of sand lance wanders up toward the shimmering undersurface. The greenish, plankton-rich water is pierced by long shafts of sunlight, and I am free of all bearings.

Eventually we arrive at a ragged line of Bull kelp and are re-oriented among the slender stipes which point upward, slightly angled by the current, from the rocky bottom.

Bull kelp—our largest algae—consists of a long, rubbery stipe, or stem, topped by a floating bulb from which four sets of long, yellow-brown blades spread. At lower tides the floats rest on the surface, the blades drifting just below. But during this very high tide the bulbs float well below the surface, the blades swaying in the upper sunlight like ragged flags.

Neighboring plants, swirled by shifting currents, tangle together like mating octopuses. The plants are attached at their base by rootlike "holdfasts"—webs of rubbery fingers strongly cemented to a rock. During winter storms, most of the kelp will be ripped from their anchors. Or small rocks they are attached to will be lifted to float onto shore with the twisted wrack.

But long before that, patches of sporangia on the Bull kelp's blades will shed enormous numbers of swimming spores into the plankton. The lucky few finding a spot to settle on subtidal rocks will overwinter as microscopic plants. In spring, sperm from a small male gametophyte plant will swim to an egg embedded in a female plant, from which the large, familiar, spore-bearing kelp will develop.

Through the summer, the stipe grows rapidly upward (up to a foot each day in clear, mineral-rich water). The hollow stipe is held up by a thick, gas-filled terminal bulb, which contains, mysteriously enough, up to 10% carbon monoxide. Eventually, the stipe will reach 40 feet or more. Pencil-thin at the base, it is so strong that Salish Indians dried and strung them together as deep-sea fishing lines capable of hauling a 100-pound halibut up from the bottom.

Bull kelp stipes create underwater forests. Fish find refuge among the stipes. Seagulls, terns, and ducks rest on and among the floating blades and feed on Kelp crabs that crawl through the blades.

Bull kelp is also very useful to boaters on Puget Sound—the stipes mark the seaward edge of reefs. And to scuba divers by indicating the direction and speed of currents. (The long stipes, though, are also a danger to the diver. It is easy to get tangled in them, and one must disentangle calmly. Divers trying to cut a stipe away with a knife have been known to cut their own air hose.)

Following a narrow stipe down to its holdfast, I work my way through the dense layer of lesser kelps and other leafy seaweeds covering the bottom rocks. Like the Eelgrass meadows, these beds of small kelps provide cover for countless organisms. "Blennies"—laterally-compressed, eel-like fishes in the gunnel and prickleback families—slither through the overlapping seaweeds. Large, shield-shaped Kelp crabs, along with two species of much smaller decorator crabs, shred and stuff the soft blades non-stop into their mouthparts. Tiny *Spirorbus* tube worms, their bright red cirri extended from hard, coiled tubes, settle on the kelp as well as on the rocks beneath.

A handsome pair of Kelp greenling—the coppery-olive male with black-edged patches of blue scattered around its head; the golden female with red-dotted, turquoise flanks—slide by. During mating season, the male's head turns bright blue as the couple vigorously defend their territory and their eggs.

Lining rocky shores, the long, hollow stipes of Bull kelp float on the surface at low tide. (Neil G. McDaniel)

Topographically, the underwater world is similar to its surroundings, though it may be hard to tell from above the waves. Far below the surface, ancient river valleys, remnants of times when sea level was hundreds of feet lower than at present, pass between submerged mountains. Some beaches extend gently outward for half a mile then slope abruptly down to great depths. On others, a beachcomber wading just past the tide line might have the beach suddenly drop out from underfoot.

Just beyond the Eelgrass meadow, this gentle slope plunges out of sight. Clearing our ears to equalize the pressure, we drift down a vertical underwater cliff.

A school of Striped seaperch, their silvery sides etched with thin horizontal blue lines, slide warily past my mask. Sea colander—a medium-size brown kelp with ragged holes in its rough-surfaced blades—grows upward, swayed by the strengthening tidal current. (The Salish

A dense school of silvery Pacific herring can contain hundreds of thousands of individuals. This keystone species feeds on plankton and is preyed on by larger fishes, seabirds, porpoises, Minke whales and people. (F. Stuart Westmorland)

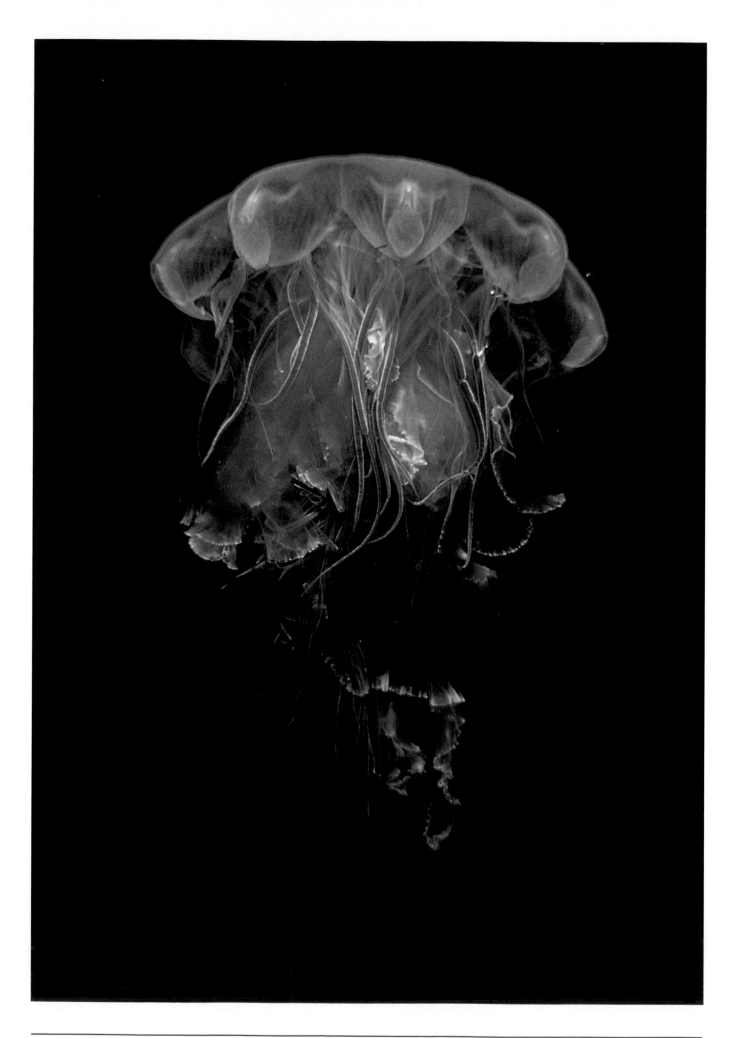

Sea's most colorful underwater areas are those with the strongest currents. Good for renewing nutrients and oxygen but a constant danger to the diver.)

As the layer of water above me thickens, shafts of cathedral light scatter on the millions of tiny particles of plankton and detritus clouding the water, cutting visibility to ten feet or so. Not far seaward, the world dissolves into an ominous, greenish void. I hug the cliff.

The cliff here is formed not of solid rock, as it might be in the San Juans or Georgia Strait, but of glacial till—a continuation of the cliffs above. The underwater wall is pocked with holes and crevices where rocks have fallen out. And from these crevices shine wary eyes. My flashlight beam reaches into a small cave within which a Quillback rockfish hides. Foot-long Buffalo sculpin, their beady eyes close-set on bulbous head, rest motionless at odd angles against the rocks.

What is most surprising to the novice diver hereabouts are the colors. Dampened as it may be by poor visibility in the plankton-rich waters, the world below the waves is not the dark, dismal one we would expect looking down from a boat or from land. In many ways it is more richly colored than the terrestrial world: constantly colorful, not just during seasons of flowering or high breeding plumage. Above water, the landscape is dominated by the green of foliage, the grays of clouds and beach stones, and, on sunny days, the blue of sky and the white of snowcapped mountains. But the dominant colors of this seacliff are reds and shocking pinks.

Pink encrusting algae (of various similar species lumped as *Lithothamnium*) form a thin crust over rocks, limpets, snail shells, and even on the softer species of seaweed. Many of the colorful encrusting and boring sponges are also pink. Since camouflage aids survival, other animals which live and feed on the pink background have taken on a pinkish exterior, at least for part of their lives. Even some of the otherwise-drab Buffalo sculpin are splashed with pink; and the juveniles of Red Irish lords are commonly so. Adding highlights to the surface of the underwater cliff are brightly banded Top shells, Pink scallops, multicolored abalone, bright Green sea anemones, and colorful sea stars.

Among the clumps of Sea colander and the waving, ragged blades of Seersucker kelp nestle two smaller red algae. One—the Iridescent seaweed—is as colorful as the corraline crusts and sponges. In the shafts of sunlight, its slick, rubbery blades reflect a rainbow of color off a reddish surface sheen; tiny new blades are a lovely blue. The other seaweed is purplish-red and is covered with hundreds of tiny stiff outgrowths called papillae, giving it the name Turkish towel. It, too, is iridescent, though less so than its neighbor.

This upper subtidal zone, between lowest tides and 60 feet or so, is richer and more varied that the intertidal above or the depths below. Light here provides energy for a thick jungle of seaweed, which in turn provides shelter and substrate for hundreds of animal species. Light on the phytoplankton and nutrient-laden river outflow creates a rich planktonic broth to feed an army of larger swimmers and filter-feeding shellfish.

It is also a transition zone. Most of the animals and plants that we find on intertidal beaches are also encountered here, as well as some that are intertidal on more exposed ocean shores. And many of the animals living

Opposite:
The Lions' mane jellyfish is the world's largest jelly, growing up to 8-feet in diameter in Arctic waters. Locally, it grows to about two feet across; in summer thousands may pulse through the upper water. Its long stinging tentacles hang down to capture small fishes, and the harpoonlike nematocysts can deliver an irritating sting even when detached. (Neil G. McDaniel)

in the depths can also seen in the upper subtidal zone—at least during part of their life cycle, or seasonally, or at night.

Attached or crawling with glacial pace over this pocked wall are an incredible variety of animals, many of which would at first glance seem more like plants. This patch of whitish fuzz resembles a terrestrial moss; but *Obelia*, a hydroid, is a colonial animal closely related to jellyfishes. Put your hand near one of the delicate red flowers blooming from gray stalks everywhere on the wall; in a flash it withdraws into its calcareous tube, quickly sealing itself with a bright red stopper (operculum) shaped like a golf tee. The flowers are actually whorls of multicolored bristles, the living plankton-nets of marine tubeworms.

Plastered against the cliff is a large sea star called the Sunflower star, easily two feet in diameter but still well under its potential size. Unlike the usual five rays of lesser sea stars, the Sunflower star has up to two dozen rays extending from a humped central disk. Two of them curl up at their tips to feel out my gloved hand with the suction cups at the end of their tiny, tubefeet. The whitish tubefeet are controlled by muscles and hydrostatic pressure, and they are all connected together through a hydraulic "water-vascular" system of larger tubes running through the arms. With them, sea stars can cling tightly to rocks or to their prey (mostly sea urchins and limpets). By a miracle of coordination, they can even move the sea star at a steady pace in a purposeful direction.

I've read that the Sunflower star has 40,000 tubefeet. Whoever counted them was surely up in a lab somewhere. Under water, twenty is about the practical limit of my math, and it takes a few counts round the massive sea star to even be sure of that number of arms. The Sunflower's pinkish-orange to reddish-purple body is flabbier than most sea stars to start with and appears even softer, almost like a fuzzy decorator cushion, because of the thousands of tiny violet pincers, which keep it clean of organisms that might want to settle on the upper surface of its substantial body. Though no speedster itself, the Sunflower star is capable of causing other normally torpid animals, such as sea cucumbers and scallops, to set dash records when it approaches.

Another sea star, the Blood star, makes up in visual intensity—a bright reddish orange—what it lacks in size (about 6 inches across). It has the five arms common to most sea stars and unlike the Sunflower star, whose rays extend from a large central disk, the Blood star's smooth, slender, tubular rays seem to join in the center with no disk at all. A female Blood star carries her fertilized eggs in her mouth until they develop. There are no eggs in the one I lift off a patch of kelp, but in the grooves under the rays is a commensal scale worm, *Arctinoe*. I replace the beautiful sea star back on its vertical perch with the clumsiness common to the gloved coldwater diver; it falls ten feet to a sand terrace.

Behind a blade of Sea colander kelp, a Keyhole limpet clamps down onto the algae-covered rock. Resembling a miniature volcano, the Keyhole's tiny clamlike siphon is visible inside the oval hole at the top of its shell. It is not a "true limpet" but, like its more advanced relatives and the related snails and chitons, the Keyhole limpet has a rough, file-like ribbon (radula) that it uses to rasp organisms off the surface of rocks or to drill through clam shells. Interestingly, the teeth on the limpet's radula are composed of hematite, which is harder than steel, while that of the common "Black Katy" chiton is composed largely of magnetite—iron oxide (lodestone)—equally hard and also magnetic.

An exquisitely etched Lined chiton grazes on the film of diatoms covering pink encrusting algae. By freshening the algae's color it aids its own camouflage. (Doug Wechsler)

At night the Keyhole limpet ventures out to graze on encrusting sponges and algae. When it senses the approach of a Sunflower star or the smaller, more common Purple sea star, it lifts its mantle up around its shell and exudes a defensive chemical. This deters the Purple sea star, but the Sunflower star just backs off for a moment. Then it climbs up over the Keyhole limpet and, mantle-be-damned, swallows it whole.

A Whitecap limpet, its shell pointed on top, attaches to an encrusted cliff pebble nearby. At night, both the Whitecap and Keyhole limpets graze on the pink encrusting algae—two of the few creatures who find the tough crust tasty. Both are often covered with the same encrusting algae that they feed upon—a clever, if ironic, camouflage.

A small but exquisitely-marked Lined chiton sticks nearby. Its pattern also echoes *Lithothamnium*'s colors, and it, too, feeds on the the pink crust. It evidently eats just the top layers; in doing so it strips away the summer film of diatoms, against which its own multicolored camouflage would be more conspicuous to predators.

Nearby, past a field of flowery tubeworms, is another grazer—the Green sea urchin. It resembles a dusty-green pincushion and is held to the rock by the combined suction of its hundreds of tube-feet. The urchin grazes on seaweeds, chewing them up with its five-part, pointed beak, called the "Aristotle's lantern," in the mouth hole beneath the center of its hemispheric shell.

Even the predators of the undersea cliff move at a snail's pace. Many of them, in fact, *are* snails. Inch-high Topshells graze hydroids and tiny algae off the pink crust. Predatory snails called whelks (genus *Nucella*) drill holes in mussels. The radula is aided by an acidic, enzyme-rich solution. After drilling the hole they insert a surprisingly long proboscis to suck up the soft tissues and juices of its prey. A whelk rarely drills into a barnacle. Instead, it pries open the plates ("valves") that protect the barnacle, then inserts its proboscis. Consequently, barnacles,

A large, multi-armed Sunflower sea star attacks a fleeing abalone. Many sea creatures have developed a strong flight response to these predatory sea stars. (Neil G. McDaniel)

A swimming scallop covered with yellow sponge resembles a costumed set of dentures. The tiny yellow photo-sensitive eyespots lining the edge of the white mantle allow it to quickly react to the shadow of a predatory sea star. By snapping its valves to expel water it can swim awkwardly but rapidly away. (Neil G. McDaniel)

though they have less meat are easier prey than mussels. It takes the whelk 60 hours to drill into and eat a medium-sized mussel; whereas a medium-sized barnacle requires just 12 hours.

Down near the bottom of the cliff, there's a veritable orgy of Purple whelks. These heavy-bodied sea snails, like most snails, are hermaphrodites, containing both male and female sex organs. They don't seem too choosy about picking a partner, or partners. In a short time, the undersides of rocks on the intertidal beach will be covered with "sea oats," the whelks' grain-sized, translucent yellow egg cases, cemented to the rocks by tiny stalks. From these will emerge a bumper crop of little whelks, resembling miniature adults, to feed upon the year's new generation of Acorn barnacles.

Other whelk shells move at a faster pace. But these are no longer occupied by the original owner. The empty shells have been comandeered by hermit crabs. Hermit crabs have soft, coiling bodies instead of the tough carapace of true crabs; and so they must occupy abandoned snail shells, moving to larger ones as they grow. There are only three common species of hermits that specialize in tide pools, but more than a dozen subtidal species inhabit the Salish Sea. This one's a beauty. Extending from its adopted shell, its legs sport alternating orange and white bands, and there's a red band below each claw. Its eyes, elevated on long stalks, are iridescent green.

Scattered along the wall are a few young Purple-hinged rock scallops, covered with a pink algal crust. At this point in their lives the rock scallops stick out from the cliff face, their valves slightly apart.

The Red Irish lord, a large sculpin, can be outrageously colorful but is surprisingly well-camouflaged against pink encrusting algae and red seaweeds. (Neil G. McDaniel)

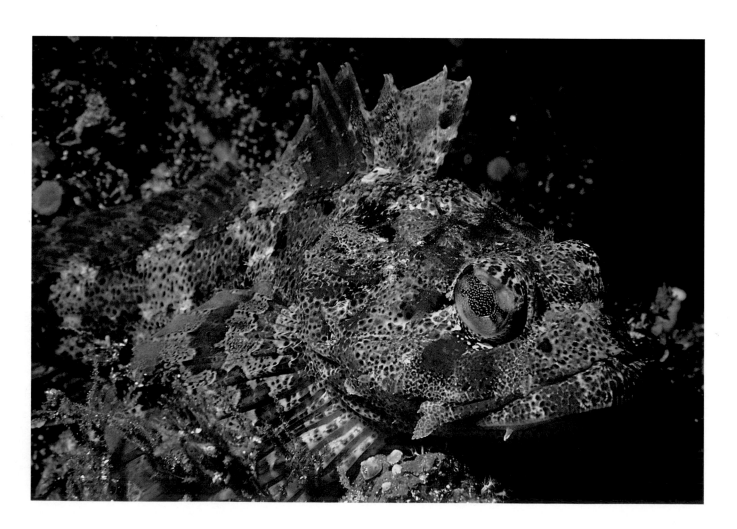

But as they grow larger, one valve will press against the rock, while the other grows thick and misshapen, barely resembling a scallop. A more delicate counterpart, the Rock oyster, or jingle shell, also lies flattened against the rock. When I approach to glimpse its red interior, it clamps down, barely distinguishable from the rock.

Among these rocky crevices I always hope to meet up with two of the region's most interesting predators: the Wolf-eel and the Giant Pacific octopus.

The Wolf-eel is a living paradox. A fairly advanced fish, it resembles a primitive eel. It lives in moderately shallow water but looks more like a creature from the abyssal ocean depths. Its four- to eight-foot length and large head lend it a definite presence, and the grotesque, stony face and large canine teeth give it a particularly ferocious visage. Yet though it can give a serious bite if annoyed, it can be easily tamed, to the point of feeding out of your hand. Both sexes look ancient even in their primes.

Young Wolf-eels are rather attractive. The long, tapering body is bluish, tinged with gold. As they age, Wolf-eels turn grayer, the numerous large black spots ringed with lighter color. The adult's head, especially the male's, enlarges relative to the long body and small beady eyes, taking on a monstrous appearance. The large mouth, strong jaws, and protruding teeth are used less for catching fish than for crushing crabs, clams, and sea urchins.

Male and female pairs often live together in the same crevice. After breeding, the two make solicitous parents. The female (or both parents,

A Wolf-eel looks fierce—and can be if one sticks a hand in its crevice. But the teeth are mostly used to crush clams, sea urchins and crabs. (F. Stuart Westmorland)

The Giant Pacific octopus is the world's largest species—reportedly to 32 feet, though 7 feet is more common locally. Active and curious, it moves rapidly over its territory, searching for crabs and other shellfish, which it cracks open with a beaklike jaw. (Neil G. McDaniel)

according to some observers) wraps her long body around the egg mass, guarding them until they hatch. This is an even worse time than usual to poke one's hand into the Wolf-eel's crevice.

Inside a similar crevice I come across a small specimen of what may be the most remarkable of all the Salish Sea's thousands of unique creatures.

The Giant Pacific octopus is a mollusk—related to clams and nudibranchs as well as to the more similar squids. But it has a sensory apparatus and intelligence that are closer to our own than to a clam's. Its sense of touch is acute, its eyes as advanced as those of mammals. In the laboratory it has shown a remarkable ability to learn and remember. It can crawl forward at high speeds or jet rapidly backwards. It can change

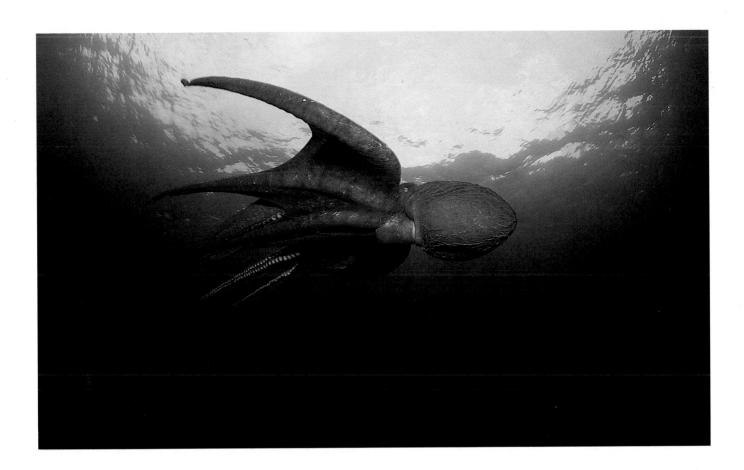

colors, seemingly at will, can slip though the tiniest of spaces, and can disappear in a cloud of ink. It is clever and coordinated enough to escape from all but the most foolproof enclosures, and it has even been reported to learn on its own how to unscrew jars to get to food.

An octopus swims by jetting water from its excurrent siphon. (Neil G. McDaniel)

The octopus's acute senses are an outgrowth of its habits. Instead of the sedentary filter-feeding of most mollusks, or even the undulations of nudibranchs or the more active darting of squids, the octopus is an active, curious, tactile hunter. Like snakes or weasels on land, it continuously searches through every crack and crevice of its territory for crabs, clams, scallops, abalone, small fishes—in short, just about anything it comes upon smaller than itself.

The octopus has been the victim of sensationalist stories and bad press. Being a lowly mollusk, it gets little respect from scuba divers who go out mainly to harvest abalones or to spear fish. I've watched dozens of these remarkable creatures brought up on the point of a spear, mostly by divers who have no great relish for their rubbery flesh. Underwater photographers and naturalists, however, are fascinated by them. Dan McLaughlin, a local diver/naturalist/writer, in his and Jak Ayres *Fieldbook of Pacific Northwest Sea Creatures*, gives a delightful description of the Giant Pacific octopus:

> There is no denying it, out of water this giant cephalopod...looks like a pile of entrails from a gutted cow...But in the water, the octopus's natural habitat, this strange creature becomes a graceful ballerina, a sleight of hand artist, a prankster. He is shy and yet very curious and exploratory. Male members of the species...are the largest of all octopuses in the world and are reputed to grow to a diameter of thirty feet...In Hood Canal the authors have seen

them measuring close to twenty feet...However, seven-foot males are the most common size.

Females do not grow over five or six feet across due to the fact that they perish while raising their young. When the females are bred, a male octopus donates with one arm a pencil-shaped, transparent, gelatinous sack of sperm to her by simply inserting it deeply inside one of her large intake ports. She then searches about for a proper lair in which to lay her eggs. She seeks a cave twice her size which has an opening so small she can barely make it through, even after extruding her body down to an amazingly thin shape. As her last legs slither from sight, they attach themselves to one or two rocks. These she pulls in with her to block the cave entrance against the intrusion of rockfishes and hungry Wolf-eels.

Octopuses' eggs are the size and color of white rice and hang from the roof of the lair like thick clumps of grapes on black stems...and it is the female's job to look after them...It can take as long as six months for the hatching process. During that time the mother uses nozzle-like funnels on the sides of her head to constantly wash water over and through the cluster of eggs to keep them clean and to constantly supply them with oxygenated water. To avoid contamination and to avoid the risk of leaving the lair unattended...she does not eat during these long months but lives on the fats and proteins of her own body tissue. The female will shrink to half her original size during the incubation period, and then, on the week when the eggs finally begin to hatch (much to the delight of rockfishes that wait outside the lair for the tiny, pulsing tidbits that try to make their escape to open water) she has so consumed herself that she dies within the cave, now no more than a pale heap of skin...

The female octopus shuts herself in a crevice to guard and aerate the rice-size eggs, usually starving in the process. (Neil G. McDaniel)

People are beginning to temper their hostile attitudes towards the octopus. This is accountable in part to the fact that this creature will often reach out and almost affectionately drape one of its arms over a diver who has settled down to watch it. Also, there is an almost human quality about an octopus's eye and eyebrow that is not seen with fishes, and often this makes people more sensitive to the creature's predicament...

Suddenly, my diving buddy, Paul, who drifted off as I focussed on this few-hundred-square-feet of seawall, appears back beside me. He is gesticulating wildly, in that compelling, utterly incomprehensible way that divers do.

(Voice is out, of course, and the stiff regulator mouthpiece and the eyes distorted by the facemask, which covers the entire forehead, combine to make normal facial expressions impossible. Everything must be done with gestures, and heavy cold-water gloves do not lend themselves to subtle signing. Though Paul and I have dived together a dozen times, we invariably find that what we thought we communicated during the dive was interpreted in two utterly different ways.)

His hand moves toward his mask, then upward. His fingers point right at his mask. He makes swimming motions. Ah. Something about a fish. Or a mermaid. I should follow him to the wondrous event. Or maybe we should get the hell out of here.

Finally, in frustration, he grabs the white scratchboard that I'm using to list species. "sealion," he scribbles. "facetoface."

Ahhh. It swam right toward him, once, twice. Paused, eyeball to eyeball. Behind the pale, expressionless face he is ecstatic; behind mine, I am envious. Ah well. I return to my intricate pink kingdom as his black fins disappear along the cliff, into the green gloom just a few yards away.

Watching him vanish reminds me of a night dive we made here at this same wall along the Tacoma Narrows a month before.

We humans dream by night and wake at day, but there are as many sea creatures active at night as there are during the day.

Intertidal creatures dance to the tides, not to the sun. Beyond the tides, some animals lie dormant or hidden during daylight, coming out only at dusk to feed then retreating at dawn. Some pelagic creatures, like the orcas, move and rest at intervals independent of daytime. Others, such as amphipods and copepods and the vast schools of fishes that feed on them (together called the "deep scattering layer") rise from the depths at dusk and return at dawn. Pacific herring and dogfish sharks, for example, might be found at 250-foot depths at noon and be seen near the surface at midnight.

And so, occasional night dives beckon, despite our instinctive reluctance to enter the sea in the dark. Who knows what lurks therein?

That night we were working our way along this same wall, sticking together quite a bit more closely than today, shining our bright lights over the surface and into crevices.

Suddenly, my light went out. Paul, thinking I had moved around a corner, kept going. When I got the light working a few seconds later, his beam had vanished. Mine traced frantic paths that were rapidly swallowed by the darkness.

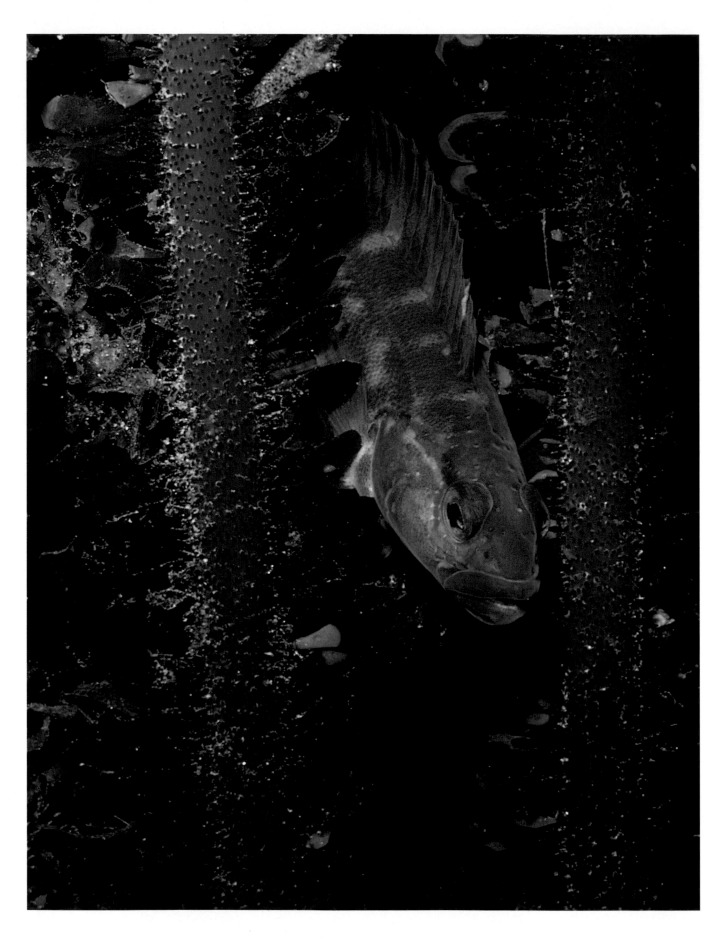

A Northern ronquil peers from the shelter of Feather boa kelp.
In early spring males develop bright colors and perform
elaborate courtship displays to entice a mate. (Doug Wechsler)

Away from the wall, the current was much stronger, and I was drifting without bearings.

Scuba diving is too recent an activity to have developed a true mythology. Yet, during a night dive in the plankton-rich murk, unexpectedly swept away by the current from the reassuring solidity of rock and seaweed, the strong flashlight beam disappearing into nothingness twenty feet away in any direction, all sense of up and down confused into vertigo, the mind is suddenly presented with all the stimulants for myth: vulnerability, fear, and the shivering glimpse into the void.

It is at that moment that you experience why Hindu philosophers picture the untrained mind as a chariot driven by a team of high-strung horses, goaded by fear or lured by desire, ready to gallop off in all directions.

It was time to rein in the horses. To slow the panicked breathing. To consult the oracle of the the wrist compass. To remember in which direction the current flowed. To kick calmly across the current. And back to the solidity of the kelp-covered wall, where Sunflower sea stars and Banded topshells pursued their stolid snail-paced lives.

When we break back through the surface, pull off our masks, and stumble up the beach into the moonlight or sunlight, it always seems as if waking from a dream. For slipping beneath the waves is a bit like passing through Alice's Looking Glass into a world where all the normal rules and limitations are transformed: gravity neutralized by buoyancy, air reduced to the tiny fraction dissolved in seawater, fire entirely absent. It is an alien world into which we are taking the first, tentative steps. A visit back into our dimmest genetic past.

Yet the dream and the world beyond the Looking Glass is just as real as our busy, human lives on the familiar terrestrial side of the aquarium's glass. And this largely invisible world is directly connected to ours—through evolution; through the harvest it offers us; and through our disruptive effects on it.

As the remarkable photos of Neil McDaniel, Stuart Westmorland, and other talented local underwater photographers clearly show, the visual rewards of entering it are extraordinary. And to anyone interested in animal behavior, it is addictive.

For the millions of us living on the watershed's slopes and streets just above this magnificent living aquarium, the responsibility for keeping it pristine and productive is enormous.

Lowlifes & Drifters

I t's easy to appreciate orcas and seals, seabirds and salmon. And it's easy to understand the importance to them of "baitfishes" such as herring, sandlance, and smelt. Orcas and eagles eat big fish. And, as we all know, big fish eat little fish

But even the largest fishes—and most other sea creatures—start as eggs or tiny larvae. How do the big fish ever get big enough to eat the little ones? And what do small creatures, such as shrimp, feed on? Or immobile or sluggish ones such as steamer clams and oysters, sea anemones and sea cucumbers, tubeworms and chitons?

The obvious answers are "plankton" and "detritus."

But these two catch-all terms cover just about everything in the sea that we don't much notice, can't see with the naked eye, or just don't understand. Or—often enough, even these days—all of the above.

Yet on closer look—with magnifying glass, microscope, or macro lens—detritus and plankton are colorful, complex worlds unto themselves, with fascinations of their own.

Opposite:
Polyorchis *is a jellyfish abundant in shallow bays in summer. Like most jellies, it is a predator, harpooning planktonic animals with the tiny nematocysts that line its hanging tentacles. Symbiotic single-celled algae give a greenish hue to its one-inch-diameter bell.*
(David Denning/Earth Images)

Amphipods dart around tidepools, feeding on algae and detritus.
(David Denning/Earth Images)

Limacina, *a minute but exquisite pteropod ("winged foot" snail), spends its entire life floating in the plankton, swimming jerkily by flapping its expanded foot. It captures smaller plankton by secreting a huge mucous net and is eaten, in turn, by the much larger shell-less pteropod,* Clione. *(Deanna Lickey)*

Of the two worlds, detritus is the harder to imagine or appreciate. Dead, decaying stuff with no form, little color, and less appeal. To our taste at least.

To hundreds of organisms, though, detritus is life itself.

True enough, detritus consists largely of dead stuff. Decaying eelgrass and seaweeds washed up on the beach. Shucked exoskeletons of metamorphosing crustaceans. Sloughed skin and scales. Eggs that never hatched. Single-celled plants by the billions that eventually overpopulated their nutrients or oxygen supply and died. Bits of half-consumed or sloppily eaten prey. Excreta. Lots and lots of excreta. A never-ending snowfall of leftovers drifting down.

Yet even before these particles of "waste" have hit the seafloor or been ground up on the beach, they have already attracted hungry hoards of microscopic recyclers eager to extract the last nutrients from this free lunch before it dissolves or leaks out into the water (to be absorbed by other lifeforms).

Bacteria soon cover the particle surfaces. Fungi break through into the interior. Different forms of bacteria take over, different fungi move in. Amoeba-like protozoans called radiolarians and forams and other single-celled animals with tiny hairlike cilia (or whiplike flagella) for movement and feeding ingest the particles and absorb the bacteria. The bits are further broken down and covered again with fungi and bacteria.

The floating tidbits, along with living single-celled plants and animals, are taken by the filter-feeders: caught in the nets of Giant barnacles and Frilled sea anemones, the mucous parachutes of pteropods, the sticky tentacles of ctenophores. Or sucked in by the incurrent siphons of clams and sponges.

Drifting particles that escape the omnivorous filter-feeders eventually clump together in a loose, active mass of plant material, excreta, protozoans, bacteria, and fungi which covers the seafloor.

The detrital mass is now very high in protein. And since plant cell walls and tough exoskeletons have been softened or penetrated, it is easily digestible.

Now the true detritus-eaters take over.

Shrimplike amphipods, cumaceans, and "harpacticoid" copepods graze detritus from the surfaces of sand and seaweed, as do "pillbug" isopods. Brittle stars extend their slender arms over the mud and Spaghetti worms extrude even slimmer feeding appendages. Giant sea cucumbers vacuum the muddy seafloor. On sandier bottoms, the Sand clam sweeps its mobile siphon over the surrounding surface.

The Lugworm resembles an earthworm, albeit with bristles along its sides. It performs the same function in muddy tideflats that the earthworm does on land, passing mud though its gut, while digesting the organic detritus. Ghost shrimps and Mud shrimps dig U-shaped tunnels into the mud, gleaning detritus from below. Even hermit crabs, while preferring to dine on an entree of dead fish garnished with Sea lettuce, get much of their protein from detritus.

Detritus passed through the gut of Giant sea cucumber becomes a beautiful, multi-armed Sunflower starfish when it dines on the cucumber. Detritus gleaned by crabs transforms into a river otter and then returns to the beach in the otter's scat.

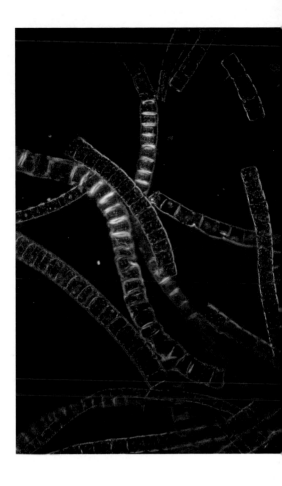

Above:
Surprisingly colorful under the microscope, these filamentous diatoms form a brown scum on rocks and seaweed. This ubiquitous coating is grazed by Lined chitons, limpets, and the Vermilion sea star. (Deanna Lickey)

A juvenile Pandalid shrimp (probably a Coon-stripe) conserves energy after a moult by hitching a ride on a tiny jellyfish. This behavior may be common, though it was only recently documented by the photographer and other local observers. (Deanna Lickey)

Though detritus can be called a major base of the marine foodweb, the broadest base is formed of living, single-celled plants called diatoms and dinoflagellates.

At first glance, some of these living forms—especially those that settle on the surface of mud, rocks, or seaweeds—look no more exciting than detritus. Under a microscope, though, in powerful light and polarizing filters, even the filamentous diatoms that form a brownish scum coating every undersea surface during the summer are as beautiful in their own way as the Lined chiton that grazes on them.

Free-floating diatoms make up a large portion of the plankton—a Greek word connoting drifters. Most plankters are plants without appendages or animals too small or weak to swim against currents (though some, like arrow worms and jellyfishes can direct their movements somewhat within the moving water "cells").

Planktonic diatoms are single-celled, chlorophyll-bearing plants encased in tiny, perforated silica cases called frustules. The cases are so finely etched that early microscope makers used to test their lenses by focusing on them. Present by the billions during the sunnier months, the silica cases cover the seafloor—and where former seafloors are now exposed, they are mined as "diatomaceous earth."

At the level of creatures no larger than a cell, the boundary between plant and animal can be rather vague. Dinoflagellates, for example, are characterized by flagella—whiplike appendages that allow the globular individual (or chains of them) to move, and in some cases capture food, as animals do. Yet many dinoflagellates have chlorophyll and produce their own nutrients, as plants do.

Most dinoflagellates use their mobility to migrate up to the sunlit surface during the day, then drop below at night. Some types are luminescent when stirred by a boat passing through (or, in somewhat warmer waters, by nighttime swimmers). *Noctiluca* is the most familiar.

Noctiluca and other, non-luminescent types, cause "red tides"—widespread stains ranging in color from pink, to deep red to brown. Though most red tides are harmless, a few are feared. For good cause.

One dinoflagellate—*Gonyaulax*—though relatively harmless to the mussels, clams, and shrimps that ingest and concentrate it, can be deadly to shrimp-eating fish, and even more so to people who eat shellfish containing its toxin. Saxitoxin, which causes Paralytic Shellfish Poisoning (PSP), is lethal to an average-size person at a dose of less than one milligram. It killed one of Vancouver's sailors and sickened two others; and dozens of people have died of it since.

Inner Puget Sound's first heavy bloom of *Gonyaulax* wasn't reported until September, 1978. It is now considered endemic at low levels in the inland waters. Another major bloom could occur anytime. Unfortunately, *Gonyaulax* doesn't produce much color, and cooking barely affects it. The only way to guard against it is for state and provincial agencies to continually test samples of mussels and clams. Though the dinoflagellate passes quickly from the bodies of some shellfish, such as mussels, it can remain for up to a year in Butter clams (*Saxidomus*, from which the toxin got its name).

Heading out of Bellingham Bay a few years back, the green water seemed to have turned, overnight, to wine. The entire bay was Burgundy, and the stain covered as far as the eye could see. As we passed the salmon net-pens off Cypress Island everything looked normal. But I found out later that despite frantic efforts to save the juvenile salmon, 95% of them died. Though the dominant organisms—a dinoflagellate and a diatom—were not poisonous, the sheer number of cells during the four-day bloom evidently clogged the fish's gills, suffocating them.

This incredible ability of single-celled creatures to multiply rapidly under the right conditions of water temperature, sunlight, and nutrients is boggling. That, the equally rapid die-off, and the resultant

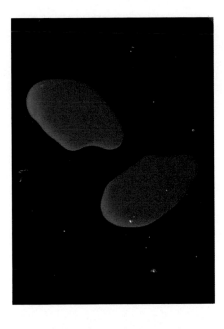

Sea stars contribute large numbers of larvae to the plankton. These Vermilion sea star larvae will eventually settle on mud/sand seafloor near Sea pens—on which they prey as adults. (Richard Strathmann/ Friday Harbor Laboratories)

A transparent shrimp larvae hints at its eventual adult shape. (David Denning/Earth Images)

patchiness of the tiny creatures makes it extremely difficult to study the plankton community. A bucket dipped in one spot at one time shows nothing, while one dipped nearby, or a few hours later, comes up full of plankton. And there may be two or three dominant species within the plankton, the percentages of each changing rapidly during the bloom.

Almost as quick as the diatoms and dinoflagellates bloom, an army of predators multiply to exploit them. It's a jungle down there, full of improbable creatures.

Some live their entire lives in the plankton. Among the most common of these predatory plankters are tiny crustaceans: "calanoid" copepods and shrimplike amphipods, euphausiids, and mysids. Voracious, transparent "arrow worms" (chaetognaths) dart among their prey like miniature barracudas. Passive-looking but just as deadly are the tiny jellyfishes, "comb jellies" (ctenophores) and pteropods (pelagic snails with expanded, winglike feet) pulsing slowly through.

Comb jellies catch their meal on sticky, trailing tentacles, with which they also weakly swim. But jellyfishes—of which there are more than 60 species hereabouts—have tiny, coiled harpoons (nematocysts) on the tentacles to stab and poison their prey.

A large proportion of the plankton, though, is just passing through. If lucky enough to survive the trip. Most marine fishes, invertebrates, and algae spend some of their lives floating in the plankton, needing to stay within the concentrations of even smaller food items.

One biologist estimates that of the more than 100,000 species of invertebrates and algae living in nearshore waters worldwide, 80% have a planktonic larval stage. The sheer numbers are astounding. A single Bull kelp plant can put out almost 4 *trillion* spores in a season, and many invertebrates put out millions at a time.

The surving spores, and the larvae of intertidal or bottom-dwelling creatures, eventually drop out of the fast lane in the plankton to settle down on rocks or bottom muds as adults. Others, such as Pacific herring

Euphysa, a tiny jellyfish found here year-round, usually stays in deep water. It is unusual because of its bright red stomach (manubrium) and only four stubby tentacles. (Claudia Mills/Friday Harbor Laboratories)

This pretty Gonionemus, with bright orange gonads, is locally abundant in shallow bays in summer. The "beads" on its tentacles are rings of stinging nematocysts. (Claudia Mills/ Friday Harbor Laboratories)

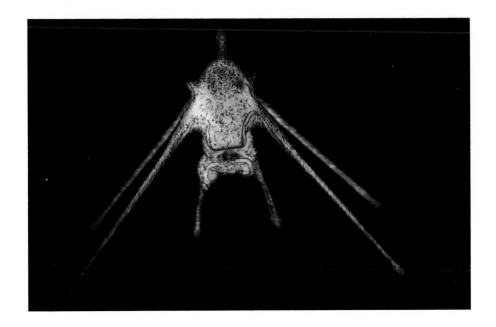

This colorful larva will develop into a Heart urchin, an inflated version of a sand dollar that lives on deep, muddy bottoms. The slender projections are a common method of keeping tiny planktonic animals and plants from sinking below the zone of light and food. (Richard Strathmann/ Friday Harbor Laboratories)

and Spot shrimps, outgrow the plankton but remain in the open water to feed on it. Other, larger fishes join the seabirds and marine mammals that feed on the fishes that feed on the amphipods that feed on the copepods that feed on the diatoms or detritus.

The next time you scoop up a handful of seawater, imagine all the invisible action going on within that small sample of the Salish Sea. How you're holding in your hand the next generation of puffins and hermit crabs and sea stars. And the ultimate source of orcas, eagles, and Kings.

A newly hatched Red octopus. It can be told from the larval stage of its Giant Pacific cousin by the single, rather than double, line of spots on its developing tentacles. (Deanna Lickey)

Gift of the Rivers

My first visit to Nisqually Delta was pure magic. I'd driven down to the newly established National Wildlife Refuge to meet some friends who were avid birders. Crawling under Interstate-5 where it bridged the marshlands, we hiked the perimeter dike built in the early 1900s to enclose the old Brown Farm. The unmaintained dike, recently breached by winter storms, was now of no use—except to robins nesting in the crabapple trees, rabbits hiding in the blackberry patches, and tangles of mating garter snakes.

Along the edge of MacAllister Creek we paused to observe the Great blue heron colony on the far side, watching the stilt-legged birds land awkwardly on swaying branches, their neighbors jabbing and squawking at them from adjacent nests. On the meandering tidal creek below, hundreds of wigeon ducks fed and rested at the edges as the tide ebbed, exposing the steep, gray mud banks.

We followed the dike for more than a mile out to the ragged edge of the delta. The view of southern Puget Sound was spectacular. Northwest, beyond the Nisqually Nature Center at the mouth of MacAllister Creek, ranged the snow-capped Olympics. Due north, past the extensive tideflats and the curve of Nisqually Reach, the tall cliffs of Devils Head stood at the southern tip of Longbranch Peninsula. Northeast, beyond Anderson, Ketron and Fox islands, the Tacoma Narrows Bridge glistened in the sun.

Seaward of the dike, fingers of sand and saltmarsh poked out into the tideflats. Parasitic dodder covered the salty pickleweed like orange spray paint, interspersed with robust yellow flowers of gumweed and delicate buttercup-like cinquefoil. Herons stalked the mudflats, among small volcanos constructed by burrowing Ghost shrimp. A flock of Caspian terns—largest of their kind, with flaming red bills—dove on crabs in the shallows. A Bald eagle perched on a half-buried log until driven off by a pesky mob of crows and gulls.

Walking back, we stopped to rest and talk, looking inward over the shallow, brackish lake created when the dike was breached by storm waves a few winters before. The lake now covered what had for a century been wheatfields laced with meandering sloughs. Across the water, framed between the farm's classic Twin Barns, Mount Rainier was gilded by the setting sun.

Conversation subsided as the evening songs of Red-wing blackbirds, Marsh wrens, and Song sparrows swelled. Gradually, the entire sky evolved from subtle green and pink pastels to lurid swaths of crimson and violet—the whole sky perfectly mirrored on the glassy lake. On the painted water floated Mallards and Northern shovelers, Blue-winged and Cinnamon teals, Canvasbacks and wigeons, each arrayed in brilliant breeding plumage.

As if this were not enough, an almost full moon popped up from behind the snow-covered peak of Mount Rainier, turning from yellow to white as it rose. Ragged chevrons of Canada geese crossed the mountain and the moon. We sat in silence, stunned by the incredible beauty of the scene.

Suddenly, a small, bright-eyed head broke through the watercolor just a few feet in front of us. Then two more. Then another three. At first the otters were as startled as we were. Then the largest began to scold us unmercifully.

Checking the dike's slope at our feet, we noticed that it was smooth as a playground slide. This is where the otter family gamboled, and where they entered and exited on daily fishing expeditions. We were blocking the way. As they moved farther along the steep dike to find another exit, they let us know in no uncertain terms that visitation time was over, and that the wildlife refuge was, as the signs pointed out, *theirs* after sunset.

Amused, we left. But I was hooked. After finishing my undergraduate program at University of Washington in Seattle, I spent a spring semester at The Evergreen State College boating out to the Nisqually mudflats and sitting on the nearby Luhr House pier, poking through petri dishes of muddy sand under a dissecting scope as part of an Environmental Impact study for Weyerhaeuser's proposal (fortunately scrapped) to build an international log-export facility adjacent to the wildlife refuge. The ensuing summer found me overseeing Young Adult Conservation Corps crews as we removed hundreds of old fence posts and miles of rusting barbed wire, renovated one of the Twin Barns for an education center, and constructed a self-guided nature

Herons and gulls feeding in the shallows off the Fraser River's huge delta, which stretches from the U.S.– Canadian border up to the edge of Vancouver. Deltaic mudflats are one of earth's richest habitats, and the Fraser's are the region's most extensive. (R. Wayne Campbell)

Great blue heron rookery. The Salish Sea still supports dozens of rookeries, though development has destroyed many. (Mark Newman/Earth Images)

trail through the sloughs and cottonwood forest along the Nisqually River. Over the years I've returned to walk the refuge trails countless times. Instead of crawling under I-5, there's now a parking lot and educational kiosk (and an entrance fee). The dike is repaired, and the interior lake is gone. But the magic remains.

Great blue herons still land awkwardly in their crowded rookery. On windy spring afternoons, Marsh hawks and Short-eared owls fight spectacular aerial battles for supremacy of good vole territory. Coyotes still dig dens near the old farmhouse orchard and howl at midnight near the Twin Barns. Killdeer lay eggs in the open along the dike and perform their broken-wing act for groups of excited schoolkids. Beavers fell alder saplings along the interior sloughs, while flickers chisel nests in drowned snags. Marsh wrens warble from cattails; hidden bitterns repeat their resonant *gung-ga-goonks*. Red-tailed hawks still nest in the tall cottonwoods along the mouth of the Nisqually River, where goldeneyes and mergansers float and Nisqually Indian fishermen in outboards set their gill nets across the current, in spots where their ancestors constructed willow fence weirs and tidal traps for returning salmon.

There is also the magic of looking up toward the Salish Sea's most impressive mountain and seeing the very source of the river and of the delta soil on which we stand: Mount Rainier's Nisqually Glacier and the ancient forest below it.

After the Puget Lobe ice sheet retreated north past The Narrows thirteen millennia ago, the Nisqually's mouth was a seven-mile-long inlet bounded by tall glacial cliffs. Over the centuries, the inlet's bottom, freed of the Puget Lobe's enormous weight, began to rise; but it was kept below sea level by the cutting river, until the seabed finally stabilized.

A delta—the name derived from the triangular form of the Greek letter—is child of both river and sea. Made up of layers of fine river sediments mixed with tidal deposits, it typically fans out from the rivermouth into the sea. Year after year, the river carried down tons of fine clays from Nisqually Glacier, fibrous organic matter from the forests, and dirt cut from meandering stream banks. Reaching tidewater, the sediments settled out to gradually filled the mouth of the inlet and fanned out a half-mile into Puget Sound. Shore currents contributed sand, transported along the coast from eroding seaside cliffs.

Eventually, Nisqually Reach, between the delta and Anderson Island, was so narrowed that its accelerated tidal currents swept away deposits as fast as they accumulated. A precarious balance was reached.

At its tidal edges, storm waves flung up beach sands and mud, building a natural levy, breached here and there by even larger waves. Behind the levy, a unique community of hardy plants colonized the marshy delta.

The river—or, more often, multiple river courses—that formed the delta meandered through it like indecisive snakes.

In active "sloughs," fresh water flows seaward at low tides. During high tides, a lens of incoming seawater wedges under the fresh. In abandoned stream courses, fresh and salt water mix in proportion to rain, evaporation, and river flow, and stormtides. The result is "brackish water," too salty to call fresh but far more diluted than seawater.

The Skagit River Delta's extensive mudflats from the air. Its delta is second only to the Fraser's in size. (Art Wolfe)

Coastal saltmarshes and sloughs such as these are often difficult to access and even harder to appreciate. Yet they constitute one of earth's most productive wildlife habitats.

Along its seaward edges, high-density populations of Lugworms, cockles, Bent-nosed clams, Mud shrimp and Ghost shrimp crowd the mud. Whimbrels—large shorebirds with exceedingly long, slender, curved bills—probe the shrimps' tunnels to extract them. At high tide, Starry flounders patrol the bottom, nipping at unwary denizens. Bay ducks dive down. Herons stab at flounders, shrimp, frogs, and aquatic snakes.

Before the riverbank was diked for farmland, periodic winter floods caused the meandering Nisqually to shift its course continuously, limited only by the steep cliffs on either side. Abandoned stream courses partially filled in with peat and sediments, leaving a braided history of narrow sloughs. Like blood vessels in a body, the network of active sloughs distributed water and nutrients throughout the delta.

A sloughs' brackish habitats differ from both river above and sea below. They function as nurseries to hundreds of aquatic species, dozens of which are of tremendous economic value. Salmon smolts, especially Coho, remain in the sloughs for weeks or months, adjusting to salt water and growing rapidly on a rich diet of copepods and other small crustaceans. Edible crabs and shrimps breed here. Ducks and geese raise their downy young among the reeds, feeding on the plant material and the small animals living in the mud.

Farmlands and saltmarsh intermingle on the Fraser River delta. (Art Wolfe)

Flocks of Snow geese overwinter on the Skagit's delta. (Peter M. Roberts)

Though salty and oxygen-poor, the dense grayish mud and dark muck of the tidal sloughs and saltmarsh are rich in nutrients. On each tide the sea brings in a high-protein broth of tiny planktonic plants, animals, larvae, and eggs. The river brings decayed needles and bark and other organic matter from the forests. Generations of marsh plants deposit layers of fibrous peat.

Above the tides, the marshy soil is saturated with salt, and so the plants ("halophytes") that survive here are necessarily salt-tolerant. Pickleweed, Brass buttons, Lyngby's sedge, Threesquare bulrush, Seaside arrowgrass, and Fleshy jaumea characterize "low salt marshes"— flooded daily by high tides. "High salt marshes"—flooded only during storms and very high tides—host fields of Saltgrass, Gumweed, Pacific silverweed, Saltmarsh bulrush, and Seaside plantain.

Each spring, hundreds of thousands of waterfowl and shorebirds— more than a million in the case of the Fraser River's delta—pause to fuel up for continent-long coastal migrations. Salish Sea deltas (along with Bowerman Basin in Washington's Gray's Harbor) are critical stops, especially for Western sandpipers and Dunlins. Nothing but rocky shores lie between here and Alaska's famed Copper River Delta.

Huge flocks of Tundra and Trumpeter swans, Snow geese, and dabbling ducks winter on the larger deltas—feeding in the shallow bays beyond the mud and among farmlands after the grasses and grains have been harvested or gone to seed. More than half of the Pacific flyway's

Brant geese used to winter here on Padilla Bay and those nearby, though their numbers have dropped precipitously during the past decade.

The Fraser River Delta's Riefel Migratory Bird Sanctuary alone hosts more than a million migrant birds each year: Mallards, Green-winged teals, American wigeons, Snow geese, and a dozen other species. Dogging these winter visitors and long-distance migrants are aerial pirates and predators. Parasitic jaegers steal fish from terns and small gulls. Bald Eagles pick off unwary ducks. Speedy, sharp-clawed Merlins dive on small shorebirds. Peregrine falcons, fastest of all birds, "stoop" in spectacular, lethal fashion on any-and-all.

In and below the grassy fields between the sloughs, vole (field mice) populations explode like lemmings in early spring, supporting families of Northern harriers (Marsh hawks) and Red-tailed hawks, along with Short-eared, Great-horned, and Barn owls. During particularly severe winters, large numbers of beautiful Snowy owls move down from the north to settle on the fields of the Skagit and Fraser deltas.

One of the many estuarine sloughs near the mouth of the Skagit River. (Art Wolfe)

The Nisqually Delta is just one of what were once dozens of wildlife-rich deltas—one at each rivermouth along the Salish Sea. The much larger Skagit River still has more saltmarsh sloughs outside its diked farmlands than the area contained inside the entire Nisqually refuge; and both are dwarfed by the remnant portions of the Fraser River's enormous delta.

What sets the Nisqually River corridor apart is its federal protection at either end. But before it could become a national wildlife refuge, Nisqually Delta had to survive the past century. The drier parts of the diked portion of the delta were planted and used for pasture for half a century. The 30% of the delta south of Interstate-5 (which cuts through the heart of the saltmarsh) was long ago developed for housing.

In the early 1970s Seattle proposed using the diked portion as a "solid waste disposal site," or, in plainer terms, a huge dump. The Port of Tacoma countered with a proposal to dredge a deepwater "superport." Other groups thought an aluminum mill on the delta would be just ducky.

Happily, these ideas were defeated by a citizens' coalition, led by the newly formed Tahoma Audubon chapter and carried on by an ad-hoc group of persistent local citizens and statewide supporters calling themselves The Nisqually Delta Association. Finally, the U.S. Fish & Wildlife Service stepped in to acquire the land.

The refuge is now one of the most popular hiking and birding areas in western Washington, quickly growing from a few thousand to more than 80,000 visitors each year (in fact, refuge staff fear that this rising usage may now be impacting the wildlife).

Similar deltas, once equally rich in saltmarsh and tideflat wildlife, have fared far worse. The marshes and tidelands of the Puyallup and Green rivers to the north lie dredged or paved beneath the loading docks and heavy industry of Tacoma and Seattle. Two-thirds of the Stillaguamish and three-fourths of the Snohomish river deltas near Everett have long been diked for farmland. Only 10% of the Lummi River's delta near Bellingham remains wild, and just 4% of the Samish River's. North of the Canadian border, the Fraser River's vast delta, a vital stop for migratory waterfowl and shorebirds, has been largely converted to farmland and is now being devoured by metropolitan Vancouver—population 1.4 million and growing.

Despite its status as a national wildlife refuge, Nisqually Delta is located between Tacoma and Olympia in the center of one of

Trumpeter swans are the most spectacular of wintering waterfowl. (Ervio Sian)

The Skagit River snakes out of the Cascade foothills through farm country toward Puget Sound. (Terry Domico/Earth Images)

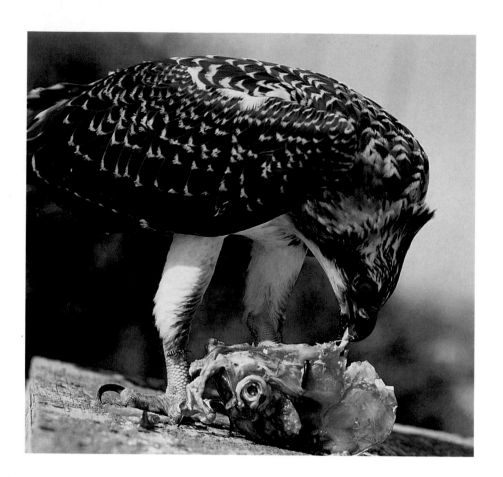

An osprey (fishhawk) devours a salmon along the lower Fraser River. (Ervio Sian)

Once considered "wasteland," fresh-water marshes along the river purify storm runoff and provide habitat for hundreds of wildlife species. Drained or filled for farm-land, housing, and malls, they are the most fragile and threatened of all habitat types. (SidneeWheelwright)

Washington's fastest-growing regions, and pressure is coming from three sides. Weyerhaeuser and Burlington Northern are developing massive housing tracts, complete with shopping malls on the uplands east and west of the refuge. In and around the Nisqually reservation at its upriver end, Indian and non-Indian housing proliferates. It is for good cause that our coastal saltmarshes are now recognized as an endangered habitat, and worthy of exceptional protection.

The rivers that created these marshy wildlife habitats meander in sweeping S-curves through flat floodplains that a century ago were planted in dairy pasture or plowed for farmland and are now being covered by a sprawl of housing developments, roads, industrial parks and malls.

Despite the ensuing degradation, these rivers still function as corridors for semi-mystical creatures that integrate the entire watershed—from the Pacific Ocean (just part of the single world sea that ultimately links all watersheds), though the Salish Sea and its esturine inlets, up the dozens of broad, shallow rivers, to branch out into thousands of streams and tens of thousands of smaller creeks and tiny rivulets.

This icon of the Pacific Northwest—all the way from northern California to coastal Alaska—is, of course, the Pacific salmon.

A species, according to biologists, is a population which keeps to its own genes. Breeding isolation—usually caused initially by geographical barriers—allows the species to develop a unique set of traits, and these further isolate it from cross-breeding, even if later brought in contact with its close relatives. Biologists divide Pacific salmon into six species: Chinook (Kings, Springs, blackmouths), Coho (Silvers); Sockeye (Reds, bluebacks); Chum (Dogs); Pink (Humpbacks, humpies); and the latest to be added—the Steelhead, or seagoing Rainbow "trout." All six are placed in a single genus (*Oncorhynchus*), implying they have only recently gone their separate ways and that they still have much in common.

Two other species in the salmonid family—Cutthroat trout and Dolly Varden char (a close relative of the eastern Brook trout) share many of the same traits.

Most salmon species can be subdivided into many geographical races. All can be finely divided into different "runs" based on river of origin and time of spawning. Thus, the Pacific salmon can be viewed as a continuum of "salmon-ness," punctuated by six sets of physical differences, such as average size, scale color, and breeding costume, and a half-dozen sets of unique behaviors.

A basic trait of salmon and sea-run trout is their flexibility. Though populations of Steelhead salmon (as stream Rainbow trout), Sockeye (as land-locked "Kokanee"), Coho (as Great Lakes introductions), and sea-run Cutthroat trout remain in fresh water throughout their lives, salmon are basically "anadromous." They breed in fresh water but live in salt water as adults. This allows them to exploit stream resources when small and then feed among the vast pastures of the sea as they mature. To do this they must go through many physiological changes during the transition—in both directions. And though the outer changes of the brightly colored, hook-jawed spawner is the more familiar and spectacular, the internal changes in the young out-migrating "smolts" are just as radical.

One amazing salmon trait is the ability to return to the particular stream of its birth after years in the ocean. Not that this homing ability is infallible—in fact, the few individuals of each run that end up in a neighboring river system are the links between separate runs that keep the species intact.

It is pretty amazing nevertheless. The largest individual King salmon circle the North Pacific for up to eight years before returning to spawn. They must therefore not only be able to sense subtle differences in water chemistry but to remember these differences years later. For Chum and Pink salmon, whose hatchlings migrate immediately to the sea, the imprinting must be particularly quick, though the memory needn't be as long-lasting. Equally remarkable is that individual streams in the same river system should be so distinctive, and the unique character of each so stable over a period of years.

A silvery Coho salmon fights its way over a spillway toward its natal spawning stream. (Tim Sharp/Earth Images)

Previous page:
A boulder-strewn river in autumn. Winter rains will soon swell its flow, allowing salmon to migrate upstream. (Chris Huss)

Each salmon species and race is essentially a way of partitioning the rivers system's resources and exploiting the unique "personality" of its natal stream system. Each run is a clever adaptation to a different set of variables: Water temperature and dissolved oxygen; streamflow and flood regime; impediments to migration; availability of food and shelter for the juveniles; avoidance of predators; and glacial events of the "recent" past still fresh in the salmon's genetic memory. Wild Steelhead that enter one river may have to leap many waterfalls; in another river, low autumn flows favor a smaller, late-season spawner; in a third, competition with Coho salmon may demand an especially aggressive fry (hatchling).

The Salish Sea and Pacific Ocean offer juvenile and adult salmon plankton blooms and schooling baitfish by the billions. But the salmon eggs are tied to stream gravels. And all but Pink and Chum feed and shelter in freshwater streams or lakes during their formative years.

Partitioning begins with the upriver migrations.

Chum salmon arrive in the Salish Sea in late fall but waste no time moving through to small coastal streams. Since the fry (like Pink salmon) don't linger in the streams after hatching, the spawners need not be too choosey.

The larger Chinook, at the other extreme, need deeper water for spawning, and their slow-developing fry are more demanding on river resources. And so they stick to the mainstem rivers. Being strong swimmers with good fat reserves, they can travel hundreds of miles up the larger river systems, surmounting seemingly impossible barriers.

Coho and Steelhead are smaller and more adaptable. They move up into every nook and cranny of the watershed. Since their juveniles will spend one to three years in the streams, they are more dependent on clean, cool, well-oxygenated streams.

Sockeye salmon are plankton specialists, even as adults in the ocean. Their juveniles, rather than fighting over the limited supply of aquatic insects in fast-moving streams, take advantage of lake plankton. The adults spawn at the edges of lakes or in nearby feeder streams so that the fry can move there directly on hatching.

The hefty adult salmon running up shallow rivers to spawn in tiny streams seem oversized and out of place—like human adults in a kindergarten playground. And this is no illusion. They *are* out of place, fighting their way briefly into a lethal environment. Once in the river, the adults do not feed. And for even the successful spawners (excluding some of the Steelhead), this arduous trip will be their last.

When spawning, a female salmon or trout turns on her side and lashes her tail to lift streambed gravels into the current. Eventually, this creates a broad, shallow depression called a "redd." Within the redd she digs a smaller but deeper nest in which to deposit hundreds of round, pink eggs.

As the female lays her eggs, a male suitor who has fought off his rivals swims alongside her. Vibrating furiously, he releases his cloudy, sperm-filled milt onto the eggs. Within seconds, a wriggling sperm penetrates the tiny hole (micropyle) in each.

The female then covers the fertilized eggs with the same violent thrashing used to dig the redd. As she moves slowly upstream she excavates a series of nests within the redd.

The spawning scene is chaotic. While the pair are mating, other males attempt to join in, to be driven off by the dominant male. Sometimes the younger, smaller, sexually precocious males, called "jacks," manage to slip into the redd to add their milt.

Some of the eggs are swept away by the current before they can be covered. These are snapped up by sculpins or resident Cutthroat and Rainbow trouts, and Dolly Varden char follow the salmon runs for this very reason. In heavily used spawning beds, later runs of spawners may uncover eggs laid by earlier runs.

Adult Chinook, Coho, Sockeye, Pink, and Chum—exhausted by the lack of food, the radical physiological changes (hooked jaws, humped backs, changes in color), and the rigors of migration and spawning— soon die. Only a small percentage of Steelhead, sea-run Cutthroat trout and Dolly Varden char survive to spawn once or twice more. Even the suvivors, called "kelts," lose up to 40% of their body weight during the spawning run. Of the Steelhead spawners sampled on one river system in Oregon, only one in six were repeat spawners, and only a fifth of those were on their third run.

The gravel-covered eggs overwinter in the streambed for one to four months, depending on species and water temperature. During this entire period they are dependent on intergravel currents to bring fresh oxygen and to remove the waste products of metabolism. If sediments settle on the gravels and block the tiny voids, intergravel currents will cease, and the eggs will die.

Salmon eggs overwinter in streambed gravels. Siltation can clog the inter-gravel spaces, smothering the eggs. (Terry Domico/Earth Images)

Coho spawners develop hooked jaws. Females excavate shallow redds in the gravel to lay eggs that the male fertilizes with milt. (Chris Huss)

Long after the large embryonic eyes have become visible through the clear outer membrane of the soft egg, the tiny hatchlings pop out from the egg case. Though no longer egg-bound, the "alevin" remains in the gravel for a few more weeks or months, living off the remains of the yolk sac bulging from its abdomen. It also gets much of its oxygen through the large veins that pulse in the sac membrane.

Finally it emerges from the gravels as a miniature "fry." Chum and Pink salmon fry immediately migrate down stream—usually at night—to rear in coastal estuaries. Sockeye fry move into nearby lakes to feed on freshwater plankton for one to three years before migrating to the sea. The tiny fry of Coho and Steelhead and Chinook are tossed into the active, competitive life of the stream, to find a niche or die.

Coho, the most wide-ranging of the stream-rearing salmon, occupy most, if not all, streams in the Salish Sea's vast watershed. The fry emerge in March or April. More tolerant of warm water than other species, they can live in the smallest of creeks during the summer months. As juveniles, Coho compete with Steelhead, but their diet is more varied, including flies and other terrestrial insects.

Stream-reared juvenile salmon feed mostly on aquatic insects. Even resident trout and sculpin and others that are predatory on smaller fish obtain most of their nutrients from the aquatic larvae of certain insect orders: mayflies, stoneflies, caddisflies, dragonflies, midges, and aquatic beetles.

The aquatic larval stages of most of these insects is much longer-lasting than the brief flying adult stage. A mayfly, for example, may live in the stream for a year, then metamorphose into a flying adult that mates and dies within a few days. Adult dragonflies patrol their stream-

A salmon alevin has broken out of its egg case, but lives off the remains of its yolk sac until able to catch aquatic insects. (Chris Huss)

side territory for a summer, but their fiercely predatory larvae may have lived in the water below for two or three years.

The insects themselves—just as their amphipod and copepod counterparts on the seafloor—ultimately depend on detritus. In this case, from fallen leaves of streamside trees rather than from Eelgrass and seaweeds. In fact, stream insects and stream-rearing fishes are far more dependent on detritus than are oceanic crustaceans or fishes. Very few planktonic animals can live in the fast-moving, one-way current of a mountain stream. Only in lakes and slow-moving sloughs does plankton contribute to the salmon's food supply.

Some of the aquatic insect larvae—especially the numerous midge (fly) larvae that attach themselves like moss to streambed rocks—are grazed directly from the streambed. But most insects are taken in the form of "drift."

To avoid salmon and trout—which are visual predators—stonefly, mayfly, and caddisfly larvae spend most of the daylight hours hidden under rocks or among the gravel. But most must come out to feed, usually at night. Despite many adaptations allowing them to avoid the current or cling to the rocks, some are inevitably swept away by the current. Others drift voluntarily, to find better spots when populations outstrip the local food supply or to escape to deeper water when the stream section starts drying up in summer.

And all aquatic insects must move to the surface when they transform into flying adults. In the process, they becoming particularly vulnerable, drifting on or just under the surface, where hungry fishes snap them up. To ensure that some will survive, entire populations tend to "hatch" at the same time, a phenomenon exploited by fly-fishers, who try to "match the hatch" with cannily crafted "flies" of feather and other materials tied onto tiny hooks.

Most insect species remain within the stream corridor as adults. Some fall into the creek from overhanging streamside trees. Others are caught by surface tension as they lay their eggs in the stream. And most of the rest drop into the stream when they die.

Salmon smolts move down into estuaries where, as striped parr, they adjust to salt water and grow large enough to compete in the sea. (Natalie B. Fobes)

One way or another, a good portion of the countless tiny insects that live around streams or lakes eventually end up as fish food.

Young salmon also require shelter. They must dart into the current to catch the drift, but to survive, they must be able to rest in slower water, hidden from predatory birds (and anglers) above, and from larger fish living nearby. The best salmon streams have complex structures—the messier the better, as long as there is a certain stability over time—with undercut banks, fallen logs, a wide range of gravel and boulder sizes, and consequent variety of currents.

Salmonids, sculpins, and darters defend sheltered spaces. They snap at and chase off rivals. And as they grow the area defended increases. This need for territorial shelter helps explain the pitfalls of introducing large populations of hatchery-reared fry into a stream system.

Though earlier residents are generally dominant over newcomers, planted hatchery fish may force the wild fry out of the area by sheer numbers, then fail to survive themselves. Their dense schools may overwhelm the local food supply. Raised in smooth concrete runways with constant current and no shelter, they waste energy fighting the current instead of sheltering from it. Instead of singly and warily slinking about on the bottom, they naively swim in tight schools near the surface, where they are easy prey for birds. While 3–6% of wild King salmon survive in healthy streams, only a quarter of 1% of hatchery releases do.

The stream's water must also be clear, well-oxygenated, and stay within the temperature range needed by the active salmon.

Intact riparian (streamside) trees are critical to all these attributes of a good salmon stream. In summer, they shade the stream and host terrestrial insects that add to the drift. In fall, leaves falling into the stream provide the basis of detritus, and those falling above the banks create duff that slows erosion from rain runoff in winter and spring. Tree rootwads slow streambank erosion; when undercut, they offer shelter for the fishes. And when streamside trees eventually die, they fall across the stream to break its flow into an alternating series of gentle pools and turbulent falls.

As they grow, salmonids drift downwards into ever larger stream reaches and deeper water. Coho, for example, gradually move

Tiny creeks like this one are critical to juvenile salmon and trout. Chum and Pink salmon hatchlings migrate immediately to the sea; tiny Coho and Steelhead feed and shelter here until ready to move downriver. (Terry Domico/Earth Images)

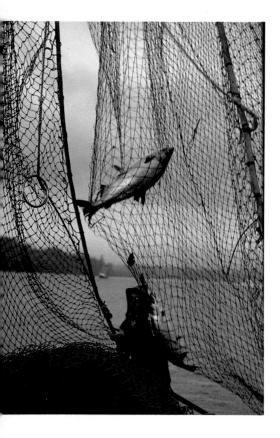

downstream into deeper water for the winter, but unlike Steelhead, which move back upstream for another year, they continue downstream toward the sea.

At a minimum size characteristic of each species the striped (parr) stage salmon juveniles migrate downstream (smolt) as they go through the internal changes that allow them to adjust from fresh water to brackish estuaries and, eventually , the salt sea.

Juvenile Coho enter the rivermouth estuaries, deltaic sloughs, and Eelgrass beds in early summer, to fatten up on small crustaceans and worms. Some remain in Puget Sound and Georgia Strait throughout

There are many nets...
(Terry Domico/Earth Images)

And orcas...
(Kelley Balcomb-Bartok)

And eagles...
between sea and spawning stream.
(Terry Domico/Earth Images

the summer before moving to the ocean. Others, like the numerous juvenile (blackmouth) Chinook caught during the winter, never leave the Salish Sea.

The more adventurous populations of Kings and Silvers, along with Sockeye and Steelhead, move out to the open Pacific to join the precocious Chum and Pink. Meanwhile, the sea-going runs of Cutthroat trout and Dolly Varden char remain in the shallows not far from the estuaries, waiting to follow the salmon hoards—driven by overwhelming urges, guided by mysterious senses, leaping all barriers, drawn to the glaciers in their genes. Upriver. Back from the sea.

Home.

Above:
Bald eagles perch in a snag above
the river in winter, waiting to feast
on spawned-out salmon.
(Mark Newman/Earth Images)

Below:
A spawned-out Coho, its mission
accomplished, becomes food for
Bald eagles, bears, and crows.
(Terry Domico/Earth Images)

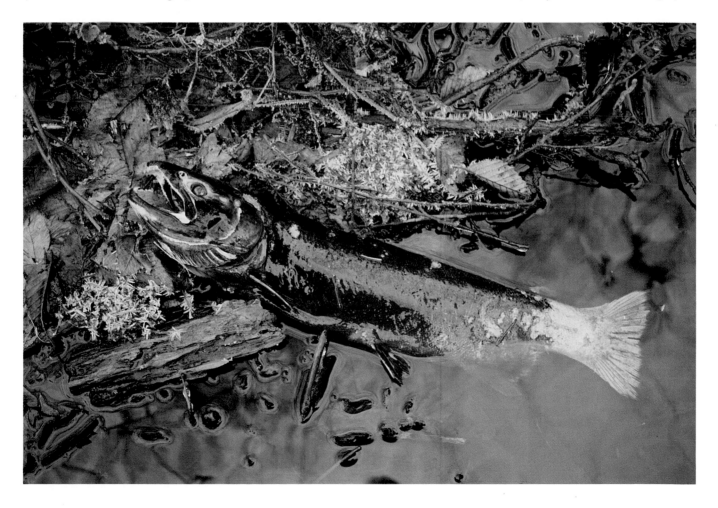

Quality of Water, Quality of Life

We were just out of Gig Harbor, riding a five knot flood-tide current past the tall cliffs of The Narrows into southern Puget Sound when we spotted the distant fins—and all at once the foggy summer morning turned magic. The tall black dorsal fins of the bull orcas cut the steamy air; the shorter, more curved fins of the females and young disappeared under water and reappeared in stately motion as the pod approached us. In our boat there was general pandemonium. Mike, Pete, and I grabbed at cameras, lenses, and film, threatening to capsize the small craft as we climbed over each other, barking conflicting orders at Chris at the wheel.

Dipping under the rippled black water, surfacing smoothly in groups of two to five, spouting their moist outbreaths into the mist, the orcas seemed to take little heed of our frantic maneuverings as we turned to follow. A large female surfaced dead off our bow, her blowhole opening with an audible *poof* as sheets of water slid off her sleek back. Chris cut the motor, dropped the wheel, and grabbed for his own camera. Up ahead, two large black heads rose vertically out of the water in synch and held there in a breathtaking double spyhop.

As we rounded Defiance Point into Tacoma's Commencement Bay, dozens of boats were fishing for salmon. I was sure the whales had had enough of boaters and would continue north up the Central Basin. But just as fishermen spot fish schools under wheeling flocks of seabirds, the spyhopping orcas must have known that where aluminum outboards gather, there are fish below. The whole pod headed for the anglers.

The orcas were soon gamboling amidst a multitude of slack-jawed spectators. Some of the onlookers hung precariously over the water; others clung to the gunnels of their open boats as the whales surfaced, splashed, and leapt partly out of the water next to them. Suddenly, twenty feet of blackness hurtled into the air not ten yards away from our boat. It seemed to hang there forever—though not quite forever enough for us to focus our telephotos—and fell back onto the water with a twisting *whump* that wetted us all with spray.

Of all the images etched in memory from that feverish hour, one other stands out—a distant orca leaping wholly out of the water against the shrouded smokestacks of Tacoma's industrial waterfront. Had the day been sunny, the contrast would not have been so stark. Snow-capped Mount Rainier would have provided a scenic backdrop for the harbor; the gray factory smoke and pulp mill steam would have been taken by the wind.

Instead, picture an exuberant whale leaping above fishing boats, awed spectators, and hidden schools of salmon—set against the smoggy skyline of one of America's most polluted ports. The image casts a troubling shadow over Puget Sound these days.

An orca breaches in Commencement Bay in front of Tacoma's heavily industrialized waterfront. (Steve Yates)

To the residents of western Washington and British Columbia, Puget Sound and Georgia Strait symbolize not just good fishing and spectacular views, freighters and ferryboats, but a unique lifestyle—less stressful and status-conscious than other parts of the country. More outdoorsy and environmentally sensitive. Heartier. Healthier.

Imagine our shock in the mid-1980s as the headlines assaulted us:

POLLUTION BLAMED FOR WHALE'S DEATH. HUGE OIL SPILL KILLS BIRDS. FISH TUMORS WORST EVER SEEN. FIRM PAYS FOR POLLUTING ELLIOTT BAY AND DUWAMISH. CHEMICAL WATER POLLUTION CAUSES GENETIC DAMAGE IN FISH. HIGH ALUMINUM LEVEL FOUND IN GRAY WHALE. PCBs THREATEN OYSTER LAGOON. RURAL CARR INLET'S BOTTOMFISH CON-TAMINATED. HIGH DISEASE RATE FOUND IN DUNGE-NESS CRABS. PART OF BAY IN TACOMA NEAR DEATH. MORE DISEASED FISH FOUND IN EAGLE HARBOR. HIGH PCBs FOUND IN GERTRUDE ISLAND HARBOR SEALS. PUGET SOUND'S TAINTED "SKIN" MAIMS FISH. FIRM ORDERED TO STOP POLLUTING HARBOR. GEO-DUCK DEATHS PUZZLE BIOLOGISTS. DON'T EAT TOO MUCH SOUND BOTTOMFISH.

Our portrait, as mirrored in the Sound's water, was not flattering. Furthermore, the stories and studies behind the headlines indicated that problems were longstanding and long ignored.

We'd clearly been negligent. Somehow, our "Fertile Fjord" was full of poisons, "God's Aquarium" clouded with toxic wastes.

Home aquarists quickly discover that fish float belly-up if water isn't filtered well. The headlines shouted that even a hundred-cubic-mile aquarium, if surrounded by 5 million people and heavy industry, had better do the same.

The Puyallup River's delta and tideflats were dredged for Tacoma's waterways. A century of unregulated effluent from pulp mills, chemical factories, oil refineries, and the recently closed ASARCO copper smelter left a legacy of poisons in the mud that now must be cleaned up at great cost. (Steve Yates)

Photographer Charles Krebs hunches in the stern of his 15-foot aluminum canoe powered by a tiny outboard, his hand on the chilly steering lever, while I hunker down in the bow. It has been raining for three hours, and the chilly spring afternoon shows no signs of clearing. Towering above us, the Port of Seattle's gigantic orange cranes lining Elliott Bay lift truck-size containers filled with motor-cycles, television sets, and baby carriages from the belly of an enormous 700-foot-long freighter inbound from Yokohama and Kowloon.

Turning into the Duwamish, we slide past the metallic screech and grind of Harbor Island, with its lead smelter, cement factory, and two major shipyards. Upstream, four-story-high cranes swing huge clamshell buckets, unloading barges of sand for bottle factories. Massive floating drydocks cradle tugs and freighters up out of the water for sandblasting and painting. Sea barges bound for Alaska float next to their loading piers, piled high with heavy machinery, pickup trucks, and 30-foot gill-netter fishing boats.

As my mind fumbles for the symptoms of hypothermia, the sun breaks out for a blessed instant. Charlie, who is shooting a magazine piece on "the working river" lets the canoe drift, breathes hard on his fingers, and grabs himself another shot of the Duwamish Waterway, the heart of the beast.

The Duwamish is the estuarine mouth of the Green River. From high in the forested Cascades, the Green flows west for 30 miles—so pure that Tacoma siphons it off for drinking water. A dozen miles south of here, the river turns north toward Elliott Bay. This lower reach was named after the Duwamish Indians who lived along its banks for thousands of years and greeted Vancouver with canoes of singers.

Just after the turn of the century the last six miles of the Duwamish were dredged and straightened to create the waterway. Dredge spoils were dumped on 3,000 acres of productive tideflats at the river's mouth, creating Harbor Island.

Heavy industry quickly moved in along the waterway. Boeing built planes; Ford built trucks. Tank farms stored gas and oil for the thriving city. Shipyards hummed during both world wars. After the Howard Hanson flood control dam was built 60 miles upriver in the 1950s, industrial parks replaced the hop and vegetable farms along the lower floodplain. The waterway now drained a jungle of food processors and metal finishers, cement companies and boatworks.

Low on the water from a small, sodden canoe looking up at Elliott Bay's humongous piers and the Duwamish's factories you get a different perspective than the usual views of Puget Sound from cliffside terrace or ferry bridge or state park.

Seattle is clearly a major industrial port city. It and competitive sisters, Tacoma and Vancouver, are three of the world's largest container ports: gateways to Alaska and the Orient. Tankers bring Alaskan crude oil for refining; ships unload fleets of Hondas and Toyotas. Old growth logs and eastern Washington apples head for Japan, along with oil from Canada's prairie provinces and petrochemicals from the entire region. Powerful tugs tow rafts of logs between local ports and pull barges transporting millions of tons of oil, gravel, chemicals, and fuel. Military shipyards service major fleets on both sides of the border; naval ships carry fuel, conventional munitions, and nuclear weapons.

The sea's scenic shorelines and towering mountains also tend to veil the fact that the Sound is heavily industrialized, and has been since Tacoma's huge ASARCO copper refinery began spewing out smoke and effluent in 1889, the very year Washington became a state.

The Salish Sea's eastern shoreline, in fact, hosts the greatest concentration of primary metals production and electrochemical factories west of the Mississippi. Five large oil refineries are clustered just south and north of the border. Ten of the continent's largest pulp and paper mills line the shore, from Shelton in southern Puget Sound to Campbell River at the northern end of Georgia Strait. Chemical plants create and ship hundreds of tons per day of chlorine to the pulp mills and municipal sewage treatment plants.

Not far upstream, we circle Kellogg Island—the last sliver of undeveloped land left after the loops of the meandering Duwamish River were sliced off by the waterway's arrow-straight path. Here, cormorants leap off rotten pilings, Great blue herons fly up squawking from the shallows. Canada geese, Mallard ducks, and four species of shorebirds nest above the beach. Charlie takes a shot of herons with the gilded city skyline in the background.

Despite the damge to its lower reaches, the Green still supports some of the largest runs of Steelhead trout and Pacific salmon of any river flowing into Puget Sound. Each year fly-fishers catch 10,000 Steelhead upriver. Anglers and Indian netters catch 150,000 Silver salmon and 50,000 Kings in the lower river as they return to the Green's streams and hatcheries to spawn. Off the rivermouth, Elliott Bay still supports a major commercial and recreational salmon fishery.

Even small remnants of undeveloped land are of value to tolerant wildlife such as this Canada goose. (Ervio Sian)

Returning downriver through the narrow East Waterway, we duck under the low Harbor Island fishing bridge. On sunnier days, dozens of folks of all ages and races would be dropping lines from the bridge, hoping to catch salmon, flounder, or cod.

Despite signs that warn of pollution, most of the anglers are unaware that one of Seattle's largest stormdrains empties into the waterway just upstream of the bridge. The fecal bacteria count of its outfall compares unfavorably with raw sewage. Bottomfish feed in the sediments below; anadromous salmon exiting and returning the Green must pass through the city's effluent.

When the National Marine Fisheries Service sampled flounder and sole along the Duwamish, the results were shocking: Up to 90% showed detectable abnormalities; 30% were cancerous. One of every four Starry flounder exhibited "fin rot." A third of the English sole, a tasty table fish, had liver tumors or precancerous lesions; more than 50% of the females in Eagle Harbor and almost 40% in the Duwamish failed to mature sexually and were unable to reproduce.

Levels of heavy metal, hydrocarbon, and PCBs (polychlorinated biphenyls: a family of long-lasting, toxic organochlorine chemicals formerly used in insulators and still created in large quantity by pulp mills) in the sampled fish were tens of times to thousands of times greater than those of similar fish in the cleaner bays.

Juvenile salmon migrating down the Duwamish were found to have "incredibly high levels" of PCBs and PAHs (polycyclic aromatic hydrocarbons: toxic petroleum breakdown products) in their stomachs and bile. Recent results indicate that such pollutants remain in Chinook smolts for at least months, harming their immune systems. What effect this has on survival of adult salmon in the sea is unknown.

In Commencement Bay, wintering Western grebes (which are fisheaters) triple their levels of PCBs over a four-month period and quadruple their levels of DDE (a breakdown product of DDT still seeping into the bay from contaminated chemical factory sites). Bottomfeeding Surf scoters accumulate cadmium and mercury.

National Marine Fisheries Service (NMFS) in Seattle—led by biochemist Donald Malins and present director, pathologist Usha Varanasi—has spent the past two decades investigating fish disease in Puget Sound. Its pioneering team of two dozen scientists have so far detected over 500 toxic compounds in Puget Sound's sediments.

Malins believes their painstaking detective work has linked the fish liver tumors to petroleum residues in the water—especially the PAHs, which come from air pollution, car exhaust, oil furnaces, and, formerly, coal-burning furnaces. Other sources include boat exhaust, spilled oil, and creosote wood preservative. Though sediment studies indicate PAH levels in Puget Sound are sharply down from peaks in the 1950s, they are still 15 times baseline levels from the 1880s.

"Our statisticians found very positive correlations between PAHs in Puget Sound and liver cancer in English sole," Malins says. "And also between concentrations of PAH metabolites in fish bile and the presence of cancerous and precancerous conditions of the fish. In areas of Puget Sound where PAHs are the overriding type of pollutant in the sediments, we get some of the highest prevalences of fish liver cancer."

Malin and Varanasi's indictment of PAHs was backed by Richard Kocan and colleagues at University of Washington's School of Fisheries, who performed an eight-year study of the effects of Puget Sound sediments on fish cells and embryos. They found that PAHs extracted from the Duwamish Estuary and other toxic hotspots caused visible chromosome damage two to three times that encountered in fish from less polluted areas.

Combined Sewer Outfalls spew urban runoff and raw sewage into the shallows after every rainstorm. (Doug Wechsler)

Harbor Island bridge at the mouth of Seattle's Duwamish Waterway remains a popular fishing spot despite signs warning of pollution. (Doug Wechsler)

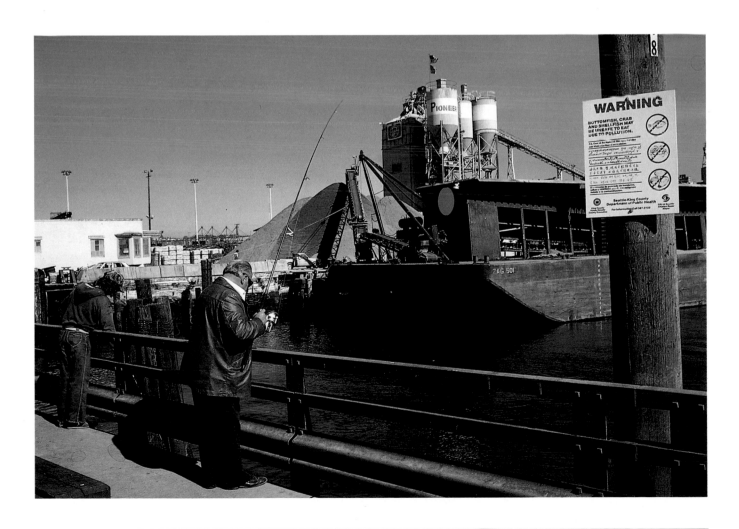

Even more ominous: the researchers found that mutations—invisible genetic effects that can be passed on to future generations—rose at a rate ten to twenty times faster than the visible chromosome damage.

"This," says Kocan," points to a problem that's slow and insidious. Unlike with oil spills, where immediate damage to birds and fish can be linked instantly to its source, it's infinitely more difficult to trace genetic damage that resulted from an environmental event or series of events occurring many years ago."

Aside from the Duwamish estuary, scientists have now mapped a half-dozen "toxic hotspots" off Seattle, some of them open-water disposal sites for contaminated soils dredged from the Duwamish.

Other chemical stews fester in Tacoma's industrialized waterways; in Everett's harbor; at Bremerton Naval Shipyard on Sinclair Inlet; and at the Navy's Undersea Warfare Engineering site at Keyport. Similar hotspots occur in the lower Fraser River near Vancouver.

Finding toxic concentrations in industrialized ports like these was not too surprising. But it was a definite shock that suburban Bainbridge Island's Eagle Harbor is badly contaminated with creosote and dioxins; that the small port of Mukilteo south of Everett is tainted with high levels of cancerous PAHs; and that Harbor seals breeding on tiny Gertrude Island in southern Puget Sound had some of the highest concentrations of PCBs in the world.

North of the border, in rural areas of Georgia Strait, "dead zones" have been found around major pulp mills. Nearby sediments have been smothered by square miles of waste pulp and poisoned by dioxin and other organochlorines from the mills' effluent.

Pollution is not limited to bottom sediments. About 10% of the solids in sewage effluent are grease or "floatables" which remain on the surface until they eventually sink or decompose. Oil from freighter bilges, exhaust from outboards, chronic oil spills, and fallout from air pollution also float. The grease and oil may be laced with toxic chemicals that are soluble in fat or oil but not in water.

In 1987, Jack Hardy and Eric Crecellius of Batelle Northwest Marine Research completed the first study of the Salish Sea's "surface microlayer."

Results indicate that large areas of the surface are contaminated to a much greater degree than the water column below. This bodes poorly for the crabs and shrimp, and fish such as sole, flounder, cod, and hake, whose planktonic eggs spend time on the water surface during early stages of development—at the time when dividing cells are most vulnerable to mutations. Studies show that 40% of all pelagic (open water) fish eggs are found in the surface microlayer. Survival of these eggs—about 90% in uncontaminated water—drops to 4% in urban bays.

Instead of burying the cancerous bottomfish in obscure government reports, Malins held a series of news conferences in the mid-1980s. The findings coincided with the closing of many inlets to shellfish harvest and the deaths of a half-dozen Gray whales (apparently from ingesting toxic sediments). Especially influential were a series of front page articles on the health of Puget Sound by Eric Pryne in the *Seattle Times*. The ensuing media flurry inspired a tidal wave of concern.

Environmentalists blamed industry for its toxic effluent—and the Department of Ecology for lax enforcement of water quality standards. Industry along Elliott Bay and the Duwamish blamed the Metro-politan Sewage Treatment Plant upriver. METRO responded that its studies showed that more that half of the waterway's pollutant loading was from "nonpoint sources"—i.e., all of us.

Bainbridge Island's picturesque Eagle Harbor is contaminated with creosote wastes. Flounder sampled in the harbor have a high incidence of liver tumors and cancerous lesions. (Terry Domico/Earth Images)

The 6-foot-diameter culvert Charlie and I passed just upstream from the Harbor Island fishing bridge, for example, funnels some of Seattle's worst "nonpoint pollution" into Puget Sound.

Stormdrains shunt rainwater off city streets and paved lots directly into our rivers or estuaries. Once-pure rainwater, corrupted into sordid urban runoff, is now a foul mix of worn tire rubber and highway asphalt, car exhaust and leaked hydraulic fluid; cat and dog droppings; solvents and scraped paint; soot from factories and home furnaces; seeps from abandoned dump sites. The city's oily sheen washes off with every rain and flows down hill, overland or through drains, untreated, directly into the drink. No place for swimming, this.

Unaware or uncaring do-it-yourselfers dump a million or so gallons of waste crankcase oil down Puget Sound basin stormdrains along with leftover paints, solvents, and pesticides from the garage. Ingredients include benzene, toluene, chloroform, napthalene, plasticizers, and a thousand unpronounceable toxics listed in small print on the labels. Owners and employees of otherwise law-abiding businesses ("midnight dumpers") also find stormdrains a convenient way to dispose of clean-ing solvents, waste paint, and other toxic chemicals.

Pollution leaks in from old gas storage tanks which are now disinte-grating. And from old waste disposal sites. Groundwater passing through old solvent dump sites near one of Tacoma's waterways contribute 75% of the total tri- and tetrachloroethylenes. On suburban Bainbridge Island, seeps from the Wycoff creosote wood-treating yard have devastated Eagle Harbor. Lumber storage yards on the lower Fraser River leak an estimated ton per year of the now-banned wood preservative pentachlorophenol—one drop of which in ten barrels of water is enough to kill a salmon.

Then there are the CSOs.

Seattle's older storm drains—like those of Vancouver, B.C., Olympia, Everett, Bellingham, and Bremerton—are combined with its sewer mains. Fifty or sixty times a year stormwater overwhelms the system. During a really big rain, half of all Seattle's sewage is dumped untreated into Elliott Bay, the Lake Washington Ship Canal, or the lower Duwamish River. Two billion gallons of excess stormwater—along with whatever icky stuff happens to be in the sewer mains at the time—is released annually through Combined Sewer Overflow pipes into nearshore waters. Metropolitan Vancouver's CSOs are even worse: an estimated 16 billion gallons go into Burrard Inlet and the lower Fraser each year.

Seattle's sewage, it should be noted, comes not only from home toilets and kitchen drains but from chemical plants, semi-conductor factories, dry cleaners, and anyone else hooked into the METRO sewer system.

According to the Puget Sound Water Quality Authority, Seattle's stormwater samples "typically exceed EPA water quality criteria for cadmium, copper, lead, nickel, and zinc," along with bacteria, viruses, mercury, pesticides, ammonia, and petroleum products. Some CSOs were "the major sources of lead and PCBs found in the sediments of Elliott Bay." The worst urban CSOs are being studied for treatment; but removing low concentrations of toxics from high volumes of stormwater is not cheap or easy.

"There are an estimated 63,000 synthetic chemicals in common use," says Malins. Many of these find their way into our estuaries. Clearly analysis of even a part of them in the marine environment is a Herculean task."

Detection methods for many new pollutants have not yet been developed. Others are known to be toxic in extremely small quantities: PCBs and oil are harmful to crab larvae in one part per million; tributyl tin (used in boat bottom paints) in parts per trillion! It is clearly easier to prevent the introduction of toxic chemicals into our waters than to locate and remove them once they have entered the waste stream.

Upriver sources add more bad news.

The Green River is no better or worse than others along the Salish Sea's eastern shore from Olympia to Vancouver. After leaving forests which are now largely clear-cut and gridded with slumping forest roads, our rivers cut through the loose glacial till blanketing the basin. The heavy load of eroded soil is greatly increased by excess runoff from tilled farm fields and construction projects.

As the riverborne sediment passes sewage outfalls and factories, its particles adsorb arsenic, cadmium, copper, lead, mercury, petroleum products, platicizers, pesticides, and PCBs. Most rivers emptying into the Salish Sea originate high in the basin's forested mountains; only the lower reaches are industrialized. The Fraser, though, drains the entire

Oppostie:
Much of the Salish Sea's contamin-ation falls from polluted air.
(Terry Domico/Earth Images)

This remarkable photo catches a Gray whale feeding on clams and worms in the nearshore sediment. Many animals burrow in the seafloor, or feed on creatures living in the polluted mud. (Neil G. McDaniel)

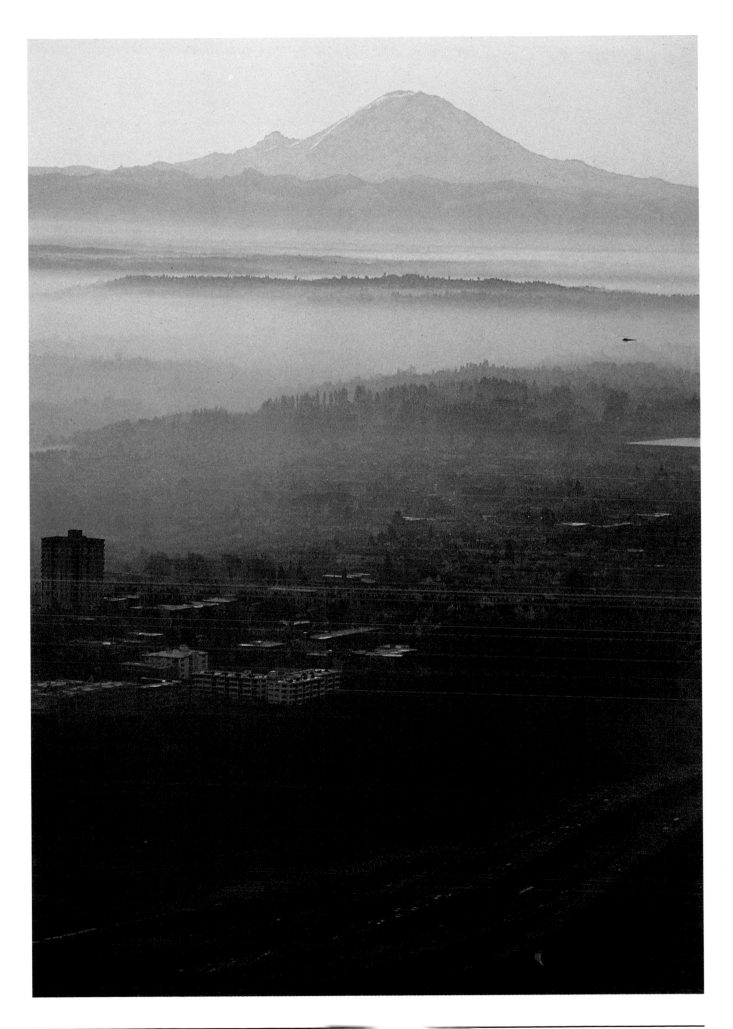

lower quarter of British Columbia, adding effluent from inland cities, mills, and factories.

When the river water meets the tidal salt, the now-toxic sediment particles clump together and sink. Before settling for good, they are held in a loose colloidal froth tonguetwistingly called the "benthic nephloid layer." Hovering just above the denser bottom muds, this layer moves with the currents and rises in plumes every time a flounder is disturbed.

For the clams, bottomfish, benthic shrimp, crabs, and a thousand other creatures—including visiting Gray whales—that feed on or burrow in the sediment, the toxic feast is inescapable. Some compounds, like PCBs, will be stored in fish and crab muscle and fatty tissue. Others, like petroleum residues, will be detoxified by the liver. Until the liver is overwhelmed, and the tumors and cancers begin.

From West Point's picturesque lighthouse the Port of Seattle's orange cranes look like carnival structures against the backdrop of Mount Rainier. On the broad sand beach south of the lighthouse, migrant Sanderlings run along the waves' edge; to the north, flocks of Black brant geese nibble on Eelgrass as the tide recedes. Farther north along the sea wall, goldeneyes and Surf scoters bob near shore; elegant male Horned grebes in breeding plumage chase each other back and forth past a diving loon. Sea lions bark from a distant bell buoy.

It used to be a great place to experience Puget Sound's spectacular spring wildlife parade.

When the U.S. Army closed Fort Lawton in 1972 Seattle snapped up most of the shoreline and surrounding bluffs to create a large city park, naming it after Vancouver's sloop Discovery (which anchored across the Sound from here exactly 200 years ago). Discovery is also the park's avowed purpose—its tidepools and glacial cliffs are priceless teaching aids for Seattle area schools.

Yet landward of the old Coast Guard lighthouse, covering much of the triangular flatland between the beaches and the sand cliffs, stands a formidable complex of buildings—Metropolitan Seattle's West Point Sewage Treatment Plant—the largest such facility north of San Francisco. Behind the chainlink fence are four huge sewage digesters, a dozen sedimentation tanks in two large concrete buildings, pre-aeration blowers, massive pumps for pushing raw sewage, grit, and effluent, and a sludge dewatering facility. Tandem dump trucks carry off slugs of sludge dropped from a conveyer chute. Eternal flames from methane stacks dance in the wind—the burning produces over 40 megawatts of electricity a day.

An even larger secondary treatment facility (in which the effluent from primary treatment is cleansed by bacterial action) is being built here. The construction covers all the remaining lowlands above tideline. Cranes and dozers work from dawn to dusk, and will do so for years to come, transforming what could have been a world-class park into a major industrial facility. Cheaper to expand here, they say, than to build elsewhere; and funds are tight these days. Ah, well...At least the effluent will be scrubbed of its metals and toxics.

Almost a billion gallons of potable water is diverted from Puget Sound's reservoirs and fish-bearing streams each day. METRO's hundreds of miles of sewer utilize a fifth of that to gather wastes from

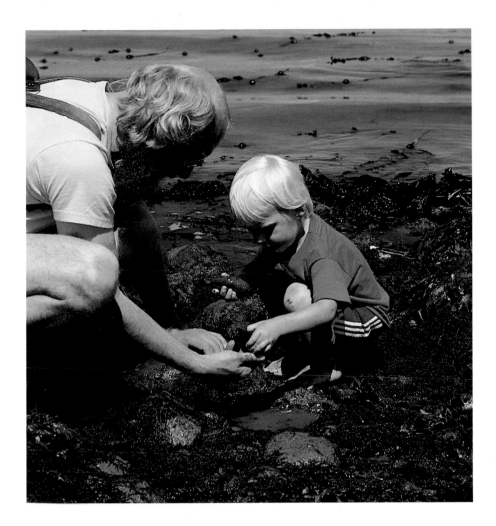

A curious youngster encounters an Orange sea cucumber in Seattle's Discovery Park. (Steve Yates)

homes, businesses, and factories. With primary treatment, huge digesters settle out the solids and skim off the surface scum from the remaining liquid, then treat the liquid with chlorine to kill bacteria. Day after day, West Point pumps almost two hundred million gallons of liquid effluent, with over four tons of chlorine, into the Sound.

The other 600 million gallons per day is utilized by shoreline pulp mills, aluminum mills, chemical plants, and oil refineries (an equal amount flows through Georgia Strait's mills and refineries). Some of this water is treated, the rest is dumped—full of acids, heavy metals, and toxic chemicals— directly into Puget Sound. Half goes into Commencement Bay, the other half into a dozen other productive estuaries, from Hammersley Inlet to Bellingham Bay.

The combined effluent from treatment plants, factories, and mills is termed "point-source" pollution since it flows through pipes from discrete sources. If the flow into Puget Sound were a single river (the Stillpollutish?), it would be the basin's fourth largest.

Though West Point contributes more than half the total sewage flowing into Puget Sound, it is just one of a hundred shoreline treatment plants lining the Salish Sea. Another 160 Canadian sewage outfalls empty into Georgia Strait. Metropolitan Vancouver's contribution, equal to West Point's, gets only primary treatment. Victoria pumps its sewage untreated into the Strait of Juan de Fuca.

Businesses that discharge into METRO's sewers are required by the federal Clean Water Act to pre-treat their effluent to certain standards. METRO charges commercial users a total of about a million dollars in permit fees. Greater Vancouver Regional District, on the other hand, does not require any pre-treatment. And it charges industry nothing for channeling 20 million gallons per day of industrial effluent through the public sewer system.

Industries that discharge directly into Puget Sound or its rivers, are subject to effluent limitations set by Washington's Department of Ecology and are also charged fees. But both the toxicant standards and enforcement (or lack thereof) are subjects of controversy—one that also rages on Boston Harbor and Long Island Sound and Chesapeake, Narragansett, and San Francisco bays.

The 1972 U.S. Clean Water Act (amended as the federal Water Quality Act of 1987) set as a major national goal that the "discharge of pollutants into the navigable waters be eliminated..." (originally by 1983). Though visible progress has been made on cleaning up our rivers and lakes, the goal for coastal estuaries is far from being met. And the Act's ultimate goal of "zero discharge" seems to be slipping farther and farther away.

The Act's Section 402 created the National Pollutant Discharge Elimination System (NPDES), which directs the U.S. Environmental Protection Agency (EPA) to administer a national program of effluent permits. The permits were designed to identify pollutant concentrations, set effluent standards, and lead to gradual reduction based on "best available technology." EPA standards are considered minimums; state and local governments were encouraged to set higher standards and to cover more types of waste.

So far, the contaminants covered in the permits have mostly been "conventional pollutants"—coliform bacteria, acidity, grease and oil, biochemical oxygen demand, and suspended solids. Though these are important, they do not directly measure heavy metals (13 categories) or toxic organic compounds (111 categories).

The NPDES process was designed to have a ratcheting effect. At each five-year permit renewal the standards were to be tightened, leading eventually to zero discharge.

Yet in 1988 Seattle Greenpeace investigators found that of the 16 major discharge permits renewed in 1985, 14 had been weakened rather than strengthened. In eight cases standards were *lowered* in three or more pollutant categories. Due to funding restraints, Washington's Department of Ecology has neglected smaller dischargers; and thousands of hidden discharge sources have not yet even been identified.

Take, for example, Pennwalt Chemical Company, one of a dozen major dischargers on the eight waterways carved from the tideflats of Tacoma's Commencement Bay (itself a federal Superfund site, with cleanup costs estimated at more than $30 million). Pennwalt produces inorganic chemicals, primarily chlorine for pulp mills. It and three neighbors—U.S. Oil, Sound Refining, and Kaiser Chemical—are consistently among Puget Sound's most frequent permit violators.

Pennwalt's "design flow" of 13 million gallons per day exceeds that of the cities of Everett or Bellingham.

Aside from the plant's permitted pollutant load (often exceeded), state inspectors discovered two unpermitted surface sewers, two groundwater seeps, and a drainage ditch. All these leaked high levels of chlorinated hydrocarbons (hexachloro-ethane and hexachlorobutadiene), pesticides (DDT and Aldrin), and heavy metals

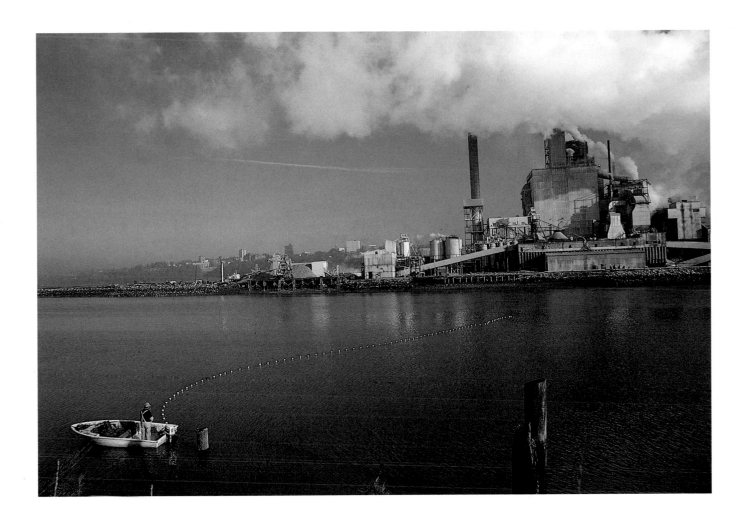

(arsenic, chromium, and mercury) directly into the bay. Mercury levels near the plant are elevated up to a hundred times, chromium a thousand times, and arsenic up to 10,000 times higher than clean seawater.

In British Columbia, similar pollutant discharge permits are issued by the Environmental Protection Division of B.C. Environment, Lands and Parks. But under its long-term Social Credit administration, standards and enforcement were even more lax than in Washington.

Bob Lyons, in his 1989 report for Greenpeace Canada called *Dire Straits*, took a look at the Woodfibre pulp mill on upper Howe Sound on the "Sunshine Coast" just north of Vancouver.

The Woodfibre mill dumps 13 tons per day of contaminated wood wastes into Howe Sound, smothering all marine life in the vicinity. Its effluent contains hundreds of pollutants, mostly organochlorines including high levels of dioxins and PCBs. (Fallout of the mill's smoke is probably not helping water quality, either: people in the surrounding area have British Columbia's highest rate of lung cancer.) Even though its permit limitations were hardly restrictive and its testing procedures lax, the Woodfibre mill was out of compliance in most categories every year.

The SoCred Environment Minister, rather than pushing for costly upgrades, gave the Woodfibre mill an unusual 5-year variance from environmental regulations starting in 1983. In 1987—despite multiple pollution charges in court and serious violations noted by the province's Waste Management Branch—the Environment Minister gave Woodfibre's owners a special Environmental Award, extolling,

A gill-netter sets for salmon in front of a pulp mill. Much of the fish and shellfish we eat lives in the effluent we release. (Doug Wechsler)

evidently without irony, "the significant contribution the company has made to the local environment."

A federal study the following year found high levels of dioxins in shrimp, prawns, and crabs up to four miles from the mill's outfall. Instead of forcing new pollution limits on the mill, the toxic zone was simply closed to shellfish harvest and fishing.

The federal "Sinclair report" (unreleased, but leaked to Greenpeace) noted in 1988, "There appears to be a substantial amount of unjustified resistance to adopting the necessary environmental controls among these mills…"

On the other hand, applauds Lyons, Woodfibre's Canadian-Japanese competitor, Howe Sound Pulp and Paper, has recently invested hundreds of millions of dollars in a chlorine-free, hydrogen peroxide pulp bleaching facility. And Randy Thomas reports in *Saving the Strait, Saving Ourselves* that Orenda Forest Products' new mill near Terrace will use a Finnish-developed "closed-loop" system to recycle its pulp chemicals. Corporate good citizenship is evidently considered good business by these two companies. Below the border, most pulpmills now employ secondary treatment.

"Toxic limits have been considered during the development of all recent permit renewals for oil refineries, pulp and paper mills, and aluminum smelters, and some limits have been included in the permits," reports the 1991 Puget Sound Water Quality Management Plan. "However, only a few municipal permits or other industrial permits include either toxic limits or monitoring improvements required by the plan." No state funds have been allocated to analyze the NPDES program or the individual permits.

Recent raising of NPDES permit fees now allows Washington's Department of Ecology to inspect most of Puget Sound's major industrial permitees on an annual basis. But these are rarely unannounced visits with rigorous check of testing and reporting.

At the enforcement level—the teeth of any permit program—the state legislature (heavily lobbied by industry) has denied Ecology the authority to prosecute midnight dumpers as felons, even "willful violators with demonstrated knowledge and intent to commit the violation." And when Ecology *has* levied fines, the state Pollution Control Hearings Board has traditionally overruled them or cut down the amount of the fine—to an average of only a few thousand dollars per violation. Fines in Canada have been even more minimal.

Compare this parking ticket approach to more vigorous action on Chesapeake Bay. In 1986, a federal judge awarded Maryland a $1.3 million penalty against meat packer Gwaltney of Smithfield, Ltd. The federal appeals court that upheld the ruling suggested district courts can impose maximum penalties of at least $300,000 *per month* for "average" NPDES permit violations.

The decision is a strong stimulant to Chesapeake Bay's shoreline industries to invest in pollution controls. It would probably do the same on Puget Sound and Georgia Strait.

Most of the insults to the Salish Sea are chronic, land-based, and often invisible. One type, though, is acute, and its deadly effects disgustingly visible. There are neither permits nor standards, and when the milk is spilled ("Oops! Sorry. Accidents happen. We're not perfect. Nature will take care of it.") all the crying in the world won't put it back in the glass.

Every year 1,500 single-hulled oil tankers enter and exit the Strait of Juan de Fuca on their way to four U. S. refineries (two near Anacortes, one each at Cherry Point and Ferndale) or three Canadian refineries near Vancouver on Burrard Inlet and the lower Fraser River.

The very largest supertankers are barred from entering farther east than Port Angeles; these transfer their cargo ("lightering") to barges. The barges themselves carry up to two million gallons.

Washington's refineries offload 10 billion gallons per year of Alaskan crude. The Port of Vancouver, aside from receiving oil from Indonesia and others, is the major transshipment point for interior Canada's oil and gas industry—shipping a *trillion* gallons of crude oil, gas, and fuel oil each year. Even the large cargo ships outgoing from Vancouver, Seattle or Tacoma—of which there are hundreds each year—may carry 800,000 gallons of diesel in their fuel tanks.

In 1989, the *Exxon Valdez* went aground in Alaska's Prince William Sound. The 11 million gallons of crude oil that spilled out covered an area virtually identical in size to that of Puget Sound. Tankers almost the size of the *Valdez* enter the Salish Sea every day, where they or the lightering barges must pass through narrow, rocky channels in strong tidal currents, sometimes in thick fog or storms.

After the *Valdez* went aground, U.S. Coast Guard Commander Greg Yarock in Seattle said of our main shipping channel through the San Juans: "The currents move through Rosario Strait so rapidly that it would be virtually impossible to set up a defensive position there against moving oil. The oil would go where it wants to go."

So far we've been spared an *Exxon Valdez*–size spill. But fear of oil fouling the shores of the Salish Sea is hardly hypothetical.

In 1964, a sunken barge leaked 300,000 gallons of bunker fuel into Howe Sound, just north of Vancouver. That same year a fuel barge off the Washington coast lost 1.2 million gallons of gas and diesel—how much washed into the Strait is not known. In 1973, a collision dumped 61,000 gallons of bunker oil into Vancouver's Burrard Inlet.

Just before Christmas, 1985, the tanker *Arco Anchorage* ran aground near Port Angeles *while at anchor!* Much of the 240,000 gallons of crude that was leaked from the ship washed up on Ediz Hook, Dungeness Spit, and Protection Island, killing at least 4,000 seabirds.

In January, 1988, a barge sank near Anacortes, leaking nearly 70,000 gallons. Later in 1988, the tug *Ocean Services* punched a hole in its barge, *Nestucca*, in heavy seas off Gray's Harbor, spilling 230,000 gallons of fuel oil. The oil not only covered Olympic National Park beaches and shores half way up Vancouver Island but entered into the Strait of Juan de Fuca as far as the San Juans. It killed an estimated 40,000 seabirds and is still visible on beaches.

In January, 1991, U.S. Oil and Refinery spilled 600,000 gallons into Commencement Bay. A month later, a pump burst while a tanker was being unloaded at March Point near Padilla Bay, spilling 210,000 gallons. Later in the year, the Japanese fish processor *Tenyo Maru*, carrying 350,000 gallons of fuel, sank just off the entrance to the Strait of Juan de Fuca. Fortunately for the strait (but not for Olympic National Park) the oil was pushed south rather than east.

Workers spent Christmas day, 1985, cleaning up some of the 240,000 gallons of crude oil spilled by the Arco Anchorage *near Port Angeles. (Doug Wechsler)*

A small oil slick spreads from a pleasure boat. Thousands of small spills, the exhaust from outboard motors, and waste crankshaft oil dumped down drains add as much oil to the Salish Sea as do major spills. (Steve Yates)

Oil isn't the only danger. Vancouver ships about a million tons of petrochemicals from Canada's prairie provinces every year; another million tons of other chemicals include 100,000 tons of asbestos. The largest pulp mills barge in 50 tons of chlorine each day.

Federal, state, and provincial governments have taken some action—belated and timid as it may be. After the *Nestucca* spill in 1988, Washington, Oregon, Alaska, and British Columbia created the States/B.C. Oil Spill Task Force. The U.S Federal Oil Pollution Act of 1990 (inspired by the *Exxon Valdez*) requires double hulls on all tankers (though not barges) by 2010—a mere two decades from now. It does establish higher liability limits for spills, creates a billion-dollar cleanup trust fund, and requires better training and higher negligence penalties for vessel staff.

Better spill prevention and response tactics than those exposed in Prince William Sound are clearly needed. Penalties for negligence should reflect both the enormity of the damage done and the level of responsibility—financial and criminal.

Yet, on average, major spills make up only a small fraction of the estimated 3 million gallons per year that leaks into the Salish Sea—from refineries, factories, leaking storage tanks, waste motor oil, and a thousand minor spills. The finger of reponsibility points everywhere, including back at ourselves.

Olympia and Victoria, the capitals of Washington and British Columbia, are fitting places to debate the fate of the Salish Sea. Overlooking the scenic intersection of Georgia Strait and Puget Sound, Victoria's beaches were routinely closed to swimming because

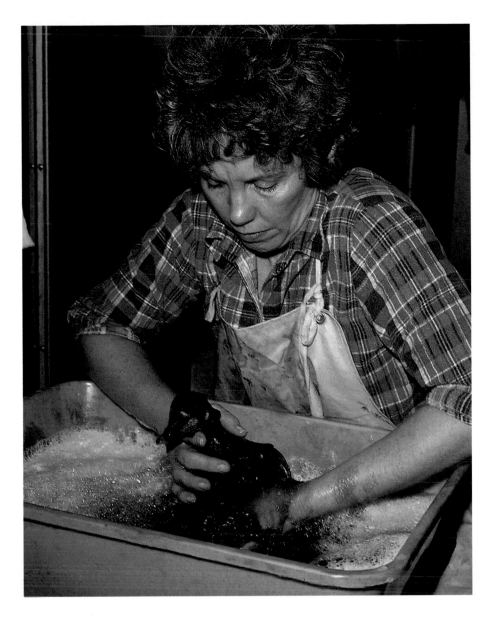

A volunteer attempts to clean an oiled Harlequin duck at a rescue center set up in Mukilteo near the Whidbey Island spill of 1985. (Doug Wechsler)

of nearby sewage outfalls. Since 1986, the Capital Region District's effluent has been screened for garbage, plastics, tampons, etc. But the untreated sewage is still pumped through a long pipe out into the Strait of Juan de Fuca. Pressed by neighboring Washington state (where secondary treatment is now mandatory), the CRD has tentatively agreed to primary treatment (settling and chlorination) in the near future, but sees no reason to go to secondary, despite Victoria's dependence on tourism and its image as the picturesque capital of scenic "Supernatural British Columbia."

Down at the southern end of the Salish Sea, Capitol Lake, in which Washington's handsome state capitol building reflects, covers what once were the tidal mudflats of Budd Inlet. Washington's earliest settlers made it through the long winters sustained by "acres and acres of clams." Nearby inlets—Henderson, Totten, Little Skookum, Hammersley—are leading producers of Olympia and Pacific oysters and Manilla clams.

"When the tide is out," the saying went, "the table is set." No more. Each of these rural inlets has seen wild native oysters wiped out (growers of the tasty native Olympia oyster blamed pulp mills effluent in the

1920s and 30s). Recently, shellfish aquaculture has been greatly curtailed as southern Puget Sound's population explodes.

South Sound is a sea within a sea. It retains most of its own wastes, while flood tides bring in half of Tacoma's effluent though The Narrows, and a fifth of Seattle's.

Previous to the 1980s, most restrictions on harvesting shellfish were due to proximity to urban areas. Lately, rural runoff has become as much of a water quality problem as the more obvious industrial effluent and urban runoff.

Rural home septic system drainfields percolate too quickly through the area's glacial tills or too slowly through its clays. Many shoreline systems were originally just temporary ones for summer homes but are now used year-round. At any given time up to 10% of the 400,000 domestic septic tanks around Puget Sound leak or overflow.

Animals on hundreds of small "hobby farms" poop in rural streams, greatly elevating bacteria counts in the nearby inlets. (Manure from 200,000 cows, the fecal equivalent of a million people, washes off the fields of northern Puget Sound's productive dairies during rainy weather. Floods sometimes cause tons of manure to break out of holding lagoons, causing massive fish kills.)

Pesticides and herbicides such as Rodeo and Roundup, 2,4-D and copper sulfate—all toxic to shellfish larvae—run off from roadside sprayings, treefarms, pastures, and gardens.

Around dozens of fast-developing towns, wetlands are being filled and paved for parking lots and malls. Stormwater—no longer retained and purified by marshes and wet meadows—washes down directly into bays and inlets.

The story of oysterman Jerry Yamashita is instructive. Forced out of Samish Bay by Bellingham's pulp mill pollution in the 1940s and from Dyes Inlet by Bremerton's sewage bacteria in the 1950s, Yamashita moved his operation to south Sound's Burley Lagoon at the head of Case Inlet.

In 1981 the state "decertified" Burley Lagoon, forcing Yamashita to truck the oysters to Henderson Inlet, east of Olympia, to purify themselves in the cleaner water there. In 1984 the state decertified parts of Henderson Inlet.

"They're closing down our last bastions," says Dave McMillan, Little Skookum Inlet shellfish grower and head of the Washington Aquaculture Council.

Since 1986, nine areas totaling 14,000 acres (almost a fifth of Puget Sound's remaining shellfish beds) have been decertified. All in all, a third of the Sound's commercial shellfish beds have been classified "conditional" or "restricted" or have been closed. "Washington state has never reopened a shellfish bed closed by bacteria," adds Greg Bonnaker, a neighboring clam farmer on Little Skookum and founder of the Aquaculture Council. "We can't just go somewhere else and find the same beds. We can't build a similar nutrient source or water temperatures."

Nearshore pollution is not just a problem for oyster growers or pier anglers. On three of ten beaches used by recreational clammers, the pollution levels would prohibit commercial harvesting. And, charges Bonnaker: "Some of the shellfish you buy in [Seattle's famous] Pike Place Market is poached from closed beds."

Assaults on the Salish Sea are so pervasive and diffuse that it would be easy to become discouraged. As National Audubon Society vice-president Brock Evans once remarked, "Puget Sound could be dying the death of a thousand cuts—no single one fatal, but added together, the consequences could be just as tragic and just as fatal." It will take time and great effort to blunt the knives, let alone heal the wounds.

Older shoreline plants and mills produce tons of toxic materials as by-products of production. Many companies, accustomed to using potable streamwater for dilution, and the sea as free sewer, resist expensive upgrades to recycle water and chemicals. Some use their considerable clout to stymie higher permit fees, tighter effluent standards, or stronger enforcement of NPDES permit violations.

Cleanup strategies demand a moderate but consistent level of funding; yet water quality must compete with other social needs, and taxpayers resist any tax increases.

The basin's human population is swelling. Conservationists struggle to preserve wildlife habitat, while competing user groups fight over vanishing forests, wetlands, rivers, and salmon.

But if you think it's hopeless, don't tell Walter Walker.

Walker grew up on the Burnette River, which runs from Burnaby Lake to the Fraser River. In his younger days, Walter and his father trapped and fished the Brunette; he remembers spawning salmon "so thick a person could literally cross the river walking on their backs." But the salmon vanished as suburban Burnaby became a part of metropolitan Vancouver, and the Brunette became an open sewer.

Walter fought back. He and the local Sapperton Fish and Game Club campaigned to clean up the river. They harassed city officials about oil in ditches. They got classrooms of kids to raise and release baby salmon. They built fish ladders to get over minor dams and installed a "fish elevator" at the main Brunette dam.

Finally salmon returned to spawn.

Now Walter walks the Brunette daily, checking pipes and spawning grounds. According to Bob Lyons, "Walter will track an oil slick right back to a company yard and bang on the boss's door to get action."

Down on central Puget Sound, Nancy Malmgren and her husband Les live above Piper's Creek. The attractive mile-long stream flows through residential north Seattle into a broad, V-shaped valley of alder and maple before becoming the heart of Carkeek Park on the edge of the Sound. By the late 1970s Piper's Creek was increasingly impacted by storm runoff from the streets and driveways of the hundreds of homes now lining its upper watershed.

Tired of seeing the creek deteriorate, Nancy, Ted Mohlendorph of Trout Unlimited, Tony Barone of nearby Shoreline Community College, and a few neighbors decided to restore the creek's watershed.

Trout Unlimited donated $500 to create a "Salmon to Sound" interpretive trail along Venema Creek, Piper's main tributary. It also helped the fledgling group obtain a $3,500 Community Action Project grant from METRO.

Incorporating as Carkeek Watershed Community Action Project in 1980, the group bought water testing kits and staff gages; rented backhoes and trucks to install bank protectors, drain tiles, and spawning gravels; cleaned out silt; and added crushed limestone to lower the creek's acidity. They organized neighbors, sports groups, Campfire and Boy Scouts, and students from local schools as workers.

Carkeek volunteers went door to door handing out brochures—designed by Shoreline Community College graphic arts students—and explained the impacts of storm runoff, waste oil, and household hazardous wastes. At one point, 350 Boy Scouts, volunteers from Trout Unlimited and other groups, and a cadre of fisheries experts were all working on restoring the creek.

Then, in late November, 1987, 20 large spawner Chum were counted in the small stream, with a hundred more milling around offshore.

"Just getting the kind of return we have now is proof that you can restore a salmon run in an urban setting," says Nancy Malmgren, who likened the project to "giving birth." "The whole experience has been extremely rewarding."

As one water quality expert involved in the state's efforts to clean up the Sound noted admiringly: "No government agency could do what CWCAP does. If there were a hundred groups like that around Puget Sound, it would make one helluva difference..."

Tom Murdoch, an urban planner working for Snohomish County—one of the country's fastest-growing counties—decided to institutionalize such stream-saving efforts. First he organized a group of biologists to inventory the county's streams. Working with Department of Fisheries' Volunteer Fisheries Resource Program (British Columbia has a

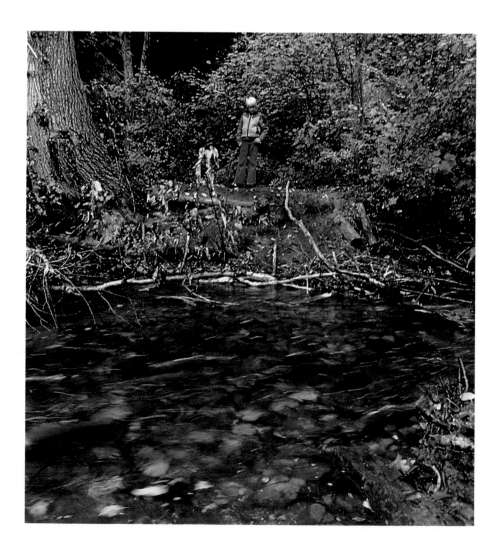

Sockeye salmon return to a clear creek in the Puget Sound watershed. (Terry Domico/Earth Images)

similar Salmonid Enhancement Program), Murdoch organized work-shops to encourage school teachers and citizen groups to become involved. Recently, he established the Adopt-A-Stream Foundation, working half-time as its director.

Based in Everett, the foundation holds workshops statewide, produces educational material and booklets on stream protection, and now even has a sister organization in Japan.

Teachers from two Snohomish County schools were early converts.

In 1984 Laurie Baker and Vicki Hill at Jackson Elementary and Neil Westover and Bill Spurling at nearby Evergreen Middle School decided to cooperate on an Adopt-A-Stream project on Pigeon Creek, which flows for about two miles, from the southeastern edge of Everett north to Puget Sound. Just below Jackson Elementary School, its last half mile cuts through the coastal bluffs in an undeveloped wooded gorge that is now a city park.

Thirty years ago Pigeon Creek supported a healthy run of Chum salmon. But over the past decades the stream was rendered almost lifeless. Pickup truck loads of trash were dumped along its banks, even within the park. A carwash near the creek's headwaters shunted detergent-laden water into the stream. Storm drains became convenient dumping spots for used oil and antifreeze. Housing construction contributed erosion sediments; faulty septic tanks and drain fields infiltrated groundwater and entered the creek.

With the aid of a small grant from the county, the teachers bused their enthusiastic students out to a state hatchery to fetch a thousand precious salmon eggs for their classroom aquarium. The enthusiasm at Evergreen Middle School spilled past school hours as they formed the Evergreen Salmon Club, which meets on Thursday evenings to care for salmon eggs and to assist at the nearby Tulalip Indian Tribe hatchery.

Meanwhile, the students cleaned 3,000 pounds of tires, mattresses, shopping carts and other junk out of Pigeon Creek. They tracked down sources of pollution in the watershed. They produced and handed out pamphlets that told how to dispose of oil, antifreeze, and household hazardous wastes in ways that would not impact the creek. They stencilled: "Outlet to Stream, Dump No Waste" on storm drains. They were determined that when the salmon returned from the sea, there would be a clean spawning stream to come home to.

"These kids have grown up around Pigeon Creek and have seen things happen that they can personally relate to," says Evergreen's Neil Westover. "They can make a connection between the things we do and how it affects the immediate environment. To them it's not an exotic concept. It's real."

After planting the first salmon eggs in the stream—covered by two local television stations and featured on a segment for a National Public Television series on river conservation—the students of both schools attended a meeting of the Everett City Council to express their views on the importance of clean streams. Everett's mayor proclaimed May 31, 1985, "Jackson Elementary School and Evergreen Middle School Students' Salmon Day."

But the reward the kids and teachers are most proud of came in December of 1987, four years after the first salmon fry were planted by the Evergreen students. A small run of Chum returned to Pigeon Creek to spawn—for the first time in 25 years.

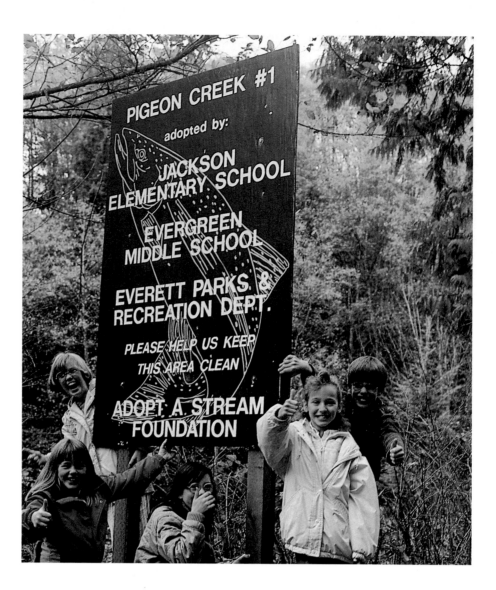

Students from Jackson Elementary and Evergreen Middle schools near Everett, Washington, celebrate their restoration of Pigeon Creek. (Sidnee Wheelwright)

Other citizens pursue similar goals, but on a larger scale.

As a teenager living on ancestral land on Nisqually Delta, and later as chairman of the Nisqually tribe, Bill Frank, Jr., was arrested and jailed many times fighting for his tribe's treaty fishing rights along the Nisqually. The confrontations and trials eventually led to the landmark "Boldt Decision" of 1974, which guaranteed the area's tribes half the salmon harvest and vested them with legal status in decisions regarding salmon habitat.

But the Boldt decision only aggravated conflict between the tribes, non-Indian recreational steelheaders, and commercial fishermen. By 1977, when Frank was appointed chairman of the Northwest Indian Fisheries Commission, it seemed that every year's state fishing regulations and allocations went straight to court, while the resource continued to go straight to hell.

The Indians won most of the court battles, but "the system was not working," Frank says. "The courtroom became irrelevant to what we were trying to do." Which was to restore the salmon runs.

In 1984, Frank convened a "Salmon Summit" that brought tribal and non-tribal fisheries officials together for the first time. It produced an agreement within Washington to manage runs cooperatively. And it provided impetus for 1985's renegotiation of the 1937 U.S.–Canada salmon-sharing treaty. In 1986, Frank helped negotiate the unlikely but innovative "Timber/Fish/Wildlife Accord" between the tribes, the state, timber companies, and environmental groups. In 1990, he was a major player as a wide array of interest groups signed a statewide accord to settle water-allocation disputes affecting salmon runs.

In 1992 Johns Hopkins University awarded Bill Frank, Jr. the Albert Schweitzer Prize for Humanitarianism. Previous winners include former president Carter and Surgeon General C. Everett Koop. In nominating him for the prize, one Seattle mediator called Frank "the Northwest's own Mahatma Gandhi."

Just a watershed north of the Nisqually, in Tacoma, Helen Engle was occupied raising seven children when she found out in 1968 that the Port of Tacoma was proposing to dredge a deepwater port on Nisqually Delta—a favorite family hiking and birding area, and the last large wildlife habitat along the eastern shore of Puget Sound. Realizing that there were no active environmental groups in the area, she organized local members of the Seattle Audubon Society into a Tahoma (the Salish name for Mount Rainier) chapter. To specifically fight for Nisqually, she and Olympia's famed "Mushroom Lady," mycologist/writer Margaret McKinney founded the Nisqually Delta Association—run after McKinney's death by Florence Brodie, whose persistence was to earn her the name "Nisqually Flo." The three women's passion and persistence paid off: Five years later, in 1974, the Brown Farm and adjacent tidelands were purchased by the U.S. Fish & Wildlife Service. The refuge is now headquarters for a statewide system that includes Dungeness Spit, Protection Island, and parts of the San Juan Islands.

In the early 1970s, just when things were looking good for Nisqually Delta, Seattle water quality activist Tom Wimmer told Helen about an 800-lot subdivision being planned on Protection Island. Leading an Audubon field trip out to the island, Helen was shocked to find that, among other insults, a bulldozer had just finished scraping the top off a hundred Rhinoceros auklet nest burrows. The pictures she brought back turned into a touring slide show that aroused birders throughout western Washington. At one point Audubon members raised money to begin buying the lots one-by-one. Eventually, it became clear that the island was one of the Northwest's most important seabird breeding areas. Not to mention that the lack of water, exposure to storms, and high costs to the county of providing services to the proposed subdivision made the platting absurd. Again, Helen Engle had helped add another gem to the National Wildlife Refuge system. In recognition of her talents, she was voted to the National Audubon Society's Board of Directors.

In 1985 and '86, Washington environmentalists rejoiced as the legislature passed a statewide water quality bill which created a Centennial Clean Water Fund endowed with $45 million (from a new tax on tobacco products). It also elevated 1983's Puget Sound Water Quality Authority (PSWQA) from an advisory board to a state agency.

The new Authority was given the daunting task of assessing Puget Sound's resources and problems, and of creating a comprehensive cleanup plan. Governor Booth Gardner turned to Kathy Fletcher to chair it.

Fletcher had done a stint in the "other Washington" in the Carter administration. Returning home, she headed Seattle City Light's Environmental Division and, as a volunteer, chaired the forerunner of

An artificially created saltmarsh near Tacoma. It takes a lot of time and labor to mitigate past damage to our nearshore environment.
(Doug Wechsler)

PSWQA. Under her leadership the new Water Quality Authority's small staff quickly produced a series of in-depth reports ("issue papers") on nine problems, ranging from "Industrial and Municipal Discharges" to "Nonpoint Source Pollution." It then held a series of public forums in communities around the Sound to discuss drafts of the issue papers, leading to the adoption of an overall Puget Sound Plan.

Starting in 1987, the Authority distributed half a million dollars per year in PIE-Fund (Public Involvement and Education) grants to dozens of community groups. It set up the Puget Sound Ambient Monitoring Program, and it issued detailed Puget Sound Water Quality Management Plans in 1987, 1989, and 1991.

This last plan was adopted as the Comprehensive Conservation and Management Plan by the Environmental Protection Agency (under the Clean Water Act's National Estuary Program).

Plans are necessary first steps, but they do not themselves keep even a thimbleful of toxic effluent out of Puget Sound. As Pam Crocker-Davis, former head of National Audubon's Washington state office, said: "We've come to the point in environmental history in which we've passed most of the basic statutes. Now we've got to fork over the bucks. It will be a tragic waste if the Water Quality Authority cleanup plan becomes just another $2 million book on the shelf."

About $5 million of the Centennial Clean Water Fund is earmarked to implement plan programs—the majority for reducing nonpoint pollution in a dozen "Early Action Watersheds." By 1997, a new Toxic Control Account (from 1988's Initiative 97, which taxes manufacture of toxic chemicals) will contribute about $4 million per year to Puget Sound cleanup. Most of the rest of the money must come from the state general fund.

So far, Washington's legislature has anted up only about half of what the Plan deemed minimally necessary ($14 million of $27 million in 1988, for example). The shortfall has meant that, among other things, insufficient funds were available for monitoring sediments; nothing for wildlife habitat; and little for identifying and dealing with "toxic hot spots." The urban stormwater program has been delayed. Very little has been done to acquire threatened wetlands, and counties have few funds available to protect them.

"Everybody's going to have to sit down and figure out how citizens can help implement and enforce our laws," said Crocker-Davis. "It's much easier to pass wonderful-sounding legislation than to follow up with the boring, complicated, frustrating job of tracking the bureaucrats. And yet that's what it's going to take. Citizen groups will have to watchdog this every step of the way."

When the Water Quality Authority was essentially merged with the Department of Ecology in 1991, Kathy Fletcher decided it was time to become a watchdog.

After a year teaching at the University of Washington's Graduate School of Public Affairs, where she studied the similar water quality situation on Chesapeake Bay, Fletcher organized a new citizen group—People for Puget Sound. Its ambitious mission: to "protect and preserve Puget Sound; its waters, the land and our common future." Its goals: to eliminate contamination of the Sound and Straits, to halt the destruction of their natural habitats, and to "sustain the Sound and Straits as a healthy source of people's livelihood, enjoyment and renewal." The organization now publishes a quarterly newsletter, *Sound & Straits*.

Given a generous seed grant by the Bullitt Foundation, People for Puget Sound literally "launched" its campaign with a 10-day voyage around the Salish Sea, holding meetings and media events in ports along the way. Shortly thereafter, Fletcher organized Puget Sound Lobby Days at the state legislature to press for water quality and habitat protections. She holds press conferences to publicize scientific findings related to the health of the Sound and coordinates efforts with Save Georgia Strait Alliance (SGSA), a sister organization across the border. Putting her body on the line—or, rather, in the chilly water—Fletcher leads a relay team which swims the 17-mile course between the Canadian mainland and Vancouver Island during SGSA's Save the Strait Marathon & Faire in August.

The Georgia Strait Marathon was the brainchild of Ernie Yacub, now a tree-planting contractor in Vancouver Island's Comox Valley. Back in 1967, Ernie had been one of the first people to successfully swim the Strait. Dismayed by the degradation of "the Gulf" over the past decades, Ernie thought that perhaps a repeat swim might draw some media attention to the damage.

So he started driving around Vancouver Island in his '75 Ford van, talking to people about the idea. A kayaker friend suggested adding kayaks; an Indian leader organized crews to paddle traditional Salish canoes. Photojournalist Randy Thomas, who lives on a trimaran, and had himself started a group called Green Islands, suggested sailboats as safety escort vessels.

The first Save the Strait Marathon & Faire in August, 1990, was so successful that it has become an annual event, drawing hundreds of participants and crafts. Some of the boats are made especially for the event, such as one beautiful canoe crafted entirely of used shopping bags.

Yacub and Thomas and Gabriola Island teacher Laurie MacBride decided to use the Marathon's impetus to start an umbrella organization for all the local groups working to save individual bays and estuaries. It soon embraced pulp mill unions and commercial fishing and clamming groups.

Immediately after the first Marathon, Save Georgia Strait Alliance members sailed around the Strait in Thomas's *Celerity*, visiting seaside communities to assess industrial pollution and public attitudes. They found that even citizens of pulp mill company towns were concerned with the health aspects of the mills' obvious air and water pollution.

The next winter they invited scientists and activists to Nanaimo for a "State of the Strait" conference, televised live on local cable. They published a handsome volume of the conference proceedings and Randy Thomas's booklet, *Saving the Strait, Saving Ourselves*. Since then the the group has created two videos and a series of fact sheets. In 1992, the Save Georgia Strait Alliance received a Bullitt Foundation grant. Members plan to prod British Columbia's recently elected New Democrats administration to live up to its campaign promises to reverse Social Credit's horrendous environmental record.

"Georgia Strait and Puget Sound are really one inseparable sea," says SGSA's director, Laurie MacBride. "What's needed is full funding of the Puget Sound Management Plan in Washington and a similar Georgia Strait Authority in B.C.—so we can have uniform standards and strong, fair enforcement. The Salish Sea should be managed under an international treaty similar to that on the Great Lakes. It's our common heritage."

The annual Georgia Strait Marathon & Faire draws hundreds of enthusiastic participants in August. (Ernie Yacub/Save Georgia Strait Alliance)

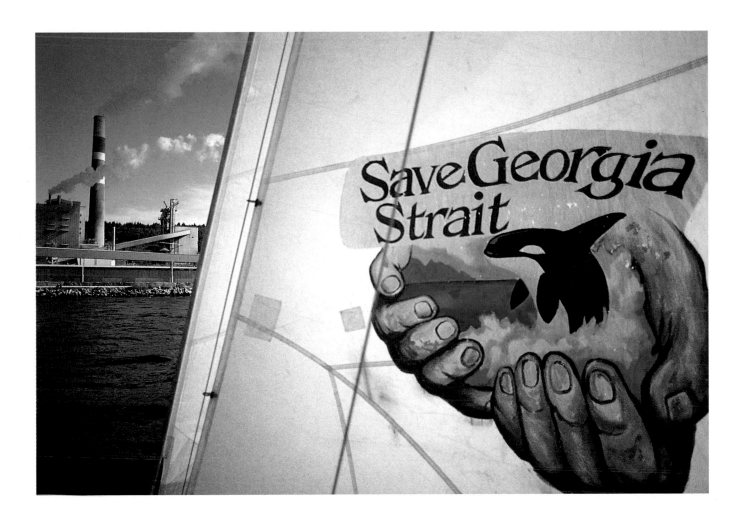

One Christmas day a friend and I took sea kayaks to the southern end of Hood Canal. A thick fog hung over the water, making ghosts of the dozen species of sea ducks that concentrate here in winter. Flocks of scoters and goldeneyes dived around us, invisible wings whistled by. A rare Yellow-billed loon appeared for a minute, then vanished in the fog.

On the way back in, we noticed dogfish sharks rising stiffly out of the water like bathtub submarines. Though I had never seen dogfish in the shallows in daylight, they seemed just a normal part of the dream-like day. Then we saw why.

The silty bottom was covered with salmon. Dead salmon.

As we beached near the mouth of Twanoh Creek, large flocks of gulls and crows rose up like clouds. Wriggling up the stream were hundreds of Chum salmon: two- to three-feet long, sleek, with greenish backs. Along their sides, splotchy vertical bars of red and brown alternated with ragged white flesh exposed by the sharp rocks of the barely flowing stream.

Hundreds of dead Chum lined the stream, while live ones powered their way through the center of the flow, slithering through small pools and fighting up chutes as gulls and crows picked at their still-flapping comrades trapped at the water's edge. We followed the winners for a half mile up into the evergreen forest and stood for a long time in the fog watching them spawn and die.

Members of Save Georgia Strait Alliance sail past pulp mill stacks near Powell River, northern Georgia Strait, on a fact-finding tour of the Strait. (Randy Thomas)

Overleaf:
Rowers explore Puget Sound in replicas of Vancouver expedition longboats sponsored by the Vashon Island-based Pure Sound Society. (Jeanne Dickinson)

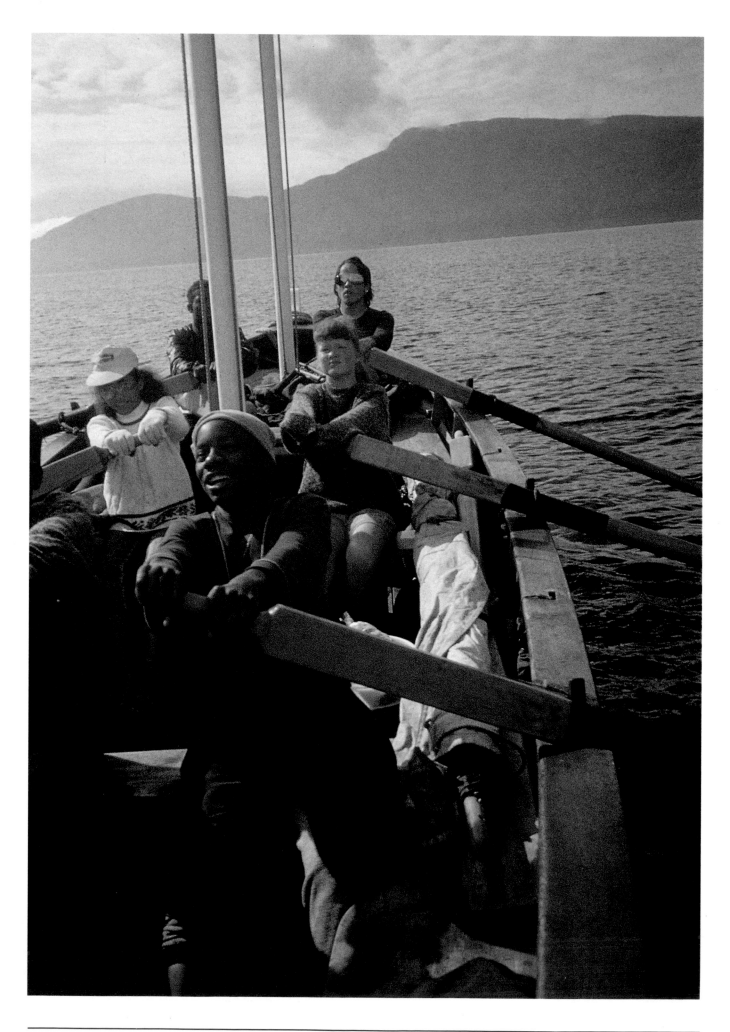

Just a week before, these same salmon were dodging orcas off Vancouver Island and gill nets in the Strait of Juan de Fuca, using their incredible sense of "smell" to find their way back after three or four years in the ocean to this tiny spawning stream at the southern end of Hood Canal. Seeing them among dense Douglas fir and cedar trees brought home to me the unity of the entire Salish Sea.

As tiny fry, these Chum fed on tiny copepods that fed on detritus in the sediments. Other salmon feed on schools of herring and sand lance, which feed on zooplankton, which feed on phytoplankton, which are nourished by the waters of both sea and land. Those that escape the predators and nets ultimately feed Bald eagles, ravens, and gulls. Their excess eggs feed sculpins and Dolly vardens. And their spawned-out bodies nourish the streams' aquatic insects—on which the salmon fry will feed.

It's a closed circle. Intricate, interlocking webs of energy and nutrients radiate through every creature in the Salish Sea's watershed. Every nutrient from each fallen leaf in the mountains—along with every chemical we loose into sewers, drains, and ditches—flows downhill and ends up in the sea. Nutrients and pollutants are transformed by metabolism or magnified by bioaccumulation. Nutrients are packaged into larger and larger animals; toxic chemicals accumulate at every step.

Sloshed back and forth by tidal currents and carried on migration paths, both nutrients and toxics are taken far out to sea and brought back upstream. To aquatic insects, eagles, and bears. To human anglers and gourmet restaurants.

It all returns—up to the huge basin's most remote and smallest creeks—to sustain us...or haunt us.

If Puget Sound is dying the death of a thousand cuts, there is no cure but to protect it from the thousand knives—the non-compliant factory, the midnight dumper, the leaking fuel storage tank, the motor oil and antifreeze lazily changed over a stormdrain, excess pesticides, faulty septic tanks, cows in the stream. A thousand cuts demand a thousand stitches. And a thousand conscious acts of caring.

Orca whales still follow salmon runs through scenic passes, breaching and spyhopping against lonely cliffs and city skylines. Anglers mooch for Kings from open boats or stand knee-deep in chilly Steelhead rivers. Eagles nest in tall fir snags above our cobbly beaches, where families below still dig for clams. There *is* a lifestyle here—an endless rhythm of tides and currents; a web of interlocking life cycles and migrations; a shared seagift.

Preserving it is more than worth the cost.

Further Reading

Angell, Tony, and Ken Balcomb. 1982. *Marine Birds and Mammals of Puget Sound.* Seattle: University of Washington, Sea Grant Publication.

Bigg, M. A., G. Ellis, J. Ford, and K. Balcomb. 1987. *Killer Whales: a study of their identification, genealogy, and natural history in British Columbia and Washington State.* Nanaimo, B.C.: Phantom Press & Publications, Inc

Burns, Robert. 1984. *The Shape and Form of Puget Sound.* Seattle: University of Washington/Sea Grant.

Calambokidis, J., et al. 1985. Biology of Puget Sound Marine Mammals and Marine Birds: populations, health, and evidence of pollution effects. Rockville, MD: NOAA Tech. Mem. NOS OMA 18.

Carefoot, Tom. 1977. *Pacific Seashores.* Seattle: University of Washington Press.

Carl, G. C., W. A. Clemens, and C. C. Lindsey. 1973. *The Fresh-water Fishes of British Columbia.* Victoria: British Columbia Provincial Museum.

Carson, Rob. 1985–1986. "Troubled Waters: a four-part series on water pollution in Puget Sound." *Pacific Northwest Magazine,* Oct. & Dec., 1985; April & June, 1986.

Chasen, Dan J. 1981. *The Water Link: A History of Puget Sound as a Resource.* Seattle: University of Washington/Sea Grant.

Cone, Molly. 1992. *Come Back, Salmon.* San Francisco: Sierra Club Books for Children.

Curtis, Edward S. 1913. *The North American Indian.* Cambridge, MA: The University Press.

Dexter, R. N. et al. 1985. Temporal trends in selected environmental parameters monitored in Puget Sound. Rockville, MD: NOAA, Tech. Memo. NOS OMA 19.

Downing, John. 1983. *The Coast of Puget Sound: Its processes and developments.* Seattle: University of Washington/Sea Grant.

Dunne, T., and W. Dietrich. 1978. Geology and hydrology of the Green River, Technical Appendix A. In: *A River of Green.* Seattle: King Co. Division of Planning.

EPA. 1991. *Beyond the Border: Environmental Management in Washington and British Columbia.* Seattle: Puget Sound Estuary Program, EPA 910/9-91-038.

Gotshall, D. W. 1981. *Pacific Coast Inshore Fishes.* Los Osos, CA: Sea Challengers.

Guberlet, M. L. 1956. *Seaweeds at Ebb Tide.* Seattle: University of Washington Press.

Haeberlin, Hermann, and E. Gunther. 1930. *The Indians of Puget Sound.* Seattle: University of Washington Press.

Haley, Delphine. 1984. *Seabirds of Eastern North Pacific and Arctic Waters.* Seattle: Pacific Search Press.

Harper-Owes. 1983. Water quality assessment of the Duwamish Estuary, Washington. Seattle: Municipality of Metropolitan Seattle (METRO).

Hart, J. L. 1973. *Pacific Fishes of Canada.* Fisheries Research Board of Canada, Bull. 180. Ottawa: Dept of Fisheries & Oceans.

Kozloff, E. N. 1983. *Seashore Life of the Northern Pacific Coast.* Seattle: University of Washington Press.

Kunze, Linda. 1984. Puget trough coastal wetlands: A summary report of biologically significant sites. Olympia: Natural Heritage/Wash. Dept. Nat. Res.

Lamb, Andy, and Phil Edgell. 1986. *Coastal Fishes of the Pacific Northwest.* Madiera, BC: Harbour Publishing.

Lewis, Mark, and Fred Sharpe. 1987. *Birds of the San Juan Islands.* Seattle: The Mountaineers.

Lyons, Bob. 1989. *Dire Straits: Pollution in the Strait of Georgia, British Columbia, Canada.* Vancouver: Greenpeace Canada.

McConnaughey, B. H., and E. McConnaughey. 1984. *Pacific Coast: Audubon Society Nature Guide.* New York: Borzoi Book/ Alfred A. Knopf.

McLachlin, D. H., and J. Ayres. 1979. *Fieldbook of Pacific Northwest Sea Creatures.* Happy Camp, CA: Naturegraph.

Malins, D. C. 1982. Chemical contaminants and abnormalities in fish and invertebrates from Puget Sound. Rockville, MD: NOAA Tech Memo. OMPA.

Meany, Edmund S. [1901] 1957. *Vancouver's Discovery of Puget Sound.* Portland: Binfords and Mort.

METRO. 1985. Duwamish industrial nonpoint source investigation. Seattle: Municipality of Metropolitan Seattle (METRO).

Miller, Bruce S., and S. F. Borton. 1980. *Geographical Distribution of Puget Sound Fishes.* 3 vols. Seattle: University of Washington Fisheries Research Institute/Washington Sea Grant.

National Geographic Society. 1987. *Field Guide to the Birds of North America.* Wash., D.C.: National Geographic Society.

Osborne, R. W., J. Calambokidis, and E. Dorsey. 1987. *Marine Mammals of Greater Puget Sound: a naturalist's field guide.* Anacortes, WA: Island Publications.

Phillips, Ron. 1984. *Ecology of Eelgrass Beds of the Pacific Northwest.* Slidell, LA: USDI/ Fish & Wildlife Service.

Puckett, James, R. Dodds, and L. Crosby. 1985. *License to pollute.* Seattle: Seattle Greenpeace.

PSWQA. 1991. 1991 Puget Sound Water Quality Management Plan. Olympia, WA: Puget Sound Water Quality Authority.

PSWQA. 1991. Puget Sound Update: Second Annual Report of the Puget Sound Ambient Monitoring Program. Olympia, WA: Puget Sound Water Quality Authority.

Scagel, R.F. 1971. *Guide to Common Seaweeds of British Columbia.* Handbook 27. Victoria: British Columbia Provincial Museum.

Simenstad, C. A., K. L. Fresh, & E. O. Salo. 1982. The role of Puget Sound and Washington coastal estuaries in the life history of Pacific salmon. In: *Estuarine Comparisons,* ed. V. S. Kennedy. New York: Academic Press.

Sinclair, W.F. 1988. Controlling Pollution from Canadian Pulp and Paper Manufacturers: A Federal Perspective. Ottawa: Environment Canada.

Smith, Marian W. 1940. *The Puyallup-Nisqually.* Contibutions to Anthropology, 32. New York: Columbia University Press.

Snively, Gloria. 1978. *Exploring the Seashore.* Vancouver: Gordon Soules Book Publ., Ltd.

Somerton, D., and C. Murray. 1976. *Field Guide to the Fish of Puget Sound and the Northwest Coast.* Seattle: Washington Sea Grant Publications.

Stern, Bernhard. 1934. *The Lummi Indians of Northwest Washington.* Contributions to Anthropology, 32. New York: Columbia University Press.

Stewart, Hilary. 1977. *Indian Fishing: Early Methods on the Northwest coast.* Vancouver: Douglas & McIntyre.

Strickland, Richard. 1983. *The Fertile Fjord.* Seattle: University of Washington/ Sea Grant.

Suttles, Wayne. 1951. Economic Life of the Coast Salish of Haro and Rosario Straits. Doctoral thesis, University of Washington.

Thomas, Randy. 1992. *Saving the Strait, Saving Ourselves.* Nanaimo, BC: Save Georgia Strait Alliance.

Thorson, R. M. 1980. Ice-Sheet Glaciation of the Puget Lowland, Washington, during the Vashon Stade (Late Pleistocene). *Quaternary Research,* 13:302-321 (1980).

Wydoski, R. S., and R. R. Whitney. 1979. *Inland Fishes of Washington.* Seattle: University of Washington Press.

Yates, Steve. 1988. *Marine Wildlife of Puget Sound, the San Juans, and Strait of Georgia.* Old Saybrook, CT: Globe Pequot Press.

_____. 1988. *Adopting A Stream: A Northwest Handbook.* Seattle: University of Washington Press.

_____. 1989. *Adopting A Wetland.* Everett, WA: Adopt-A-Stream Foundation.

Index

Savoring Italy

WILLIAMS-SONOMA

Savoring Italy

Recipes and Reflections on Italian Cooking

Recipes and Text
MICHELE SCICOLONE

General Editor
CHUCK WILLIAMS

Recipe Photography
NOEL BARNHURST

Travel Photography
STEVEN ROTHFELD

Illustrations
MARLENE McLOUGHLIN

Oxmoor
House®

SVIZZERA

AUSTRIA

SLOVENIA

FRANCIA

CRO

TRENTINO-
ALTO ADIGE

TRENTO

FRIULI-
VENEZIA
GIULIA

TRIESTE

VALLE D'AOSTA

VARESE

VENETO

VENEZIA

AOSTA

LOMBARDIA

PIEMONTE

MILANO

VERONA

TORINO

EMILIA-ROMAGNA

BOLOGNA

SAN MARINO

GENOVA

LE MARCHE

ANCONA

LIGURIA

FIRENZE

MARE

TOSCANA

PERUGIA

UMBRIA

ABRUZZO

PESCARA

LIGURE

MARA

ELBA

L'AQUILA

MOLISE

CORSE

ROMA

LAZIO

CAMPOBASSO

CAM

NAPOLI

P

MARE

TIRRENO

SARDEGNA

CAGLIARI

MARE MEDITERRANEO

PALERMO

SICI

KM
0   50   100   150   200

0   50   100
MILES

TUNISIA

6°

9°

12°

42°

39°

36°

Contents

14
INTRODUZIONE
the Italian table

22
ANTIPASTI E PANI
antipasti, pizzas, and breads

64
PRIMI
pastas, risotti, and soups

116
SECONDI
fish, poultry, meat, and frittatas

172
CONTORNI
seasonal vegetables and salads

210
DOLCI
cakes, cookies, and fruit desserts

246
GLOSSARIO
basic recipes and ingredient glossary

INTRODUZIONE

The Italian Table

IF A MAGICAN COULD CAPTURE the essence of Italy and place it in a bottle, it would indeed be precious to me. For if my day was dreary, I could uncap it and feel the warmth of the country's golden sunshine, hear the romance of its language and music, and taste the goodness of its wines. Looking into my bottle, I could see the beauty of Italy's ancient ruins, medieval cities, and timeless landscapes contrasted with the contemporary style of its people. But perhaps best of all, if I was hungry, I could draw from my bottle the delicious Italian *cucina,* from a humble slice of good bread rubbed with garlic and drizzled with fruity green Tuscan olive oil to a plate of exquisite egg-rich *tajarin* (tagliatelle) tossed with butter and crowned with shavings of white truffles.

Unfortunately, my magic bottle is only a dream, so when I want to conjure up thoughts of Italy, I do the next best thing. I head for the kitchen and start to plan an Italian meal. So much of the story of Italy's past and present is captured in its food that, as I pour myself a glass of wine and begin to cook, I imagine I am there.

A great deal has been written about the regional nature of Italian cooking. While modern times have dulled the differences somewhat, regional cuisines remain deeply rooted, and I do not believe they will ever die out completely. Why is it that Italian recipes are not standardized across the country, or that northern Italian cooking is based on butter, meat, and fresh pasta, while

Left: This sienna-toned Tuscan farmhouse sits nestled among the vineyards and gentle hills surrounding the small town of Borgo San Felice. **Above top:** A cheese shop in Bolzano, the Tyrolean capital of Alto Adige. **Above bottom:** A woman sells her greens at a local market in Abruzzo. Forming the "ankle" of the Italian boot, the sparsely populated Abruzzo and Molise harbor some of Italy's last wilderness areas.

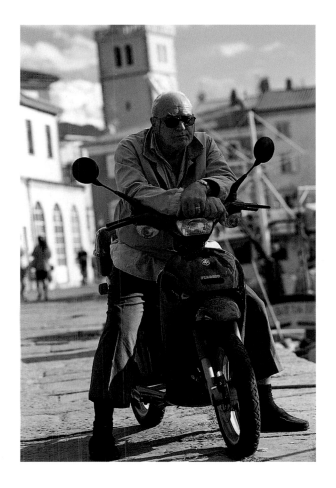

southern cooks rely on olive oil, vegetables, and dried pasta? The reasons for these regional differences and their evolution make sense when you consider Italy's geography and history.

For centuries, the Italian peninsula was divided into numerous city-states, each with its own language, culture, arts, government, laws, and currency. Over the years, invaders had conquered different areas of what is now Italy, eventually establishing settlements. In Sicily, for example, first it was the Greeks, then the Arabs, then later the Normans and the Spaniards. Portions of northern Italy were at various times controlled by the French and the Austrians. Many of these trespassers were eventually absorbed into the local population, introducing new foods, plants, and cooking methods.

Finally, in the 1860s, thanks to the efforts of statesmen like Cavour and Mazzini, the regions were united to form the Republic of Italy. Giuseppe Garibaldi and his troops, under the direction of the King of Savoy, who ruled what is now Piedmont and Sardinia, swept through Italy and garnered support for the unification. Despite the success of their plan, the psychological boundaries dividing the regions lingered. It was easier to change the laws to form a new country than to change people's attitudes toward their neighbors. Many citizens did not welcome unification and remained suspicious of "foreigners" from other parts of the country. Changes came slowly. Transportation, especially in southern Italy, was rudimentary, so products from the north never reached the south, and vice versa. Many people, especially southerners, lived in poverty imposed by a centuries-old feudal system known as the *mezzadria*.

When it came to eating, people had little choice but to rely on foods produced locally. The limited amount of pastureland in southern Italy made it impossible to raise herds of beef cattle, so smaller animals like pigs, sheep, and

goats became staples. The milk of the latter two was used to make cheese. Butter was scarce, so lard rendered from pork fat or oil pressed from the fruits of the olive trees that thrived in the hot, dry terrain was the typical cooking medium. A small plot of carefully tended land was sufficient to raise vegetables like tomatoes, squashes, peppers (capsicums), and eggplants (aubergines) to feed a large family. In the north, dairy cattle thrived on the rich flood plains of the Po River, which meant that veal, beef, milk, butter, and cow's milk cheeses were available and widely used. In both the north and south, foraged greens, wild mushrooms, fish, and game enhanced the menu.

One of the best ways to appreciate these regional differences is to visit local food markets. In large cities, the major *mercati* are usually open daily, except Sundays and holidays, and are centrally located in large warehouse-type buildings or in a series of outdoor stalls that wind through the streets. In small towns and villages, the market is often a weekly event, with vendors setting up portable carts or

Left: Sicily's Romanesque architecture, characterized by rich colors, patterns, and traditional Islamic motifs, rose during the rule of the Normans, who hired local Arab craftsmen, Greek mosaicists, and French sculptors to construct their monumental buildings. **Right:** A gentleman astride his Piaggo *motocicletta* observes fishermen at work in the Adriatic port of Muggia.

Above top: Italians love to linger at the table, enjoying laughter and conversation over an afternoon *aperitivo*.
Above bottom: The Leaning Tower of Pisa, which started to tilt even before its completion in 1274, has attracted visitors for centuries, among them Galileo, who conducted his experiments on the velocity of falling objects from the top of the tipping *torre*. **Right:** Portofino, the most exclusive of the Italian Riviera towns, is filled with elegant shops and yachts. Indeed, boats are a convenient way to reach the village, which does not permit cars to enter its narrow streets.

wooden stalls. Some of the more modern stands are specially equipped vans complete with awnings and refrigeration. Every market has its own character, and although they all sell standard items like celery and carrots, garlic and onions, packaged biscuits and dried beans, you can learn a great deal about the local food and what is in season.

One of my favorites is the sprawling San Lorenzo market in Florence. I came upon it quite by accident on an early trip to that city. It was a chilly day in spring, and I was feeling saturated after a morning of looking at the magnificent artworks housed in the Uffizi galleries. Headed vaguely in the direction of my *pensione*, I found myself in a swirl of housewives bound for the market. Inside the enormous space, I picked a likely looking produce stand and stood nearby, listening and watching as people came and went and negotiated with the vendors. Since I did not have access to a kitchen, I bought only those things that didn't need preparation, but were new to me: a slice of local pecorino cheese; a few *nespole,* a delicious fruit I later learned is called loquat in English; and some *tarocchi,* or blood oranges. I had heard of the exotic citrus with dark red

pulp and juice, but up to that point had never tasted one.

I discovered that visiting markets such as San Lorenzo, the sprawling street market in Bologna, or the bountiful outdoor market near the Rialto Bridge in Venice provided an opportunity to learn about local foods. At the Rialto, for example, many varieties of seafood are sold that are found only in the Venice area and are an important part of the local cooking. I counted at least five kinds of clams, two kinds of scallops, and three types of crabs, plus a variety of shrimp (prawns), sea snails, and fin fish.

Markets are also excellent places to get cooking advice, recipes, or even tips on good restaurants. A few rudimentary words of Italian will generally yield a wealth of suggestions from a friendly vendor or other customers.

In Italy, one thing always seems to have a way of leading to another. At the market in Florence some years ago, I spoke with a man selling fresh herbs and salad greens. He recommended a suburban restaurant that he supplied, an establishment owned by his cousin. The next day, I enjoyed a fine meal there and chatted with the *padrona*. When I complimented her on the olive oil she served, she offered to introduce me to the oil's producer, a friend of hers who had a farm near Siena. I gladly accepted her invitation, and a few days later went to see him, quickly discovering he also made excellent wines. He proudly showed me around his property, including several apartments that he rented out under the system known as *agriturismo* (agricultural tourism), which allows guests to stay on a working farm and participate in its activities. I promptly booked a charming apartment in an old stone tower.

I spent the next several days watching as he prepared the winery for the coming harvest. His wife let me tag along as she tended the hens and her bountiful vegetable garden. But best of all, she let me help her in the kitchen.

It was there that I learned the secret to good Italian cooking. Guided by the seasons, Italians prefer to use locally produced fresh foods. Their goal is to start with the finest ingredients and showcase them by gently enhancing their flavors. Italian cooks have a gift for making the most of what they have. Even when the range is limited, the variety of flavors they are able to coax from a handful of common ingredients never ceases to amaze me.

To capture the true character of the Italian table even when I am not in Italy, I look for markets in my area that offer imported Italian cheeses, olive oil, and pasta and always avoid out-of-season produce. Since no Italian meal would be complete without wine, even if it is just a simple glass or two of *vino da tavola*, I select a bottle with origins similar to the food I am serving. I think regionally, so if my menu is Tuscan, I might choose a Chianti or Brunello di Montalcino. In contrast, a southern menu will prompt me to pour a voluptuous Aglianico del Vulture from Basilicata or a crisp Sicilian white.

By cooking and sharing an Italian meal with family and friends, I am transported to Italy and have no need for a magic potion. I invite you to join me on that culinary journey.

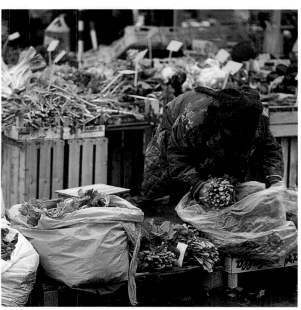

Left top: The Pantheon is considered the most extraordinary and best-preserved building in Rome. Its vast dome, its radius equal to its height, exemplifies the harmonious proportions of the structure. **Left bottom:** Rome, the Eternal City, houses ancient treasures—temples, paintings, and statues—from every architectural age and artistic era. **Above top:** Venice's Grand Canal is the longest waterway in the city, and visitors who travel its length in a *vaporetto* are treated to magical views. **Above bottom:** At a Tuscan *mercato*, a vendor pulls greens from bags and arranges them in a display to attract passing shoppers.

ANTIPASTI E PANI

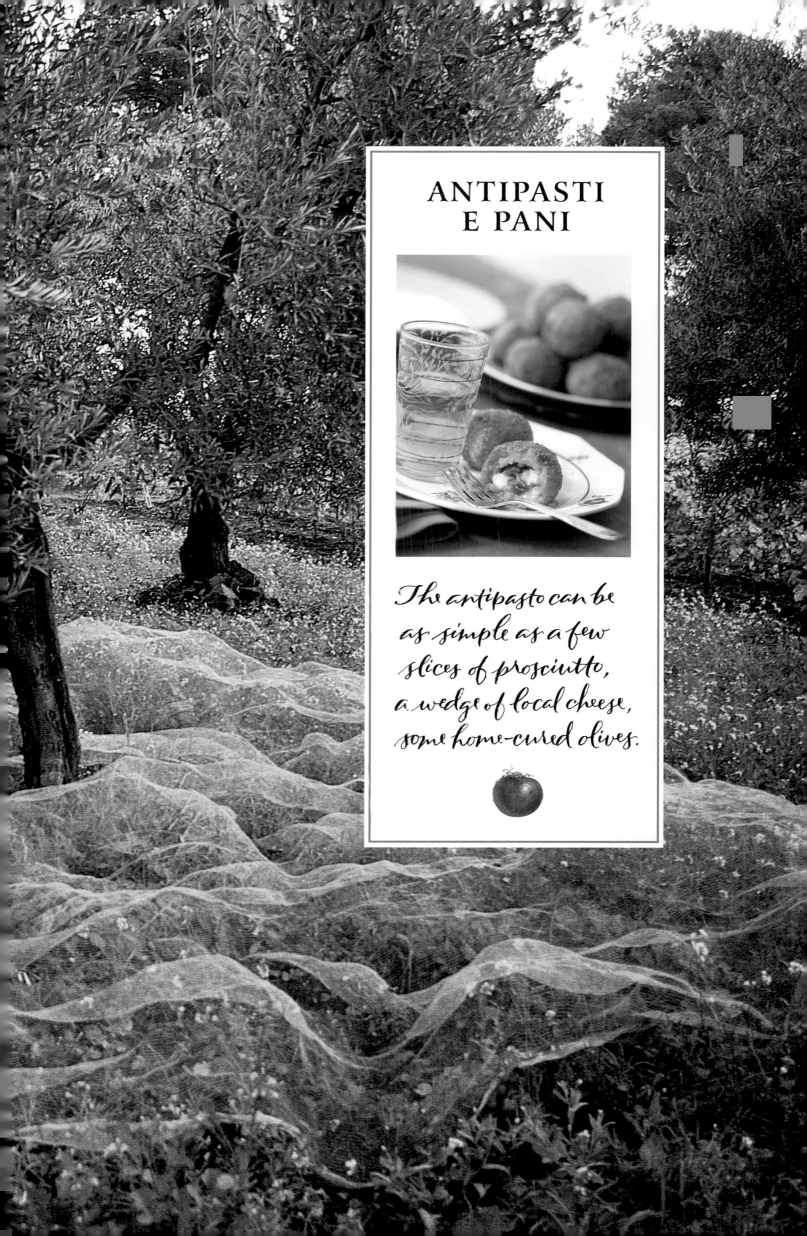

The antipasto can be as simple as a few slices of prosciutto, a wedge of local cheese, some home-cured olives.

MANY YEARS HAVE PASSED, but I can still remember the first time I saw a classic Italian antipasto table. It was in a little trattoria in Rome, and my husband and I arrived just as the cook was arranging her display of the freshly cooked salads and vegetables that were available for that day's lunch. We stopped to admire the selection and were amazed at the bounty of choices: tomatoes stuffed with herbed rice, a frittata laced with cheese and greens and baked golden brown, a salad of lemony seafood and crunchy celery, white anchovy fillets marinated with vinegar and garlic, salami of various types and sizes, a whole leg of prosciutto on a special stand, a bowl of fresh mozzarella balls, and an enormous wedge of Parmigiano-Reggiano.

We considered our options, but finally let our helpful host choose for us. As a result we sampled a little of everything. I have no doubt the rest of the meal was delicious, but I will always remember the details of the antipasto table, its appearance so alluring that it seemed to pull us right into the restaurant.

Not every Italian meal begins with an antipasto—literally, "before the meal"—although most restaurant meals do. In Italian homes, the antipasto can be as simple as a few slices of prosciutto, dried salami or other cured meat, a wedge of local cheese, or some home-cured olives. Vegetable, seafood, and grain salads are popular, as are *crostini,* made either with toasted bread or grilled sliced polenta and various toppings. Stuffed vegetables are frequently served, and mushrooms turn up in every imaginable form.

The character of the antipasto changes as you travel from one region to another and pass from one season to the next. Piedmont, in northwestern Italy, is arguably the capital of antipasto. Meals may begin with as many as a dozen different small tastes, and I have been told of banquets and special occasions where far more are served. Thin shavings of *tartufi bianchi,* the coveted, highly aromatic, and pricey white truffles for which the region is renowned, are sometimes used to top the local antipasti. Typical Piedmontese dishes are *carne cruda,* lean, tender veal chopped and mixed with garlic, oil, and lemon; *bagna cauda,* literally a "hot bath" of anchovies, garlic, butter, and olive oil served as a dip for cardoons, peppers (capsicums), celery, and other vegetables; and *salame de la duja,* a soft pork sausage preserved in a covering of lard. Another favorite is *fonduta,* a creamy blend of Fontina and eggs. When you arrive at the table, you may also find long, crisp *grissini* (bread sticks) laid across the center. They are the most typical bread of the region and are thicker, crispier, and tastier than the packaged *grissini* found elsewhere in Italy.

To the south of Piedmont, Ligurians favor antipasti from the garden. Dishes made with mushrooms or stuffed vegetables predominate, but you will also be served marinated anchovies and a vast variety of *focacce* and savory *torte.* The *torta pasqualina,* typically made at Easter, consists of thirty-three layers of pastry, one for each year of Christ's life, alternating with eggs, cheeses, and all kinds of spring vegetables. Focaccia is served at every meal, topped with olive oil, herbs, onions, or other flavorings. A famous version from the town of Recco bakes soft stracchino cheese between two paper-thin layers of dough.

Whenever I order an antipasto in Tuscany, I always ask for *finocchiona,* a salami made from

Preceding spread: Olive pickers spread nets below the trees, then, from atop ladders, carefully loosen the ripened fruits from the branches with simple handheld rakes. **Left:** In an ideal marriage of form and function, three sundials decorate the façade of the Palazzo del Governatore on Piazza Garibaldi in Parma. **Right top:** On a sunny afternoon in Parma, an espresso taken at an outdoor *caffè* with a ringside view of this elegant city's lively street life is a favorite pastime of locals and visitors alike. **Right middle:** Padua has long enjoyed a reputation as a major cultural center, warmly welcoming artists such as Petrach and Giotto. Its bakers are artisans as well, as evidenced by their hand-shaped loaves of freshly baked bread. **Right bottom:** Tuscans are reputed to have an exquisite eye for composition and color, apparent in even the simplest aspects of everyday life, like these vibrant hydrangeas framed in an archway.

ground pork seasoned with fennel seeds. My Tuscan friends advise me that it is best in the wintertime, but I enjoy it whenever I can get it. It is common to serve a few slices alongside *crostini di milze,* toasted bread spread with a pâté made of spleen. The simplest Tuscan antipasto, however, is *fettunta,* literally "oiled slice," a thick cut of unsalted Tuscan bread toasted and rubbed with a garlic clove, then drizzled with a thread of extra-virgin olive oil and sprinkled with coarse salt.

Versions of *fettunta* exist in many regions of Italy, all made with local bread and olive oil. In Rome, for example, it can come in the form of toasted garlic bread smeared with thick, fruity oil and accompanied with small chunks of grana, a hard cheese similar to Parmigiano-Reggiano, although lacking its distinguished pedigree.

In the Marches, *olive all'ascolana,* large pitted green olives stuffed with ground meat and seasonings, coated with bread crumbs, and deep-fried, are a favorite antipasto, the flavorful, fleshy local olive ensuring their fame. Farther south, the antipasti begin to focus more on

Above top: In the spring, brightly colored flowers dot the mountain ranges of Sicily's interior. **Above middle:** Girolamo Savonarola, a fanatical monk who ordered the Bonfire of the Vanities in Florence's Piazza della Signoria, was himself burned at the stake in the same square in 1497 by his own disillusioned followers. **Above bottom:** Wedges of Parmigiano-Reggiano cheese stand ready to be consumed. **Right:** Outside a Turin bakery, a woman proudly cradles an armful of *grissini.*

Above top: Modena, birthplace of Luciano Pavarotti and Enzo Ferrari, is also famous for delicacies such as *zampone* (stuffed pig's trotter), balsamic vinegar, and Lambrusco wine, all easily purchased at a *salumeria.* **Above bottom:** Aromatic and leafy basil, the basis of Liguria's celebrated pesto, also contributes its distinctive flavor to many other Italian preparations, especially those containing tomatoes, seafood, and poultry.

seafood. Grilled shrimp (prawns), stuffed clams, mussels steamed in white wine, seafood salads made with octopus, calamari, and shrimp: these are just a few of the dishes I have sampled in Campania, Calabria, and Apulia.

These regions offer excellent vegetables, too, either fried, stuffed, or in salads. Eggplants (aubergines) are marinated raw, or dusted with crumbs and fried, or layered in a gratin with tomatoes and cheese. Roasted pepper salad is often served with anchovies or sharp pro-volone. Fresh mozzarella, particularly the extra-fine *mozzarella di bufala,* is served Capri style, with slices of ripe tomatoes, basil, and olive oil, or baked on pizza. Indeed, pizza, the ultimate snack food, is a common antipasto in Neapolitan restaurants.

The breads of southern Italy, invariably the perfect complements to myriad antipasti, are among my favorites. I love the enormous golden Neapolitan loaves with their crisp, crackling crust. Apulian breads, especially those made in the town of Altamura, are appreciated all over Italy, where they are known as *pani pugliesi.* In addition to the big, crusty, chewy disks typical of Altamura, Apulians bake other distinctive breads, including delicious focaccia flavored with tomatoes, and *taralli,* hard, round rings made in all sizes. The larger versions are often split horizontally and used as a base for chopped tomato salads or seafood stews.

The most famous Sicilian antipasto is *caponata,* an addictive sweet-and-sour combination of eggplants, onions, and tomatoes flavored with sugar and vinegar. Some cooks add raisins and pine nuts, others add chocolate (a Spanish contribution), and still others add peppers. There is also an artichoke *caponata,* and one made with seafood.

A number of foods that at one time were sold as snacks in *friggitorie* (fry shops) or *focacerie* are now served as antipasti. At the home of Sicilian friends, I was served chilled Sicilian spumante, a crisp, dry sparkling wine made in the champagne method, with *panelle,* fried wafers fashioned from chickpea (garbanzo bean) flour. But in a *friggitoria* or *focacceria,* you can still get *panelle* sandwiches layered with ricotta and grated pecorino, served on a crusty roll; with anchovies, two or three different cheeses, and bread crumbs; or with tomatoes and a dusting of oregano.

The breads in Sicily are a creamy yellow from semolina flour and are sometimes shaped to resemble birds, braids, or other objects. Sesame seeds, a legacy of the Arabs who ruled the island for several hundred years, are often sprinkled on top before baking. Sicilians also make delicious thick-crust pizzas called *sfincioni,* topped with onions, anchovies, and olives. These same shops also typically carry *arancine* (fried stuffed rice balls, recipe page 38) as well as various vegetables—cauliflower, squash blossoms, eggplant—that have been dipped in batter and deep-fried, all snacks that commonly double as antipasti.

I have included pizzas in this chapter not because they are exclusively antipasti, but because they are sometimes served as such. Breads and bread sticks traditionally appear on the Italian table at the beginning of the meal, and in the case of many antipasti are also essential ingredients. The best hosts routinely replenish the supply throughout the repast.

Below top: Eggplant (aubergine) is familiar fare on the tables of southern Italy, where it is eaten marinated, fried, or baked as an antipasto or with pasta as a *primo.* **Below bottom:** A *salumiere* in Alba admires a white truffle, *tartufo bianco,* one of the world's rarest, most prized, and most expensive delicacies.

Toscana

Insalata di Fagioli con Tonno e Radicchio

warm bean salad with tuna and radicchio

Radicchio is arguably the most prestigious member of the chicory family, a large group of leafy greens that grows wild throughout Italy. About a hundred years ago, gardeners in the Veneto began to cultivate wild radicchio in a manner similar to that used to grow Belgian endive. The method is a complicated one that involves sprouting the seeds, then growing them in a carefully controlled environment. Now there are many types of radicchio available, both red and green. Most red radicchio, radicchio rosso, is cultivated in the Veneto, which specializes in several varieties. Indeed, the towns of Castelfranco, Chioggia, Treviso, and Verona each boasts its own distinct type. All of them are crisp and bittersweet and can be eaten raw in salads or cooked in a frying pan, on a grill, or in the oven. Red radicchio grows in heads with leaves that range from creamy to greenish white near the base to wine red at the tips. The Treviso variety has elongated leaves, while the other types are more or less round.

Here, smooth, creamy traditionally Tuscan beans are a perfect complement to the slightly bitter flavor of grilled radicchio. If you don't have the time to cook the beans, 3 cups (18 oz/560 g) canned may be substituted. Rinse the beans and warm them gently over medium-low heat before using.

BEANS

1 rounded cup (8 oz/250 g) dried cannellini or borlotti beans

2 tablespoons extra-virgin olive oil

1 or 2 cloves garlic

1 fresh sage sprig

salt to taste

2 small heads radicchio

extra-virgin olive oil for brushing, plus 2 tablespoons

salt and freshly ground pepper to taste

1 cup (5 oz/155 g) chopped celery, including some of the leaves

½ small red (Spanish) onion, chopped

pinch of dried oregano

1–2 tablespoons fresh lemon juice

1 can (7 oz/220 g) tuna in olive oil, drained and separated into chunks

To prepare the beans, pick over the beans and discard any misshapen beans or stones. Rinse the beans under cold running water and drain. Place in a large bowl with cold water to cover and let soak for at least 4 hours at room temperature, or as long as overnight in the refrigerator.

Drain the beans and place them in a large saucepan with fresh water to cover by about 1 inch (2.5 cm). Bring to a simmer over high heat. Add the olive oil, garlic, and sage sprig. Cover, reduce the heat to low, and simmer until the beans are tender but not falling apart, about 1 hour. Once cooked, season the beans with salt. Remove from the heat and let stand for 10 minutes.

Preheat a broiler (griller), or prepare a fire in a charcoal grill.

Cut each radicchio into 4–6 wedges through the core, so that the wedges will keep their shape. Brush with olive oil and sprinkle with salt and pepper. Broil or grill the radicchio, turning once, until wilted and lightly browned, about 5 minutes total.

Meanwhile, drain off the excess liquid from the beans. Add the celery, onion, oregano, the 2 tablespoons olive oil, 1 tablespoon lemon juice, salt, and pepper. Toss well. Taste and adjust the seasonings with more lemon juice, salt, and pepper.

Arrange the radicchio wedges on a platter. Pile the warm beans in the center and top with the tuna. Serve immediately.

serves 4–6

The Tuscans have created hundreds of recipes for beans, a culinary archive that has earned them the nickname i mangiafagioli— "the bean eaters".

Il Pane

Fresh bread, *pane*, appears on the table at every Italian meal, a venerable symbol of sustenance and prosperity. It is always served alone, without butter or olive oil, and leftovers are rarely wasted. Instead they are made into crumbs for stuffings or a pasta topping, or sliced and toasted for *crostini* (croutons) for soups or salads.

Every region has its own unique breads, and religious feasts and holidays are often celebrated with special loaves. In Sicily, for example, intricately shaped *pani* are baked for St. Joseph's Day. Some, fashioned into birds or flowers, are used for decorations. Others, like the *bastone di San Giuseppe,* a long, twisted loaf thought to resemble the saint's walking staff, are blessed by the village priest and eaten by everyone. Tuscans bake *pani coi santi* for All Saints' Day on November 1. Traditionally eaten for breakfast or snacks, they are made from a basic yeast dough to which is added sugar, raisins, walnuts, and black pepper.

Toscana

Bruschetta di Pomodori

fresh tomato toasts

Bruschetta *can be made with different toppings, the simplest being a rub of garlic and a drizzle of extra-virgin olive oil. This version, which demands summertime's finest vine-ripened tomatoes, is one of the best. A bit of balsamic vinegar brings out the sweetness of the tomatoes. You can also add some chopped garlic, if you like. A thin slice of ricotta salata laid on top of the tomatoes is a nice addition and can turn this antipasto into a light lunch.*

2 tomatoes, chopped

6 fresh basil leaves, torn into small pieces

¼ cup (2 fl oz / 60 ml) extra-virgin olive oil

1 teaspoon balsamic vinegar

coarse salt to taste

8 slices coarse country bread, each about ½ inch (12 mm) thick

2 large cloves garlic

❦ Preheat a broiler (griller), or prepare a fire in a charcoal grill.

❦ In a bowl, combine the tomatoes, basil, olive oil, vinegar, and salt. Toss well.

❦ Place the bread on a baking sheet or grill rack and broil or grill, turning once, until lightly toasted on both sides, about 2 minutes total. Remove from the broiler or grill and immediately rub one side of each slice with the garlic cloves.

❦ Arrange the grilled bread, garlic side up, on a serving platter and spoon on the tomatoes, dividing evenly. Serve at once.

serves 4

Piemonte

Bagna Cauda

hot anchovy and garlic dip

In Piedmont, eating bagna cauda (sometimes caôda) is a fall and winter ritual, commonly accompanied with a fresh, young Barbera wine. The name means "hot bath," and the dish is so-called because the mixture of garlic and anchovies is traditionally kept warm in a chafing dish or fondue pot. Bagna cauda is served with small pieces of assorted vegetables for dipping and crusty bread to catch the drips. Among the possible vegetables are raw Jerusalem artichokes, cardoons, bell peppers (capsicums), carrots, spinach, green onions, or celery; cooked potatoes; roasted onions or beets; and blanched cauliflower or broccoli. Some cooks prefer to simmer the garlic first in a little milk to tame the flavor. The cloves are then mashed to a paste and mixed with the anchovies, olive oil, and butter.

¾ cup (6 fl oz/180 ml) olive oil

8–10 cloves garlic, very finely chopped

12 anchovy fillets

¼ cup (2 oz/60 g) unsalted butter

about 8 cups (2½ lb/1.25 kg) trimmed, cut-up vegetables (see note)

slices of coarse country bread

☙ In a small saucepan over low heat, combine the olive oil, garlic, and anchovies. Cook, mashing the anchovies with the back of a wooden spoon, until smooth, about 5 minutes. Remove from the heat and stir in the butter.

☙ Pour the mixture into a warmed chafing dish or fondue pot set over a warming candle or spirit lamp. Serve immediately with vegetables for dipping. Pass the bread slices at the table.

serves 6–8

Sicilia

Caponata

sweet-tart eggplant and peppers

In this well-known Sicilian dish, eggplants, peppers, celery, and onions are cooked separately so that they retain their individual character, then simmered together with tomatoes in a sweet-and-sour sauce.

The sweet and sour flavors of the dish reflect its Arabic heritage. Some versions include chopped almonds instead of pine nuts, and in Syracuse the tomatoes are traditionally replaced by chocolate, one New World import standing in for another. Indeed, there are nearly as many different recipes for caponata *as there are Sicilian cooks, with eggplant the only true constant and everything from boiled shrimp to boiled octopus to boiled eggs, from tuna roe to lobster claws, turning up in the mix. Even the name can vary, with the diminutive* caponatina *used as the common moniker in Catania and a number of other places. Finally,* caponata *can be served hot or cold, and as an antipasto or a side dish.*

Caponata *tastes best the day after it is made, once the flavors have had a chance to blend and mellow. It keeps well in the refrigerator, but should be brought to room temperature before serving. Accompany it with crusty sesame-seed-topped Sicilian bread for soaking up the fragrant sauce.*

vegetable oil for frying

2 eggplants (aubergines), about 1 lb (500 g) each, cut into 1-inch (2.5-cm) cubes

2 red or yellow bell peppers (capsicums), seeded and cut into ¾-inch (2-cm) cubes

2 large yellow onions, cut into ¾-inch (2-cm) cubes

3 tender celery stalks, sliced

3 tomatoes, chopped

1 cup (5 oz/155 g) chopped pitted green olives

⅓ cup (2 oz/60 g) raisins

2 tablespoons capers

2 tablespoons sugar

2 tablespoons red wine vinegar

pinch of salt

¼ cup (1 oz/30 g) pine nuts, lightly toasted

☙ In a deep, heavy frying pan, pour in vegetable oil to a depth of ½ inch (12 mm). Place over medium heat and heat until a piece of the eggplant dropped into the pan sizzles and swims around in the oil.

☙ Dry the eggplant well with paper towels. Working in batches, and adding additional vegetable oil to the pan as needed, carefully arrange the eggplant pieces in the pan in a single layer. Cook, stirring occasionally, until the eggplant is tender and browned on all sides, 7–8 minutes. Using a slotted spoon, transfer to paper towels to drain.

☙ When all of the eggplant has been cooked, fry the bell peppers in the same way until tender and lightly browned, 4–6 minutes, then drain on paper towels. Finally, fry the onions and celery together in the same way until tender and golden, 7–8 minutes, and drain on paper towels.

☙ In a large saucepan over low heat, combine the tomatoes, olives, raisins, capers, sugar, and vinegar. Stir well and add the fried vegetables and salt. Cover and cook over low heat, stirring occasionally, until thickened, about 20 minutes. Add a little water if the mixture begins to dry out. Remove from the heat, transfer to a serving dish, and let cool. If time permits, cover and refrigerate overnight to allow the flavors to marry.

☙ Bring to room temperature before serving. Just before serving, sprinkle with the pine nuts.

serves 8–10

Lazio

Insalata di Fave, Rucola, e Pecorino

fava bean, arugula, and pecorino salad

In Italy, this salad is made with a more flavorful pointed-leaved cousin of the arugula commonly found elsewhere. Fresh fava beans are at their best in the spring, when the pods are small and the beans are tender. Romans like to eat them right out of the pods, accompanied with wedges of sharp pecorino romano cheese and Frascati wine. If the beans are small, peeling them may not be necessary. The pecorino romano, one of the best known of Italy's many sheep's milk cheeses, is traditionally made from March through June, primarily in the provinces of Rome, Cagliari, Sassari, Nuoro, Grosseto, Latina, and Viterbo, and is prized for its sharp taste and dense texture.

1 lb (500 g) fava (broad) beans, shelled

3 tablespoons extra-virgin olive oil

2 tablespoons fresh lemon juice

salt and freshly ground pepper to taste

4 cups (4 oz / 125 g) arugula (rocket) leaves

wedge of pecorino romano cheese

⚜ Bring a small saucepan three-fourths full of water to a boil. Add the fava beans, blanch for 1 minute, and drain. Cool under cold running water. Using your fingertips or a small knife, slit the fava bean skins and then gently pinch them to free the beans.

⚜ In a large bowl, whisk together the olive oil, lemon juice, salt, and pepper. Add the arugula and fava beans and toss to coat evenly. Taste and adjust the seasonings.

⚜ Divide the salad among 4 individual plates. Using a vegetable peeler, shave thin curls of the cheese over the salads. Serve immediately.

serves 4

Emilia-Romagna

Insalata di Funghi e Parmigiano

mushroom and parmesan salad

On hot summer days, restaurants in Bologna serve this refreshing salad. The mushrooms of choice are the rare and costly white ovoli, so-called because of their egg shape. Ordinary white mushrooms can be substituted with good results. Be sure to cut all the vegetables into very thin slices. A mandoline or food processor is useful for this step.

½ cup (4 fl oz / 125 ml) extra-virgin olive oil

1 tablespoon fresh lemon juice

1 tablespoon balsamic vinegar

salt and freshly ground pepper to taste

½ lb (250 g) fresh ovoli or firm white button mushrooms, brushed clean and sliced paper-thin

2 tender celery stalks, sliced paper-thin

1 carrot, peeled and sliced paper-thin

wedge of Parmigiano-Reggiano cheese

⚜ In a bowl large enough to accommodate all the ingredients, whisk together the olive oil, lemon juice, vinegar, salt, and pepper.

⚜ Add the mushrooms, celery, and carrot. Transfer the salad to a serving platter.

⚜ Using a vegetable peeler, shave thin curls of the cheese over the top. Taste and adjust the seasonings. Serve immediately.

serves 4

The character of the antipasto course changes as you travel from one region to another and pass from one season to the next.

Sicilia

Arancine

fried stuffed rice balls

*T*hese savory little rice balls are known as arancine, or "little oranges," due to their golden crust, which gives them the appearance of their namesakes. The classic filling is a rich meat and tomato sauce with peas—although stuffing them with various types of cheese, with cheese and prosciutto, or with chopped vegetables in a white or cheese sauce, is also popular. Similar to the Roman supplì al telefono, arancine are served as snack food in bars and caffès all over Sicily. They can be assembled up to an hour in advance and fried at the last minute, or they can be fried and kept warm in a slow oven for up to an hour.

2½ cups (20 fl oz/625 ml) chicken stock

pinch of saffron threads, crumbled

1 cup (7 oz/220 g) medium-grain white rice such as Arborio

1 tablespoon unsalted butter

salt to taste

½ cup (2 oz/60 g) grated Parmigiano-Reggiano cheese

1 whole egg, plus 1 egg yolk

1 cup (5 oz/155 g) all-purpose (plain) flour

2 cups (8 oz/250 g) fine dried bread crumbs

3 egg whites

2 oz (60 g) prosciutto, chopped

2 oz (60 g) fresh mozzarella cheese, chopped

vegetable or light olive oil for deep-frying

❧ In a saucepan over high heat, combine the stock and saffron and bring to a boil. Stir in the rice, butter, and salt. Cover, reduce the heat to low, and cook until tender, 18–20 minutes.

❧ Transfer the rice to a bowl and stir in the cheese. Let cool slightly, then stir in the whole egg and egg yolk. Let cool completely.

❧ Spread the flour and bread crumbs separately on 2 dinner plates. In a shallow bowl, lightly beat the egg whites.

❧ Moisten your hands with water. Scoop up ¼ cup (1¾ oz/50 g) of the rice mixture and place it in the cupped palm of your hand. Flatten out the mixture slightly and place about one-twelfth of the prosciutto and mozzarella in the center. Mold the rice over the filling, adding a bit more rice if needed to cover it completely. Shape the rice into a ball. Roll the ball in the flour, and then in the egg whites to coat completely. Finally, roll the ball in the bread crumbs. Place on a rack to dry for at least 15 minutes. Continue with the remaining ingredients to make 12 balls. Rinse your hands frequently to prevent the rice from sticking to them.

❧ In a heavy saucepan or deep-fat fryer, pour in enough oil to cover the rice balls by 1 inch (2.5 cm) once they are added. (This much oil is necessary so that the balls cook evenly and do not burst.) Heat the oil to 375°F (190°C) on a deep-frying thermometer, or until the oil sizzles when a bit of the egg white is dropped into it. With a slotted spoon or wire skimmer, gently lower a few of the rice balls into the pan; do not crowd the pan. Fry until golden brown and crisp all over, about 2 minutes. Using a slotted spoon, transfer to paper towels to drain. Keep warm while you fry the remaining balls in the same way.

❧ Arrange the *arancine* on a warmed platter and serve immediately.

makes 12

Campania

Insalata di Peperoni

roasted pepper salad

Campania's plains and hillsides are regarded as some of the country's best areas for growing fruits and vegetables. Much of the soil is volcanic, courtesy of the region's still-active Mount Vesuvius, and even the ancient Romans envied the bountiful crops of their neighbors to the south, where the contadini enjoyed a year-round growing season. Here, Campania's sweet peppers balance the saltiness of anchovies. Serve the salad with bread for soaking up the delicious juices.

6 large red, yellow, or green bell peppers (capsicums), or a mixture

¼ cup (2 fl oz/60 ml) extra-virgin olive oil

6 large fresh basil leaves, torn into small pieces

2 cloves garlic, halved

2 tablespoons capers

salt and freshly ground pepper to taste

12 anchovy fillets

☙ Preheat a broiler (griller). Place the bell peppers on a broiler pan and slip under the heat. Broil (grill), turning as needed, until the skins are evenly blistered and lightly charred; do not allow the flesh to burn. Transfer to a bowl, cover with plastic wrap or aluminum foil, and let cool.

☙ Working with 1 pepper at a time and holding it over a sieve placed over a bowl to catch the juices, remove the stem, seeds, and ribs, then peel away the charred skin. Cut or tear the peppers into long strips ½ inch (12 mm) wide.

☙ Add the cut peppers to the bowl of captured juices along with the olive oil, basil, garlic, capers, salt, and pepper. Cover and refrigerate for at least 1 hour or for as long as overnight. (If left to chill overnight, the oil and juices will solidify. Let stand at room temperature for about 30 minutes to liquefy slightly before continuing.)

☙ Place half the peppers into a serving dish. Layer the anchovy fillets on top. Arrange the remaining peppers over the anchovies. Serve immediately.

serves 6

Campania

Vongole Ripiene

stuffed clams

While visiting the tiny island of Procida, off the coast of Naples, my husband and I asked a local woman which of the nearby restaurants she recommended. She looked at us blankly for a moment before replying that she had no recommendation. She never ate out. We took our chances on a little port-side establishment where we had seen a fisherman deliver a basketful of just-caught fish and shellfish. Our instincts were right, and we were rewarded with a heaping platter of fresh clams dusted with a crunchy crumb topping. This is my approximation of that recipe.

36 hard-shell clams, well scrubbed

⅓ cup (1½ oz/45 g) fine dried bread crumbs, preferably homemade from coarse country bread

3 tablespoons grated Parmigiano-Reggiano or pecorino romano cheese

3 tablespoons chopped fresh flat-leaf (Italian) parsley

1 clove garlic, minced

6 tablespoons (3 fl oz/90 ml) olive oil

salt and freshly ground pepper to taste

lemon wedges

♛ Working with one clam at a time, and protecting your hand with a heavy towel, hold the clam in one hand with the hinge facing you. Push a round-tipped knife gently into the crack between the halves of the shell. Once the shell opens slightly, slide the knife around from side to side to separate the halves. Holding the clam over a bowl to catch the juices, scrape the flesh from one shell into the other. Discard the empty shell. Arrange the clams in a shallow baking pan. Strain the juices and pour a little over each clam.

♛ Preheat a broiler (griller). In a bowl, combine the bread crumbs, cheese, parsley, garlic, 3 tablespoons of the olive oil, salt, and pepper. Spoon the crumb mixture onto the clams. Do not pack the crumbs down or they will become soggy. Drizzle evenly with the remaining 3 tablespoons oil.

♛ Broil (grill) until the crumbs are lightly browned, about 4 minutes. Remove from the broiler and immediately arrange on warmed individual plates. Serve with the lemon wedges.

serves 6

Veneto

Pane di Olive e Rosmarino

olive and rosemary bread

Olives are grown all over Italy, with many varieties reserved specifically for pressing into oil and others for eating out of hand. A visit to a market stall specializing in olives will reveal a bounty of different kinds. Not only do they range dramatically in size, but in color as well: green, black, brown, red, or purplish. Some are cured in brine and others are cured in oil, resulting in distinct textures and flavors. Soft, meaty Gaeta olives are popular in the Rome area, while Sicilians are fond of wrinkled oil-cured black olives and large green garlicky ones. A favorite from Apulia is the very large and bright green Bella di Cerignola.

Green and black olives can be used in this bread. Use several varieties or only one, as you prefer. Most olives can be pitted easily. Lay a few at a time on a solid work surface, place the flat side of a large, heavy knife on them, and then smack it with the heel of your hand. The olives will split open and the pit can be quickly removed. This flavorful bread is made with a starter, a mixture of yeast, water, and flour, that gives the loaf an excellent flavor.

2½ teaspoons (1 package) active dry yeast

2 cups (16 fl oz/500 ml) warm water (105°–110°F/43°–46°C)

4 cups (1¼ lb/625 g) unbleached all-purpose (plain) or bread (hard-wheat) flour

1 cup (5 oz/155 g) whole-wheat (wholemeal) flour

1 tablespoon chopped fresh rosemary leaves, or 1 teaspoon dried rosemary

2 teaspoons salt

1½ cups (7½ oz/235 g) mixed olives such as Sicilian green olives, Gaeta, and Niçoise, in any combination, pitted and coarsely chopped

In a bowl, sprinkle the yeast over 1 cup (8 fl oz/250 ml) of the warm water and let stand until creamy, about 5 minutes. Stir until dissolved. Whisk in 1 cup (5 oz/155 g) of the all-purpose or bread flour. Cover this starter with plastic wrap and let stand in a cool place until bubbly and thick, about 1 hour or for as long as overnight.

In a large bowl, using a wooden spoon, stir together the remaining 3 cups (15 oz/470 g) all-purpose or bread flour, the whole-wheat flour, the rosemary, and the salt. Add the starter and the remaining 1 cup (8 fl oz/250 ml) warm water and stir until a soft dough that holds it shape forms, about 2 minutes. Turn out the dough onto a lightly floured work surface and knead until smooth and elastic, about 10 minutes. The dough should be slightly sticky. Form into a smooth ball.

Oil a large bowl, place the dough in it, and turn it once to oil the top. Cover the bowl with a kitchen towel and let rise in a warm, draft-free place until doubled in bulk, 1–1½ hours.

Oil a large baking sheet. Punch down the dough and turn out onto a lightly floured work surface. Cut the dough in half. Using your hands, flatten each half into an oval about 8 by 12 inches (20 by 30 cm). Scatter the olives evenly over them. Working with one piece at a time, tightly roll up each oval to form loaves, each about 12 inches (30 cm) long. Place the loaves several inches (8–12 cm) apart on the prepared baking sheet. Cover with plastic wrap and let rise until doubled in bulk, about 45 minutes.

Preheat an oven to 400°F (200°C).

Using a single-edge razor blade or a serrated knife, make 3 or 4 diagonal slashes ½ inch (12 mm) deep on the surface of each loaf. Bake until golden brown, 40–45 minutes. To test, rap on the bottom of a loaf; you should hear a hollow ring.

Slide the loaves onto a wire rack and let cool before serving. Once cool, the loaves may be wrapped tightly in aluminum foil and frozen for up to 1 month. To thaw, loosen the foil and heat in a 350°F (180°C) oven for 20 minutes. Then unwrap completely and bake for 10–15 minutes longer.

makes 2 loaves

Bread—crusty country loaves, intricately shaped rolls, crisp grissini—appears on the table with the antipasti and is replenished throughout the meal.

ANTIPASTI E PANI 47

Lazio

Fiori di Zucca Fritti

fried stuffed zucchini flowers

*O*ne of the pleasures of summer in Rome is being able
to eat fried stuffed zucchini flowers to my heart's
content. I love the way the cheese and anchovies ooze
out of the thin, crisp fiori. At home, I serve them in
batches just as they come out of the pan, so they don't
get soggy. Use the blossoms as soon as possible after
picking, as they will wilt within a day.

1 cup (5 oz/155 g) all-purpose (plain) flour

1 teaspoon salt

2 eggs

½ cup (4 fl oz/125 ml) cold sparkling mineral
water

1 tablespoon vegetable oil, plus oil for deep-frying

2 oz (60 g) fresh mozzarella cheese

10 anchovy fillets, cut in half crosswise

20 large squash blossoms

꽃 In a small bowl, stir together the flour and salt.
Add the eggs, mineral water, and the 1 tablespoon
vegetable oil and whisk just until blended. Cut the
mozzarella into sticks 1 inch (2.5 cm) long by ¼ inch
(6 mm) wide by ¼ inch (6 mm) thick. Pat the
anchovies dry with paper towels.

꽃 In a heavy frying pan at least 3 inches (7.5 cm)
deep or in a deep-fat fryer, pour in oil to a depth
of 1 inch (2.5 cm). Heat to 375°F (190°C) on
a deep-frying thermometer or until a bit of the batter sizzles when dropped into the oil.

꽃 While the oil is heating, gently spread open the
petals of each flower and carefully pinch out the filaments inside. Insert a piece of the cheese and the
anchovy into each flower. Press the petals closed.

꽃 One at a time, dip the flowers into the batter,
turning to coat completely. Lift out and drain off the
excess. Working with a few at a time, slip the flowers
into the hot oil and fry until golden brown on all
sides, about 4 minutes. Using a slotted spoon, transfer to paper towels to drain. Continue with the
remaining flowers. Serve immediately.

makes 20

Piemonte

Crostini di Polenta con Funghi

grilled polenta with mushrooms

The cooking of the Piedmont is divided into two distinct cuisines, one of the cities and lowlands and one of the higher altitudes. Polenta, well known for its rib-sticking properties, holds a place of honor on the mountain table. Cubes of cooked cornmeal and Fontina cheese—breaded, deep-fried, and skewered together on small sticks—are a favorite antipasto, and polenta grassa—cornmeal and the local Fontina layered in a dish and baked—is a popular primo piatto. *Polenta is also cut into slices and crisped in the broiler or on a grill. Here, the slices are topped with sautéed mushrooms, but other toppings such as sautéed peppers (capsicums), pesto sauce, or Gorgonzola would also be good. In fact, polenta* crostini *can be a wonderful substitute for bread* crostini *in nearly any recipe, especially as a base for stews.*

POLENTA

4 cups (32 fl oz/1 l) water

1 cup (5 oz/150 g) polenta (coarse yellow cornmeal)

1 teaspoon salt

3 tablespoons unsalted butter

1 tablespoon olive oil, plus more as needed

1 clove garlic, finely chopped

¾ lb (375 g) fresh white mushrooms, brushed clean and halved or quartered if large

1 teaspoon chopped fresh thyme or rosemary

salt and freshly ground pepper to taste

1 tomato, chopped

1 tablespoon chopped fresh flat-leaf (Italian) parsley, plus extra for garnish

❧ To make the polenta, bring the water to a boil in a large saucepan. Add the polenta in a slow, steady stream, whisking constantly to prevent lumps from forming. Add the salt. Reduce the heat to low and cook, stirring frequently, until the polenta thickens and begins to pull away from the sides of the pan, 30–40 minutes.

❧ Meanwhile, oil a 12-by-9-inch (30-by-23-cm) baking pan.

❧ When the polenta is ready, pour it into the prepared pan, spreading it evenly with a spatula dipped in cold water. Let the polenta cool at room temperature until firm, about 1 hour, or cover with plastic wrap, place in the refrigerator, and chill overnight.

❧ In a large frying pan over medium heat, melt the butter with the 1 tablespoon olive oil. Add the garlic and cook, stirring, until lightly golden, about 30 seconds. Stir in the mushrooms, thyme or rosemary, salt, and pepper. Cook, stirring frequently, until the mushrooms are browned, about 10 minutes.

❧ Add the tomato and cook until the juices have evaporated, about 10 minutes more. Stir in the 1 tablespoon parsley and remove from the heat. Cover and keep warm.

❧ Preheat a broiler (griller).

❧ Cut the polenta into 8 pieces and brush on both sides with olive oil. Arrange on a heavy baking sheet.

❧ Broil (grill) 4 inches (10 cm) from the heat source, turning once, until crisp and golden on both sides, about 3 minutes on each side.

❧ Place 2 polenta *crostini* on each plate. Top with the mushroom mixture, dividing evenly, and sprinkle with parsley. Serve hot.

serves 4

Sicilia

Panelle

chickpea fritters

I remember eating these crisp-edged fritters, accompanied with glasses of chilled Chardonnay, at the home of Anna Tosca Lanza, whose family owns the Regaleali wine estate in central Sicily. In Palermo, panelle are sometimes tucked into sandwich rolls with fresh ricotta cheese for a quick lunch.

3½ cups (28 fl oz / 875 ml) water

2 cups (8 oz / 250 g) Italian chickpea (garbanzo bean) flour

2 teaspoons salt, plus salt to taste

freshly ground pepper to taste

vegetable oil for frying

❀ Line two 15-by-10-by-1-inch (38-by-25-by-2.5-cm) jelly-roll (Swiss-roll) pans with plastic wrap.

❀ Pour the water into a saucepan, then slowly whisk in the chickpea flour, a little at a time, to prevent lumps from forming. Whisk in the 2 teaspoons salt and the pepper. Place over medium-low heat and bring to a simmer, stirring constantly. Reduce the heat to low and cook, stirring, until the mixture is very thick, about 5 minutes.

❀ Pour the batter into the prepared pans, dividing evenly. With a rubber spatula dipped in water, quickly spread to a thickness of about ¼ inch (6 mm). Let cool completely to set the mixture. (The recipe can be prepared up to this point, covered, and refrigerated for up to 1 day before continuing.)

❀ Using a knife, cut the cooled sheets into 3-by-2-inch (7.5-by-5-cm) strips, then peel the strips off the plastic wrap. In a large, deep frying pan, pour in vegetable oil to a depth of ½ inch (12 mm). Place over medium heat and heat until the oil sizzles when a small piece of a strip is dropped into it. Carefully lower a few of the strips into the hot oil; do not crowd the pan. Fry, turning once, until golden brown and slightly puffed, 3–4 minutes. Using a slotted spoon, transfer to paper towels to drain. Keep warm while you fry the remaining pieces.

❀ Arrange the fritters on a warmed platter, season with salt, and serve immediately.

serves 8–10

Toscana

Gamberi in Salsa Verde

shrimp in green sauce

Viareggio is one of several towns along the Tuscan coast popular with Italian vacationers. Row after row of identical bathing establishments line the sandy beaches, the brilliant colors of their umbrellas and beach chairs the only way to tell one from the other. Viareggio became a resort around the middle of the nineteenth century, and its Belle Epoque buildings lend the community an elegant atmosphere. There's a large park on each side of town filled with palm trees, tamarisks, and oleanders, and both destinations are popular with families taking their evening passegiata, or predinner stroll.

It was in one of the town's many seafood restaurants that my husband and I ate shrimp prepared this way. If tomatoes are not at their peak of ripeness, serve the shellfish in cups of radicchio leaves.

GREEN SAUCE

½ cup (¾ oz / 20 g) finely chopped flat-leaf (Italian) parsley

¼ cup (1½ oz / 45 g) finely minced yellow onion

2 tablespoons capers, chopped

2 anchovy fillets, chopped

½ cup (4 fl oz / 125 ml) extra-virgin olive oil

2 tablespoons fresh lemon juice

½ teaspoon grated lemon zest

salt to taste

1 lb (500 g) shrimp (prawns), peeled and deveined

4 tomatoes, sliced crosswise

lemon wedges

❀ To make the green sauce, on a cutting board, chop together the parsley, onion, capers, and anchovies until very fine. Transfer to a bowl. Whisk in the olive oil, lemon juice and zest, and salt.

❀ Bring a saucepan three-fourths full of water to a boil. Add salt and the shrimp and cook just until they turn bright pink, about 2 minutes. Drain.

❀ Arrange the tomato slices, slightly overlapping, on a large platter. Place the warm shrimp on top. Drizzle with some of the sauce and garnish with lemon wedges. Pass the remaining sauce at the table.

serves 6

Panzanella

bread and summer vegetable salad

Much of the success of this recipe, which some cooks identify as a soup rather than a salad, depends on the bread—it should be chewy and quite firm. The Tuscans, of course, use their beloved unsalted bread, known as pane sciocco, *meaning insipid. This bland bread takes some getting used to for the outsider, and it is made in no other region. Some observers attribute its origin to the traditionally frugal Tuscans who wanted to avoid paying the high government salt taxes. Others insist that it was born out of the need for a plain loaf to pair with the often salty and spicy dishes of the area.*

The salad can be made several hours ahead of time, but it is at its best when no more than a couple of hours old. You can vary the flavors by adding arugula (rocket) or capers.

2 tomatoes, cut into bite-sized pieces

1 small cucumber, peeled and sliced

1 small red (Spanish) onion, thinly sliced

1 cup (1 oz/30 g) fresh basil leaves, torn into small pieces, plus whole leaves for garnish

½ cup (4 fl oz/125 ml) extra-virgin olive oil, or as needed

3 tablespoons red wine vinegar, or to taste

salt and freshly ground pepper to taste

6–8 slices coarse country bread

❦ In a bowl, combine the tomatoes, cucumber, onion, and torn basil. Drizzle with ½ cup (4 fl oz/125 ml) olive oil and 3 tablespoons vinegar and season with salt and pepper. Toss well to coat evenly.

❦ Cut or tear the bread into bite-sized pieces. Place half the bread in a wide, shallow bowl. Spoon on half of the vegetables. Layer the remaining bread on top and then the remaining vegetables. Cover and refrigerate for 1 hour.

❦ Toss the salad, then taste and adjust the seasonings. If the bread is dry, add a little more oil or vinegar. Garnish with a few basil leaves. Serve immediately.

serves 6

Veneto

Pizza di Cipolle, Prosciutto, e Mozzarella

pizza with onion, prosciutto, and mozzarella

At a lively pizzeria near Piazza Bra in Verona, I ate a wonderful crisp pizza crust topped with this inspired combination. Since it is made without tomatoes, it's considered a pizza bianca, *or "white pizza." If you like, scatter a handful of arugula (rocket) leaves on top of the hot pizza as it emerges from the oven.*

pizza dough (page 58)

1 red (Spanish) onion, thinly sliced

2 tablespoons olive oil

salt to taste

¼ lb (125 g) mozzarella cheese, preferably fresh, thinly sliced

2 or 3 thin prosciutto slices

❦ Prepare the pizza dough as directed on page 58 through setting it aside for the second rising. Place a pizza stone, unglazed quarry tiles, or a baking sheet on the lowest rack of an oven and preheat the oven to its hottest setting (500° or 550°F/260° or 290°C) 30–60 minutes before baking.

❦ Meanwhile, in a frying pan over medium heat, sauté the onion in the olive oil until tender and golden, about 5 minutes. Sprinkle lightly with salt and remove from the heat. Set aside to cool.

❦ Uncover the dough and, using your fingers, stretch and flatten it into a 12-inch (30-cm) round, turning the round over once or twice as you work. Dust a baker's peel or the back of a baking sheet with flour. Place the dough round on the peel and shake the peel once or twice to be sure the dough isn't sticking. If it is, lift the round and dust the peel or baking sheet with more flour.

❦ Spread the onion on the dough. Immediately slide the pizza onto the baking stone. Bake for 3–4 minutes. Remove from the oven and arrange the mozzarella on top. Bake until the edges are puffed and the crust is crisp and golden brown, 4–5 minutes longer. Remove from the oven and arrange the prosciutto slices on top. Transfer the pizza to a cutting board. Cut into wedges to serve.

makes one 12-inch (30-cm) pizza; serves 2–4

La Vera Pizza Napoletana

Although pizza is available in nearly every corner of the world, nowhere does it achieve the status bestowed upon it in Naples, where the modern pie was born. A few years ago, Neapolitan pizza makers, alarmed at what they saw as the degradation of their culinary art, established *La Vera Pizza Napoletana,* an organization dedicated to defining and defending genuine Neapolitan pizza.

The classic pizza is a subtle masterpiece—a no-frills pie that showcases only a handful of the best ingredients. It is thin crusted, but never too thin, crisp and chewy at the same time. Crushed vine-ripened tomatoes, fresh mozzarella, a thread of fruity green olive oil, and a leaf or two of fresh basil crown the popular *Margherita,* named for a beloved queen. *Pizza marinara,* yet another traditional pie, is topped with nothing more than tomatoes, garlic, oregano, and olive oil. Both respect the legacy of simplicity that separates the true Neapolitan pie from its gaudy competitors.

Pomodori Ripieni di Riso Verde

tomatoes stuffed with green rice

During the summer months, ripe red tomatoes bursting with a rice stuffing are a staple antipasto of Roman trattorie. They can also be served as a first course.

½ cup (3½ oz/105 g) medium-grain white rice such as Arborio

salt to taste

4 large tomatoes

2 tablespoons olive oil

¼ cup (⅓ oz/10 g) finely chopped fresh basil, plus whole leaves for garnish

2 tablespoons chopped fresh flat-leaf (Italian) parsley

2 tablespoons grated Parmigiano-Reggiano cheese

1 small clove garlic, finely chopped

freshly ground pepper to taste

☙ Bring a saucepan filled with water to a boil. Add the rice and salt and simmer until the rice is about half cooked, 9–10 minutes. Drain, place in a large bowl, and set aside.

☙ Preheat an oven to 350°F (180°C). Oil a baking dish just large enough to hold the tomatoes snugly.

☙ Cut off a slice ½ inch (12 mm) thick from the top of each tomato and reserve. Using a small spoon, scoop out the tomato seeds and juice and place in a sieve set over a bowl. Arrange the tomatoes in the prepared baking dish.

☙ Add to the rice the strained tomato juice, the olive oil, chopped basil, parsley, cheese, garlic, salt, and pepper and mix well. Spoon the rice mixture into the hollowed-out tomatoes, dividing evenly. Cover each tomato with its top.

☙ Bake until the rice is tender, about 20 minutes. Remove from the oven and serve hot or at room temperature, garnished with the whole basil leaves.

serves 4

Emilia-Romagna

Fagottini di Asparagi al Forno

baked asparagus bundles

Although not a tourist mecca like some regions, Emilia-Romagna has much to offer the traveler. Each summer, the sandy beaches along the Adriatic coast attract visitors from all over Europe. Ravenna, at one time the capital of the Byzantine Empire in the west, has magnificent seventh-century mosaics in the Basilica di Sant'Apollinare in Classe, some of the finest I have ever seen. Inland, the flat countryside turns rich and green, and dairy and produce farms are everywhere. At the center of this agricultural bounty stands Modena, famous for its fast cars (both Maserati and Ferrari are headquartered here), fat sausages (this is the birthplace of zampone, *forcemeat-stuffed pig's foot, and* cotechino, *a husky pork sausage traditionally eaten with lentils all over Italy on New Year's), and fizzy red Lambrusco wine, a perfect partner to the rich local food. Housewives in the area still make fresh egg pasta every day, and pork, veal, butter, cream, and cheese are used with abandon.*

Parma is a beautiful small city in Emilia-Romagna, with elegant shops and a fine opera house, the Teatro Regio. My husband and I like to explore the surrounding countryside with its cheese factories and prosciutto producers during the day, and eat in the local restaurants at night. It was springtime when we were last there, and asparagus was abundant and so good that we ate some every single day. We had it stuffed into pasta and omelets, and simply gratinéed with butter and Parmigiano-Reggiano. This dish, though, was my favorite preparation: topped with creamy mozzarella cheese and sweet local prosciutto. To transform it into a light meal, serve the bundles alongside a couple of fried eggs or a few slices of frittata. If pencil-thin asparagus are in the market, you will need the larger number of spears.

16–24 asparagus spears

salt to taste

4 thin prosciutto slices

4 fresh mozzarella cheese slices

1 tablespoon unsalted butter, cut into bits

❦ Preheat an oven to 375°F (190°C). Butter a 9-inch (23-cm) square baking dish.

❦ Trim off any tough ends from the asparagus, cutting at the point at which they begin to turn white. Thicker spears benefit from a light peeling to within about 3 inches (7.5 cm) of the tips.

❦ Bring a large saucepan three-fourths full of water to a boil. Add the asparagus and salt, reduce the heat to medium, and simmer until the spears are just beginning to bend when they are lifted by the stem end, 4–8 minutes; the timing will depend on the thickness of the asparagus. Using tongs, transfer to a platter and pat dry with paper towels.

❦ Divide the asparagus evenly among the prosciutto slices, centering the spears across the end of each slice. Roll up the prosciutto, encasing the asparagus inside, to form 4 neat bundles.

❦ Place the bundles in the prepared dish. Lay a mozzarella slice on top of each bundle. Dot the ends and tips of the asparagus with the butter.

❦ Bake until the cheese is melted, about 10 minutes. Transfer to warmed individual plates and serve hot.

serves 4

PRIMI

Pasta, risotto, minestra—
the primo sets the pace
of the meal, reflecting
the region, the season,
the market.

ONE OF MY EARLIEST childhood memories is of visiting my grandmother on holidays and watching her make homemade ravioli. Her old-fashioned kitchen would be filled with the aroma of slowly simmering *ragù*, a Neapolitan-style tomato sauce made with beef and pork. My sister and I would watch her as she worked, barely able to contain our anticipation of what was to come.

Nonna began by piling a mound of flour in the middle of her big pasta board and mixing in some eggs. Then, with patient, rhythmic movements, she kneaded the mass into a smooth cushion of supple dough. With her enormous rolling pin, she stretched the dough into sheets as sheer and smooth as pale yellow silk. After placing mounds of creamy ricotta filling over half of the surface, she folded over the other half, molding it around the filling with her cupped hands. Then, with a small, heavy drinking glass, Nonna would cut out the plump, round ravioli. She made dozens of them every time, and would lay them out to dry on clean white cloths spread over the kitchen table.

Pasta is only one of the typical *primi*, or first courses, that may begin an Italian meal, although it surely is the most beloved. The two main types are *pasta fresca*, "fresh pasta," which can be homemade or store-bought, and *pasta secca*, dried flour-and-water pasta, which is made commercially and available everywhere in boxes or bags.

Pasta all'uovo, "fresh egg pasta," is the most common fresh pasta. It is more typical of northern Italy, where the land is fertile, the people are prosperous, and eggs have generally been plentiful and affordable. Southern Italians, who have traditionally been less affluent, rely on *pasta secca*, long an important staple because it is far less expensive to produce and keeps well in the hot, dry climate. Italians do not compare fresh egg pasta and dried pasta—that is, one is not considered better than the other. They are simply different, and directions for cooking and saucing them respect that difference.

Fresh egg pasta is often cut into ribbons, usually fettuccine, tagliatelle, or *pappardelle*, which vary in width. But the true glory of this

silky dough is stuffed pasta, such as ravioli or *tortelli*, which can be square or round, large or small, with a fluted or straight edge. Then there are tortellini and *tortelloni*, small and large versions respectively of a ring-shaped stuffed pasta said to have been invented by a cook inspired by the beauty of the goddess Venus's navel. Cappelletti are similar in shape to tortellini, but because the tips are turned up they resemble little peaked caps, from which they take their name.

Lovers of *pasta all'uovo* should go to Emilia-Romagna, where exquisite fresh pasta is still made daily in many homes and restaurants. The forms and fillings are countless, and every

Preceding spread: The vast and productive rice fields of the Po Valley supply much of the grain used in risotto throughout the country. **Left:** Bologna is a wonderful place for taking a stroll, whether along its stall-lined alleys or its miles of stone arcades that form a continuous pedestrian zone in the historic center. **Below:** Shopkeepers in Padua wind their delicate strands of fresh pasta into nests to create an appealing display.

time I visit I discover something new. On a recent trip it was colorful *caramelle.* Shaped like paper-wrapped candies, the pasta was striped green and white and filled with bright orange carrot-flavored ricotta. Most often in Emilia-Romagna, the pasta is sauced with melted butter accented with sage, but cream sauces are popular, too, and vegetable and tomato sauces are eaten in the warmer months. Parmigiano-Reggiano, made in this region, is the crowning touch, grated at the last possible moment to retain its nutty flavor.

Piedmont is another region known for fresh egg pasta. The Piedmontese use egg yolks only for dough with a particularly refined flavor

and texture, and most often cut it into ribbons called *tajarin,* dialect for tagliatelle. The finest pastas are served simply with butter and a shower of shavings from a fresh *tartufo bianco,* the aromatic white truffle found in the region.

Although *pasta secca* is more common than fresh egg pasta in southern Italy, stuffed pastas like ravioli and cannelloni are popular for holidays and special occasions. The finest dried pasta is made from golden semolina flour ground from durum wheat. Typical sauces for dried pasta are based on olive oil or lard rather than butter. Tomato sauces prevail in southern Italy, and they may be plain or with meat, seafood, or other vegetables.

The fresh pasta category also includes a number of pastas made without eggs, and practically every region has its unique version. In Apulia, *orecchiette,* little ear-shaped disks, and *cavatelli,* narrow shell-shaped pasta, are made with semolina flour mixed with water. Sicilians make a type of *cavatelli* or gnocchi from flour mixed with soft, fresh ricotta cheese. Ligurians are known for *trofie,* small, round, bumpy-surfaced pasta made with chestnut flour and white wine. In Lombardy, *pizzoccheri,* pasta ribbons of buckwheat flour, wheat flour, and water, are eaten with butter, soft Bitto cheese, and sautéed greens. Venetians make *bigoli,* thick whole-wheat pasta strands cranked out of a meat-grinder-like device called a *torchio* and eaten with a rich duck *ragù.* Tuscans have their hand-rolled *pici,* thick pasta strings that are coated with a mix of garlicky bread crumbs and olive oil.

Of course, many other first course possibilities exist in addition to pasta. Risotto, made from special varieties of medium-grain rice grown in northern Italy, is at its best in Piedmont, Lombardy, Veneto, and Emilia-Romagna. Although no one knows for sure

Left top: Emilia-Romagna is a highly prosperous and gastronomically diverse region of Italy. Its fertile plains are a prolific source of *grano* (wheat), *granturco* (corn), and *orzo* (barley). **Left bottom:** A stone arcade in the town of Poppi, renowned for its winding porticoed lanes, partially shades glass jars from the rays of the Tuscan sun. **Right:** The majestic snow-capped Dolomites provide the backdrop for vineyards near Breitbach, in Alto Adige. These dramatic mountains are dotted with castles, churches, and ski resorts.

its origin, the Italian method of first sautéing the rice in a little butter or other fat, then slowly and gradually stirring in liquid in the form of stock, wine, or water, is traditional.

Risotto takes on seasonal and regional characteristics wherever it is eaten and is readily adapted to whatever is available. In the Veneto, it is made with springtime's asparagus or peas, with burgundy-leaved radicchio, and with mixed seafood. In Friuli, it is cooked with *sclupit,* a slightly bitter wild green known as silene in English. The Piedmontese make risotto with their famed local wines, such as Barbera and Barolo. The classic risotto in Lombardy is *alla milanese,* with saffron and veal marrow. In the Alto Adige, I ate a memorable risotto that combined tart apples and Parmigiano-Reggiano cheese.

When people were too poor to afford pasta or risotto, they could always make soups *(minestre),* mainstays of the Italian kitchen that, during hard times, could be fashioned from foraged vegetables or kitchen scraps. Just the name *acquacotta,* "cooked water," is an indica-

tion of how little goes into this Tuscan soup made with leftover bread and wild mushrooms. In Apulia, *zuppa di pesce scappata,* "soup of the escaped fish," probably invented by the wife of an unlucky fisherman, is made by boiling seaweed-covered rocks from the ocean floor to create a flavorful broth. The Calabrian *millecosedde,* "a thousand little things," is a thrifty housewife's way of clearing out the pantry at the end of winter. It is made with a handful of dried beans or peas, broken scraps of pasta, and whatever vegetable odds and ends are on hand. Two things amaze me about such soups: so much flavor and nourishment is coaxed from truly basic ingredients, and their yield can be extended almost magically. *Pasta fagioli,* for example, can be pasta with a bean sauce or bean soup with pasta—just add more water or stock.

Although polenta, or cornmeal mush, is usually thought of as a northern Italian dish,

Above top: A baker and his assistant carry a tray laden with *panini* along a street in Abruzzo. In the south, superb breads are made from *semolino di grano duro* (semolina flour milled from the center of the durum wheat berry). **Above bottom:** *Pici,* a Tuscan specialty, are rustic hand-rolled noodles made from durum wheat, water, and olive oil. Traditionally a dish of the poor, *pici* are tossed with bread crumbs, garlic, *peperoncini,* olive oil, and pecorino cheese, or simply with a tomato sauce. **Right:** The process for making Parmigiano-Reggiano is so lengthy and arduous that the valuable wheels are traditionally aged in highly secure cheese bank vaults, where they are sometimes used as collateral for loans.

it is served in southern Italy as well. Unlike pasta or risotto, polenta may be offered as an accompaniment, usually to a stew of game, meat, fish, or mushrooms. Often the soft, creamy, freshly cooked polenta is poured out of the cooking pot onto a round wooden serving board. Indentations are made in the surface, and it is topped with the stew and sauce. A length of string is used to cut the polenta into serving portions.

In Friuli–Venezia Giulia, I ate a polenta dish known in dialect as *toc' in braide,* very soft polenta topped with smoked ricotta, melted butter, and toasted cornmeal. Elsewhere polenta is layered and baked with cheeses, sauce, and vegetables to form a hearty *pasticcio,* which can be served as a first course or main dish.

Perhaps because it reminds me of my grandmother's kitchen, or because it is the most uniquely Italian part of a meal, but the *primo piatto* is always the course I look forward to with the greatest anticipation.

Lombardia

Tortelli di Zucca

golden squash tortelli with sage butter

The Antica Locanda Mincio arguably has the most idyllic setting for a restaurant in all of Italy. The garden looks out on an old watermill and the fast-moving Mincio River, and you can dine there under a canopy of trees. The food is simple: two or three homemade pastas, including these lovely tortelli *filled with golden squash accented with amaretti, roasted meats, fish from the river, and for dessert, local peaches poached in a simple syrup or perhaps a creamy* semifreddo.

The restaurant began operations as an inn around 1600, and Napoleon is reported to have stopped there with his troops in 1796. The town of Valeggio sul Mincio, where it is located, is actually in the Veneto, but this stuffed pasta is more typical of nearby Lombardy.

FILLING

1 small winter squash such as Hubbard, butternut, or pumpkin, 1½ lb (750 g)

1 cup (4 oz/125 g) grated Parmigiano-Reggiano cheese

¼ cup (1 oz/30 g) fine dried bread crumbs

¼ cup (1 oz/30 g) crushed amaretti (about 8 small cookies)

1 egg

¼ teaspoon ground nutmeg

salt to taste

PASTA DOUGH (ABOUT 1¼ LB/625 G)

about 3 cups (15 oz/470 g) unbleached all-purpose (plain) flour

5 eggs

SAUCE

½ cup (4 oz/125 g) unsalted butter

4 fresh sage leaves

½ cup (2 oz/60 g) grated Parmigiano-Reggiano cheese

❀ Preheat an oven to 400°F (200°C). Oil a large baking pan. To make the filling, cut the squash in half lengthwise and scoop out the seeds and fibers. Place the halves, cut sides down, in the prepared baking pan. Bake until tender when pierced with a knife, about 1 hour. Remove from the oven, let cool, and scoop the flesh out of the shell. Purée the flesh in a

food processor or by passing through a food mill placed over a bowl. Stir in the cheese, bread crumbs, amaretti, egg, nutmeg, and salt until smooth. Cover and refrigerate until needed.

❀ To make the pasta dough, follow the directions on page 249, using the quantity of ingredients given. Roll out the pasta by hand or by machine. Cut into long strips about 4 inches (10 cm) wide.

❀ Line 3 baking sheets with kitchen towels and dust the towels with flour. Keeping the remaining strips covered with another kitchen towel, lay out 1 strip on a lightly floured work surface. Fold it in half lengthwise to mark the center, then unfold. Place small spoonfuls of the filling in a straight row the length of one-half of the strip about 1 inch (2.5 cm) in from the edge and spaced about 2 inches (5 cm) apart. Using a pastry brush, lightly paint cool water around each mound. Fold the other half of the strip over the filling, pressing firmly to eliminate air bubbles. Using a pastry wheel or a sharp knife, cut between the mounds to form the *tortelli*. To be sure they are well sealed, press firmly all around the edges with a fork. As the *tortelli* are cut, arrange them in a single layer on the prepared baking sheets. Cover with another towel and refrigerate until ready to cook. Repeat with the remaining dough and filling. (The *tortelli* can be made up to 3 hours in advance. Refrigerate, turning them several times so that they do not stick to the towels.)

❀ Bring a large pot three-fourths full of water to a boil. Add salt to taste, then gently slip in half of the *tortelli* and cook until al dente, 2–3 minutes if very fresh or for up to 5 minutes if drier. Using a slotted spoon, lift the *tortelli* from the pot, draining them well.

❀ Meanwhile, make the sauce: In a small frying pan over low heat, melt the butter. Add the sage leaves and gently sauté, swirling them around in the pan, until fragrant and lightly browned at the edges, about 3 minutes. Spoon about half of the sage butter into a warmed shallow serving bowl, add the cooked *tortelli,* and turn gently to coat. Cook the remaining *tortelli* in the same way and add to the bowl with the remaining sage butter, again turning gently to coat. Sprinkle with the cheese and serve immediately.

serves 6

Toscana

Insalata di Farro

farro salad

An ancient grain in the same family as wheat, farro, which long ago fell out of use in the Italian kitchen, has become popular again. Its appeal comes not only from its nutty flavor, but also because it is healthful and easy to digest, even by many people who are allergic to wheat. Residents of the Garfagnana area of eastern Tuscany where farro is grown claim that the grain is also an effective aphrodisiac well into old age.

Farro, which is commonly translated as "spelt" in English, may be ground up for flour for bread or pasta or cooked whole in soups or for salads. If it is not available, hulled wheat berries can be substituted here. You may need to adjust the cooking time depending on how long the berries have been stored.

1 cup (5 oz/155 g) farro (spelt)

4 cups (32 fl oz/1 l) water

1 teaspoon salt, plus salt to taste

4–6 radishes, trimmed and thinly sliced

2 tomatoes, chopped

1 small cucumber, chopped

⅓ cup (2 oz/60 g) chopped pitted Gaeta or other Mediterranean-style black olives

¼ cup (¼ oz/7 g) fresh basil leaves, cut into narrow strips

3 tablespoons extra-virgin olive oil

freshly ground pepper to taste

lettuce leaves

4 hard-boiled eggs, peeled and quartered

☙ In a bowl, combine the *farro* with water to cover. Let soak for 2 hours. Drain and pour into a large pot with the 4 cups (32 fl oz/1 l) water. Bring to a boil and add the 1 teaspoon salt. Reduce the heat to low and cook, uncovered, until very soft, about 40 minutes. (Cooking time may vary as much as 10–20 minutes.)

☙ Drain and pour into a large bowl. Add the radishes, tomatoes, cucumber, olives, basil, olive oil, salt, and pepper and toss well. Line a platter with lettuce leaves and spoon or pour the *farro* mixture into the center. Arrange the egg quarters around the edge of the platter and serve.

serves 4

Valle d'Aosta

Zuppa alla Valpellinentze

cabbage, bread, and cheese soup

High up in the Alps between France and Switzerland sits Italy's smallest region, the Valle d'Aosta. The cows that graze on the mountain slopes produce the milk for Fontina, one of the country's finest cheeses. Fontina Valle d'Aosta is aged in caves and has a natural rind, so it is easy to distinguish from its many wax-coated imitators. Here, it is used in a rustic soup made with the local dark rye bread, pane nero.

1 small Savoy cabbage, about 1 lb (500 g)

salt to taste

¾ lb (375 g) Fontina cheese

6 cups (48 fl oz/1.5 l) chicken or meat stock

pinch of ground nutmeg

pinch of ground cinnamon

freshly ground pepper to taste

12 slices crusty rye, whole-wheat, or other bread, toasted

2 teaspoons unsalted butter, cut into bits

☙ Cut the cabbage lengthwise into quarters and trim the core and outer leaves. Bring a large pot three-fourths full of water to a boil over high heat. Add salt and the cabbage. Reduce the heat to low and cook, uncovered, until tender, about 30 minutes. Drain well and let cool.

☙ Preheat an oven to 350°F (180°C).

☙ Thinly slice the cabbage crosswise. Coarsely shred enough cheese to measure ½ cup (2 oz/60 g). Thinly slice the remainder. In a saucepan, combine the stock, nutmeg, cinnamon, salt, and pepper. Bring to a simmer.

☙ Arrange 4 slices of the bread in the bottom of a deep 3-qt (3-l) baking dish. Cover with half each of the cabbage and the cheese slices. Repeat the layers, then cover with the remaining bread. Pour the hot stock over the contents of the baking dish. Sprinkle with the shredded cheese and dot with the butter.

☙ Bake until bubbling and browned, about 45 minutes. Remove from the oven. Let rest for 5 minutes. Ladle into warmed soup bowls to serve.

serves 4–6

Lazio

Penne con Salsa di Pomodoro Piccante

penne with spicy tomato sauce

Anchovy fillets give this quick uncooked pasta sauce a salty tang. The best anchovies come packed in salt and are usually sold by weight from a large tin. They have a firm, meaty texture and rich flavor, but they must be filleted and rinsed before using. To do so, carefully pull apart the fillets to reveal the bony frame. Discard the frame and rinse the fillets in cool water. Oil-packed anchovies can be good, too. Look for them packed in jars rather than tins, so that you can judge their quality before you buy.

Frascati, a very dry white wine sold in a handsome funnel-shaped bottle and produced in the Castelli Romani, a picturesque cluster of small communities set in the sloping hills just south of Rome, makes a good accompaniment to this robust pasta.

12 anchovy fillets, chopped (see note)

3 tomatoes, chopped

½ cup (2½ oz/75 g) chopped Gaeta or other Mediterranean-style black olives

2 tablespoons capers, chopped

1 large clove garlic, chopped

2 tablespoons chopped fresh flat-leaf (Italian) parsley

2 tablespoons chopped fresh basil

1 small dried red chile, crushed, or pinch of red pepper flakes

salt to taste

¼ cup (2 fl oz/60 ml) extra-virgin olive oil

1 lb (500 g) penne

❦ In a large serving bowl, combine the anchovies, tomatoes, olives, capers, garlic, parsley, basil, chile, salt, and olive oil. Stir well to blend the flavors. Let stand for 1 hour.

❦ Just before serving, bring a large pot three-fourths full of water to a boil. Add the penne and salt to taste and cook, stirring frequently, until al dente.

❦ Drain the pasta, add to the sauce, and toss well. Taste and adjust the seasoning. Serve immediately.

serves 6

I Capperi

The caper bush is a perennial that has long grown wild all around the Mediterranean. In the springtime in Italy, hardy foragers climb tall ladders or reach over stone walls to gather the unopened flower buds of the bush, which are eaten fresh or preserved in salt or vinegar. The salted ones are preferred because vinegar interferes with the caper's delicate flavor and makes the texture unpleasantly mushy. The most sought-after *capperi* are said to be those with a pink crown, an indication of high quality.

Italian farmers now cultivate the plants, and the best capers come from plots on the islands off Sicily, especially Pantelleria and Salina. Since the berries are naturally resistant to pests, most capers are grown organically. The same plants also produce milder-tasting, long-stemmed fruits known as caperberries, which are usually preserved in brine and can be eaten like olives or used in any way that you would use capers.

Risotto di Biete
e Parmigiano

risotto with beets and parmesan

*Roasted beets stain this risotto a brilliant ruby red.
Instead of grating the Parmigiano, it is shaved into
thin curls or flakes that melt into the rice.*

4 beets

3 oz (90 g) wedge of Parmigiano-Reggiano cheese

6 cups (48 fl oz / 1.5 l) chicken stock

3 tablespoons unsalted butter

1 tablespoon olive oil

1 yellow onion, finely chopped

*2 cups (14 oz / 440 g) medium-grain rice such as
Arborio, Carnaroli, or Vialone Nano*

¾ cup (6 fl oz / 180 ml) dry white wine

salt and freshly ground pepper

❧ Preheat an oven to 450°F (230°C). Trim the
beets. Place on a large sheet of aluminum foil and
fold the ends to seal. Bake in a small roasting pan
until tender when pierced, 45–60 minutes. Let cool,
slip off the skins, chop the beets, and set aside.

❧ Using a vegetable peeler, shave off thin curls of
the cheese, using about half (1½ oz / 45 g) of the
wedge. Grate the remaining cheese. Set aside.

❧ Bring the stock barely to a simmer in a saucepan.

❧ In a large saucepan over medium heat, melt
2 tablespoons of the butter with the oil. Add the
onion and sauté until tender, about 5 minutes. Stir in
the rice and cook, stirring, until the grains are hot
and coated, about 2 minutes. Add the wine and
continue to cook and stir until the liquid is absorbed.
Add the beets and cook, stirring, for 1 minute.

❧ Add the stock ½ cup (4 fl oz / 125 ml) at a time,
stirring constantly and making sure the liquid has
been absorbed before adding more. When the rice is
about half cooked, stir in the salt and pepper. The
risotto is done when the rice grains are creamy on
the outside and firm, yet tender to the bite, 20–25
minutes total.

❧ Stir in the grated cheese and the remaining
1 tablespoon butter. Spoon into warmed soup plates,
strew with the shaved cheese, and serve immediately.

serves 4–6

Basilicata

Zuppa di Patate, Zucchini, e Menta

potato and zucchini soup with mint

This soup is a classic example of the elemental cooking of Italian peasants, or la cucina povera, literally, "poor cooking." The tradition draws a remarkably satisfying flavor from a few basic ingredients and has historically sustained the country's less fortunate through hard times.

Basilicata has long been among the most remote and poverty stricken regions of Italy. Much of the land is rocky and arid, yielding few agricultural riches. In recent years, though, tourists have been attracted to the area's narrow strip of Mediterranean coast and have brought their wealth along with them. One of Italy's respected red wines, Aglianico del Vulture, is a product of grapes raised in the local volcanic soil. It has a deep red color and sharp, intense flavor that mellows beautifully with age.

1 yellow onion, chopped

3 tablespoons olive oil

8 cups (64 fl oz / 2 l) chicken stock

3 potatoes, peeled and diced

salt and freshly ground pepper to taste

3 small zucchini (courgettes), trimmed and thinly sliced

1 cup (3 oz / 90 g) small dried pasta shapes such as ditalini or tubetti

2 tablespoons chopped fresh mint

⅓ cup (1½ oz / 45 g) grated pecorino romano cheese

❧ In a large saucepan over medium heat, sauté the onion in the oil until tender, about 5 minutes. Add the stock, potatoes, salt, and pepper. Bring to a simmer, add the zucchini, and cook until the vegetables soften, about 10 minutes. Add the pasta and cook, stirring frequently, until al dente. Stir in the mint.

❧ To serve, ladle the soup into warmed bowls and sprinkle with the cheese. Serve immediately.

serves 6

Toscana

Gnocchi Verdi

spinach gnocchi

Gnocchi made with potatoes may be the most familiar form of these dumplings, but many other types are popular as well. In Trentino–Alto Adige, gnocchi stuffed with small plums or apricots are typical, while in the Veneto, puréed winter squash goes into the dough. In the northeast, they are made with bread crumbs and served in broth. These green gnocchi from Tuscany feature spinach, but Swiss chard can be substituted.

GNOCCHI

2 lb (1 kg) spinach, tough stems removed

¼ cup (2 fl oz/60 ml) water

2 tablespoons unsalted butter

1 small yellow onion, finely chopped

2 oz (60 g) prosciutto, finely chopped

2 cups (1 lb/500 g) ricotta cheese

1½ cups (7½ oz/235 g) unbleached all-purpose (plain) flour

1 cup (4 oz/125 g) grated Parmigiano-Reggiano cheese

2 eggs

¼ teaspoon salt

¼ teaspoon freshly ground pepper

¼ teaspoon ground nutmeg

SAUCE

½ cup (4 oz/125 g) unsalted butter

6 fresh sage leaves

pinch of salt

½ cup (2 oz/60 g) grated Parmigiano-Reggiano cheese

☙ To make the gnocchi, in a saucepan, combine the spinach and water. Cover, place over medium heat, and cook until wilted and tender, about 5 minutes. Drain in a colander, pressing out excess water with the back of a spoon, and let cool. Wrap in a clean kitchen towel and squeeze out any remaining liquid. Finely chop the spinach.

☙ In a medium frying pan over medium-low heat, melt the butter. Add the onion and sauté until tender, 5–6 minutes. Add the prosciutto and sauté for 30 seconds. Stir in the chopped spinach. Transfer to a large bowl. Using a wooden spoon, beat in the ricotta cheese, the flour, the Parmigiano-Reggiano cheese, the eggs, salt, pepper, and nutmeg. The mixture will be soft.

☙ Line baking sheets with waxed paper and dust lightly with flour. Dampen your hands with cool water and shape the spinach mixture into balls about ¾ inch (2 cm) in diameter. As the balls are shaped, place on the prepared baking sheets. Cover with plastic wrap and refrigerate until ready to cook. (The gnocchi can be refrigerated for up to several hours before cooking.)

☙ Preheat an oven to 350°F (180°C). Butter a large baking dish.

☙ To make the sauce, in a small saucepan over low heat, melt the butter. Add the sage leaves and salt. Cook until the butter is lightly browned, 4–6 minutes. Keep warm over very low heat.

☙ Meanwhile, bring a large pot three-fourths full of water to a boil. Add salt to taste. Working in 2 batches, drop in the gnocchi a few at a time to prevent sticking. After they rise to the surface, boil gently until cooked through, 1–2 minutes.

☙ Using a slotted spoon, transfer the gnocchi to the prepared baking dish. (At this point, the gnocchi can be covered and chilled for up to 24 hours before baking.) Drizzle evenly with the sauce and sprinkle with the cheese. Bake until heated through, about 15 minutes. Serve hot directly from the dish.

serves 6–8

Veneto

Zuppa di Fagioli alla Veneta

bean soup with ditalini

An Italian chef I once met insisted that the bean soup served in the Veneto is the only bean soup in Italy. The Venetian version is very good, but cooks in every region have their own delicious recipe for zuppa di fagioli. What sets the Venetian soup apart is the type of bean used, typically dark pink or marbled borlotti (similar to cranberry beans) rather than the white cannellini used elsewhere.

2¼ cups (1 lb/500 g) dried borlotti, cranberry, pinto, or other pink beans

¼ lb (125 g) pancetta, coarsely chopped

1 yellow onion, finely chopped

2 celery stalks, finely chopped

salt and freshly ground pepper to taste

¼ lb (125 g) ditalini, *elbow macaroni, or other small pasta shape*

extra-virgin olive oil

❦ Pick over the beans, discarding any stones or mis-shapen beans. Rinse and place in a bowl with cold water to cover by 2 inches (5 cm). Let soak for 4 hours at room temperature or for up to overnight in the refrigerator.

❦ Drain the beans and place in a large pot with water to cover by 1 inch (2.5 cm). Place over medium heat and bring to a simmer. Reduce the heat to low. Add the pancetta, onion, and celery and cook, covered, until the beans are completely tender, 1–1½ hours. Add water if needed to keep the beans immersed.

❦ Strain the beans through a sieve, reserving the liquid. In batches, transfer the beans to a food processor or blender. Process until smooth. Return the purée and liquid to the pan. Season with salt and pepper.

❦ Bring a saucepan three-fourths full of water to a boil. Add the pasta and salt and cook, stirring, until nearly al dente.

❦ Meanwhile, gently reheat the bean purée. Drain the pasta, reserving about 1 cup (8 fl oz/250 ml) of the cooking water. Add the pasta to the beans. Stir in the pasta cooking water if the soup is too thick. Ladle into warmed soup plates and drizzle with olive oil. Serve immediately.

serves 8–10

Toscana

Pappa al Pomodoro

tomato and bread soup

Like panzanella (page 55), this soup is a creative way the frugal Tuscans use up scraps of day-old bread. Most Italian cooks feel that many foods, including most soups, taste best when they are neither too hot nor too cold. Moderate temperatures don't shock the taste buds and allow all of the flavors to come through. This soup tastes good at any temperature, fresh off the stove, at room temperature, or in between.

1 yellow onion, chopped

2 tender celery stalks, chopped

4 tablespoons (2 fl oz/60 ml) extra-virgin olive oil

2 cloves garlic, minced

2 lb (1 kg) fresh tomatoes, peeled, seeded, and chopped

4 cups (32 fl oz/1 l) water

4 slices day-old coarse country bread, crusts removed and torn into small pieces (about 2 cups/4 oz/125 g)

4 fresh basil leaves, torn into small pieces

salt and freshly ground pepper to taste

❦ In a large saucepan over medium heat, sauté the onion and celery in 2 tablespoons of the olive oil until tender, about 7 minutes. Add the garlic and sauté until fragrant, about 1 minute longer. Add the tomatoes and water and bring to a simmer. Cook uncovered, stirring occasionally, until the vegetables are soft, about 20 minutes.

❦ Pass the contents of the saucepan through a food mill placed over a bowl, or purée it in batches in a blender or food processor. Return it to the pan. Add the bread, basil, salt, and pepper. Cook until the bread is soft, about 10 minutes longer. Stir in a little more water if the soup becomes too thick.

❦ Serve hot, warm, or room temperature ladled into bowls. Divide the remaining 2 tablespoons olive oil among the servings, drizzling over the top.

serves 4

La Raccolta delle Olive

During late fall and early winter, the olive harvest, *la raccolta delle olive*, takes place all over Italy. Large drop cloths or nets are spread out, looking like so many picnic blankets, under the silvery-leaved trees. But there are no picnickers, only workers armed with handheld rakes for removing the ripe olives. They prop ladders against the gnarled trunks of the ancient trees and carefully free the ripe fruits from the branches. Once harvested, the olives are rushed to the presses to prevent them from spoiling, which can happen within a matter of days.

Only the best-quality olives are used to make extra-virgin oil. They are crushed between large millstones, and the drawn liquid is centrifuged to eliminate water. Some producers also filter it to remove sediment. Finally, the oil is ready to be bottled, but not before it is tasted. The thick, green liquid is drizzled onto slices of hot toasted bread to bring out all of its subtle flavor. The taste depends on the ripeness of the olives, the mix of varieties, where they were grown, and how they were handled. If the oleic acid content of the newly pressed oil is found to be too high, it cannot be labeled extra virgin. By law, an extra-virgin oil must have an acidity level of less than 1 percent. Lesser-grade oils are sold as virgin oil or simply olive oil.

Campania

Spaghetti alla Bucaniera

spaghetti, pirate's style

In Naples, very ripe cherry tomatoes called pendolini, *"little hanging ones," are used to make quick sauces like this one. They grow in bunches, and the entire stalk of ripe tomatoes is harvested and hung in a cool, dry place to use over time.*

6 tablespoons (3 fl oz/90 ml) olive oil

½ lb (250 g) medium shrimp (prawns), peeled, deveined, and cut into ½-inch (12-mm) pieces

salt to taste

1 lb (500 g) squid, cleaned and cut into rings ½ inch (12 mm) wide (see page 250; about ½ lb/250 g cleaned)

3 large cloves garlic, lightly crushed

¼ cup (⅓ oz/10 g) chopped fresh flat-leaf (Italian) parsley

pinch of red pepper flakes

1 lb (500 g) small hard-shell clams, soaked in cool water for 30 minutes and well scrubbed

1 lb (500 g) ripe cherry tomatoes, halved, or plum (Roma) tomatoes, seeded and chopped

1 lb (500 g) spaghetti or linguine

✢ In a frying pan large enough to hold the cooked pasta and sauce, heat 3 tablespoons of the oil over high heat. Add the shrimp and a pinch of salt. Sauté just until the shrimp are pink, about 1 minute. Using a slotted spoon, transfer to a plate. Add the squid and a pinch of salt to the pan and sauté until opaque, about 1 minute. Transfer to the plate.

✢ Add the remaining 3 tablespoons oil, the garlic, the parsley, and the pepper flakes to the pan and cook over medium heat until the garlic is golden, about 1 minute. Add the clams (discard any that do not close to the touch) and tomatoes, cover, and cook over low heat, stirring occasionally, until the clams open, about 5 minutes. Discard any that failed to open. Add the seafood and remove from the heat.

✢ Meanwhile, bring a large pot three-fourths full of water to a boil. Add the pasta and salt and cook until al dente. Drain, reserving a ladleful of the water.

✢ Add the pasta to the sauce and stir and toss over medium heat, adding some of the cooking water if too dry. Transfer to a warmed serving bowl and serve.

serves 6

Sicilia

Pasta con Tonno e Briciole

pasta with tuna and bread crumbs

Many southern Italian pastas are topped with toasted bread crumbs, a custom that probably dates to a time when cheese was too costly for many of the locals to afford. The crumbs add a pleasing crunch and rich, toasty flavor to vegetable and fish sauces. In some recipes, they are first sautéed with olive oil and mashed anchovies for a salty tang and extra flavor. I like to serve this pasta with a clean, fruity white wine such as one bottled by Regaleali.

1 small yellow onion, finely chopped

¼ cup (2 fl oz/60 ml) olive oil

2 cloves garlic, finely chopped

1 small dried red chile, crushed, or pinch of red pepper flakes

¼ cup (2 fl oz/60 ml) dry white wine

1 can (7 oz/220 g) tuna in olive oil, drained and flaked

¼ cup (⅓ oz/10 g) chopped fresh flat-leaf (Italian) parsley

1 lb (500 g) linguine or spaghetti

salt to taste

½ cup (2 oz/60 g) toasted fine bread crumbs

♛ In a frying pan large enough to hold the cooked pasta and the sauce, sauté the onion in the olive oil over medium heat until tender, about 5 minutes. Add the garlic and chile and cook until the garlic is golden, about 1 minute. Add the wine and cook until the liquid is reduced by half, about 1 minute. Stir in the tuna and parsley and remove from the heat.

♛ Meanwhile, bring a large pot three-fourths full of water to a boil. Add the pasta and salt and cook, stirring frequently, until al dente. Drain, reserving a ladleful of the cooking water.

♛ Add the drained pasta to the sauce and stir and toss well over medium heat, adding some of the cooking water if too dry. Transfer to a warmed serving bowl, sprinkle with the bread crumbs, and serve immediately.

serves 4

Emilia-Romagna

Ravioli all'Uova con Tartufi

giant egg ravioli with truffles

At San Domenico restaurant in Imola, near Bologna, this exquisite pasta is a specialty of the house. Each diner is served a single large raviolo. Inside each pasta package, a ring of seasoned ricotta holds an egg yolk. When the raviolo is cooked, the yolk remains soft, so that once the pasta is cut, the egg oozes out and blends with the truffles and sauce.

Making the ravioli is not difficult, but they must be handled very carefully to avoid breaking the egg yolks. Also, they must be assembled just before cooking. Be sure to use very fresh, pliable pasta. If you like, you can roll the pasta out slightly thicker than you might for other stuffed pastas to make it easier to handle. If truffles are not available, the ravioli are still delicious without them.

FILLING

1 cup (8 oz/250 g) ricotta cheese

2 tablespoons grated Parmigiano-Reggiano cheese

2 tablespoons chopped fresh flat-leaf (Italian) parsley

pinch of ground nutmeg

salt and freshly ground pepper to taste

4 eggs

PASTA DOUGH (ABOUT ½ LB/250 G)

about 1¼ cups (6½ oz/200 g) unbleached all-purpose (plain) flour

2 eggs

SAUCE

½ cup (4 oz/125 g) unsalted butter

2 tablespoons grated Parmigiano-Reggiano cheese

1 small fresh white truffle, brushed clean

To make the filling, in a small bowl, combine the ricotta cheese, Parmigiano-Reggiano, parsley, nutmeg, and salt and pepper. Stir until well mixed. Cover and refrigerate until needed. Reserve the eggs for later use.

To make the pasta dough, follow the directions on page 249, using the quantity of ingredients given. Roll out the pasta by hand or by machine. Cut into four 8-by-4-inch (20-by-10-cm) strips. Keeping the other strips covered with a kitchen towel, lay out 1 strip on a lightly floured work surface. Fold in half crosswise just to mark the center, then unfold.

Scrape the filling into a pastry (piping) bag fitted with a ½-inch (12-mm) plain tip, or into a heavy-duty plastic bag and snip off a corner to create a ½-inch (12-mm) opening. Leaving a ½-inch (12-mm) border all around and using about one-fourth of the cheese mixture, pipe a circle of the mixture to one side of the crease in the pasta strip. Separate 1 egg, reserving the white for another use. Carefully slip the yolk inside the circle. Using a pastry brush, lightly paint around the cheese with cool water. Fold the other half of the pasta dough over the filling. Using a fork, press the edges of the pasta together firmly to seal. Repeat with the remaining dough and filling.

Bring a large pot three-fourths full of water to a boil. Add salt to taste. Carefully slip the ravioli into the water and cook until the pasta is just done and the yolk is still soft, about 3 minutes. Using a slotted spoon, lift the ravioli from the pot, draining well.

Meanwhile, make the sauce: In a small saucepan over medium-low heat, melt the butter. Continue to heat, swirling the butter in the pan, until it begins to brown around the edges, about 3 minutes.

Transfer the ravioli to individual plates. Gently blot them dry with a kitchen towel. Drizzle with the browned butter and sprinkle with the cheese. Using a truffle shaver or vegetable peeler, shave the truffle over the top, if using. Serve immediately.

serves 4

Lazio

Linguine alle Vongole

linguine with clam sauce

Many types of clams are harvested all over Italy, from the long brownish razor clams to thumbnail-sized vongole veraci. These small, sweet-tasting hard-shell clams are considered the best kind for this familiar dish. To capture all of their flavorful juices, Romans cook the clams in their shells right in the sauce. As you eat the pasta, typically linguine or spaghettini, remove the clams from the shells with your fork, or eat them directly from the shells. Be sure to provide bowls in which to discard the shells. Small mussels can also be prepared this way.

As some clams can be sandy, it's a good precaution to soak them in cool water for a half hour or so to help them disgorge any grit.

3 lb (1.5 kg) small hard-shell clams, soaked in cool water for 30 minutes and well scrubbed

2 large cloves garlic, finely chopped

1 small dried red chile, crushed, or pinch of red pepper flakes

⅓ cup (3 fl oz/80 ml) olive oil

¼ cup (⅓ oz/10 g) finely chopped fresh flat-leaf (Italian) parsley

½ cup (4 fl oz/125 ml) dry white wine

1 lb (500 g) linguine or spaghetti

salt to taste

❦ Discard any clams that do not close to the touch. In a large saucepan over medium heat, warm the garlic and the chile in the olive oil until the garlic is golden, about 1 minute. Stir in the parsley.

❦ Add the clams and wine, cover, and cook over medium heat, shaking the pan occasionally, until the clams open, about 5 minutes. Discard any clams that fail to open.

❦ Meanwhile, bring a large pot three-fourths full of water to a boil. Add the pasta and salt and cook, stirring frequently, until al dente. Drain, reserving a ladleful of the cooking water.

❦ Transfer the pasta to a warmed serving bowl. Add the clams and their juice and stir and toss well. Add a little of the cooking water if the pasta seems too dry. Serve immediately.

serves 4–6

Lazio

Zuppa di Pesce alla Romana

roman-style fish soup

Every region of Italy with a coastline has a characteristic fish soup. This Roman version is spicy with garlic and hot chile. It contains a minimum of liquid, so it is more like a stew than a soup. Use whatever fish varieties are available with the exception of strong-flavored oily fish, which would overwhelm the delicate shellfish.

2 cloves garlic, chopped

pinch of red pepper flakes

⅓ cup (3 fl oz/80 ml) olive oil

2 lb (1 kg) squid, cleaned and cut into rings ½ inch (12 mm) wide (see page 250; about 1 lb/500 g cleaned)

1 cup (8 fl oz/250 ml) dry white wine

2 tomatoes, peeled, seeded, and chopped

2 tablespoons chopped fresh flat-leaf (Italian) parsley

pinch of salt

2 cups (16 fl oz/500 ml) water

1 lb (500 g) small hard-shell clams or cockles, soaked in cool water for 30 minutes and well scrubbed

1½ lb (750 g) assorted firm-fleshed fish fillets such as whiting, monkfish, turbot, porgy, bream, red snapper, and sea bass, cut into chunks

4 slices coarse country bread, toasted and rubbed on one side with a garlic clove

❦ In a large saucepan over medium heat, sauté the garlic and pepper flakes in the olive oil until the garlic is golden, about 2 minutes. Using a slotted spoon, remove the garlic and discard. Add the squid and cook and stir until opaque, about 2 minutes. Add the wine and simmer for 1 minute longer. Add the tomatoes, parsley, and salt and cook until the juices evaporate, about 10 minutes longer.

❦ Add the water and bring to a simmer. Add the clams (discard any that do not close to the touch) and fish, cover, and cook until the clams open and the fish is opaque throughout, about 5 minutes. Discard any clams that failed to open. Adjust the seasonings.

❦ Place a bread slice in each warmed soup plate. Ladle the soup over the bread and serve.

serves 4

Veneto

Risotto agli Zucchini e Fiori

risotto with zucchini and flowers

Any type of squash blossom can be used for this risotto. Look for ones that are tightly closed. If squash flowers are not available, the risotto will still be delicious. Try substituting a handful of shredded spinach leaves or some fresh fava (broad) beans.

about 5 cups (40 fl oz/1.25 l) chicken stock

3 tablespoons unsalted butter

1 tablespoon olive oil

1 yellow onion, chopped

1 clove garlic, chopped

1 cup (7 oz/220 g) medium-grain rice such as Arborio, Vialone Nano, or Carnaroli

½ cup (4 fl oz/125 ml) dry white wine

1 zucchini (courgette), sliced

salt and freshly ground pepper to taste

6–8 zucchini (courgette) flowers, filaments removed and chopped

⅓ cup (1½ oz/45 g) grated Parmigiano-Reggiano cheese

❧ Pour the stock into a saucepan and bring barely to a simmer.

❧ In a large saucepan over medium heat, melt 2 tablespoons of the butter with the oil. Add the onion and sauté until tender, about 5 minutes. Add the garlic and rice and stir until the kernels are hot and coated, about 2 minutes. Add the wine and continue to cook and stir until the liquid is absorbed.

❧ Add half of the zucchini and cook, stirring, for 1 minute. Add the stock ½ cup (4 fl oz/125 ml) at a time, stirring constantly and making sure the liquid has been absorbed before adding more. When the rice is about half cooked, stir in the remaining zucchini and the salt and pepper. The risotto is done when the rice grains are creamy on the outside and firm, yet tender to the bite, 20–25 minutes total. Rice varies, so you may not need all of the stock or you may need more. If more liquid is required, use hot water. Stir in the flowers just until wilted.

❧ Remove from the heat and stir in the remaining 1 tablespoon butter and the cheese. Spoon into warmed soup plates and serve.

serves 4

L'Ombra

When Venetians want a little wine and a light snack, they often head for a wine bar, or *bacaro*. There, they can order wine by the glass, known as *l'ombra,* meaning "the shadow." I have heard two explanations of how this midday beverage got its name. One is that the wine was originally sold by itinerant street merchants who operated in the shadows cast by tall buildings on hot days. As the sunlight shifted, they followed the shade to keep the wine cool. Another story credits the city's hardworking gondoliers, who stopped periodically for some refreshment and stood in the shade as they sipped a glass of wine. Both explanations make sense to me, and a visit to a *bacaro* is a sure way to sample a true taste of Venice.

To accompany your *ombra,* order *cicchetti,* (sometimes *cichetti* or *cicheti*), traditional Venetian snacks that run the gamut from the simple—cubes of local cheese, *coppa* and bread, a saucer of pungent olives—to the more elaborate—creamy *baccalà mantecato* (page 165), seafood salad, flavorful *polpettini,* sticks of fried polenta, braised tripe, *sarde in saor* (marinated sardines).

Near Teatro La Fenice, the charming Vino Vino wine bar pours a fine Soave or Chiaretto for enjoying with an appealing array of little plates. To enjoy your snacks amid a clatter of Venetian dialect, head to the Castello quarter for the plain-jane Osteria da Dante, with its *cicchetti* of plump sea snails, tiny fish, and fried squid.

Campania

Polenta Pasticciata con Ragù di Carne

polenta casserole with meat sauce

Immediately after cooking in liquid, polenta is soft and creamy and can be served as is, usually as a bed for stews or sauces. Or it can be allowed to set up in a shallow pan or bowl and then cut into slices or wedges. These firm pieces can be grilled or fried and used in place of bread for crostini *(see page 49) or layered, as in this dish, and baked with a meat sauce and cheese. Other cheeses, such as Fontina or young pecorino, can replace the mozzarella, and a plain tomato sauce or mushroom sauce can stand in for the ragù.*

Although polenta is usually associated with northern Italy, this is a southern Italian dish. It's perfect to double or triple for a crowd, and can be assembled a day or two ahead of time and baked just before serving.

POLENTA

8 cups (64 fl oz/2 l) water

2 cups (10 oz/315 g) polenta (coarse yellow cornmeal)

1 tablespoon salt

SAUCE

2 tablespoons unsalted butter

2 tablespoons olive oil

1 yellow onion, chopped

1 carrot, peeled and chopped

1 celery stalk, chopped

1 clove garlic, chopped

½ lb (250 g) ground (minced) beef or veal

½ cup (4 fl oz/125 ml) dry red wine

1 can (28 oz/875 g) plum (Roma) tomatoes with juice

salt and freshly ground pepper

½ lb (250 g) fresh mozzarella cheese, sliced

¼ cup (1 oz/30 g) grated Parmigiano-Reggiano cheese

♨ To make the polenta, in a saucepan, bring the water to a boil. Dribble the cornmeal into the water in a very thin, steady stream, stirring constantly with a wooden spoon to prevent lumps. Add the salt. When the polenta begins to boil, reduce the heat to low. Cook, stirring frequently, until it is thick and pulls away from the sides of the pot, 30–40 minutes.

♨ Meanwhile, oil two 8-inch (20-cm) square baking pans. Pour the polenta into the prepared pans, dividing it evenly and spreading it flat with a rubber spatula moistened with cold water. Let cool until firm. (The polenta can be made up to 24 hours ahead. Cover with plastic wrap and refrigerate.)

♨ To make the sauce, in a large saucepan over medium heat, melt the butter with the olive oil. Add the onion, carrot, and celery and cook, stirring, until tender but not browned, about 10 minutes. Stir in the garlic. Add the meat and cook, stirring to break up any lumps, until browned, about 10 minutes. Add the wine and cook until the liquid evaporates, about 2 minutes more. Pass the tomatoes and their juice through a food mill or sieve directly into the saucepan. Add salt and pepper and simmer, uncovered, until thickened, 30–45 minutes.

♨ Preheat an oven to 400°F (200°C). Oil a large square or rectangular baking dish.

♨ Cut the polenta into eight 4-inch (10-cm) squares and arrange half of the squares in the bottom of the baking dish. Spoon on half of the sauce, covering evenly, and top with half of the mozzarella cheese slices. Repeat the layers using the remaining ingredients. Sprinkle the Parmigiano-Reggiano cheese evenly over the top.

♨ Bake until the cheese melts and the sauce is bubbling, about 40 minutes. Let stand for 5 minutes, then serve hot directly from the baking dish.

serves 4

Soft, creamy polenta is typically poured out of its cooking pot onto a round wooden board. A length of string smoothly "slices" it into servings.

Liguria

Trenette al Pesto

trenette with potatoes, green beans, and pesto

Ligurians make uncooked pasta sauces from various herbs, nuts, or anchovies. Traditionally made by hand in a mortar, this type of sauce is called pesto, from pestare, *which means "to pound." The best known of this family of sauces is composed of basil, garlic, pine nuts, and cheese and is usually served over* trenette *or* linguine *tossed with thin green beans and sliced potatoes, perfect foils for the rich sauce.*

PESTO

1½ cups (2 oz/60 g) firmly packed fresh
basil leaves

3 tablespoons pine nuts

1 clove garlic

pinch of coarse salt, plus salt to taste

⅓ cup (3 fl oz/80 ml) extra-virgin olive oil

1 cup (4 oz/125 g) grated Parmigiano-Reggiano
cheese

2 tablespoons unsalted butter, at room temperature

½ lb (250 g) new potatoes, peeled and sliced

½ lb (250 g) thin green beans, trimmed

1 lb (500 g) trenette *or* linguine

To make the pesto, in a food processor or blender, combine the basil, pine nuts, garlic, and a pinch of salt. Process until very finely chopped. With the machine running, gradually add the olive oil in a steady stream and process until smooth. Turn off, add the cheese and butter, and pulse a few times just until the ingredients are blended. Set aside.

Bring a large pot three-fourths full of water to a boil. Add salt to taste, the potatoes, and the green beans and cook until the vegetables are just tender, about 8 minutes. Using a skimmer, transfer the vegetables to a warmed serving bowl and keep warm.

Add the pasta to the boiling water and cook, stirring frequently, until al dente. Drain, reserving a ladleful of the cooking water.

Add the pasta and the pesto to the vegetables. Toss well, adding the reserved pasta water as needed to thin the sauce. Serve immediately.

serves 4–6

Campania

Lasagne di Magro

meatless lasagne

In northern Italy, lasagne usually is made with besciamella, a white sauce, and meat ragù. In this southern version, ricotta and mozzarella cheeses are substituted for the besciamella and a meatless tomato sauce replaces the ragù. The result is lighter and less rich, but no less delicious. You will end up with a generous amount of sauce. Serve the remainder alongside the baked lasagne, or toss it with pasta for another meal.

SAUCE

3 tablespoons unsalted butter

1 tablespoon olive oil

1 yellow onion, finely chopped

5 lb (2.5 kg) fresh tomatoes, peeled, seeded, and chopped, or 2 cans (28 oz/875 g each) plum (Roma) tomatoes seeded and chopped, with juice

salt and freshly ground pepper to taste

6–8 fresh basil leaves, torn into small pieces

PASTA DOUGH (ABOUT 1¼ LB/625 G)

about 3 cups (15 oz/470 g) unbleached all-purpose (plain) flour

5 eggs

FILLING

1 egg

3 cups (1½ lb/750 g) ricotta cheese

¼ cup (⅓ oz/10 g) finely chopped fresh flat-leaf (Italian) parsley

salt and freshly ground pepper to taste

1 cup (4 oz/125 g) grated Parmigiano-Reggiano cheese

½ lb (250 g) fresh mozzarella cheese, thinly sliced

❀ To make the sauce, in a large, heavy saucepan over medium heat, melt the butter with the olive oil. Add the onion and sauté until tender, about 5 minutes. Add the tomatoes and salt. Bring to a simmer, and cook, stirring occasionally, until thickened, about 45 minutes. Stir in the basil and pepper. Let cool to room temperature. You should have about 7 cups (56 fl oz/1.75 l).

❀ To make the pasta, follow the directions on page 249, using the quantity of ingredients given. Roll out the pasta by hand or by machine. Cut into eight 12-by-4-inch (30-by-10-cm) strips.

❀ Bring a large pot three-fourths full of water to a boil. Add salt to taste and the pasta strips, a piece at a time, stirring gently so that they do not stick together. Boil until almost tender, about 1 minute. Drain off about two-thirds of the water, leaving the pasta in the pot. Refill the pot with cold water and set aside.

❀ To make the filling, in a bowl, lightly beat the egg until blended. Stir in the ricotta, parsley, salt, and pepper.

❀ Preheat an oven to 375°F (190°C). In a 9-by-12-by-2-inch (23-by-33-by-5-cm) baking dish, spread about ¼ cup (2 fl oz/60 ml) of the sauce. Remove 2 of the lasagne noodles from the pot, spread them on a kitchen towel, and pat dry. Place the pasta in the pan in a single layer. Spread evenly with about 1 cup (8 oz/250 g) of the ricotta mixture, and sprinkle with ¼ cup (2 oz/60 g) of the grated cheese. Scatter about one-fourth of the mozzarella slices on top. Make a second layer using 2 noodles and spread it with sauce. Layer again with the cheeses as described. Repeat the layers. Make a final layer with the remaining noodles, spread with a thin layer of sauce, and top with the remaining mozzarella and grated cheese. (At this point the dish can be covered and refrigerated for several hours or for up to overnight before baking.)

❀ Bake until the sauce is bubbling, the top is browned, and the center is heated through, about 45 minutes. (If the lasagne has come straight from the refrigerator, it will need to bake for about 1¼ hours.) Remove from the oven and let stand for 10 minutes. Meanwhile, reheat the remaining sauce over low heat. Cut the lasagne into squares and serve. Pass the remaining sauce and grated cheese at the table.

serves 8

Although pasta is but one of the traditional primi, it is surely the most beloved.

Il Pecorino Romano

What Parmigiano-Reggiano is to northern Italy, pecorino romano is to the south. Pecorino, from *pecora*, or "sheep," is made from ewe's milk. The animals thrive on rocky hillsides, but much of the grazing land that once surrounded Rome, where the cheese is traditionally made, has been lost to progress. Many cooks must now substitute pecorino sardo from Sardinia, a similarly processed cheese with the same characteristics and only a modest difference in taste due to local variations in the milk. Sharp and salty, pecorino romano is primarily eaten as a grating cheese on pastas and soups, and is also delicious on salads of bitter greens. One of my favorite combinations is arugula with sliced sweet pears or apples and thin flakes of pecorino romano.

When to use pecorino romano and when to use Parmigiano-Reggiano? Dishes of southern Italian origin and those made with olive oil, garlic, and vegetables go best with pecorino, while butter or cream sauces are complemented by Parmigiano. Sometimes the two grating cheeses are combined for a balance of sweetness, sharpness, and pure cheese flavor.

Milder forms of pecorino can be found all over Italy. In Tuscany and Umbria, for example, sweet young pecorino is eaten after meals with a drizzle of fine olive oil and a dusting of black pepper or with a drizzle of honey.

Lazio

Bucatini all'Amatriciana

bucatini with tomatoes, pancetta, and chile

Guanciale—*pork cheek that resembles unsmoked bacon and is cured with salt, pepper, and sometimes garlic*—is typically used in this dish from Amatrice, a small town near Rome known for its excellent pork products. Pancetta, rolled pork belly cured in a similar manner, can be substituted. Tomatoes, onion, garlic, and chile complete the sauce, which is served over bucatini, a thick rod-type pasta with a hole in the center.

¼ lb (125 g) guanciale or pancetta, chopped

2 tablespoons olive oil

1 small yellow onion, chopped

2 cloves garlic, chopped

1 small dried red chile, crushed, or pinch of red pepper flakes

2½ cups (15 oz/470 g) peeled, seeded, and chopped tomatoes (fresh or canned), passed through a food mill or sieve

pinch of salt, plus salt to taste

1 lb (500 g) bucatini, perciatelli, or rigatoni

⅓ cup (1½ oz/45 g) grated pecorino romano cheese, plus more for passing

⚜ In a saucepan large enough to hold the cooked pasta and sauce over medium heat, cook the *guanciale* or pancetta in the olive oil, stirring often, until golden, about 10 minutes. Add the onion and sauté until tender and golden, about 5 minutes. Add the garlic and chile and sauté until the garlic is golden, about 1 minute longer.

⚜ Add the tomatoes and salt, bring to a simmer, and cook uncovered, stirring occasionally, until the sauce thickens, about 15 minutes.

⚜ Meanwhile, bring a large pot three-fourths full of water to a boil. Add the pasta and salt to taste and cook, stirring frequently, until al dente. Drain the pasta, reserving a ladleful of the cooking water.

⚜ Pour the pasta into the saucepan and stir and toss well. Add a little of the cooking water if the pasta seems dry. Sprinkle with the cheese and toss again. Transfer to a warmed bowl and serve immediately. Pass additional cheese at the table.

serves 4–6

Lombardia

Risotto ai Funghi, Piselli, e Salsiccia

risotto with mushrooms, peas, and sausage

The secret to making risotto is to cook it slowly, stir it often, and add as much liquid as the rice requires. Since the pot will need almost constant stirring, have all of the ingredients ready in advance and be prepared to devote your undivided attention to cooking the rice. The texture and flavor are best when the risotto has been carefully made and is served fresh from the stove.

Soft, creamy risotto usually is served as a first course, followed by meat or fish. Top this risotto with shavings of Parmigiano-Reggiano cheese and serve with Barbera, a red wine from the Piedmont region that complements mushrooms and sausages.

6 cups (48 fl oz/1.5 l) meat stock

3 tablespoons unsalted butter

1 tablespoon olive oil

1 yellow onion, finely chopped

½ lb (250 g) Italian pork sausages, casings removed and meat chopped

½ lb (250 g) fresh white mushrooms, brushed clean and sliced

2 cups (14 oz/440 g) medium-grain rice such as Arborio, Carnaroli, or Vialone Nano

½ cup (4 fl oz/125 ml) dry white wine

½ cup (2½ oz/75 g) shelled peas (fresh or frozen)

salt and freshly ground pepper to taste

⅓ cup (1½ oz/45 g) grated Parmigiano-Reggiano cheese

❦ Pour the stock into a saucepan and bring barely to a simmer.

❦ In a large saucepan over medium heat, melt 2 tablespoons of the butter with the oil. Add the onion and sauté until tender, about 5 minutes. Add the sausages and cook, stirring frequently with a wooden spoon to break up the lumps, until lightly browned, about 5 minutes. Add the mushrooms and cook, stirring, until just wilted, about 2 minutes. Stir in the rice and cook, stirring, until the kernels are hot and coated with oil, about 2 minutes. Add the wine and continue to cook and stir until the liquid is absorbed.

❦ Add the stock ½ cup (4 fl oz/125 ml) at a time, stirring constantly and making sure the liquid has been absorbed before adding more. When the rice is about half cooked, stir in the peas and the salt and pepper. The risotto is done when the rice grains are creamy on the outside and firm, yet tender to the bite, 20–25 minutes total. Rice varies, so you may not need all of the stock or you may need more. If more liquid is required, use hot water.

❦ Remove from the heat. Stir in the remaining 1 tablespoon butter and the cheese. Spoon into warmed soup plates and serve immediately.

serves 4–6

Lombardia

Zuppa di Porri e Bietole

leek and swiss chard soup

Soup making does not have to be complicated, as this recipe shows. With just a few ingredients and not much time, you can have a flavorful, satisfying dish.

2 tablespoons unsalted butter

1 tablespoon olive oil

2 small leeks, white part and about 2 inches (5 cm) of green, cut into slices ½ inch (12 mm) thick

½ lb (250 g) Swiss chard, trimmed and cut into 1-inch (2.5-cm) pieces

6 cups (48 fl oz/1.5 l) chicken stock

½ cup (3½ oz/105 g) medium-grain rice such as Arborio

salt and freshly ground pepper to taste

½ cup (1 oz/30 g) grated Parmigiano-Reggiano cheese

❦ In a large saucepan over low heat, melt the butter with the olive oil. Add the leeks and cook, stirring occasionally, until tender and golden, about 10 minutes. Add the Swiss chard and stock, raise the heat to medium, and bring to a simmer. Cook, stirring occasionally, until the chard wilts, about 10 minutes.

❦ Add the rice and salt and pepper. Cover and cook over low heat until the rice is tender, about 20 minutes. Stir in the cheese. Adjust the seasonings.

❦ Ladle into warmed bowls and serve immediately.

serves 4

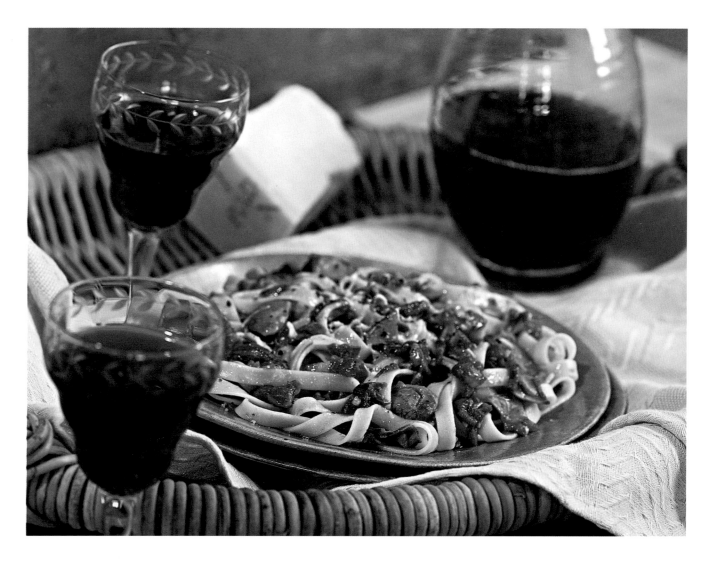

Lazio

Fettuccine con Fegatini

fettuccine with chicken livers

The towns of Castelli Romani outside of Rome are a favorite destination for city dwellers on a Sunday outing. The restaurants there cater to big family groups, and the food, including dishes such as this one, is often served on large platters at long tables. A typical meal includes homemade fettuccine, a secondo of porchetta (suckling pig laced with rosemary) served with roasted potatoes and spinaci in padella, and an endless stream of the local white wine.

This sauce for fettuccine calls for pancetta, a cut of pork similar to bacon that is seasoned, rolled, and cured like a salami. Although it can be eaten raw, it is more often used as a cooking ingredient, as in this sauce. It is also used to wrap game birds, chickens, or rabbits to keep them moist during roasting or grilling. Variations on this tasty pasta dish abound; some are made with chicken giblets and prosciutto, while others call for fresh white mushrooms instead of dried porcini.

PASTA DOUGH (ABOUT 1 LB/500 G)

about 2½ cups (12½ oz/390 g) unbleached all-purpose (plain) flour

4 eggs

SAUCE

1 oz (30 g) dried porcini mushrooms

2 cups (16 fl oz/500 ml) warm water

2 slices pancetta, about 2 oz (60 g), finely chopped

2 large shallots, finely chopped

3 tablespoons olive oil

1 clove garlic, minced

½ cup (4 fl oz/125 ml) dry white wine

2 large tomatoes, peeled, seeded, and chopped

salt and freshly ground pepper to taste

½ lb (250 g) chicken livers, trimmed and quartered

¼ cup (1 oz/30 g) grated pecorino romano cheese

✻ To make the pasta dough, follow the directions on page 249, using the quantity of ingredients given. Roll out the pasta by hand or by machine and cut into strips about ⅜ inch (1 cm) wide for fettuccine.

✻ To make the sauce, place the mushrooms in a bowl with the warm water. Let soak for at least 30 minutes to soften. Drain the mushrooms, reserving the liquid. Strain the liquid through a paper coffee filter or fine-mesh sieve lined with dampened cheesecloth (muslin). Rinse the mushrooms well under running water, paying special attention to the stem pieces, which may have bits of soil clinging to the base. Drain well, pressing out any excess water, and chop. Set aside.

✻ In a large frying pan over medium heat, sauté the pancetta and shallots in the olive oil until golden, about 5 minutes. Stir in the garlic and cook for 1 minute longer. Add the mushrooms and their liquid and the wine. Bring to a simmer and cook until most of the liquid evaporates.

✻ Add the tomatoes and season with salt and pepper. Cook, stirring occasionally, until the sauce is thickened, about 15 minutes. Add the chicken livers and simmer, stirring occasionally, until just cooked through, about 5 minutes longer.

✻ Meanwhile, bring a large pot three-fourths full of water to a boil. Add the pasta and salt to taste and cook, stirring frequently, until al dente.

✻ Drain the pasta and place in a warmed shallow serving bowl. Add the sauce and toss gently to combine. Sprinkle with the cheese; toss lightly again and serve immediately.

serves 4

Fresh pasta is never considered better than dried pasta. They are simply different, and directions for cooking and saucing them respect that difference.

Mostra del Fungo

Every year in the town of Ceva, in Piedmont, lovers of wild mushrooms gather for a fair, called the *Mostra del Fungo*. Most of the varieties that grow abundantly in the region are assembled and labeled for inspection. Amateur hunters and expert mycologists alike gather to inspect and study the displays, which are set up on outdoor tables in the town center. The most common varieties are the *ovoli*, egg-shaped specimens, and porcini, or "little pigs," so-called because of their chubby shape and meaty texture.

Nearby restaurants celebrate the season by offering all-mushroom menus, with tables reserved far in advance. The mushrooms are sautéed, fried, or roasted; used in soups, breads, pasta sauces, and stuffings; and cooked with meats. The finest porcini are reserved for grilling, like a juicy steak. One memorable version cloaks them with a cream-and-prosciutto sauce.

The local mushrooms are also preserved for use during the seasons when they are not available fresh. The most common method is to slice and dry them, although they are also frozen, pickled, canned, or processed into sauces and pâtés sold in jars.

SECONDI

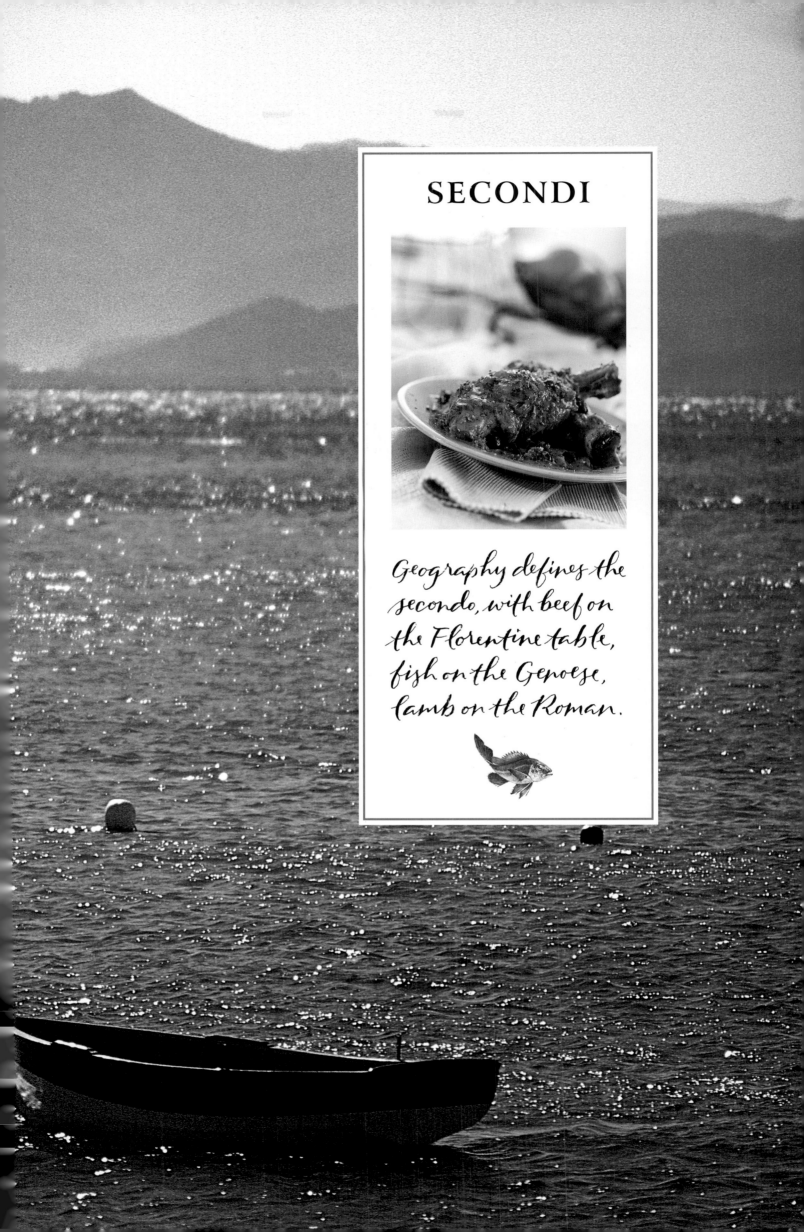

Geography defines the secondo, with beef on the Florentine table, fish on the Genoese, lamb on the Roman.

ACCORDING to an old Italian adage, *carne e pesce ti fanno vivere a lungo,* "meat and fish make you live a long time." Although modern medical findings may have put the veracity of that statement in doubt, there was a time when those foods were so expensive and difficult to come by that only the wealthiest Italians could afford to eat them on a regular basis.

At a luxurious feast prepared for Pope Pius V by the great chef Bartolomeo Scappi in 1570, the second course included roasted and fried meats, poultry, and game. The menu was obviously a special one and a blatantly excessive display of wealth. Among the highlights of the *secondo piatto* were skylarks with lemon sauce, stuffed pigeons roasted with sugar and capers, pastries filled with veal sweetbreads, spit-roasted veal and kid, and a soup of almond cream with the flesh of pigeons.

Preceding spread: A lone fishing boat floats on the glittering azure water of the Ligurian Sea near the medieval fishing village of Santa Margherita Ligure. **Above:** The *salsamenteria,* or *salumeria,* is a shop-cum-delicatessen that sells *salumi,* cheeses, pasta, prepared salads, and specialty foods. **Right:** Throughout Florence, elements of contemporary life bump against treasures of antiquity, like these modern-day scooters propped against centuries-old sculptures.

Until recently, poor people, and they were in the majority, ate meat, fish, or poultry rarely—only on holidays, or if they were sick—if at all. Even now, most Italians consume relatively small amounts of these protein-rich foods. Because of the scarcity and expense of meat, every scrap was precious and put to use, with the result that the less choice cuts, often the most flavorful, have come to be preferred. The Romans, for example, eat every type of offal, as well as feet, tails, and snouts. These parts are known collectively as the *quinto quarto,* the "fifth quarter," a humorous reference to the fact that butchered animals are typically divided into quarters. The trimmings are thus extra, like a fifth quarter.

A popular dish at the traditional restaurants located in the city's Testaccio neighborhood, where the old slaughterhouse was located, is *pajata,* the milk-filled intestines of newborn calves cooked in a tomato sauce with rigatoni. *Coda alla vaccinara,* a delicious stew of oxtails simmered with celery, tomatoes, and wine in a rich brown gravy, is practically synonymous with Roman cooking.

In Emilia-Romagna, *zampone,* spiced ground pork encased in a pig's foot, is a popular sausage. According to legend, it was invented in the Middle Ages to feed a starving population while their city was under siege by an invading army. Little did those early patriots know that today Modena, the site of the invention, would be celebrated throughout Italy for its superb *zampone.*

Pork is especially delicious in Italy, whether roasted, grilled, or made into prosciutto and fresh and dried sausages. A feature of every market, fair, and festival throughout Lazio and Umbria is *la porchetta,* a whole pig generously stuffed with a mix of rosemary, wild fennel, mint, garlic, and plenty of black pepper and roasted on a spit. Each *porchettaro,* as the cook who specializes in this preparation is called, has his or her own favorite blend of the traditional seasonings. Enormous animals weighing up to two hundred pounds (100 kg) each are used, and the roasted meat is sliced to be eaten as is or in sandwiches. *La porchetta* is also made at home using suckling pigs.

In southern Italy, lamb is particularly popular, roasted whole on a spit or cut into chunks for stew. One of my favorite stews from Apulia calls for simmering chunks of lamb with white wine and aromatic vegetables until very tender. Just before serving, a combination of beaten eggs, cheese, peas, and parsley is poured over the stew, known as *agnello con i piselli,* and baked until the custard sets.

A popular street food in Sicily is *stigghiole,* lamb's intestines wrapped around green (spring) onions on sticks and flavored with grated

Left: As they sip their drinks, young boys watch fishermen go about their work in the tiny village of Vernazza, the second link from the north in the chain of the Cinque Terre. **Right top:** The Venetian lagoon is the source of an extraordinary variety of fish and shellfish, and Venice's Rialto fish market is a sight to behold with its beautiful displays, often labeled in the local dialect, of *bisato* (eel) and *caparozzoli* (clams), *ghizzo* (goby) and *seppie* (cuttlefish). **Right middle:** In Muggia, a small harbor town minutes away from Trieste on the northern Adriatic, a fishmonger's hand-painted sign—"Fish always fresh"—attracts attention and customers. **Right bottom:** A young fisherman, just returned from an early morning venture, proudly shows off his catch.

cheese and pepper. The meat is grilled over charcoal braziers set up on Palermo's street corners and in her labyrinthine Vucciria, an animated marketplace that recalls the souks of nearby North Africa.

Tuscany is home to a special breed of massively built white cattle known as Chianina, which produces the best beef in Italy and some of the best in the world. It is the source of the classic *bistecca alla fiorentina,* T-bone steak charcoal-grilled rare, *al sangue,* and served with lemon wedges and a generous sprinkling of salt. In Piedmont, cooks prepare *brasato al Barolo,* a thick cut of beef braised for hours in Barolo wine. Southerners eat beef, too, although typically it is cut into thin slices and rolled around a tasty filling, or ground up and seasoned to make meatballs or loaves.

Rabbit is popular all over Italy, no doubt a testimony to the ease of raising it. Its mild flavor makes it the perfect mate for more pungent ingredients like bell peppers (cap-sicums), garlic, and anchovies in Piedmont, or tomatoes and olives in Campania. In Venice, rabbits are cut up and deep-fried for a dish called *coniglio fritto dorato.* Palermitans, in contrast, favor *coniglio in agrodolce,* punctuated with capers and olives.

Capon is the centerpiece of many holiday meals, and it is customary for a Roman family to sit down to a plump roast capon on Christmas Day. The bird is also sometimes used to make a rich and flavorful broth for stuffed pasta. Turkey, too, is roasted whole and often its cavity is filled with ground meats, nuts, and other flavorings, although Bolognese cooks favor thick slices of turkey breast breaded, fried, and topped with prosciutto and cheese before they come off the fire.

In the Veneto and a handful of other regions, horsemeat, known as *carne di cavallo,* is regularly eaten, purchased in butcher shops that specialize in its sale. Cooks in Verona are famous for their *pastissada di cavallo,* a rich horsemeat stew served with polenta, while in Apulia, *involtini* of horsemeat are sometimes served.

Italians will eat fish only if it is absolutely fresh, and many fish restaurants are closed on Mondays for good reason: no fishing boats go out on Sundays. I once met a woman living in landlocked Umbria who, to be sure that she got the freshest seafood, drove once a week to a distant town to meet the fishmonger's van, rather than wait for him to arrive in her area late in the day. Even though the vendor kept the fish chilled, she feared that its quality suffered en route.

The kinds of fish available change from one region to the next, but Italian cooks agree on the two most popular ways to prepare them: grilled simply with olive oil and a squeeze of lemon juice or deep-fried in a light, crispy crust.

Shellfish also are often simply grilled or fried, although clams, mussels, squid, and cuttlefish frequently turn up in pasta sauces and risotti. The sweetest clams I have ever eaten are the tiny *vongole veraci,* prized for pasta sauces in Rome and throughout the south.

Simply cooked or richly sauced, *secondi* cooked the Italian way are so satisfying that a small portion always seems sufficient, especially after an antipasto and a *primo.*

Far left: The Italians generally consume less meat than they do pasta and vegetables, and they are highly discerning when they shop at the local *macelleria* (butcher shop). A good butcher must be precise when cutting his customers' selections, be it *vitello* (veal), *manzo* (beef), or *agnello* (lamb). **Left:** Beach chairs and umbrellas await the tide of vacationers at Monterosso, one of Italy's many popular coastal resort towns. **Above top:** Alassio, an ancient Ligurian maritime center with a mild winter climate, has welcomed a steady stream of international tourists since the late 1800s. Ceramic reproductions of the autographs and handprints of visiting celebrities are embedded in its Muretto (little wall), and quirky artwork decorates other facades of this friendly resort town. **Above middle:** This sign hangs on the shop of a pork butcher in Greve, Tuscany. Although in Italy pigs are commonly slaughtered for processing into *salumi,* fresh pork and *porchetta* (whole roast pig) are also popular. **Above bottom:** In a city abundant with relics, Rome's tombstones offer just one of many glimpses into the past.

Umbria

Agnello a Scottadito

grilled lamb ribs

After a visit to Orvieto's magnificent cathedral and fascinating Etruscan museum, my husband and I were tired and hungry. We let our noses lead us through the winding medieval streets to a trattoria where a roaring fireplace was used to grill steaks, chops, chicken, sausages, and these simple rib chops, bathed with an olive oil and garlic marinade brushed onto them with rosemary branches. The crisp, brown chops are best when eaten sizzling hot off the fire, so the Italians call them scottadito, meaning "burned fingers."

3 large cloves garlic, finely chopped

2 tablespoons chopped fresh rosemary

¼ cup (2 fl oz/60 ml) olive oil

freshly ground pepper to taste

8–12 rib lamb chops, well trimmed of fat

salt to taste

lemon slices (optional)

☙ In a small bowl, stir together the garlic, rosemary, olive oil, and pepper. Place the lamb chops in a shallow dish and brush the mixture over them. Cover and refrigerate for at least 2 hours or as long as overnight.

☙ Prepare a fire in a charcoal grill, or preheat a broiler (griller). Brush the grill rack or the rack of a broiler pan with oil. Place the chops on the rack and grill or broil, turning as needed, until browned and crisp on the outside yet still pink and juicy inside, about 10 minutes.

☙ Transfer to warmed individual plates, sprinkle with salt, and serve immediately with lemon slices, if using.

serves 4

Until recently, poor people —and they were the majority— ate meat, poultry, and fish rarely, if at all.

Sicilia

Frittata di Verdura e Formaggio

wild greens and cheese frittata

It is not unusual to drive by a meadow in Italy and see someone foraging for wild greens. Country people know just which ones are the tastiest and where to find them. If they pick more than they can use, they often bring the extra to the market to sell.

In Sicily, this frittata is commonly made with wild greens, but cultivated vegetables won't disappoint you.

about 1 lb (500 g) leafy greens such as spinach, chard, broccoli rabe, or arugula (rocket), tough stems removed

1 cup (8 fl oz/250 ml) water

8 eggs

salt and freshly ground pepper to taste

¼ cup (2 fl oz/60 ml) olive oil

1 clove garlic, minced

¼ lb (125 g) ricotta salata or young pecorino cheese, thinly sliced

☙ In a large saucepan, combine the greens and water. Cover, place over medium heat, and cook until tender, about 5 minutes for spinach or up to 10 minutes for tougher greens. Drain well in a colander, pressing out the excess liquid. Place in a kitchen towel and squeeze dry. Chop the greens and set aside.

☙ Preheat a broiler (griller).

☙ In a bowl, beat the eggs just until blended. Season with salt and pepper.

☙ In a 9-inch (23-cm) flameproof frying pan over low heat, warm the olive oil. Add the garlic and sauté until fragrant, about 30 seconds. Add the greens and a pinch of salt, and stir and toss to coat the greens well. Lightly stir in the eggs and arrange the cheese slices on top. Cook, lifting the edges as needed to allow the uncooked egg to flow underneath, until set around the edges but still moist in the center, about 10 minutes. Slip under the broiler until the top is puffed and golden and the cheese is slightly melted, about 1 minute.

☙ Remove from the broiler and transfer to a serving plate. Serve hot, cut into wedges.

serves 4

Campania

Bistecca alla Pizzaiola

steak in the style of the pizza maker

Ripe, sweet tomatoes and aromatic garlic are the signature ingredients of Neapolitan cooking, often accented with a bit of peperoncino, the fiery little red chile beloved by many southern Italian cooks. The tomatoes, like other fruits and vegetables that grow in Campania, are unrivaled for flavor, their character a product of the hot sun and the rich volcanic soil around Mount Vesuvio. Even the ancient Romans recognized the inherent productivity of the soil, calling the area Campania Felix, the Fortunate Country.

In Naples, one of the most popular toppings for a pizza is simply crushed fresh tomatoes, chopped garlic, and a sprinkling of oregano. The same ingredients can be used as a sauce for simmering small steaks, which is how this dish got its name. A similar specialty of Neapolitan cooks, costolette di maiale alla pizzaiola, uses pork in place of the beef.

4 small beef chuck steaks or similar small steaks

2 tablespoons olive oil

2 cloves garlic, finely chopped

4 fresh tomatoes, peeled, seeded, and chopped, or 2 cups (12 oz/375 g) seeded and chopped plum (Roma) tomatoes, with juice

2 tablespoons chopped fresh flat-leaf (Italian) parsley

½ teaspoon dried oregano

salt and freshly ground pepper to taste

Pat the steaks dry. In a large frying pan over medium-high heat, warm the olive oil. Add the steaks and cook, turning once, until browned on both sides, about 10 minutes.

Reduce the heat to low, scatter the garlic around the steaks, and cook for 1 minute. Add the tomatoes, parsley, oregano, salt, and pepper. Cover partially and simmer, turning the steaks occasionally, until tender and the sauce is thickened, about 30 minutes.

Transfer to warmed individual plates and serve.

serves 4

Lombardia

Petto di Vitello Ripieno

breast of veal stuffed with spinach and mushrooms

An inexpensive cut of veal, the breast is nonetheless full of flavor. Ask the butcher to cut a pocket between the meat and the bones, forming a perfect cavity for a delicious stuffing. The meat is cooked slowly until it is very tender and the flavors of the stuffing permeate it. Serve with mashed potatoes and accompany the meal with a first-rate Barbera wine.

1 lb (500 g) spinach, tough stems removed

½ cup (4 fl oz/125 ml) water

salt to taste

2 tablespoons unsalted butter

1 tablespoon olive oil

2 yellow onions, chopped

½ lb (250 g) fresh white mushrooms, brushed clean and chopped

freshly ground pepper to taste

½ cup (2 oz/60 g) fine dried bread crumbs

¼ cup (1½ oz/45 g) golden raisins (sultanas)

½ cup (2 oz/60 g) grated Parmigiano-Reggiano cheese

1 bone-in veal breast (6 ribs), 5½ lb (2.75 kg), cut with a pocket (see note)

1 carrot, peeled and chopped

1 celery stalk, chopped

6 fresh sage leaves

1 cup (8 fl oz/250 ml) meat or chicken stock

½ cup (4 fl oz/125 ml) dry white wine

☙ In a saucepan, combine the spinach, water, and salt. Cover, place over low heat, and cook until the spinach is wilted and tender, about 5 minutes. Drain in a colander, pressing out excess water with the back of a spoon, and let cool. Wrap the spinach in a clean kitchen towel and squeeze out any remaining liquid. Chop finely and set aside.

☙ In a large frying pan over medium heat, melt the butter with the olive oil. Add half of the onions and cook, stirring occasionally, until tender, about 5 minutes. Add the mushrooms and cook, stirring frequently, until the mushrooms are tender and their liquid has evaporated, about 10 minutes longer.

Stir in the reserved spinach, salt, and pepper. Remove from the heat and stir in the bread crumbs and raisins. Let cool slightly, then stir in the cheese.

☙ Preheat an oven to 450°F (230°C). Oil a large ovenproof pot.

☙ Stuff the spinach mixture into the veal pocket, and sew up the opening with kitchen twine. Sprinkle the veal with salt and pepper. Scatter the carrot, the celery, the remaining onion, and the sage in the prepared pot. Add the veal, bone side down.

☙ Roast, uncovered, until browned, about 45 minutes. Reduce the heat to 350°F (180°C). Add the stock and wine. Cover and cook, basting the meat occasionally, until it is very tender, about 2 hours.

☙ Transfer the veal to a warmed platter and cover to keep warm. Strain the pan juices through a fine-mesh sieve into a small saucepan. Skim off the fat from the surface. Bring the juices to a simmer over medium heat and reduce until the liquid is syrupy, about 3 minutes. Season with salt and pepper.

☙ Carve the veal by cutting between the rib bones. Serve with the pan juices.

serves 6

Sicilia

Tonno con Capperi e Cipolle

braised tuna with capers and onions

The tuna hunt is a centuries-old tradition in Sicily. Called la mattanza, *the hunt still takes place every May on the west coast of the island, pursuing the fish as they migrate from the Atlantic to the warmer waters of the Mediterranean. The fishermen set out in a fleet of small boats and lay out huge nets, stringing them from one boat to the next. As they go about their work, they sing ancient chants led by their leader, the* rais. *The chants, which are believed to date back to the Arab domination of Sicily, help the men to work in unison to maneuver the large fish into the nets. Once they are trapped, the chanting becomes louder and louder as the men haul the enormous tunas onto their boats.*

In Sicily, tuna is roasted, grilled, and cooked in sauces. The finest cut, which comes from the tender belly of the fish, is called ventresca. *Much of it is preserved in olive oil and sold in jars to be eaten as an antipasto.*

2 tablespoons olive oil

1 large red (Spanish) onion, thinly sliced

½ cup (4 fl oz / 125 ml) dry white wine

2 tablespoons capers, chopped

1 bay leaf

salt and freshly ground pepper to taste

4 thick tuna or swordfish steaks, each about
6 oz (185 g)

chopped fresh flat-leaf (Italian) parsley

☙ In a large frying pan over medium heat, warm the olive oil. Add the onion and sauté until tender, about 5 minutes; do not allow to brown. Add the wine, capers, bay leaf, salt, and pepper and stir well. Rinse the fish steaks and pat dry. Push the onion mixture to one side of the pan and add the fish. Cook, turning once, until opaque throughout, about 5 minutes total. Transfer the fish to a warmed serving platter and sprinkle with salt and pepper.

☙ Continue to cook the onions until most of the liquid has evaporated, just a few minutes. Pour the onions over the tuna. Sprinkle with parsley and serve hot or at room temperature.

serves 4

Sicilia

Calamari Imbottiti alla Griglia

grilled stuffed squid

Calamari, or squid, belong to the family of cephalopods that in Italy includes meaty seppie, *or cuttlefish;* polpo, *or octopus; and* moscardini, *tiny octopus with tightly curled tentacles. Squid are the most versatile members of the family. They can be deep-fried, boiled quickly and tossed with lemon juice and olive oil for a seafood salad, cooked with tomatoes and garlic for a pasta sauce, roasted, or grilled.*

8 squid, each 6–8 inches (15–20 cm) long

1 cup (4 oz / 125 g) fine dried bread crumbs

¼ cup (2 fl oz / 60 ml) olive oil

1 tablespoon chopped fresh flat-leaf
(Italian) parsley

salt and freshly ground pepper to taste

2 oz (60 g) cooked ham, cut into narrow strips

1 tablespoon raisins

1 clove garlic, minced

1 lemon, sliced

☙ Prepare a fire in a charcoal grill, or preheat a broiler (griller).

☙ To prepare each squid, gently pull the head and tentacles away from the body. Cut off the tentacles just above the eyes; discard the lower portion. Squeeze the base of the tentacles to extract the hard, round beak. Squeeze the viscera out of the body and pull out the long, plasticlike quill. Cut a small slit in the pointed end of the body sac and rinse to eliminate any sand. Rinse the tentacles. Drain and pat dry.

☙ In a bowl, toss together the bread crumbs, olive oil, parsley, salt, and pepper. Set aside ¼ cup (1 oz / 30 g) on a plate. In a bowl, mix together the remaining crumbs, the ham, raisins, and garlic. Stuff loosely into the body sacs. Tuck a set of tentacles into each sac and secure the top with a toothpick. Roll each squid in the reserved crumbs to coat evenly.

☙ Place the squid on the grill rack or on a broiler pan. Grill or broil, turning once, until opaque and lightly browned, about 2 minutes on each side.

☙ Serve on a warmed platter with lemon slices.

serves 4

Toscana

Pesce al Forno con Pinoli e Uva Passa

roasted fish with rosemary, pine nuts, and raisins

Tuscans are known for their simple techniques for cooking meats, often marinating them first with fresh rosemary. But along the region's Mediterranean coastline, fish is also flavored with the highly aromatic herb. In this recipe, it permeates the flesh, while the vinegar balances out the sweetness of the raisins. Any leftovers are good served cold. A red wine from the Chianti region makes a surprisingly good partner.

2 tablespoons olive oil

2 small red snappers or sea bass, 1¼–1½ lb (625–750 g) each, cleaned with heads and tails intact

2 tablespoons chopped fresh rosemary, plus sprigs for garnish

salt and freshly ground pepper to taste

⅔ cup (4 oz/125 g) raisins

¼ cup (1¼ oz/37 g) pine nuts

¼ cup (2 fl oz/60 ml) balsamic vinegar

¼ cup (2 fl oz/60 ml) water

❧ Preheat an oven to 400°F (200°C). Oil a large roasting pan with a little of the olive oil.

❧ Rinse the fish, pat dry, and place in the prepared pan. Drizzle the inside of each fish with the remaining oil and sprinkle the insides with the rosemary and the salt and pepper. Scatter the raisins inside the fish, then sprinkle the pine nuts over the tops. In a small bowl, stir together the vinegar and water and pour evenly over the fish.

❧ Roast until the flesh is opaque when cut near the bone, 25–30 minutes.

❧ Transfer the fish to a large warmed platter. Spoon the pine nuts, pan juices, and any raisins that tumbled from the cavities over the fish. Garnish with rosemary sprigs and serve immediately.

serves 4

Le Gastronomie

Gastronomie, the fancy food stores of Italy, are easy to spot, whether they anchor a piazza or are tucked away on a narrow *vicolo*. Golden loaves of bread are invariably piled against the windows, and wheels of Parmigiano-Reggiano are stacked next to the doorway, twin invitations difficult to turn down. Inside, refrigerator cases are filled with all kinds of cheeses: balls of fresh mozzarella swimming in milky liquid, swirled mounds of buttery mascarpone, ricotta molded in little basket shapes. Trays of fresh pasta, in various shapes and sizes, curled into loose skeins or stuffed and arranged in neat rows, are lined up below a canopy of *salumi*, cured meats hung from the rafters, their mouthwatering aromas perfuming the air.

Many *gastronomie* sell delicious prepared foods, too, such as salads, stuffed vegetables, and roasted chickens and other meats, perfect fare for a picnic or a quick supper. At the more elegant shops, such as Milan's Gastronomia Peck, you will find plump stuffed squabs, rosemary-scented *porchetta*, chestnut brown spit-roasted rabbits, vegetable flans made of greens or asparagus, sautéed porcini, and more.

Agnello Arrosto all'Erbe e Patate

herbed roast leg of lamb with potatoes

At an inn outside of Orvieto, my husband and I feasted on lamb seasoned with herbs and garlic and roasted on a spit over glowing coals. A pan of potatoes and onions placed under the lamb caught the dripping juices and flavored the potatoes as they turned a delicious crusty brown. Since I do not have a fireplace to use for cooking, I devised the following method to attain similar results.

1 bone-in leg of lamb, about 7 lb (3.5 kg)

2 oz (60 g) pancetta, sliced

6 fresh sage leaves

4 cloves garlic

1 tablespoon fresh rosemary leaves

salt and freshly ground pepper to taste

6–8 boiling potatoes, peeled and cut into 1-inch (2.5-cm) chunks

2 yellow onions, thinly sliced

¼ cup (2 fl oz / 60 ml) olive oil

❀ Preheat an oven to 450°F (230°C). Trim off the excess fat from the lamb. Finely chop together the pancetta, sage, garlic, and rosemary. With the tip of a small knife, make slits ½ inch (12 mm) deep all over the surface of the lamb. Push a little of the herb mixture into each slit. Sprinkle with salt and pepper.

❀ Choose a roasting pan about the same size as the lamb. Put the potatoes and onions in the pan and drizzle with the olive oil. Sprinkle with salt and pepper. Position a large cake rack over the potatoes and onions. Place the lamb, fat side down, on the rack.

❀ Roast for 20 minutes. Reduce the oven temperature to 350°F (180°C). Turn the lamb over and roast for 1 hour longer for medium-rare or 1¼–1½ hours for well done, or until an instant-read thermometer inserted into the thickest part away from the bone registers 135°F (57°C) for medium-rare or 170°F (77°C) for well done. Transfer to a cutting board, cover with aluminum foil, and let rest for 15–20 minutes. Leave the potatoes in the oven to brown, raising the heat to 450°F (230°C), if necessary. Cut the lamb lengthwise into thin slices. Serve with the potatoes and onions.

serves 8–10

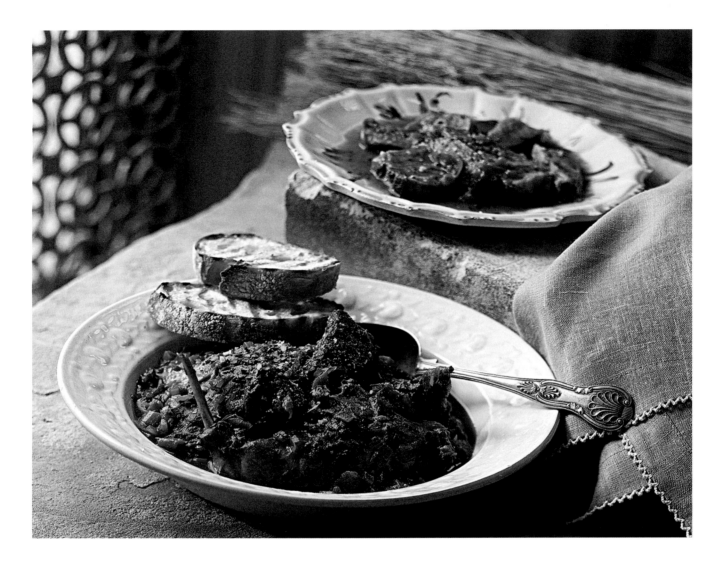

Friuli-Venezia Giulia

Stinco al Forno

roasted veal shanks

Rather than cut veal shanks into thick slices for ossobuco as they do in Lombardy, cooks in Friuli prefer to roast or braise the shanks whole. The large shank bone, its end wrapped with a white napkin, makes a perfect handle to grasp while carving.

2 veal shanks, about 2 lb (1 kg) each

2 tablespoons unsalted butter

3 tablespoons olive oil

salt and freshly ground pepper to taste

2 celery stalks, chopped

1 carrot, peeled and chopped

1 yellow onion, chopped

2 cloves garlic, chopped

2 tablespoons chopped fresh sage

1 cup (8 fl oz/250 ml) dry white wine

2 cups (16 fl oz/500 ml) chicken or meat stock

✤ Pat the veal shanks dry. In a heavy pot over medium heat, melt the butter with the olive oil. Add the shanks and cook, turning occasionally, until browned, about 15 minutes total. Sprinkle the veal with salt and pepper. Scatter the celery, carrot, onion, garlic, and sage around the meat. Cook until wilted, about 5 minutes longer.

✤ Add the wine to the pan and cook for 1 minute. Add the stock and bring to a simmer. Reduce the heat to low, cover partially, and cook, turning the shanks occasionally, until the meat is tender and coming away from the bone, about 2 hours.

✤ Transfer the shanks to a plate and cover to keep warm. Skim the fat from the pan juices, then pass the contents of the pan through a food mill placed over a clean saucepan. Bring it to a simmer over medium heat. If it is too thin, raise the heat slightly and boil until reduced.

✤ Carve the meat from the shanks and divide among warmed individual plates. Spoon the pan juices over the meat.

serves 4–6

Scottiglia all'Aretina

arezzo-style hunter's stew

While Tuscans along the coast prepare cacciucco, *a stew made with many types of fish, cooks in the landlocked Arezzo area make a similar dish called* scottiglia *with meats and game. Just like the fish version, the latter calls for tomatoes, garlic, and wine and is served over slices of toasted bread. And also like the fish version, it is made from whatever is on hand, usually what the hunters were able to bring home supplemented by veal, pork, or chicken. The greater the variety of meats you use, the better the stew will taste. In addition to the meats listed, you can add or substitute pheasant, pigeon, hare, boar, or other game.*

2 lb (1 kg) lean pork spareribs, cut into individual ribs

4 tablespoons (2 fl oz/60 ml) olive oil

salt and freshly ground pepper to taste

1 chicken, about 3½ lb (1.75 kg), cut into serving pieces

1 lb (500 g) boneless veal shoulder, cut into 2-inch (5-cm) chunks

1 rabbit, cut into serving pieces

4 quail, cut in half

2–2½ lb (1–1.25 kg) fresh tomatoes, peeled, seeded, and chopped, or 1 can (28 oz/875 g) plum (Roma) tomatoes, seeded and chopped, with juice

2 yellow onions, chopped

2 carrots, peeled and chopped

1 celery stalk, chopped

2 cloves garlic, chopped

1 small dried red chile, crushed, or pinch of red pepper flakes

2 tablespoons chopped fresh flat-leaf (Italian) parsley

1 tablespoon chopped fresh rosemary

juice of 2 lemons

1 cup (8 fl oz/250 ml) dry red wine

1–2 cups (8–16 fl oz/250–500 ml) meat stock

GARNISH

8 slices coarse country bread

2 cloves garlic

2 tablespoons chopped fresh flat-leaf (Italian) parsley

❧ Pat the pork ribs dry. In a large frying pan over medium-high heat, heat 2 tablespoons of the olive oil. Add the ribs to the pan and cook, turning as needed, until well browned on both sides, about 10 minutes. Transfer to a plate. Sprinkle with salt and pepper. In batches, add the chicken, veal, rabbit, and quail to the same pan and brown in the same way. Spoon off the excess fat as it accumulates in the pan.

❧ Meanwhile, pass the tomatoes through a food mill or sieve placed over a bowl. In a heavy pot large enough to hold all of the meats, warm the remaining 2 tablespoons olive oil over medium heat. Add the onions, carrots, celery, garlic, chile, parsley, and rosemary and sauté until softened but not browned, about 5 minutes. Add the tomatoes and lemon juice, bring to a simmer, reduce the heat to low, and cook, stirring occasionally, until slightly thickened, about 10 minutes.

❧ When all of the meats have been browned, drain off the fat from the frying pan and place the pan over medium heat. Add the wine and deglaze the pan, scraping with a wooden spoon to remove any browned bits from the pan bottom. Cook for 2 minutes. Pour the liquid into the pot holding the tomatoes and add 1 cup (8 fl oz/250 ml) of the stock. Add the browned meats and any accumulated juices. Cover partially and cook over low heat until all of the meats are tender, about 1 hour. Add more stock if the liquid evaporates too quickly. The sauce should not be too thick.

❧ Just before serving time, prepare the garnish: Toast the bread slices, then rub them on one side with the garlic cloves. Place the bread slices in a large serving platter. Spoon on the meats and sauce. Alternatively, divide the meats and sauce among individual soup plates and place the toasted bread alongside. Sprinkle with the parsley and serve immediately.

serves 8

The memorable flavors the Italian cook can coax from a handful of everyday ingredients never cease to amaze me.

Liguria

Salmone in Cartoccio

salmon baked in paper

Although not native to their waters, salmon has become a popular fish among Italian cooks. Naturally, they have adapted it to Italian tastes, as this recipe, with its fresh herbs, tomatoes, and olive oil, illustrates.

The steam that forms inside the paper envelope infuses the fish with the flavor of the seasonings and keeps it moist and tender. I like to serve my guests the unopened packets and let them unwrap them themselves, releasing the fragrant steam. You could, however, transfer the fish and sauce to dinner plates in the kitchen. Aluminum foil, although not as attractive, can be substituted for the parchment.

3 tomatoes, seeded and chopped

2 shallots, finely chopped

2 tablespoons chopped fresh marjoram or oregano or ½ teaspoon dried

3 tablespoons fresh lemon juice

2 tablespoons olive oil, plus extra for oiling paper

salt and freshly ground pepper to taste

6 skinless salmon fillets, about 6 oz (185 g) each and of uniform shape

✤ Preheat an oven to 400°F (200°C).

✤ In a small bowl, stir together the tomatoes, shallots, marjoram or oregano, lemon juice, the 2 tablespoons olive oil, salt, and pepper.

✤ Rinse the fish and pat dry. Cut 6 sheets of parchment (baking paper) about 12 inches (30 cm) square. Fold each sheet in half. Open each sheet like a book, and brush the paper to one side of the crease with olive oil. Place a fillet on each oiled side. Spoon the tomato mixture over the fish, dividing it evenly.

✤ Fold the parchment paper over the fish. Tightly seal each package by folding the edges over several times and creasing firmly. Place the packages on 2 baking sheets.

✤ Bake until the salmon is opaque throughout, about 15 minutes. To check for doneness, open a package and pierce the fish with a knife.

✤ Slide the packages onto individual plates and allow the diners to open their own packages.

serves 6

Sicilia

Pesce Spada alla Griglia

swordfish on the grill with lemon and mint

The Romans called swordfish xiphias gladius, *gladius being the name of the short sword carried by soldiers. The fish, which can grow to over a thousand pounds (500 kg), are quite fearless and have been known to attack ships with their built-in weapons. Fish sellers in Italy are always careful to display the head with its awesome sword, often several feet long, alongside the trimmed swordfish. Not only is it an eye-catching sight, but it also ensures purchasers that they are getting the real thing.*

1 lemon

⅓ cup (3 fl oz/80 ml) olive oil

salt and freshly ground pepper to taste

¼ cup (⅓ oz/10 g) chopped fresh mint, plus sprigs for garnish

2 large cloves garlic, chopped

4 thin swordfish, shark, or tuna steaks, about 6 oz (185 g) each

lemon slices

✤ Grate the zest from the lemon, then halve the lemon and squeeze the juice from the halves. In a small bowl, whisk together the zest, juice, olive oil, salt, and pepper. Stir in the chopped mint and garlic.

✤ Rinse the fish steaks and pat dry. Place in a shallow nonaluminum container and pour the lemon mixture evenly over the top. Turn to coat well. Cover and refrigerate for 1 hour.

✤ Prepare a fire in a charcoal grill, or preheat a stove-top griddle or griddle pan. Remove the fish from the marinade and place on the grill rack or griddle. Cook, turning once, until just opaque throughout, 2–3 minutes on each side.

✤ Transfer to warmed individual plates and garnish the fish with the mint sprigs and lemon slices. Serve immediately.

serves 4

Il Paese del Vino

Grapes have been cultivated in Italy from the earliest times. The Etruscans left evidence that they made and drank wine, and the Greek colonizers are known to have built pipelines for transporting it to the peninsula's southern ports, from which it was shipped to dinner tables in Athens. Today grapes are grown and wine is made in every region of this age-old *paese del vino,* "country of wine."

To ensure standards of quality, in 1963, the Italian government established the *Denominazione di Origine Controllata,* a designation granted only to those wines that meet specific requirements covering every aspect of grape cultivation and wine production. In the 1970s, wines of extraordinarily high quality were further distinguished by the institution of a new category, DOCG (the G stands for *garantita,* or guaranteed authenticity). Wines outside of these two designations are labeled simply *vino da tavola,* "table wine," although the finest of these fall under yet another category, *indicazione geografica tipica,* which classifies them by color or grape variety. Fine wines are produced everywhere, but Piedmont and Tuscany are especially known for their great reds, while the whites from the Veneto and Friuli–Venezia Giulia are highly prized.

It is not necessary to use an expensive wine for cooking. You should, however, use something that you enjoy drinking and that complements the dish you are making and the wine you will be serving with it. I always use Italian wine in my Italian recipes, just as I never stray from Italian olive oil.

Umbria
Quaglie con Uva e Salsiccia
quail with grapes and sausage

Grapes grow in every region of Italy, so it is not surprising that they find their way into a number of savory dishes. I have eaten pork loin cooked with grapes and onions in Sicily and tomatoes baked with grapes in Tuscany. Another Tuscan use is in this classic preparation, which combines quail, pork sausages, and wine grapes. If wine grapes are not available, substitute table grapes and add a bit of lemon juice to balance out the sweetness of the fruit.

4 quail
salt and freshly ground pepper to taste
4 fresh rosemary sprigs, plus extra for garnish
2 tablespoons olive oil
4 mild pork sausages
½ cup (4 fl oz/125 ml) dry white wine
1 cup (8 fl oz/250 ml) meat stock
1 lb (500 g) white wine grapes (about 3 cups), stems removed

♨ Rinse the quail and pat dry. Sprinkle with salt and pepper. Tuck the wing tips underneath the breasts. Stuff a sprig of rosemary inside each cavity. Tie the legs together with kitchen string.

♨ In a large frying pan over medium heat, warm the olive oil. Add the sausages and quail and cook, turning frequently, until the meats are browned on all sides, about 15 minutes.

♨ Add the wine and simmer for 1 minute. Add the stock and bring to a simmer. Reduce the heat to low, cover, and cook, turning the sausages and quail occasionally, until the quail are tender, 25–30 minutes.

♨ Add the grapes to the pan and cook until hot and slightly collapsed, about 5 minutes. Transfer the quail and sausages to a warmed serving dish. Using a slotted spoon, scatter the grapes over the meats. If the liquid in the pan is thin, raise the heat to high and reduce until thickened and syrupy. Pour the juices over the meats. Garnish with rosemary and serve immediately.

serves 4

Lombardia

Ossobuco

braised veal shanks

Thick slices of veal shank are called ossobuco in Italian, or "bone with a hole." The tender meat is often served with saffron-flavored risotto, but I prefer to accompany it with fresh vegetables such as peas, asparagus, and baby carrots, cooked in a little butter. Be sure to provide narrow spoons or knives for removing the rich marrow from its hollows.

½ cup (2½ oz/75 g) all-purpose (plain) flour

6 slices veal shank, each 1½ inches (4 cm) thick, tied with kitchen string

2 tablespoons unsalted butter

2 tablespoons olive oil

1 small yellow onion, finely chopped

salt and freshly ground pepper to taste

1 cup (8 fl oz/250 ml) dry white wine

2 cups (16 fl oz/500 ml) meat stock

¼ cup (⅓ oz/10 g) chopped fresh flat-leaf (Italian) parsley

1 small clove garlic

½ teaspoon grated lemon zest

❧ Spread the flour on a plate and dust the veal, tapping off the excess. In a large, heavy pot over medium heat, melt the butter with the olive oil. Add the veal and cook on the first side until golden brown, about 4 minutes. Turn the meat and add the onion to the pan, scattering it around the pieces of veal. Sprinkle with salt and pepper. Cook until browned on the second side, about 4 minutes longer.

❧ Add the wine, bring to a simmer, and cook for 1 minute. Add the stock and bring to a simmer. Reduce the heat to low and cook, covered, turning occasionally, until the meat is tender, 1½–2 hours. (The dish can be prepared up to this point, cooled, covered, and refrigerated for up to 24 hours. To continue, reheat gently over low heat for 20 minutes.)

❧ Combine the parsley and garlic clove on a cutting board and finely chop together. Transfer to a bowl, add the lemon zest, and toss together. Scatter the mixture over the veal. Baste the veal with the sauce and simmer for 5 minutes longer.

❧ Transfer to a warmed serving dish or individual plates. Serve at once.

serves 6

Trentino-Alto Adige

Stufato di Cervo

venison stew with tomatoes and capers

After World War II, the two regions of Trentino and the Alto Adige in the north of Italy were linked politically, although they have little but their location in common. Alto Adige shares its northern border with Austria, so it is not surprising that this mountainous region has many Austro-Hungarian influences, including the language. Many of the residents speak German fluently and Italian badly. The food also has an alpine inflection. Rather than pasta, for example, people here often eat knödel (canederli), bread dumplings flavored with ham, liver, or cheese. Goulash and stews flavored with sweet spices like cinnamon or cloves are prepared with venison, chamois, kid, or roebuck. Strudel containing apples or poppy seeds is the most popular dessert.

I find this stew especially appealing because of its combination of flavors: game accented with cloves cooked with two typically southern Italian ingredients, capers and tomatoes.

3 lb (1.5 kg) boneless venison stew meat, cut into 2-inch (5-cm) pieces

½ cup (2½ oz/75 g) all-purpose (plain) flour

salt and freshly ground pepper to taste

2 tablespoons unsalted butter

1 tablespoon olive oil

2 oz (60 g) pancetta, chopped

2 carrots, peeled and chopped

1 celery stalk, chopped

1 yellow onion, chopped

1 clove garlic, chopped

2 tablespoons chopped fresh flat-leaf (Italian) parsley, plus extra for garnish

4 fresh sage leaves, chopped

1 teaspoon chopped fresh rosemary

1 cup (8 fl oz/250 ml) dry white wine

2 cups (16 fl oz/500 ml) meat stock

1 cup (6 oz/185 g) peeled, seeded, and chopped tomatoes (fresh or canned)

1 tablespoon capers, chopped

2 whole cloves

❦ Pat the meat dry a few pieces at a time. Spread the flour on a plate and lightly dust the pieces, shaking off the excess. Season with salt and pepper.

❦ In a large, heavy pot over medium heat, melt the butter with the oil. Add the meat in batches and cook, turning as needed, until well browned on all sides, about 15 minutes. As the meat is ready, transfer it to a plate.

❦ Add the pancetta, carrots, celery, onion, garlic, parsley, sage, and rosemary to the pot and cook over medium heat, stirring occasionally, until the vegetables have softened, about 5 minutes. Add the wine, bring to a simmer, and deglaze the pot, stirring and scraping with a wooden spoon to remove the browned bits from the pot bottom. Cook for 1 minute longer.

❦ Return the venison to the pot. Add the stock, tomatoes, capers, and cloves and bring to a simmer. Reduce the heat to low, cover, and cook the meat, turning occasionally, until tender, about 2 hours. Add a little water if the liquid reduces too much.

❦ Using a slotted spoon, transfer the meat to a plate. Pass the contents of the pot through a food mill or a sieve placed over a bowl. Return the sauce to the pot and bring back to a simmer. If it seems too thin, raise the heat and boil until reduced. Return the meat to the pot and reheat gently.

❦ Transfer to a warmed deep platter or serving bowl, sprinkle with parsley, and serve at once.

serves 4

Liguria

Coniglio in Vino Rosso

rabbit in red wine

Since Liguria is known for its white wines, I was surprised to find this rabbit dish cooked with red wine. But then I discovered a number of other variations as well, including pine nuts instead of walnuts and sage instead of thyme. The rabbit and the olives are the two constants. The most typical olive in Liguria is the small, dark Taggiasca, used for both eating and for oil. Another brine-cured Mediterranean olive can be substituted.

1 rabbit, about 2½ lb (1.25 kg), cut into 8 serving pieces

3 tablespoons olive oil

salt and freshly ground pepper to taste

1 yellow onion, finely chopped

1 celery stalk, chopped

2 teaspoons chopped fresh rosemary

1 teaspoon chopped fresh thyme

1 bay leaf

½ cup (4 fl oz/125 ml) dry red wine

2 tablespoons chopped walnuts

⅓ cup (2 oz/60 g) brine-cured Mediterranean olives (see note)

1 tablespoon chopped fresh flat-leaf (Italian) parsley

❧ Rinse the rabbit pieces and pat dry. In a large frying pan over medium heat, warm the olive oil. Add the rabbit and cook until well browned on all sides, about 10 minutes. Sprinkle with salt and pepper. Add the onion, celery, rosemary, thyme, and bay and cook, stirring occasionally, until the vegetables are softened, about 5 minutes. Add the wine and cook for 1 minute. Add the walnuts, cover, and cook, turning occasionally, until the rabbit is tender when pierced with a fork, about 30 minutes. Add a little water if the juices evaporate too quickly.

❧ Add the olives and heat through. Transfer to a warmed platter, sprinkle with the parsley, and serve.

serves 4

Toscana

Pollo alla Diavola

deviled chicken

If you visit Tuscany, you might want to look into buying a mattone *("brick"), a heavy glazed terracotta disk that looks like a flat pot lid and is used for weighting down a chicken as it cooks. This recipe is sometimes called* pollo al mattone, *since it uses a* mattone *to hold the bird close to the heat so that it cooks crisply and evenly. Of course, you don't need a special gadget at all. A heavy roasting pan filled with bricks will do the job as well.*

This chicken is especially delicious grilled over charcoal. Garnish with strips of orange or lemon zest for an attractive presentation.

¼ cup (2 fl oz/60 ml) fresh lemon juice

¼ cup (2 fl oz/60 ml) olive oil

2 small dried red chiles, crushed, or 1 teaspoon red pepper flakes, or to taste

salt and freshly ground pepper to taste

1 small chicken, about 3 lb (1.5 kg)

❧ In a shallow baking dish, whisk together the lemon juice, olive oil, chiles, salt, and pepper.

❧ Split the chicken in half through the breast bone. Rinse and pat dry. With a meat pounder, pound each half gently to flatten it out. Place the chicken halves in the lemon juice mixture, turning to coat well. Cover and let stand at room temperature for at least 1 hour or as long as 24 hours in the refrigerator.

❧ Prepare a fire in a charcoal grill, or preheat a stove-top griddle or griddle pan. Cover the bottom of a heavy roasting pan with aluminum foil. Place a heavy object such as a brick in the pan.

❧ Remove the chicken from the marinade, and place it on the grill rack or griddle skin-side up. Place the foil-covered pan on top to keep it flat against the grill. Cook, removing the weight occasionally and turning the chicken over to be sure it does not burn. The chicken is done when the juices run clear when the thigh is pierced with a knife, about 30 minutes. It may be necessary to move the chicken to a cooler part of the grill or reduce the heat under the griddle to prevent it from browning.

❧ Transfer to individual plates (or halve first if serving 4) and serve hot or at room temperature.

serves 2–4

Campania

Frittata di Patate, Peperoni, e Prosciutto

pepper, potato, and prosciutto frittata

Frittate are served as both primi *and* secondi *all over Italy. They may be thick or thin, individual size or as large as a cake, eaten hot or cold. Such versatility makes them ideal for picnics, sandwiches, and all kinds of portable meals. They are also the perfect vehicles for leftover pasta, vegetables, cheeses, or meats.*

¼ cup (2 fl oz/60 ml) olive oil

1 yellow onion, thinly sliced

2 red, yellow, or green bell peppers (capsicums), seeded and thinly sliced crosswise

2 potatoes, unpeeled, thinly sliced

salt and freshly ground pepper to taste

8 eggs

½ cup (3 oz/90 g) chopped prosciutto

❧ In a large flameproof frying pan, warm the olive oil over medium heat. Add the onion and sauté until tender, about 5 minutes. Add the bell peppers and potatoes and cook, stirring occasionally, until the potatoes are tender, about 20 minutes. Sprinkle with salt and pepper.

❧ Meanwhile, in a bowl, beat the eggs until well blended. Season with salt and pepper.

❧ Preheat a broiler (griller).

❧ When the potatoes have become tender, scatter the prosciutto over the vegetables, then pour in the eggs. Cook, lifting the edges as needed to allow the uncooked egg to flow underneath, until set around the edges, but still moist, about 10 minutes. Slip under the broiler until the top is set and golden, about 1 minute. Watch the pan closely that the frittata does not brown.

❧ Remove from the broiler and transfer to a serving plate. Serve hot, warm, or at room temperature, cut into wedges.

serves 4

Liguria

Spigola al Forno

sea bass with potatoes and olives

More than any other herb, I associate the scent of marjoram with Ligurian cooking. Similar to oregano, although more delicate and with a hint of citrus, fresh marjoram is used in stuffings, sauces, and marinades for both fish and meat. It is a perennial with small green to golden leaves and tiny white or pale pink flowers in summer. Striped bass and red snapper are also good prepared this way.

2 sea bass, 1½–2 lb (750 g–1 kg) each, cleaned with heads and tails intact

2 tablespoons chopped fresh flat-leaf (Italian) parsley

1 tablespoon chopped fresh marjoram

6 tablespoons (3 fl oz/90 ml) olive oil

2 tablespoons fresh lemon juice

salt and freshly ground pepper to taste

4 lemon slices

2 lb (1 kg) waxy boiling potatoes, peeled and sliced

½ cup (2½ oz/75 g) Gaeta or other Mediterranean-style black olives

✲ Preheat an oven to 450°F (230°C).

✲ Rinse the fish and pat dry. Using a sharp, heavy knife, make slashes on both sides of each fish, cutting down to the bone. In a small bowl, stir together the parsley, marjoram, 4 tablespoons (2 fl oz/60 ml) of the olive oil, the lemon juice, salt, and pepper. Rub the mixture inside the cavities and over the outside of each fish. Tuck the lemon slices inside. Cover and let stand while you prepare the potatoes.

✲ Rinse the potato slices under cold running water and pat dry. Place in a bowl and add the remaining 2 tablespoons oil, the salt, and pepper. Toss well, then spread them in a roasting pan large enough to hold them in a shallow layer.

✲ Bake until the potatoes begin to brown, 25–30 minutes. Turn the potatoes, stir in the olives, and place the fish on top. Continue to bake until the flesh is opaque when cut near the bone and the potatoes are tender, 20–30 minutes longer.

✲ Transfer the fish to a warmed platter. Surround with the potatoes and olives. Serve at once.

serves 4

I Mangiapolenta

Corn, or maize, is native to the Americas, so it was not until after Columbus's voyages to the New World that the grain was planted in Europe. Because it grew easily and was cheap, corn, ground into meal and cooked into a mush, became a mainstay of poor people, especially in northern Italy, where both the milled and cooked forms were called polenta. The peasants simmered the ground grain with milk or ate it with beans or vegetables, and it became so closely associated with northern Italy that southern Italians, who prefer pasta, sometimes call northerners by the disparaging name of *mangiapolenta,* or "polenta eaters."

Today polenta is eaten in many forms, soft and creamy as a side dish with meats or fish, or chilled and cut into slices to fry or grill as a base for mushrooms, cheese, or a meat *ragù.* It is even eaten for dessert: in the Alto Adige polenta is sweetened and fried in butter and accompanied with baked apples, while in Liguria it is drizzled with extra-virgin olive oil, sprinkled with sugar, and eaten with blood oranges.

Yellow cornmeal is used in most regions, although white is preferred in the Veneto because its delicate flavor is believed to be more complementary to fish. Polenta is traditionally cooked in a special copper pot called a *paiolo.* Housewares stores in Italy sell electrified versions that eliminate the need for tedious stirring.

Toscana

Stracotto con Cipolle

beef pot roast with onions

In Florence, pot roast tender enough to cut with a fork is served with creamy white beans, cooked al fiasco, in an old wine bottle, with sage and garlic. The plentiful onion gravy from the beef is also good over soft polenta or mashed potatoes. Pour a fine Chianti or Brunello di Montalcino.

1 beef pot roast, about 4 lb (2 kg)

2 cloves garlic, thinly sliced

2 oz (60 g) pancetta, chopped

3 tablespoons olive oil

salt and freshly ground pepper to taste

1 cup (8 fl oz/250 ml) dry red wine

6 red (Spanish) onions, thinly sliced

2 carrots, peeled and thinly sliced

1 celery stalk, sliced

2 tablespoons chopped fresh flat-leaf (Italian) parsley

2 cups (16 fl oz/500 ml) meat stock

2 cups (16 fl oz/500 ml) tomato purée

❦ Make small slits about ½ inch (12 mm) deep all over the meat. Insert some of the garlic and pancetta into each slit.

❦ In a large, heavy pot over medium heat, warm the olive oil. Add the beef and brown well on all sides, about 15 minutes. Season with salt and pepper. Spoon off the fat. Add the wine and cook over medium heat until most of the liquid evaporates, about 2 minutes.

❦ Add the onions, carrot, celery, parsley, stock, and tomato purée. Cover partially and bring to a simmer. Reduce the heat to low and cook the meat, turning occasionally, until tender, about 3 hours.

❦ Transfer the meat to a plate and keep warm. Using a slotted spoon, lift out the solids from the pot juices and place in a food processor or blender. Purée until smooth. Return the purée to the liquid in the pot and reheat gently. If too thin, raise the heat and boil to reduce. Taste and adjust the seasonings.

❦ Slice the beef and arrange on a warmed platter. Spoon some of the sauce on top, and pass the remaining sauce at the table.

serves 8

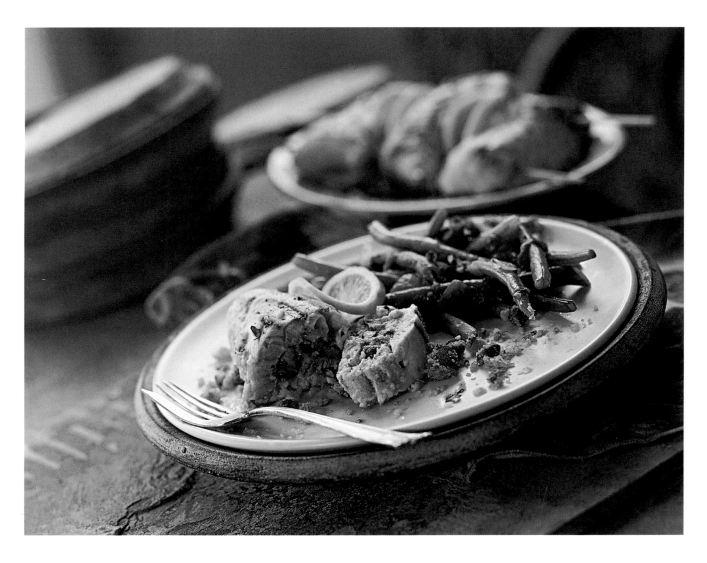

Sicilia

Involtini di Pesce Spada

stuffed swordfish rolls

This is a typical Sicilian way to serve swordfish. Thin slices are wrapped around a tasty stuffing of bread crumbs, tomatoes, and capers. To keep the rolls from falling apart as they cook, thread them onto pairs of bamboo or wooden skewers held side by side.

½ cup (3 oz/90 g) seeded and chopped tomato

½ cup (1 oz/30 g) fresh bread crumbs

2 tablespoons capers, chopped

1 large clove garlic, finely chopped

½ teaspoon dried oregano

salt and freshly ground pepper to taste

4 tablespoons (2 fl oz/60 ml) olive oil

4 thin swordfish steaks, about 1 lb (500 g) total weight, skinned

2 tablespoons fresh lemon juice

lemon slices

♕ Preheat a broiler (griller), or prepare a fire in a charcoal grill.

♕ In a bowl, combine the tomato, bread crumbs, capers, garlic, oregano, salt, and pepper. Add 2 tablespoons of the oil and mix well.

♕ Rinse the fish and pat dry. Working with 1 fish steak at a time, place between 2 sheets of plastic wrap and pound gently with a meat pounder to flatten to ¼ inch (6 mm) thick. Cut each steak in half. Place one-eighth of the bread-crumb mixture near one end of a piece of fish. Roll up the fish, tucking in the sides to make a neat package. Repeat with the remaining fish and stuffing. Using one hand, hold 2 skewers parallel to each other about 1 inch (2.5 cm) apart. Thread 4 rolls onto each pair of skewers so they are lightly touching. In a small bowl, stir together the remaining 2 tablespoons oil and the lemon juice. Brush on the rolls.

♕ Place the skewers on a rack on a broiler pan or on a grill rack. Broil or grill, turning once, until just firm to the touch, 3–4 minutes on each side. Slide the rolls off the skewers onto a warmed platter. Serve hot with lemon slices.

serves 4

Friuli-Venezia Giulia

Fagiano Ripieno

stuffed pheasant

The hardworking and hospitable Friulani, tucked away in the far northeast corner of the country, have experienced a checkered history, enjoying both great glory—for years the town of Aquileia was the second most important city in the Roman Empire—and much hardship—centuries of grinding poverty and countless invaders. La cucina friulana is known for its gnocchi of potato or squash; cialzòn, pasta stuffed with a variety of mixtures, from spinach and citron to ricotta and herbs; and the legendary prosciutto di San Daniele, a prosciutto that connoisseurs declare surpasses that of Parma. Other traditional cured pork products, such as prosciutto affumicato and muset (pork sausage flavored with cinnamon), are appreciated beyond the local table, and game, including venison, trout, and the pheasant dish presented here, are popular in the area's mountainous regions.

Since the lean meat of pheasant can be dry, cooks wrap the birds with pancetta. Frequent basting helps, too, as does a savory meat stuffing. The pancetta gets brown and crisp while the pheasant stays moist and juicy. Chicken or guinea fowl can also be roasted this way.

2 slices white bread, crusts removed

¼ cup (2 fl oz/60 ml) milk

2 tablespoons unsalted butter

1 small yellow onion, chopped, plus 1 medium onion, thinly sliced

1 bay leaf

¼ lb (125 g) ground (minced) beef

1 Italian pork sausage, about 3 oz (90 g), casing removed and crumbled

1 pheasant liver or chicken liver, chopped

salt and freshly ground pepper to taste

1 pheasant, about 2½ lb (1.25 kg)

4 slices pancetta

2 fresh rosemary sprigs

½ cup (4 fl oz/125 ml) dry white wine

❧ In a small bowl, soak the bread in the milk until the milk is fully absorbed. Squeeze the bread to remove excess moisture, then chop it.

❧ In a small frying pan over medium heat, melt the butter. Add the chopped onion and bay leaf and sauté until the onion is tender, about 5 minutes.

❧ Discard the bay leaf. Transfer the onion to a bowl and add the bread, beef, sausage meat, liver, salt, and pepper. Mix well.

❧ Preheat an oven to 375°F (190°C). Oil a roasting pan just large enough to hold the pheasant.

❧ Rinse the pheasant and pat dry. Sprinkle with salt and pepper. Stuff the beef mixture into the cavity, and lay the pancetta slices over the breast and legs. Tuck the wings under the body and pass a 3–4 foot (90–120 cm) piece of kitchen string under the bird at the wing ends. Cross the ends over the breast, securing the pancetta in place, then cross again at the tail end. Finally, tie the drumsticks securely. Place in the prepared pan. Scatter the sliced onion and the rosemary in the pan and pour in the wine.

❧ Roast for 30 minutes, basting occasionally with the pan juices. Raise the heat to 450°F (230°C). Continue to roast until the juices run clear when the flesh is pierced near the joint between the leg and the body, 15–30 minutes. Transfer the pheasant to a warmed platter, cover with aluminum foil, and let rest for 10 minutes.

❧ Strain the pan juices through a fine-mesh sieve into a small saucepan. Skim off the fat from the surface, then reheat the juices.

❧ Carve the pheasant and arrange on the platter. Pass the juices at the table.

serves 4

Toscana

Arista

roast loin of pork with rosemary

A group of bishops assembled in Florence in 1439 to discuss church matters. At a banquet one night, the guests were served a succulent pork roast flavored with rosemary and garlic. The Greek delegates were so impressed that they proclaimed it aristos, "the best." The name stuck and to this day the roast is known by the Italianized arista.

4 large cloves garlic

2 tablespoons fresh rosemary

salt and freshly ground pepper to taste

1 bone-in pork loin roast, about 5 lb (2.5 kg)

¼ cup (2 fl oz/60 ml) olive oil

2 carrots, peeled and chopped

1 celery stalk, chopped

1 cup (8 fl oz/250 ml) dry white wine

❦ Preheat an oven to 325°F (165°C).

❦ Very finely chop together the garlic and rosemary. Transfer to a small bowl, season with salt and pepper, and mix well to form a paste. Make slits ½ inch (12 mm) deep all over the pork roast and insert some of the mixture into each slit. Rub the roast all over with the remaining seasoning, then rub with the olive oil. Place the meat in a roasting pan just large enough to hold it.

❦ Roast the meat for 1 hour. Scatter the carrots and celery around the meat. Continue to roast until an instant-read thermometer inserted into the thickest part of the roast away from the bone registers 155°F (68°C) or the meat is pale pink when cut into at the center, about 1¼ hours longer. Transfer to a warmed platter and cover loosely with aluminum foil to keep warm. Let rest for 15 minutes before carving.

❦ Place the roasting pan over low heat. Add the wine and deglaze the pan, stirring with a wooden spoon to scrape up any browned bits from the pan bottom. Pour through a fine-mesh sieve into a small saucepan. Skim off the fat. Reheat to serving temperature, if necessary.

❦ Carve the roast and arrange on a warmed platter or individual plates. Pour the pan juices into a warmed bowl and pass at the table.

serves 8

Sardegna

Insalata di Gamberi alla Sarda

shrimp salad with tomatoes and capers

Until recently, most Sardinians did not eat much fish or shellfish, so not many traditional seafood recipes exist. Even though Sardinia is an island, the largest in the Mediterranean Sea, few people lived along the shore. Anyone who did had to endure the malarial mosquitoes that thrived in the coastal marshes and frequent attacks by pirates. Except for those who settled in the few port cities, Sardinians made their homes in the center of the island, where they labored as shepherds and farmers. In the 1950s, malaria was eradicated, and not long after wealthy land developers arrived. Now the northeastern coast, known as the Costa Smeralda, is rimmed with beautiful beaches and expensive resorts.

Some of the most delicious shrimp I have ever sampled were served to me on Sardinia. They were simply prepared, often with the excellent local tomatoes.

1¼ lb (625 g) shrimp (prawns), peeled and deveined

1 teaspoon salt, plus salt to taste

2 tomatoes, chopped

3 green (spring) onions, including tender green tops, chopped

2 tender inner celery stalks, thinly sliced

¼ cup (2 oz/60 g) capers, chopped

2 tablespoons chopped fresh mint

¼ cup (2 fl oz/60 ml) extra-virgin olive oil

2 tablespoons fresh lemon juice

lettuce leaves

Bring a large saucepan of water to a boil. Add the shrimp and the 1 teaspoon salt. Cook just until the shrimp turn pink and begin to curl, 1–2 minutes. Drain and rinse under cold water. Pat dry.

In a bowl, combine the shrimp, tomatoes, green onions, celery, capers, and mint. In a small bowl, whisk together the olive oil, lemon juice, and salt to taste. Pour over the shrimp mixture and toss well. Let stand for 15 minutes, stirring once or twice.

Arrange the lettuce on a platter and spoon the salad on top. Serve immediately.

serves 4

Lazio

Coda di Rospo Piccata

monkfish with lemon and capers

Lemon, capers, and parsley are frequently served as a sauce for thin veal cutlets, so I was surprised to find this version made with medallions of monkfish at a Roman restaurant renowned for its fish. Since monkfish is firm and meaty, it makes perfect sense, of course, and later I learned that some fishermen call it "the veal of the sea." Serve this simple dish with buttered asparagus or broccoli.

1½ lb (750 g) monkfish fillets

½ cup (2½ oz/75 g) all-purpose (plain) flour

salt and freshly ground pepper to taste

2 tablespoons olive oil

3 tablespoons unsalted butter

½ cup (4 fl oz/125 ml) dry white wine

3 tablespoons fresh lemon juice

2 tablespoons capers, chopped

2 tablespoons chopped fresh flat-leaf (Italian) parsley

lemon slices

Cut the fish fillets on an angle into slices ½ inch (12 mm) thick (or have the fishmonger do this for you). Rinse the fish and pat dry. Working with 1 slice at a time, place between 2 sheets of plastic wrap and pound gently with a meat pounder to ¼ inch (6 mm) thick.

Spread the flour on a plate and season with salt and pepper. Lightly dust the fish slices with the flour, shaking to remove the excess.

In a large frying pan over medium heat, melt the butter with the olive oil. Add the fish in batches and cook, turning once, until browned on both sides, about 4 minutes total. Transfer to a warmed platter and keep warm.

When all the fish is cooked, pour the wine and lemon juice into the pan and add the capers. Raise the heat and cook until the liquid is reduced and slightly thickened, about 1 minute. Stir in the parsley. Pour the sauce over the fish and garnish with the lemon slices. Serve immediately.

serves 4

Il Prosciutto

Prosciutto is ham that has been air-dried and cured with salt and spices. It is sometimes called *prosciutto crudo,* or "raw ham," to distinguish it from *prosciutto cotto,* which is cooked, usually boiled, ham.

Prosciutto crudo is made in many different regions of Italy, but the most famous version comes from near the town of Parma in Emilia-Romagna. The pigs raised for *prosciutto di Parma* are fed on the whey left over from the making of Parmigiano-Reggiano cheese. Sweet and tender, this prized ham is typically served thinly sliced as an appetizer with fresh butter and crusty bread, luscious ripe melon or figs, or as an accompaniment to soft, milky mozzarella. No part of a prosciutto is wasted. Small bits of meat are chopped and added to pasta dishes, and the bone is treasured for flavoring soups, particularly those made with beans.

Prosciutto from Friuli–Venezia Giulia is renowned as well, especially that cured in the town of San Daniele, easily recognized by its attached hoof. Smoked prosciutto from Savris, a lovely alpine village, is also celebrated. In Sardinia, *prosciutto di cinghiale,* made from the wild boars that live in the island's mountainous center, is a specialty sought out by both locals and mainlanders.

Lazio
Scaloppine di Vitello con Funghi e Peperoni

veal scallopini with mushrooms and peppers

Veal scallops are one of the nicest cuts because they go with so many different ingredients and cook so quickly. I like this tasty version that I first enjoyed in a little Roman trattoria with some Frascati wine. It is a perfect quick meal for a busy-day supper. The secret to browning scallopini—or any meat or fish—is to dust them with flour just seconds before cooking them. If the meat is coated in advance, the flour will become gummy and not brown properly.

8 veal scallops, almost 1 lb (500 g) total weight and ⅓–½ inch (9–12 mm) thick

⅓ cup (2 oz/60 g) all-purpose (plain) flour

salt and freshly ground pepper to taste

2 tablespoons unsalted butter

3 tablespoons olive oil

1 red bell pepper (capsicum), seeded and thinly sliced

½ lb (250 g) fresh white mushrooms, brushed clean and sliced

½ cup (4 fl oz/125 ml) white wine

2 oz (60 g) thinly sliced prosciutto, cut into narrow strips

1 tablespoon chopped fresh flat-leaf (Italian) parsley

❦ One at a time, place the veal scallops between 2 sheets of plastic wrap and pound gently with a meat pounder until ¼ inch (6 mm) thick. Spread the flour on a plate and season with salt and pepper. Lightly dust the veal scallops, shaking off the excess.

❦ In a large frying pan over medium heat, melt the butter with the olive oil. Add the veal and cook, turning once, until browned on both sides, about 6 minutes total. Transfer the veal to a plate.

❦ Add the pepper slices and mushrooms to the frying pan over medium heat and cook, stirring occasionally, until the pepper slices are tender, about 10 minutes. Add the wine and cook, stirring, until the liquid evaporates, about 2 minutes. Stir in the prosciutto. Season with salt and pepper. Return the veal to the pan, spooning the vegetables and prosciutto over it, and cook for about 1 minute longer.

❦ Transfer to a warmed platter or individual plates and scatter the parsley over all. Serve immediately.

serves 4–6

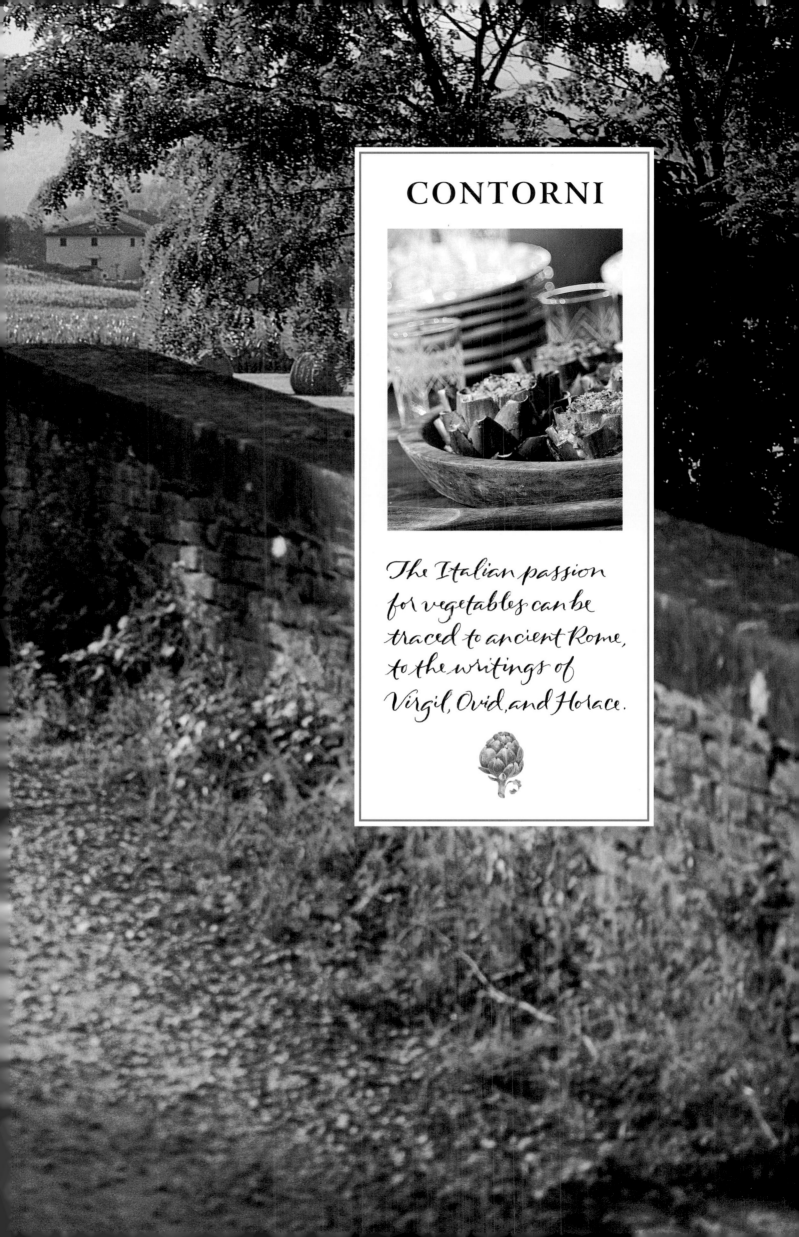

CONTORNI

The Italian passion for vegetables can be traced to ancient Rome, to the writings of Virgil, Ovid, and Horace.

CONTORNI are the vegetables that typically accompany the *secondo*. The term comes from the Italian word for "contours" or "outlines," a reflection of the Italian belief that vegetables give shape and structure to a meal. A vast variety of vegetables are grown in Italy, yielding many choices for this respected element of the Italian diet, and the combination of rich volcanic soil, skillful farming, and a long growing season makes them particularly flavorful.

In city and country markets, locally raised vegetables are proudly displayed with signs saying *nostrale*, "local," since vendors are aware that shoppers prefer produce that comes from nearby. Knowing that they will not have to ship their harvests over long distances, farmers plant the most tender varieties and pick them when they are at their peak of ripeness, flavor, and nutrition. Many Italians are avid home gardeners as well, and during the growing season every little plot is planted with a profusion of tomatoes, peppers (capsicums), artichokes, eggplants (aubergines), onions, and basil.

But what makes Italian vegetables extraordinary is the way in which they are handled in the kitchen. Arguably, no other cooks are as creative as the Italians when it comes to preparing *le verdure*. A look at the common zucchini (courgette) helps to illustrate the claim. In general, small zucchini are preferred for their fewer seeds and fuller flavor, and are often sold with their flowers still attached as an indication of freshness. The versatile squashes are cut into chunks, strips, or rounds, and deep-fried, sautéed, steamed, stewed, marinated,

Preceding spread: According to legend, it was on this stone bridge in Vicchio, Tuscany, that Cimabue discovered the young Giotto, then a shepherd. So impressed was he by Giotto's sketches of sheep that Cimabue whisked him off to Florence, launching his artistic career. **Left:** A veritable rainbow of fruits and vegetables—plums, apricots, peaches, arugula (rocket), zucchini (courgette) blossoms—is displayed at one of Bologna's famed maketplaces. **Right top:** Originally a Roman temple to the gods, the Pantheon was consecrated as a Christian church in the seventh century. Its interior is now lined with the tombs of Italian monarchs and artists. **Right middle:** *Pomodori secchi sott'olio,* sun-dried tomatoes in olive oil, is a popular ingredient throughout southern Italy. **Right bottom:** Two friends, shielding themselves from a light Abruzzo rain, pause to discuss the news of the day.

Above: Shoppers stroll through Padua's bountiful Piazza delle Erbe, perusing the season's fresh produce and pondering which fruits and vegetables to buy for the evening meal. **Near right:** For the serious cook and gardener, seeds for radicchio, squash, parsley, and other vegetables are available at most markets. **Far right top:** For cooks with neither the land nor the time to garden, a wide selection of beans, lettuces, radishes, and peppers (capsicums) appear in nearby stalls. **Far right bottom:** In the south, older women spend hours stringing *peperoncini* and then hanging them out to dry in the sun. Chiles are dried for a year or more and are then often fried in hot oil until crunchy for adding a spicy accent to many dishes.

stuffed, grilled, or baked. In Rome, the blossoms that do not bear fruit are stuffed and fried until they are *croccante,* or "crispy," while in Tuscany, the blossoms are poached in a delicate tomato sauce. Sicilians even make use of zucchini vines, known as *tennerumi,* cooking them in a delicious soup. The Genoese stuff the squashes with herbed mashed potatoes, while in other areas meat, tuna, or bread crumbs form the basis of the stuffing.

When we think of tomatoes we usually think of southern Italy, but northern cooks regularly use them, too. Garibaldi, the general whose armies were responsible for the unification of the country in the late nineteenth century, once gave a fiery speech proclaiming, "It will be spaghetti, I swear to you, that will unite Italy." Today, everyone in Italy eats spaghetti, once a regional dish, and it is usually tossed with some form of tomato sauce. But tomatoes also turn up as *contorni,* baked Sicilian style with anchovies, parsley, capers, bread crumbs, and olive oil;

braised Roman style with green beans, onion, and parsley; or prepared Tuscan style with cannellini beans.

Leafy greens fill many market stalls and produce shops, an indication of their popularity. Some vendors sell precooked chicory, chard, or spinach, ready to be sautéed with garlic and dressed with lemon juice and good olive oil. Strong or bitter greens such as broccoli rabe are cooked in much the same way, their flavors enhanced by marrying them with other sharp tastes such as anchovies, chiles, and olives. *Cavolo nero,* a Tuscan kalelike cabbage with curly, dark bluish green leaves, is cooked with the local cannellini beans or added to soups.

Certain spring vegetables are treated almost reverently, not only because they are so beloved, but also because their arrival signifies the end of the long, dark winter. All over Italy, tender shoots of greens are gathered and eaten raw or cooked as a kind of spring tonic. One of my favorites is the Roman *puntarelle,* crisp, young shoots of curled, pale green Catalan chicory that are tossed with an anchovy, garlic, and vinegar dressing and eaten as a salad. In

Above top: *Radicchio di Treviso,* a bitter, pale red chicory, is widely cultivated in the Veneto, where it is served raw in salads, grilled, or as an ingredient in risotto. **Above bottom:** While the higher elevations of the Friuli–Venezia Giuila and Alto Adige are not conducive to large-scale farming, some vegetables grow well there, such as potatoes and squash. **Right top:** The Trevi Fountain, Rome's largest, depicts Neptune flanked on either side by Tritons, one attempting to control a bucking seahorse and the other leading a more placid animal. **Right bottom:** In the Chianti region, vineyards and olive groves, rolling hills and stone farmhouses have long enchanted visitors. Even a rustic door, opened to the outside, holds the promise of a pleasing vista.

Friuli–Venezia Giulia, *bruscandoli,* which look something like skinny asparagus, and silene, a spinachlike vegetable known locally as *sclupit,* regularly appear on dinner tables.

The arrival of the first peas is celebrated with special dishes—*risi e bisi* in the Veneto, *piselli al prosciutto* in Lazio, *minestra di fave* in Sicily. Asparagus festivals are held not long after the first spears appear in the market. Some cooks prefer them green and slender, while others claim that thick, white stalks with purplish tips are the finest. The town of Bassano celebrates the first days of springtime and asparagus with an annual *sagra,* a kind of country fair. In Rome, it is not unusual to make a meal of *la vignarola,* a stew of artichokes, fava (broad) beans, and peas eaten when these seasonal vegetables are at their peak.

Mushrooms, too, have a special place in the Italian culinary repertory. Because the most flavorful varieties are not cultivated, foragers must gather them. Stories are told of secretive mushroom hunters who sneak out in the predawn hours to visit the special places they know harbor the best varieties. Their actions are covert because wild mushrooms, especially the coveted *funghi porcini,* have become scarce and expensive as forests have been cut down to make way for homes and businesses.

Because of their meaty texture and flavor, *porcini* and other sizable, fleshy mushrooms are often eaten in place of meat. In Turin, large mushroom caps are sautéed and sauced with cream and prosciutto and eaten like a steak. Romans slice *porcini* and roast them with garlic and olive oil or cook them together with anchovies, garlic, tomatoes, and mint. In many regions, small mushrooms are dipped in batter and deep-fried and then sometimes served as part of a grand *fritto misto di verdura,* a delicious mixed fry of seasonal vegetables.

Ordinary white mushrooms are elevated to new heights by cooking them with garlic, olive oil or butter, and parsley, a preparation that appears on Italian menus as *trifolati.* Although the term prompts thoughts of the truffle, *tartufo* in Italian, it does not mean that the rare and precious fungus, a member of the same family as the lowly white mushroom, would ever be cooked in such an extravagant manner. Rather it implies that a dish prepared in this style would be as rich and delicious as one that contains truffles. In fact, truffles, both the black and highly esteemed white varieties, often are not cooked at all, but merely shaved into paper-thin slices and scattered over hot cooked pasta, eggs, risotto, or polenta. The steamy heat alone is sufficient to bring out all the flavor of the truffle without damaging its delicacy.

In the south, eggplants, which thrive in the hot, dry summers, come in many shapes, colors, and sizes, and, like zucchini, may be stuffed, grilled, roasted, fried, or stewed. Campania, the region that includes Naples, has some especially interesting eggplant preparations, including combining it raw with garlic, chile, and wine vinegar. Eggplants even turn up among the *dolci;* the beautiful town of Amalfi is known for a tart made with chocolate, candied fruits, and the versatile eggplant.

Whether your taste runs to cabbages or cardoons, *alga marina* (seaweed) or *scorzonero* (black salsify), you are certain to find it expertly prepared on the Italian table.

Liguria

Melanzana alla Griglia con Maggiorana

grilled eggplant with marjoram sauce

Mela insana, "mad apple," was the name given to eggplants by early Italian botanists because it was believed they were poisonous and capable of causing insanity. They were cultivated for the beauty of their flowers and glossy fruits rather than for the kitchen. Today, there are many varieties of eggplant, both solid and striped, in a rainbow of skin colors, including purple, violet, white, and green.

Salting eggplants is a precautionary step to eliminate bitter juices. If your eggplants are very fresh, you can skip this step. Fresh marjoram complements grilled eggplant. If it is not available, fresh basil, parsley, mint, or oregano are appropriate alternatives.

2 eggplants (aubergines), about 12 oz (375 g) each, cut crosswise into slices ½ inch (12 mm) thick

salt to taste

¼ cup (2 fl oz/60 ml) extra-virgin olive oil, plus extra for brushing

2 tablespoons chopped fresh marjoram

1 clove garlic, minced

¼ teaspoon grated lemon zest

freshly ground pepper to taste

☙ Layer the eggplant slices in a colander, sprinkling each layer with salt. Top with a plate and a heavy weight such as a pot. Let stand for 1 hour to drain off the bitter juices. Rinse off the salt and pat the slices dry with paper towels.

☙ Prepare a fire in a charcoal grill, or preheat a broiler (griller).

☙ To prepare the marjoram sauce, in a small bowl, stir together the ¼ cup (2 fl oz/60 ml) oil, marjoram, garlic, zest, and pepper. Set aside.

☙ Brush the eggplant slices on both sides with olive oil. Place on the grill rack or on a broiler pan and grill or broil, turning once, until browned and tender, about 5 minutes on each side.

☙ Arrange the slices, overlapping them, on a serving plate. Spoon on the marjoram sauce and let stand until serving. Serve warm or at room temperature.

serves 6

Toscana

Fagiolini alla Fiorentina

florentine green beans with fennel

I have found that one of the best ways to discover new recipes is to visit an Italian market. All you need to do is ask how to prepare something, and invariably either the shopkeeper or another shopper will tell you all you need to know. Sometimes you don't even have to ask. Many shopkeepers will throw in some cooking advice as they tuck in a gratis bunch of fresh parsley or some rosemary branches with your purchase.

That is how I acquired this recipe. As I admired some extra-long green beans in a market in Florence, the saleswoman saw my interest and volunteered the way she cooks them—an excellent sales pitch! I bought the ingredients and hurried back to my kitchen to try it.

1 lb (500 g) green beans, trimmed

salt to taste

1 yellow onion, chopped

1 teaspoon fennel seeds

3 tablespoons olive oil

1 tomato, peeled, seeded, and chopped

freshly ground pepper to taste

☙ Bring a saucepan three-fourths full of water to a boil. Add the beans and salt and cook until softened, about 3 minutes. The timing will depend on the thickness of the beans. Drain and rinse under cold running water to halt the cooking. Drain well and pat dry with paper towels.

☙ In a saucepan over medium heat, sauté the onion and fennel seeds in the olive oil until the onion is tender, about 5 minutes. Add the tomato and cook, stirring occasionally, until the tomato is soft and the juices have evaporated, about 10 minutes.

☙ Add the green beans, salt, and pepper and simmer, uncovered, until the beans are very tender, about 10 minutes longer. Transfer to a serving dish and serve hot or at room temperature.

serves 4–6

CONTORNI *181*

Il Diavolillo

In Abruzzo, a small hot red chile, known elsewhere in Italy as the *peperoncino*, is called *diavolillo*, or "little devil." Local cooks add the fiery tiny peppers to practically everything, from eggs and meats to vegetables. Bottles of *olio santo*, "holy oil" made by infusing olive oil with chopped *diavolilli*, are placed on dining tables all over the region, for drizzling on foods.

One way to experience the *diavolillo* is to attend a *panarda*, a traditional Abruzzese feast. It is held to celebrate a special event such as a wedding, a reunion, or the feast day of a saint, and it classically consists of thirty-six dishes, although sometimes there are as many as sixty. Among them are roasted goat, crepes in broth, *maccheroni alla chitarra* (square spaghetti made with a special guitarlike cutter), stuffed turkey, grilled lamb, veal rolls in tomato sauce, soups, cheeses, pastries, and on and on.

Traditionally, the opening courses of the *panarda* are *magro,* that is, "lean," consisting primarily of fish and vegetables. The final plates are cheeses, fruits, cakes, and sugared almonds. A cellar of wines is poured throughout the banquet. When the meal is finished, most diners are anxious for a *digestivo,* usually the local herb-loaded Centerbe, a product of Tocco Casauria that comes in two forms, *forte* and *dolce.*

Abruzzo

Cavolo al Peperoncino

cabbage with pancetta and chile

Cavolo cappuccio is the Italian name for common pale green cabbage, while verza *is the crinkly leaved and somewhat more delicate savoy cabbage. Either type can be used for this recipe, which I like to serve with grilled fresh sausages or pork ribs.*

2 tablespoons olive oil

¼ lb (125 g) pancetta, salt pork, or bacon, chopped

1 yellow onion, chopped

1 small dried red chile, crushed, or pinch of red pepper flakes

1 clove garlic, finely chopped

½ head cabbage, about 1½ lb (750 g), sliced

¼ cup (2 fl oz/60 ml) water

pinch of salt

In a large saucepan over medium heat, combine the oil, pancetta, onion, and chile and cook, stirring often, until the onion is golden and tender, about 10 minutes. Stir in the garlic and cook until fragrant, about 1 minute longer.

Add the cabbage, water, and a pinch of salt. Reduce the heat to low, cover, and cook, stirring occasionally, until the cabbage is tender and browned, about 30 minutes. Add more water if necessary to prevent sticking. Serve hot.

serves 6

Italian vegetables owe their remarkable flavor to a combination of rich volcanic soil, skillful farmers, and a benevolent Mediterranean sun.

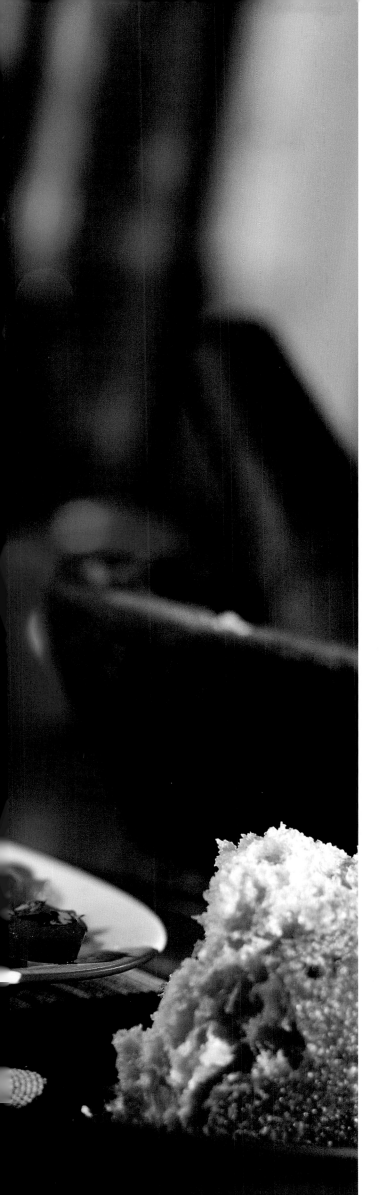

Peperonata

peppers with tomatoes and onion

Like eggplants (aubergines), potatoes, and tomatoes, peppers traveled to Italy after Columbus's voyages to America and were at first cultivated for decorative purposes only, their edibility regarded with suspicion. Now they are grown all over Italy, although the peppers from Asti in Piedmont, called quadri *because of their four sides, are justifiably famous. They are the biggest and meatiest peppers I have ever seen.*

In the Piedmont, peppers are roasted for salads, and they are an important part of bagna cauda *(see page 34). They are also served stuffed with tuna or preserved in vinegar and in oil. Peperonata, a combination of bell peppers, onions, and tomatoes, is popular too, although it may not be native to the region since similar dishes are prepared in Sicily as well as other parts of the country.*

1 yellow onion, thinly sliced

¼ cup (2 fl oz/60 ml) olive oil

1 clove garlic, sliced

4 red, yellow, or green bell peppers (capsicums), seeded and thinly sliced crosswise

2 tomatoes, peeled, seeded, and chopped, or 1 cup (6 oz/185 g) seeded and chopped canned plum (Roma) tomatoes

salt and freshly ground pepper to taste

2 tablespoons chopped fresh basil or flat-leaf (Italian) parsley

☙ In a large frying pan over medium heat, sauté the onion in the olive oil until tender, about 5 minutes. Add the garlic and cook until fragrant, about 1 minute longer.

☙ Stir in the bell peppers and cook until just beginning to brown, about 10 minutes. Add the tomatoes and cook until the peppers are tender and the sauce thickens, about 20 minutes longer. Season with salt and pepper.

☙ Transfer to a serving dish and sprinkle with the basil or parsley. Serve hot or at room temperature.

serves 4

Campania

Insalata di Rinforzo

reinforcement salad

At Christmastime, this salad is a favorite in Neapolitan homes. It appears over and over throughout the holiday season, "reinforced" each time with another handful of vegetables, more dressing, some chopped anchovies, or whatever else is needed to stretch it for another meal or the arrival of unexpected guests. The bright colors and lively flavors brighten up the menu, not only at holiday time, but all through the winter months when fresh vegetables are scarce.

1 cauliflower, about 1½ lb (750 g)

salt to taste

2 tender inner celery stalks, thinly sliced

2 carrots, peeled and shredded

½ cup (3 oz/90 g) pickled sweet red peppers, cut into narrow strips

2 tablespoons capers, chopped

2 tablespoons chopped fresh flat-leaf (Italian) parsley

¼ cup (2 fl oz/60 ml) olive oil

¼ cup (2 fl oz/60 ml) white wine vinegar

❦ Cut the cauliflower into bite-sized florets and discard the tough stalk.

❦ Bring a large pot three-fourths full of water to a boil. Add the cauliflower and salt and cook until tender when pierced with a knife, about 7 minutes. Drain and place under cold running water to halt the cooking.

❦ In a bowl, combine the cauliflower, celery, carrots, red peppers, capers, parsley, olive oil, and vinegar and toss well. Cover and refrigerate for at least 1 hour or as long as overnight.

❦ If the salad is very cold, let it stand at room temperature for 30 minutes before serving. Then toss gently, taste for seasoning, and serve.

serves 6

Puglia

Fave e Cicoria

fava beans with chicory

Dried fava beans are a staple of Apulian cooking. They are simmered until they soften into a thick creamy paste and are typically eaten with sautéed dandelions, chicory, or other wild greens and slices of country bread, often toasted and slicked with olive oil.

Dried favas have a thick skin that must be removed. Peeled ones are usually available. If you cannot locate any, unpeeled favas may be used, but you will need to double the quantity. Soak the unpeeled beans overnight in cold water to cover to loosen the skins. The next morning, they will slip off easily.

Serve this dish as an accompaniment to roast pork or pork chops, or as a vegetarian main course.

1 rounded cup (8 oz/250 g) dried peeled fava (broad) beans

1 baking potato, unpeeled, cut into chunks

salt to taste

½ cup (4 fl oz/120 ml) olive oil

freshly ground pepper to taste

1½ lb (750 g) chicory (curly endive), tough stems removed and cut into 1-inch (2.5-cm) pieces

8 slices coarse country bread, toasted

extra-virgin olive oil

❦ In a large saucepan over medium heat, combine the fava beans and potato with water to cover. Bring to a simmer, reduce the heat to low, and cook, stirring occasionally, until the favas and potato chunks are very soft, about 1 hour. Add salt and continue to cook, stirring frequently and mashing the beans and potato, until thick and creamy, about 2 minutes. Watch carefully to prevent scorching. Stir in ¼ cup (2 fl oz/60 ml) of the olive oil and the pepper.

❦ While the beans are cooking, bring a large saucepan three-fourths full of water to a boil. Add the greens and salt and cook until tender, about 10 minutes. Drain in a colander, pressing out any excess water, and transfer to a bowl. Add the remaining ¼ cup (2 fl oz/60 ml) oil and toss well.

❦ Spread the bean purée on a warmed platter. Top with the greens. Serve immediately with the toasted bread. Pass the extra-virgin olive oil at the table for drizzling on the bread.

serves 4–6

Toscana

Fagioli all'Uccelletto

beans in the style of little birds

Quail, thrushes, and other small birds are often prepared with tomatoes, garlic, and sage, which is how these beans got their name. Sometimes Tuscans cook beans al fiasco, in a thick, narrow-necked glass bottle that they place in a large pan of water in the oven. The shape of the bottle ensures that the beans will become tender without the need for a lot of liquid that can dilute their flavor. At the same time, the water bath allows them to cook slowly and evenly so they keep their shape and still turn out as creamy and soft as possible.

1 rounded cup (8 oz/250 g) dried cannellini or Great Northern beans

3 cloves garlic, chopped

4 fresh sage leaves

¼ cup (2 fl oz/60 ml) olive oil

1 large tomato, peeled, seeded, and chopped

salt and freshly ground pepper to taste

☙ Pick over the beans and discard any misshapen beans or stones. Rinse the beans and drain. Place in a bowl, add plenty of water to cover, and let soak for at least 3 hours or as long as overnight.

☙ Drain the beans and place in a heavy saucepan with water to cover by 1 inch (2.5 cm). Bring to a simmer over medium heat. Cover partially, reduce the heat to very low, and cook until the beans are tender, about 1 hour. The cooking time will vary according to the variety and age of the beans.

☙ Drain the beans, reserving the liquid. In a large saucepan over medium heat, sauté the garlic and sage in the olive oil until the garlic is pale gold, about 1 minute. Add the beans, tomato, salt, and pepper and simmer to blend the flavors, about 20 minutes. Add a little of the reserved liquid if the beans become too dry.

☙ Transfer to a serving dish and serve hot or at room temperature.

serves 6

Campania

Zucchini a Scapece

marinated fried zucchini

Zucchini, winter squashes, carrots, and eggplants (aubergines) all can be prepared a scapece, that is, fried and marinated with garlic, vinegar, and mint. Some historians believe that the name is derived from that of Apicius, author of the earliest known cookbook, De re coquinaria.

Use only small, firm zucchini for this recipe. The flavors need time to marry and mellow, so prepare it at least a day ahead of serving. The dish keeps well for several days. It also makes a fine antipasto.

olive oil or vegetable oil for frying

6 small zucchini (courgettes), trimmed and cut crosswise into slices ¼ inch (6 mm) thick

2 large cloves garlic, minced

¼ cup (⅓ oz/10 g) chopped fresh mint or basil

salt and freshly ground pepper to taste

¼ cup (2 fl oz/60 ml) red wine vinegar

☙ In a saucepan, pour in oil to a depth of 1 inch (2.5 cm) and heat to 375°F (190°C) on a deep-frying thermometer.

☙ Pat the zucchini slices dry. Using a slotted spoon and working in batches, carefully lower the slices into the hot oil. Cook until golden brown, about 4 minutes. With the slotted spoon, transfer to paper towels to drain.

☙ Meanwhile, in a small cup or bowl, stir together the garlic and mint or basil. When all the zucchini have been cooked, transfer them to a large bowl, sprinkling some of the garlic-herb mixture and salt and pepper between each layer. Pour the vinegar evenly over the top. Cover and refrigerate overnight.

☙ Remove from the refrigerator about 30 minutes before serving. Serve at room temperature.

serves 4

Le Erbe

Herbs are employed judiciously in Italian cooking. Flat-leaf (Italian) parsley is the most widely used, added to everything from meats to vegetables to sauces, although its most important application is for fish. The character of fresh fish is subtle, making parsley, with its refreshing, uncomplicated flavor, the obvious choice.

Basil is the second most widely used. It marries perfectly with a variety of foods, especially tomatoes and garlic. Rather than chopping and thus bruising the leaves, it is often torn into pieces. Frequently it is added at the end of cooking so the warmth of the food will release the herb's flavor without expending it. Basil is commonly preserved for the winter months by packing it in salt or under olive oil.

Southern Italians use oregano, particularly in its dried form, for sauces, including a tasty concoction for fish called *salmoriglio,* made with olive oil and lemon juice. Sage and rosemary are used everywhere for roast meats, poultry, and game. Mint is popular in Lazio with artichokes and throughout the south, especially on vegetables and dark-fleshed fish such as bluefish or mackerel. Marjoram flavors vegetables, sauces, and stuffings in Liguria.

For mushrooms, the herb of choice is often *nepitella,* or calamint. Bay leaf, thyme, and tarragon also turn up in the kitchen, although not with the frequency of those already mentioned.

One distinctive characteristic of Italian cooking is that herbs often are used singly in dishes, to preserve their clear, fresh flavors and not overwhelm the profile of the other ingredients.

Funghi in Salsa di Pomodori

mushrooms in tomato sauce

In the midnineteenth century, Francesco Cirio, a fruit-and-vegetable merchant in Turin's Porta Palazzo market, had a brilliant idea. Since Neapolitan tomatoes were so plentiful in season, yet so perishable, why not pack them in tins, so that they could be available to everyone the year-round. Working in a rented room in his native city, Cirio was the first Italian to can not just tomatoes, but all kinds of fruits and vegetables. His idea met with immediate success, and within a few years trains loaded with his products were leaving from Turin, and eventually Naples, for cities all over Europe.

Now canned tomatoes and tomato products are available throughout Italy. They are a convenient shortcut for fresh tomatoes (which must be peeled) or an alternative when good-quality vine-ripened ones are nowhere to be found.

¼ cup (2 fl oz/60 ml) olive oil

2 large cloves garlic, lightly crushed

1 lb (500 g) fresh white mushrooms, brushed clean and halved or quartered if large

salt and freshly ground pepper to taste

2 tomatoes, peeled, seeded, and chopped, or 1 cup (6 oz/185 g) seeded and chopped canned plum (Roma) tomatoes

2 tablespoons chopped fresh flat-leaf (Italian) parsley

❧ In a large frying pan over medium heat, warm the olive oil with the garlic. When the garlic is golden, after about 2 minutes, add the mushrooms, salt, and pepper. Cook, stirring occasionally, until the mushroom juices have evaporated and the mushrooms are lightly browned, about 10 minutes. Add the tomatoes and cook, stirring frequently, until the sauce thickens, about 10 minutes more.

❧ Stir in the parsley and transfer to a warmed serving dish. Serve hot or at room temperature.

serves 4

Emilia-Romagna

Finocchio al Forno

oven-braised fennel

*Crisp fennel is usually eaten raw in salads or after
meals as a digestivo, that is, a digestive aid. It is also
good cooked in a sauce for pasta, or prepared as it
is here, topped with Parmigiano-Reggiano cheese, as a
side dish with meat, fish, or chicken.*

2 fennel bulbs, about 12 oz (375 g) each

½ cup (4 fl oz/125 ml) meat or chicken stock

salt and freshly ground pepper to taste

*½ cup (2 oz/60 g) grated Parmigiano-Reggiano
cheese*

3 tablespoons unsalted butter, cut into small bits

❦ Preheat an oven to 350°F (180°C). Butter a 9-by-
13-by-2-inch (23-by-33-by-5-cm) baking dish.

❦ Trim off the stems from each fennel bulb, leaving
½ inch (12 mm) intact. Discard any bruised outer
stalks. Shave a thin slice off the root end. Cut each
bulb lengthwise into 8 wedges.

❦ Arrange the fennel wedges in a single layer in the
prepared baking dish. Pour the stock over the fennel
and sprinkle with salt and pepper. Scatter the cheese
over the top and dot with the butter.

❦ Place in the oven and braise, uncovered, until the
fennel is tender when pierced with a knife, about 45
minutes. Serve hot directly from the baking dish.

serves 4

*Spring arrives early in Sicily,
and with it the feathery
green stalks of wild fennel
that are eagerly clipped for
flavoring soups and sauces.*

Toscana

Patate Fritte alla Salvia

potatoes fried with garlic and sage

*Vipore was one of my favorite restaurants in the
Lucca area, although it was very hard to find. The
first two times my husband and I tried to go there, we
gave up in frustration after driving around for what
seemed like hours. The third time, however, we would
not surrender, and we stopped and asked directions
from everyone we saw along the narrow, badly paved,
hilly road. They all gave us the same instructions:
sempre diritto, "straight ahead," with a
sideways wave of the hand.*

*Finally we came to a landslide that completely
blocked the road. We parked our car beside
it and then clambered over the pile of rocks and dirt,
edged our way along a cliff, and suddenly we were
there. The restaurant was packed, although how
everyone else arrived we will never know. Sadly, Vipore
is closed now, but whenever I make these delicious
potatoes, I think of the restaurant and its wonderful
rustic cooking. A garden planted with all kinds of herbs
sloped away from the rear of the dining room, and the
cooks used them to their best advantage.*

*2 lb (1 kg) new potatoes, unpeeled, cut into bite-
sized pieces*

½ cup (4 fl oz/125 ml) olive oil

4 large cloves garlic, lightly crushed

12 fresh sage leaves

1 tablespoon chopped fresh thyme

salt and freshly ground pepper to taste

❦ Dry the potatoes with paper towels to remove any
natural moisture.

❦ In a large frying pan over medium heat, warm the
olive oil. Add the potatoes and cook, stirring frequently, until they begin to brown, about 10 minutes. Add the garlic, sage, thyme, salt, and pepper.
Reduce the heat to low, cover, and cook, stirring
occasionally, until golden brown and tender when
pierced with a fork, about 15 minutes.

❦ Using a slotted spoon, transfer the potatoes to a
warmed serving dish. Serve hot.

serves 4

Carciofi Ripieni

stuffed artichokes

Artichokes lend themselves to stuffing. I have had them filled with canned tuna in Abruzzo, sausage meat in Calabria, rice in the Veneto, and ricotta and salami in Sicily. This filling, with minor variations, is popular throughout southern Italy.

After trimming, artichokes are often rubbed with a cut lemon or immersed in acidulated water to prevent darkening. I regularly skip this step, since the artichokes will darken anyway during cooking.

6 artichokes

⅔ cup (2½ oz/75 g) fine dried bread crumbs

½ cup (2 oz/60 g) freshly grated pecorino romano cheese

¼ cup (⅓ oz/10 g) chopped fresh flat-leaf (Italian) parsley

1 clove garlic, chopped

salt and freshly ground pepper to taste

about 4 tablespoons (2 fl oz/60 ml) olive oil

✤ Working with 1 artichoke at a time, snap off the small, tough leaves around the base. Cut off the stem flush with the bottom and set aside. Cut off the pointed leaf tips. Using a small spoon, scoop out the prickly choke and discard. Repeat with the remaining artichokes. Peel the stems, then chop them.

✤ In a bowl, combine the chopped stems, bread crumbs, cheese, parsley, garlic, salt, and pepper. Add about 2 tablespoons of the olive oil, or just enough to moisten the mixture. Gently spread open the leaves of an artichoke and push a little of the stuffing mixture between them. Repeat until all the artichokes are stuffed.

✤ Place the artichokes upright in a pot just large enough to hold them. Add water to reach about one-third of the way up the sides of the artichokes. Drizzle with the remaining 2 tablespoons olive oil.

✤ Cover the pot and place over low heat. Bring to a simmer and cook until the artichoke hearts are tender when pierced with a knife and a leaf is easily pulled out, about 45 minutes. Add a little more water if the liquid evaporates too quickly.

✤ Serve warm or at room temperature.

serves 6

Le Sagre

A *sagra,* the Italian version of a country fair, is often, although not always, timed to coincide with the harvest of a local product. Artichokes, peaches, peppers, grapes, and beans each have their own special *sagra,* but so do sardines, snails, goose salami, stockfish, and sheep's cheese.

Some *sagre* commemorate the feast day of a beloved local saint. One such is the *Festa di San Ilario,* patron saint of Parma. The holy man, who was extremely poor, went about doing his good works wearing a pair of broken shoes. A kind shoemaker took pity on Ilario and gave him a new pair in exchange for the old. The next day, the broken shoes were found renewed, and the townspeople immediately attributed miracles to them. To celebrate, biscotti shaped like shoes are baked in the local pastry shops.

A typical *sagra* lasts for a day or two, with local residents cooking special foods in the town's central piazza or nearby fairgrounds. Usually, tastes of the foods are given away, although sometimes a small fee is charged. The day often begins with special church services, followed later by fireworks, music, and folk dancing. One of the best *sagre* to visit is the almost half-century-old Sagra del Pesce in the picturesque seaside Ligurian town of Camogli. On a Sunday in mid-May, local fishermen fry up nearly two tons (2,000 kg) of small fish in an immense frying pan that weighs close to half that amount itself.

Lazio

La Vignarola

artichokes, peas, and pancetta

Romans take great pride in their locally grown artichokes, an especially flavorful variety known as Romanesco. They do not have spiny leaves, so they are easier to prepare for cooking. The choicest artichoke on every plant is the central one on top, known as the cimarolo, *which is sold by the piece, not by the bunch, and costs more than the* braccioli, *or artichokes from farther down on the bush.*

There are any number of ways to prepare artichokes, but to me this lovely stew, the essence of springtime, is one of the best. I can make a whole meal of it, as the Romans often do.

2 lb (1 kg) fava (broad) beans, shelled

4 artichokes

¼ lb (125 g) sliced pancetta, chopped

¼ cup (2 fl oz/60 ml) olive oil

1 yellow onion, chopped

½ cup (4 fl oz/125 ml) chicken stock

salt and freshly ground pepper to taste

1¾ cups (8 oz/250 g) shelled peas (about 1¾ lb/875 g unshelled)

❦ Bring a saucepan three-fourths full of water to a boil. Add the favas and boil for about 2 minutes. Drain, rinse under cold running water, and slip the beans from their tough skins. Set aside.

❦ Working with 1 artichoke at a time, snap off all the tough outer leaves. Peel the stem and shave off a thin layer from the base. Cut in half lengthwise, then cut off the top third of each half. Using a pointed spoon, scoop out the choke from each half. Cut each half lengthwise into 3 or 4 wedges.

❦ In a large frying pan over medium heat, cook the pancetta in the olive oil, stirring frequently, until it begins to brown, about 5 minutes. Add the onion and cook, stirring, until tender, 5–6 minutes longer.

❦ Add the artichokes, fava beans, stock, salt, and pepper. Cover, reduce the heat to low, and cook until the artichokes are almost tender when pierced with a knife, about 10 minutes. Add the peas and cook until all the vegetables are tender, about 5 minutes longer. Serve hot or at room temperature.

serves 6

Sardegna

Carciofi e Patate

artichokes and potatoes

Choosing a wine for a menu that features artichokes is always a challenge. They are naturally high in tannin and the chemical cynarin, which gives the vegetable its characteristic bittersweet flavor. Both play havoc with the flavor of wine, altering its flavor and making it taste sweet. When artichokes are on the menu, it is wise to avoid serving a fine wine.

This delicious stew is excellent with roasted or grilled fish or chicken.

4 artichokes

1 large yellow onion, chopped

3 tablespoons olive oil

1 clove garlic, chopped

2 tablespoons chopped fresh flat-leaf (Italian) parsley

4 boiling potatoes, unpeeled, cut into 1-inch (2.5-cm) chunks

salt and freshly ground pepper to taste

½ cup (4 fl oz / 125 ml) water

❦ Working with 1 artichoke at a time, snap off all the tough outer leaves. Peel the stem and shave off a thin layer from the base. Cut in half lengthwise, then cut off the top third of each half. Using a pointed spoon, scoop out the choke from each half. Cut each half lengthwise into 3 wedges. Set aside.

❦ In a saucepan over medium heat, sauté the onion in the olive oil until tender but not browned, about 5 minutes. Stir in the garlic and parsley and cook until fragrant, about 1 minute longer.

❦ Add the artichokes and potatoes and stir well. Sprinkle with salt and pepper and add the water. Cover, reduce the heat to low, and cook until the vegetables are tender, about 20 minutes.

❦ Transfer to a serving bowl and serve hot or at room temperature.

serves 4

Campania

Crocche' di Patate

potato croquettes

Neapolitans love to snack as they walk through the streets on their way to work or school or while out shopping. The habit began long ago when the city was so overcrowded that many people lived in tiny apartments without cooking facilities. Itinerant vendors would set up their portable stoves on street corners and cook up calzone, spaghetti, and all kinds of fritters and croquettes that passersby purchased for pennies. Although the menu has changed somewhat, the tradition continues to this day, with the nomadic vendors replaced by restaurants with outdoor stands.

5 large boiling potatoes, 2 lb (1 kg) total weight, peeled and cut into 1-inch (2.5-cm) chunks

salt to taste

¾ cup (3 oz / 90 g) grated Parmigiano-Reggiano cheese

3 eggs, separated

2 tablespoons chopped fresh flat-leaf (Italian) parsley

freshly ground pepper to taste

1½ cups (6 oz / 185 g) fine dried bread crumbs

vegetable oil for frying

❦ In a saucepan, combine the potatoes and water to cover. Bring to a simmer over medium heat, add salt, and cook until tender, about 15 minutes. Drain well and mash until smooth. Let cool slightly.

❦ Stir in the cheese and egg yolks. Add the parsley, salt, and pepper. Using about 3 tablespoons of the potato mixture for each croquette, shape into logs 2½ inches (6 cm) long and 1 inch (2.5 cm) in diameter. In a shallow dish, beat the egg whites until frothy. Spread the bread crumbs on a sheet of waxed paper. Dip the potato logs into the egg whites, coating evenly, then roll them in the bread crumbs. Pat the crumbs into the logs to help them to adhere. Place on a rack to dry for 30 minutes before frying.

❦ In a deep, heavy frying pan, pour in vegetable oil to a depth of ½ inch (12 mm) and heat over medium heat. Add the croquettes, a few at a time, and fry, turning as needed, until golden brown on all sides, about 4 minutes. Using a slotted spoon, transfer to paper towels to drain briefly. Arrange on a warmed platter and serve immediately.

serves 6–8

Emilia-Romagna

Tortino di Patate

baked mashed potatoes

Bologna is often called La Grassa, "The Fat One," because cooks there use rich ingredients like butter, eggs, and cheese in generous quantities. Here, even simple mashed potatoes get the classic Emilia-Romagna treatment. For the best flavor and texture, mashed potatoes should be prepared just before serving. This cheesy mashed potato tortino is appealing because it can be prepared as much as a day ahead of time and refrigerated until you are ready to bake it. Serve with a roast capon or turkey for a festive holiday dinner.

4 baking potatoes, 1¼ lb (625 g) total weight, peeled and cut into 1-inch (2.5-cm) chunks

salt to taste

½ cup (4 fl oz/125 ml) milk

2 tablespoons unsalted butter

freshly ground pepper to taste

6 tablespoons (1½ oz/45 g) grated Parmigiano-Reggiano cheese

1 egg, beaten

☙ Preheat an oven to 350°F (180°C). Butter a 4–cup (1–l) baking dish.

☙ Place the potatoes in a saucepan and add water to cover. Bring to a simmer over medium heat, add salt, and cook until tender when pierced with a fork, about 15 minutes.

☙ Drain the potatoes well and pass them through a ricer placed over a bowl, or place in a bowl and mash with a fork or a potato masher until smooth. Stir in the milk, butter, and pepper, mixing well. Add 4 tablespoons (1 oz/30 g) of the cheese and the egg.

☙ Spoon the potato mixture into the prepared baking dish. Smooth the surface, then sprinkle with the remaining 2 tablespoons cheese.

☙ Bake until heated through and the top is golden, about 25 minutes (or about 45 minutes if previously refrigerated). Serve hot directly from the baking dish.

serves 4

Veneto

Piselli alla Menta

peas with onions and mint

Every year during the first week of June, the town of Peseggia, near Verona, hosts the Festa dei Bisi, the Sweet Pea Festival. Bisi is Venetian dialect for "peas," or piselli in Italian. The best-known dish of the region is risi e bisi, a mixture of fresh new peas and local Vialone rice cooked with stock, butter, and onion and sprinkled with Parmigiano-Reggiano. This is another popular way to prepare the local crop.

3 tablespoons unsalted butter

¼ cup (1½ oz/45 g) minced yellow onion

2 cups (10 oz/315 g) shelled peas (about 2 lb/1 kg unshelled)

1 teaspoon sugar

salt to taste

¼ cup (2 fl oz/60 ml) water

2 tablespoons chopped fresh mint, basil, or flat-leaf (Italian) parsley

☙ In a saucepan over medium heat, melt the butter. Add the onion and sauté until just tender, about 5 minutes. Add the peas, sugar, salt, and water. Reduce the heat to low, cover, and simmer until the peas are tender, about 5 minutes.

☙ Remove from the heat and stir in the mint or other herb. Transfer to a warmed serving dish and serve hot.

serves 4

The first peas of the season are celebrated with special dishes — risi e bisi in the Veneto, piselli al prosciutto in Lazio, minestra di fave e piselli in Sicily.

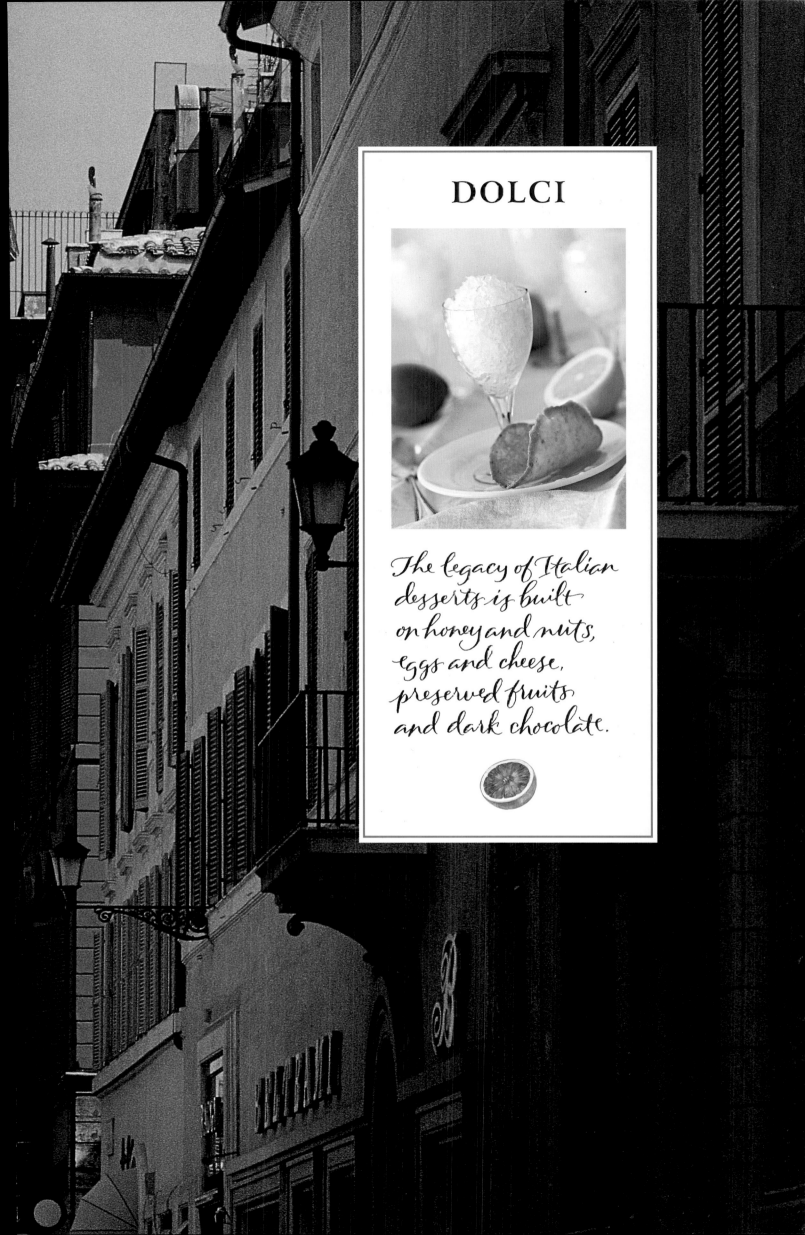

DOLCI

The legacy of Italian
desserts is built
on honey and nuts,
eggs and cheese,
preserved fruits
and dark chocolate.

NOTHING FOR ME is more evocative of Italy than the sight of a fig tree heavy with late-summer fruit. A few years ago, on a trip to Tuscany, I saw spreading, gnarled fig trees everywhere, carefully tended in front yards and in garden plots and growing wild along the roadside. Warmed by the relentless sun, the fruits were plump and bursting open, with honeylike juice oozing from the fissures. Stopping at one tree, I peeled and ate a handful of figs that were still hot from the sun.

Figs and other fruits of all kinds are one of the supreme delights of the Italian table. Nowhere have I eaten grapes as sweet or peaches as juicy. The aromas of the melons and strawberries are intoxicating. Even the oranges, especially the dark red blood oranges from Sicily, seem to have their own special flavor. And each *fruttivendolo* in the market has come up with a distinctive and appealing way of displaying them, often with their leaves still attached as a sign of freshness.

Not surprisingly, with such an abundance of luscious choices, nearly every lunch and dinner in Italy ends with fruit. Even when more elaborate dessert pastries or cakes are to follow, most diners expect to have some fruit as a palate cleanser and *digestivo*.

Italian hosts traditionally serve an assortment of fruit with a bowl of cold water alongside. Each diner dips his or her choice into the water to clean and refresh it. Once retrieved, the fruit is peeled and eaten with a knife and fork. Removing the skin from a ripe, slippery peach can be challenging, but Italians always seem to do it with aplomb.

Cut-up fresh fruits or whole berries are often sprinkled with fresh lemon juice, wine, or balsamic vinegar and sugar. The combination of acidity and sugar sharpens the fruit flavor. Whole fruits are poached in syrup or stuffed and baked in the oven. After a number of years, I still dream about the magnificent amaretti-filled peaches baked in a vanilla custard that I once ate in Parma.

Fruits, of course, are also primary ingredients in many pastries and other desserts. Fresh fruit *crostate,* or "tarts," are popular all over Italy, as are many cakes and cookies filled with fresh, dried, or candied fruits. In Friuli, for example,

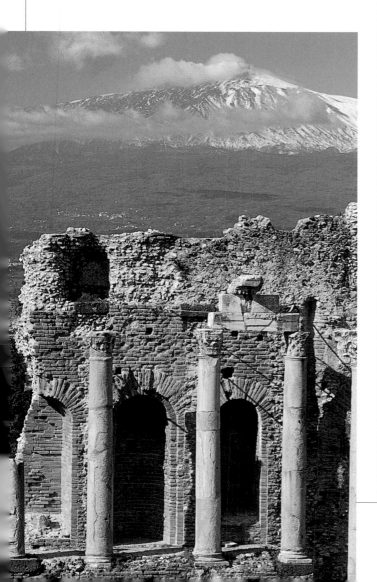

Left: Taormina's spectacularly situated Greek theater offers a magnificent view of Mount Etna, one of the world's largest active volcanoes. **Above top:** The ancient Romans believed figs imported from Greece were superior to those grown in local soil. Italians today are happy with their own harvests, sometimes serving them with prosciutto as an antipasto, baking them into breads, or mixing them with nuts and honey for filling cookies. **Above bottom:** Casks of Chianti DOCG, Italy's famous red wine.

a delicious cake called *gubana* is made by combining dried fruits and nuts and wrapping them in pastry. Rolled into a spiral, the cake is often doused with grappa before serving. At Christmastime, Sicilians wrap dried fruits, nuts, and spices in rich pastry doughs, shape them into birds and rings, flowers and fans, and strew them with candy confetti.

Nuts, too, figure prominently in desserts. After a visit to my husband's family in Sicily, we were not allowed to leave without an enormous sack of almonds grown on his uncle's farm. We were glad to have them, since they were the largest and finest we had ever tasted. Almonds are used to make cookies, including soft, sweet, cakelike almond *biscotti* from Apulia, and the Piedmont's crisp, airy meringues strongly flavored with bitter almonds.

Piedmont is known for delicious hazelnuts (filberts) and chestnuts as well, which are eaten roasted or mixed into desserts. A favorite flavor combination of the region is hazelnuts and chocolate, known as *gianduja* (sometimes spelled *gianduia*). You can find *gianduja* ice cream, cakes, and candies, and all are superb.

As you head south, desserts change dramatically, becoming sweeter and richer. Neapolitan desserts are among my favorites, especially *sfogliatelle*, which can be a ricotta-filled tartlet or a crisp pastry turnover. The Neapolitans also make a delicious *babà au rhum; bignè,* or cream puffs; and *struffoli,* little balls of crisp fried dough coated while still warm with honey. At Easter, *la pastiera,* a rich pie filled with wheat berries, ricotta, eggs, and candied fruits, appears on countless holiday tables.

Cannoli, pastry tubes fried crisp in lard and filled with sweetened *ricotta di pecora,* soft, fresh cheese made from tangy sheep's milk, are classic Sicilian sweets. Ricotta is also used to make *cassata,* a layer of sponge cake filled with the sweetened cheese, wrapped in almond paste, and topped with colorful glazed fruits, and *cassatedde di ricotta,* fried turnovers concealing the sweetened cheese dotted with chocolate

Left: Piedmont boasts a wide range of desserts, from simple butter cookies, to *ciliegie al Barolo,* sour cherries simmered with wine and sugar and topped with whipped cream, to chocolates filled with hazelnut cream. **Above:** On a warm day in Turin, a waitress carries a tray of cold drinks to a trio of waiting customers.

morsels and flecks of cinnamon. The Sicilians also bake *biscotti regina,* sometimes called *reginette,* delicious, not-too-sweet cookies generously coated with tiny ivory sesame seeds, reminders of the island's long ago Arab rulers. The Arabs also are believed to have invented the forerunner of the *granita,* a water-based ice traditionally flavored with lemon, coffee, or jasmine. The ices, which they called *sarbat,* were frozen in snow brought from the high peaks of Mount Etna, which remained snow-capped even in summer.

Italian *gelato* is perhaps the finest ice cream in the world. No wonder you will see everyone from infants to grandparents eating cones full of the creamy concoction all day long during the hot summer months. Whether made with fruit, nuts, or chocolate, *gelati* capture and intensify the full flavor of the ingredients. When visiting Italy, always look for a *gelateria* that displays a sign indicating *produzione propria*—made by the proprietor—for a superior product.

One dessert that has gained popularity all over Italy in recent years is *tiramisù*. It is usually made with *savoiardi* (ladyfingers) that have been soaked in espresso and rum and layered with sweetened mascarpone cheese. Numerous conflicting stories describe its origin, including one that asserts it was concocted by a chef in a Treviso restaurant in the 1960s and another that it was created to celebrate the visit of Grand Duke Cosimo de'Medici III to Siena in the early eighteenth century.

Many fine Italian dessert wines pair well with the simpler desserts. Ripe strawberries and thin delicate cookies are excellent with a lightly sparkling *(frizzante)* Moscato from Piedmont. A glass of Vin Santo from Tuscany is traditionally served with *biscotti di Prato,* hard almond cookies that are dipped into the wine before eating. Marsala is a fine accompaniment to cheeses, especially rich, creamy Gorgonzola. Any of these and the many other fine dessert wines would make a perfect ending to an Italian meal.

Left top: The best grappas, produced by a handful of distillers in northern Italy, carry the strong, pure fragrance and flavor of a single grape variety. **Left middle:** Pomegranates are labor-intensive fruits, but the tiny, edible seeds surrounded by bright red, sweet-tart pulp are well worth the effort. Eat them out of hand, press them to extract the juice, or use the seeds as a garnish. **Left bottom:** Exquisitely graceful angels perch on the Ponte Sant'Angelo in Rome. **Above:** The awning of the Pasticceria San Lorenzo in Alassio reads, *"I veri baci di Alassio,"* announcing the celebrated chocolate-and-hazelnut cookie of the seaside Ligurian town.

Piemonte

Torta di Nocciola

hazelnut cake

At the home of wine makers in Piedmont, I was served slices of this simple cake with glasses of Moscato d'Asti, a lightly sparkling dessert wine with a lovely floral aroma. The cake, which is traditional in the region, is made with only the whites of the eggs and contains no butter; thus the pure flavor of the hazelnuts comes through.

2 cups (10 oz/315 g) hazelnuts (filberts)

1¼ cups (10 oz/310 g) sugar

⅓ cup (2 oz/60 g) all-purpose (plain) flour

8 egg whites, at room temperature

½ teaspoon salt

1 teaspoon vanilla extract (essence)

☙ Preheat an oven to 350°F (180°C). Butter a 9-inch (23-cm) springform pan with 3-inch (7.5-cm) sides. Dust the pan with flour and tap out the excess.

☙ In a food processor, combine the nuts with ½ cup (4 oz/125 g) of the sugar and process to chop finely. Add the flour and pulse to blend. Transfer to a large bowl and set aside.

☙ In another bowl, using an electric mixer set on low speed, beat together the egg whites and salt until foamy. Increase the speed to high and gradually beat in the remaining ¾ cup (6 oz/185 g) sugar until the whites form soft peaks. Add the vanilla and beat until stiff, about 2 minutes longer.

☙ Using a rubber spatula, fold about one-third of the egg whites into the ground nut mixture to lighten it. Gradually fold in the remaining whites just until no white streaks remain. Spoon the mixture into the prepared pan, spreading it evenly.

☙ Bake until a wooden toothpick inserted into the center comes out clean, about 55 minutes. Transfer to a wire rack and let cool in the pan for 10 minutes. Release and remove the pan sides and slide the cake off the base onto the rack. Let cool completely before serving.

serves 8

Sicilia

Arance Marinate

marinated oranges

I like to make this simple dish with two kinds of oranges, but it also works well with just one. Sicilian blood oranges, known as sanguinelli, *with their deep red color, are especially attractive. Serve this light dessert after a rich dinner or one that features fish.*

4 navel oranges

2 blood oranges

10 cups (80 fl oz/2.5 l) water

¾ cup (6 oz/185 g) sugar

☙ Using a serrated knife, remove the zest in wide strips from 2 of the navel oranges and both blood oranges; avoid including the white pith as much as possible. Set the oranges aside. Scrape away any pith from the zest. Stack the zest pieces and cut into narrow matchstick strips.

☙ In a small saucepan, bring 3 cups (24 fl oz/750 ml) of the water to a boil. Add the orange zest, blanch for 1 minute, then drain and rinse under cool water. Repeat two more times, using 3 cups (24 fl oz/750 ml) fresh water each time, to eliminate any bitterness in the zest.

☙ In the same small saucepan over medium heat, combine ½ cup (4 oz/125 g) of the sugar and the remaining 1 cup (8 fl oz/250 ml) water. Bring to a boil, stirring to dissolve the sugar. Add the blanched zest and cook, uncovered, until the syrup thickens slightly, 5–10 minutes. Remove from the heat, let cool completely, cover, and refrigerate until serving.

☙ Using the serrated knife, trim away all of the white pith from the 4 oranges from which the zest has been removed. Cut the oranges crosswise into slices ¼ inch (6 mm) thick and place in a bowl.

☙ Halve the remaining 2 navel oranges and squeeze the juice from the halves into the bowl. Sprinkle with the remaining ¼ cup (2 oz/60 g) sugar and toss well. Cover and refrigerate for 1 hour.

☙ To serve, spoon the orange slices into shallow bowls or glasses, dividing evenly. Top each serving with the orange zest and syrup.

serves 4

Lombardia

Torta di Cioccolata alle Mandorle

chocolate amaretti cake

Amaretti are combined with almonds and fine chocolate in this delicious Lombardian cake. Be sure to use crisp, crunchy amaretti. The cake keeps very well for a few days in the refrigerator, or it can be wrapped airtight and frozen for up to a month. Serve it plain or with ripe berries and whipped cream.

6 oz (185 g) semisweet (plain) chocolate such as Perugina or Callebaut, broken up

1 cup (5½ oz/170 g) almonds

1 cup (3 oz/90 g) crumbled amaretti (about 16)

½ cup (4 oz/125 g) unsalted butter, at room temperature

⅔ cup (5 oz/155 g) sugar

4 eggs

cocoa powder

☙ Preheat an oven to 350°F (180°C). Butter a 9-inch (23-cm) round cake pan with 2-inch (5-cm) sides. Line the bottom of the pan with parchment (baking) or waxed paper. Butter the paper. Dust the pan with flour and tap out the excess.

☙ Place the chocolate in a heatproof bowl placed over (not touching) simmering water in a saucepan. Heat until softened, then remove the bowl from over the water and stir the chocolate until smooth.

☙ In a food processor, process the almonds and cookie crumbs until finely ground. Transfer to a bowl. Process the butter and sugar until smooth. With the motor running, add the eggs, one at a time, and blend well, stopping occasionally to scrape down the sides of the bowl. Add the nut mixture and the chocolate. Pulse to blend. Pour batter into the pan.

☙ Bake until the center is slightly puffed, about 30 minutes. Let cool in the pan on a wire rack for 15 minutes. Invert onto a serving plate. Lift off the pan, then peel off the paper. Let cool completely.

☙ Just before serving, place cocoa powder in a small sieve and dust the top of the cake.

serves 10–12

Il Bar-Caffè

The Italian bar-*caffè* is driven by ritual. From early until midmorning, businessmen and barbers, movie actors and car mechanics alike stream in, newspapers tucked under their arms. They stop first at the *cassa* (cashier) to secure a receipt for their breakfast. Then they place the receipt, anchored with a 100-lire-coin tip, on the counter, and, catching the eye of the white-jacketed *barista*, call out their order. They drink, eat, scan the newspaper, and are out the door again.

By late morning, many of these same customers have returned for *panini* (sandwiches) concealing prosciutto or *pomodoro e mozzarella* to quell prelunch hunger pangs or for the energy boost guaranteed by a short, inky espresso. In the late afternoon, another coffee and perhaps a slice of *torta di cioccolata* or a couple of *biscotti* are in order. After the initial cup of the day, however, the Italian never takes coffee in the form of a milk-rich cappuccino, relying instead on the wealth of nuances offered by the espresso: *lungo*, made with more water; *ristretto*, with less water; *corretto*, with a shot of grappa or other liquor; *macchiato*, "stained" with a streak of steamed milk; or Hag, made with decaffeinated beans.

Of course, an *aperitivo* (Cinzano, Campari, Cynar), a *spremuta d'arancia* (fresh orange juice), or a *birra alla spina* (draft beer) can also be taken standing up at the counter or sitting down at one of the small tables.

One of my favorite coffee bars in Rome is the Tazza d'Oro near the Pantheon. I can't walk past it without yielding to the lure of an espresso. The doors slide open automatically as customers approach, and a gust of coffee aroma swirls out and pulls them in over the threshold. Inside, amid the continually hissing and rising steam of the shiny four-piston espresso machine, customers pause briefly at the counter to down a powerful espresso in no more than two quick gulps.

In summer, I treat myself to their *granita di caffè*, a grainy coffee ice that cools and refreshes as the crystals melt in my mouth. If I feel like splurging, I order it *con panna*, topped with a cloud of softly whipped cream. It melts slowly into the icy mass and the *granita* seems to last forever, giving me time to watch the *baristi* flirt with the young girls, gossip with one another, and argue endlessly about their beloved *calcio* (soccer).

Campania

Bignè al Limone

lemon cream puffs

Along the Amalfi coast, at a restaurant high on a hilltop, my husband and I found ourselves to be the only lunch guests. We felt like royalty as we sat on the sunny terrace overlooking the Bay of Naples. The high point of the meal was this dessert, a pile of still-crisp cream puffs filled with lemon custard and topped with lemon cream.

CREAM PUFFS

½ cup (4 oz/125 g) unsalted butter

1 cup (8 fl oz/250 ml) water

½ teaspoon salt

1 cup (5 oz/155 g) all-purpose (plain) flour

4 eggs

TOPPING AND FILLING

2 cups (16 fl oz/500 ml) milk

⅔ cup (5 oz/155 g) sugar

3 egg yolks

2 tablespoons all-purpose (plain) flour

1 teaspoon vanilla extract (essence)

1 teaspoon grated lemon zest

1 cup (8 fl oz/250 ml) heavy (double) cream

tiny strawberries or raspberries (optional)

❧ Preheat an oven to 400°F (200°C). Butter a large baking sheet. Dust the baking sheet with flour and tap out the excess.

❧ To make the cream puffs, in a saucepan over medium-low heat, warm the butter, water, and salt until the butter melts and the mixture reaches a boil. Remove from the heat. Add the flour all at once and stir well with a wooden spoon until the flour is completely incorporated.

❧ Return the saucepan to the stove over medium heat. Cook, stirring constantly and turning the dough often, until the dough begins to leave a thin film on the bottom of the saucepan, about 3 minutes. (This step dries out the dough to ensure crisp puffs.) Transfer the dough to a large bowl.

❧ Add the eggs, one at a time, beating thoroughly after each addition. Continue to beat until the mixture is smooth and shiny.

❧ Drop the dough by rounded spoonfuls onto the prepared baking sheet, forming 12 mounds spaced about 3 inches (7.5 cm) apart. With your fingers, pat the tops to give them a nice round shape.

❧ Bake until golden brown, 40–45 minutes. Turn off the oven and remove the puffs. With a small knife, make a hole in the side of each puff to allow steam to escape. Return the puffs to the oven for 10 minutes to dry.

❧ Using a serrated knife, cut the puffs part way through in half horizontally. Do not cut into 2 separate pieces. Open like a book and scoop out and discard the soft dough inside. Transfer to a wire rack and let cool completely. (The cream puffs can be made ahead and frozen in a plastic bag for up to 2 weeks. Crisp the frozen puffs in a 350°F/180°C oven for 5–10 minutes before proceeding.)

❧ To make the topping and filling, in a saucepan over low heat, stir together the milk and sugar just until the sugar dissolves and the milk is steaming, about 5 minutes. Remove from the heat.

❧ In a large bowl, whisk together the egg yolks and flour until pale yellow. Slowly add the warm milk mixture in a thin stream, whisking constantly. Pour the mixture back into the saucepan and place over low heat. Cook, stirring constantly with a wooden spoon, until the mixture comes to a boil and begins to thicken, about 2 minutes. Then cook for 1 minute, remove from the heat, and strain through a fine-mesh sieve into a bowl. Let cool slightly. Stir in the vanilla and lemon zest. Cover with plastic wrap, pressing it against the surface to prevent a skin from forming, and chill well.

❧ In a chilled bowl, using chilled beaters, whip the cream until soft peaks form. Cover with plastic wrap and chill until needed.

❧ Just before serving, using about half of the custard in all, place a spoonful inside each cream puff. Arrange the puffs in a mound on a large serving platter. Using a rubber spatula, fold the whipped cream into the remaining lemon custard just until no white streaks remain. Spoon the mixture over the cream puffs. Then scatter the berries, if using, over the top. Serve immediately.

serves 6–8

Pere alle Spezie

spiced pears

Anjou or Bartlett (Williams') pears are perfect for this recipe. As the mixture of red wine and sugar cools after baking, it thickens into a syrup that glazes the fruits a rich ruby red. For a truly decadent dessert, serve the pears with warm zabaione, *a foamy custard sauce made with egg yolks, Marsala, and sugar.*

1½ cups (12 fl oz/375 ml) fruity red wine such as Barbera

¾ cup (6 oz/185 g) sugar

6 whole cloves

8 firm, yet ripe whole pears (see note)

♛ Preheat an oven to 450°F (230°C).

♛ In a baking dish just large enough to hold the pears upright, stir together the wine, sugar, and cloves. Stand the pears in the dish and spoon the wine mixture over them.

♛ Bake the pears, basting occasionally with the pan juices, until the pears are tender when pierced with a knife and the wine is slightly thickened, 45–60 minutes. Add a little water to the dish if the liquid begins to evaporate too quickly.

♛ Remove from the oven and let cool to room temperature, basting occasionally with the wine.

♛ To serve, stand the pears on individual plates and drizzle the syrup over the top.

serves 8

Fruits are among the delights of the Italian table. Nowhere have I eaten grapes as sweet or peaches as juicy.

Le Fragole di Nemi

The little town of Nemi, not far from Rome, has long been famous for its strawberries. They grow practically the year-round in the rich volcanic soil of the green hillsides that surround the nearby lake of the same name. Just twenty families are said to hold the secret to cultivating the legendary dark red fruits, a secret that they carefully pass down through the generations.

The locals will proudly tell you that the Emperor Caligula journeyed to Nemi to worship at the temple of Diana and to eat the berries. Visitors still come to the town to see the placid lake, known as the Mirror of Diana, to visit the ruins of the temple, and, of course, to eat the strawberries.

Each year in June, a festival honoring the town's most important product is held. A homey parade of children turned out in imaginative strawberry costumes is part of the festivities, as are young women who walk through the streets carrying baskets filled with ripe, fragrant berries. Attendees consume their fill of the fruits, either fresh from the bush or folded into a rich and creamy *gelato,* and then pack shopping bags with wonderful strawberry jams and liqueurs. Romans and other savvy visitors also know to stop at the street-side vendors selling slabs of peppery *porchetta* from the nearby town of Ariccia.

Sicilia

Biscotti all'Arancia

orange biscotti

I love to buy candied orange peel in Italy. Because of its frequent use in baking, the demand for the fruit is high, and it flies off the shelves of local gastronomie. The Italians make it from high-quality citrus fruits grown along the Amalfi coast, and it is always very fresh and full of flavor.

Fine yellow cornmeal gives these biscotti *a pleasant crunch, while fresh and candied orange peel add a zesty flavor. They keep a long time in a tightly sealed tin and are nice to have on hand for afternoon tea or with ice cream or fruit desserts. Or enjoy them with a glass of dessert wine such as Moscato di Pantelleria, a honeylike wine from an island off Sicily.*

2 cups (10 oz/315 g) all-purpose (plain) flour
¾ cup (4 oz/125 g) fine yellow cornmeal
1½ teaspoons baking powder
1 teaspoon salt
3 eggs
1 cup (8 oz/250 g) sugar
1 tablespoon grated orange zest
⅓ cup (2 oz/60 g) very finely chopped candied orange peel

�™ Preheat an oven to 325°F (165°C). Butter 2 large baking sheets. Dust the baking sheets with flour and tap out the excess.

☙ In a large bowl, stir together the flour, cornmeal, baking powder, and salt.

☙ In another bowl, using an electric mixer set on medium speed, beat together the eggs and sugar until foamy and pale yellow. Beat in the grated orange zest. Reduce the speed to low and stir in the flour mixture and the chopped candied orange peel just until blended. The dough should be soft and sticky.

☙ Using 2 rubber spatulas, scoop the dough into 3 logs about 12 inches (30 cm) long and placed about 2 inches (5 cm) apart on the prepared baking sheets. Moisten your hands with cool water and pat the surface of the dough until smooth.

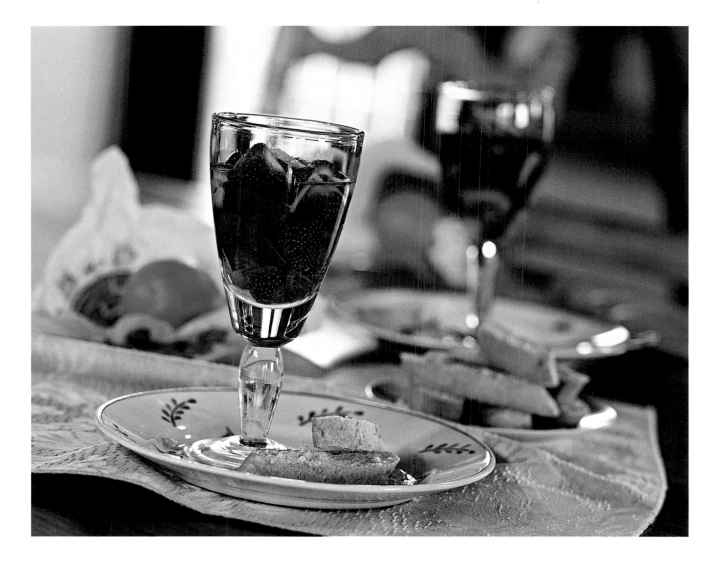

❦ Bake until lightly browned, 25–30 minutes. Remove the baking sheets from the oven, leaving the oven on.

❦ Slide the logs onto a cutting board. With a heavy chef's knife, cut the logs on the diagonal into slices ½ inch (12 mm) thick. Stand the slices on a cut side on the baking sheets, arranging them about ½ inch (12 mm) apart.

❦ Return the baking sheets to the oven and bake until the slices are lightly toasted, about 15 minutes. Transfer the *biscotti* to racks to cool completely. Store in an airtight container at room temperature for up to 2 weeks.

makes about 6 dozen

Lazio

Fragole al Vino Bianco

strawberries in white wine

White wine, sugar, and lemon zest bring out the sweet perfume of fresh strawberries. My friend Roberto recalls that his mother would keep a bowlful of these berries hidden away for him in the back of the refrigerator, waiting to satisfy the urge for a late-night snack.

1 cup (8 fl oz/250 ml) dry white wine

2 tablespoons sugar, or to taste

2 lemon zest strips

2 pints (1 lb/500 g) strawberries, hulled and quartered or sliced if large

❦ In a large bowl, combine the wine, sugar, and lemon zest. Stir to dissolve the sugar. Add the berries and toss well. Cover and refrigerate for 1 hour, tossing the berries occasionally. Serve in shallow glass bowls or stemmed glasses.

serves 4

Lazio

Crostata di Ricotta e Cigliegie

ricotta cherry tart

Rome's Jewish quarter is a tiny zone of narrow streets and medieval palazzi, where Jews were confined by papal decree for almost three hundred years. Isolated behind locked gates, and with meager food supplies, the people lived with few changes during this time. When the ghetto walls finally came down in the middle of the nineteenth century, outsiders were attracted to the area in search of authentic Roman cooking. Even today, the trattorie in the old ghetto are the best place for Roman specialties like baccalà and fried artichokes.

Bakeries in the quarter are known for their delicious pastries, especially cheesecakes. I particularly like this two-layered version that combines sour cherry jam with a creamy ricotta topping. Seek out the smoothest and creamiest ricotta you can find.

PASTRY

1¾ cups (9 oz/280 g) all-purpose (plain) flour

¼ cup (2 oz/60 g) sugar

½ teaspoon salt

grated zest of 1 lemon

½ cup (4 oz/125 g) chilled unsalted butter, cut into bits

1 whole egg, plus 1 egg yolk

1 teaspoon vanilla extract (essence)

FILLING

1½ cups (12 oz/375 g) whole-milk ricotta cheese

2 eggs

¼ cup (2 oz/60 g) sugar

1 teaspoon vanilla extract (essence)

1 cup (10 oz/315 g) sour cherry jam

To make the pastry, in a large bowl, stir together the flour, sugar, salt, and lemon zest. Using a pastry blender or a fork, work in the butter until the mixture resembles coarse crumbs.

In a small bowl, whisk together the egg, egg yolk, and vanilla. Pour over the dry ingredients and stir just until the liquid is incorporated. If the mixture seems dry, add a tablespoon or so of cold water, or just enough to bring the dough together. Shape the dough into a disk. Wrap in plastic wrap and refrigerate for at least 30 minutes or for up to overnight.

Position a rack in the lower third of an oven and preheat to 350°F (180°C).

Place the dough between 2 sheets of plastic wrap and roll out into a 12-inch (30-cm) round. Transfer to a 10-inch (25-cm) tart pan with a removable bottom, pressing it smoothly against the bottom and sides. Trim the edges, leaving a ½-inch (12-mm) overhang. Fold the overhang over against the inside of the rim of the pan. Refrigerate the dough-lined pan while you prepare the filling.

To make the filling, in another large bowl, whisk together the ricotta cheese, eggs, sugar, and vanilla until well blended. Spread the jam evenly in the bottom of the pastry shell. Pour the ricotta mixture over the jam and spread it evenly.

Bake until the top is puffed and golden, 55–60 minutes. Remove from the oven and transfer to a wire rack to cool in the pan for 10 minutes. Remove the pan rim and let cool completely.

Slide the tart off the pan base onto a serving plate. Serve chilled or at room temperature. Store any leftovers in the refrigerator.

serves 8

As you head south, desserts change dramatically, becoming sweeter, richer, more whimsical, more baroque.

Friuli-Venezia Giulia

Torta di Mele al Burro

buttery apple cake

At the home of wine maker Livio Felluga, I was served this delicious torta *made of tender apple slices bound together with a small amount of buttery cake. It was perfectly matched with Signor Felluga's Picolit, a honeylike dessert wine that tastes like nectar. This cake is also good made with pears instead of apples.*

½ cup (4 oz/125 g) plus 1 tablespoon unsalted butter

3 Renette or Golden Delicious apples, peeled, cored, and cut into slices ¼ inch (6 mm) thick

⅔ cup (3½ oz/105 g) all-purpose (plain) flour

½ teaspoon baking powder

½ teaspoon salt

2 whole eggs, plus 1 egg yolk

1 teaspoon vanilla extract (essence)

1 cup (8 oz/250 g) granulated sugar

½ teaspoon grated lemon zest

confectioners' (icing) sugar

☙ Preheat an oven to 375°F (190°C). Generously butter a 9-inch (23-cm) round cake pan with 2-inch (5-cm) sides.

☙ In a large frying pan over low heat, melt the butter. Pour 6 tablespoons (3 fl oz/90 ml) of it into a small bowl or cup and set aside. Add the apple slices to the butter remaining in the frying pan and cook, stirring occasionally, until the apples are tender, about 10 minutes. Remove from the heat.

☙ In a small bowl, stir together the flour, baking powder, and salt. In a large bowl, beat the whole eggs and egg yolk until blended. Add the 6 tablespoons (3 fl oz/90 ml) melted butter, the vanilla, the granulated sugar, and the lemon zest. Stir in the flour mixture and the apples. Spoon into the prepared pan, smoothing the top.

☙ Bake until the cake is browned, 30–35 minutes. Transfer to a wire rack and let cool in the pan for 5 minutes. Invert the cake onto a plate and lift off the pan, then invert the cake again onto the rack and let cool completely.

☙ Just before serving, place confectioners' sugar in a small sieve and dust the top of the cake.

serves 8

Lombardia

Coppa di Mascarpone alle Pesche

mascarpone and peaches

Sweet white or yellow peaches bathed in liqueur and layered with clouds of rich, velvety mascarpone are the perfect summer dessert. Although not a cheese in the true sense of the word (as it is made without a starter), mascarpone is often consumed like one. Because it is highly perishable, it was traditionally made only in the cold fall and winter months and packed into muslin bags for sale. Today, of course, it is produced year-round. It can be served with fresh or cooked fruits or used in baking cakes. A favorite way to eat it is on toasted slices of panettone, Milanese sweet bread popular at Christmastime.

4 large, ripe peaches

⅓ cup (3 fl oz/80 ml) amaretto or orange-flavored liqueur

1 tablespoon fresh lemon juice

½ lb (250 g) mascarpone

¼ cup (2 oz/60 g) sugar

1 cup (8 fl oz/250 ml) heavy (double) cream

½ cup (1½ oz/45 g) finely crushed amaretti (about 8)

2 tablespoons sliced (flaked) almonds, lightly toasted

☙ Bring a saucepan three-fourths full of water to a boil. Using a slotted spoon and working with 1 peach at a time, slip a peach into the water and blanch for 30 seconds. Lift it out and drop it into a bowl of cold water. Repeat with the remaining peaches. Using a small knife, lightly score the peaches lengthwise and pull off the skins. Halve, pit, and then cut into thin wedges. Place in a bowl, add the liqueur and lemon juice, and toss to coat evenly.

☙ In a large bowl, whisk together the mascarpone and sugar until well blended and fluffy. In a chilled bowl, using chilled beaters, whip the cream until stiff peaks form. Using a rubber spatula or whisk, fold the cream into the mascarpone just until combined. Spoon half of the cream mixture into parfait glasses, dividing evenly. Top with the peaches and then amaretti, again dividing evenly. Spoon on the remaining cream mixture. Cover and chill well.

☙ Sprinkle with the almonds just before serving.

serves 6

Sicilia

Granita di Limoni e Cedro

lemon-lime ice

Ices made from various citrus fruits are popular all over southern Italy. Nothing is more refreshing on a hot day than this simple tangy granita. Use both lemons and limes, as is done here, or only one fruit. For a smoother-textured ice, freeze the ingredients in a solid block, cut it into chunks, and then process in a food processor until smooth. The granita can also be frozen in an ice cream maker. Serve with a splash of grappa, if desired, for a sophisticated lift.

3 cups (24 fl oz/750 ml) water

¾ cup (6 oz/185 g) sugar

¼ cup (2 fl oz/60 ml) fresh lime juice

¼ cup (2 fl oz/60 ml) fresh lemon juice

½ teaspoon grated lime zest

½ teaspoon grated lemon zest

❧ In a small saucepan over medium heat, combine the water and sugar. Cook, stirring occasionally, until the sugar dissolves, about 3 minutes. Remove from the heat, pour into a bowl, let cool slightly, then cover and chill well.

❧ Add the lime and lemon juices and zests to the chilled sugar syrup and stir well. Pour the mixture into a 9-by-12-by-2-inch (23-by-30-by-5-cm) baking pan or other metal pan. Place in the freezer until ice crystals form around the edges, about 30 minutes. Remove from the freezer and, using a metal spoon, stir the ice into the center of the pan. Continue freezing and stirring the mixture every 30 minutes until frozen solid, about 2½ hours total.

❧ To serve, using the side of a spoon, scrape off ice crystals. (If the *granita* is too firm to scrape, let stand at room temperature for about 15 minutes to soften slightly.) Spoon into wine goblets or parfait glasses.

serves 8

Valle d'Aosta

Tegoline

roof tile cookies

Thin and crisp, these curved cookies are named for their resemblance to the roof tiles used on houses in Valle d'Aosta. They are very delicate, so they need to be handled with care. Don't make the cookies on a damp day, or they may turn out limp instead of crisp. If you prefer, cool the hot rounds over small bowls to make cups for serving ice cream.

½ cup (2½ oz/75 g) pine nuts

½ cup (4 oz/125 g) sugar

¼ cup (2 oz/60 g) unsalted butter, at room temperature

2 egg whites, at room temperature

⅓ cup (2 oz/60 g) all-purpose (plain) flour

❧ Preheat an oven to 400°F (200°C). Butter 3 large baking sheets. Dust the baking sheets with flour and tap out the excess. Have ready 2 rolling pins or wine bottles for molding the cookies.

❧ In a food processor, process the pine nuts and 2 tablespoons of the sugar until finely ground.

❧ In a bowl, using an electric mixer set on medium speed, beat the butter until light. Add the remaining 6 tablespoons (3 oz/90 g) sugar and beat until fluffy. Beat in the egg whites until well blended. Stir in the ground pine nuts and flour just until combined.

❧ Drop the batter by level tablespoons 6 inches (15 cm) apart onto the prepared baking sheets. With a spatula, spread the batter as thinly as possible into rounds about 3 inches (7.5 cm) in diameter.

❧ Bake the cookies, one sheet at a time, until spotted with brown in the center and browned around the edges, 5–6 minutes. Remove from the oven and let the cookies cool until just firm enough to move them without breaking, about 30 seconds. One at a time, slide a thin metal spatula under each cookie and immediately drape over the rolling pin or bottle. As the cookies cool, they will become crisp. Work quickly. If they should become too brittle to mold, return the cookies to the oven briefly until they warm and soften. Let cool until set.

❧ Store the cookies in an airtight container at room temperature for up to 3 days.

makes about 2 dozen

La Grappa

I watched spellbound as Romano Levi dropped a tiny vial, no bigger than a thimble, tied with a long string down into the bunghole of a wooden barrel. It filled with clear liquid, and then he drew it out, poured a drop into his palms, and rubbed vigorously, indicating that I should do the same. Opening his hands, he took a long, deep sniff. "Ah, grappa!" he proclaimed. I sniffed, too, and indeed it was the essence of grappa: warm, woody, and inviting. The heat and friction of our hands had released all of its subtle fragrance.

Romano Levi is a renowned grappa maker from the old Roman town of Neive in Piedmont. He distills his heady brew with painstaking care from only the finest *vinacce*, the grape solids that are left over after making wine. His *distilleria* is tiny, and his equipment seems ancient. He does most of the work himself, including drawing the labels for his bottles with pen and ink. Although Levi's production is small, the demand for it is great. Wineshop owners chuckle when you request it, saying that they are waiting for their new shipments or that their allotment is promised to longtime customers before it even arrives.

Distilled in many different regions of northern Italy, grappa was traditionally a peasant's liquor, a raw, rough potion, often poured into a cup of hot coffee to warm farmers and hunters on a cold morning. Made today with modern techniques and equipment, grappa is a sophisticated and expensive after-dinner drink. Some producers, like the Veneto's Jacopo Poli, present their grappa in elegant blown-glass bottles. In Friuli–Venezia Giulia, the Nonino family is famous for its *grappa monovitigno*, made from single grape varieties, and *acquavite*, a similar beverage made from whole fruits like apricots, cherries, or peaches.

Grappa is usually sipped straight up after meals, although it is occasionally added to desserts. One typical use in Friuli is to pour a glassful over portions of *gubana*, a delicious fruit-and-nut-filled cake. In the Alto Adige, a mixture of hot coffee, grappa, lemon, and sugar is passed around after meals in what is called the *coppa dell'amicizia,* or "friendship cup," a special carved wooden bowl with several spigots. According to legend, it is bad luck to leave the table until all of the beverage has been consumed.

Veneto

Frappe

venetian carnival fritters

Every region of Italy has its own variety of crunchy fried cookies. Some are shaped into balls or cartwheels, some are sprinkled with nuts or dried fruit, and some are drizzled with honey or dusted with sugar. In this version from the Veneto, a splash of fiery grappa is used for flavoring. Substitute a favorite brandy or a liqueur, if you prefer.

1 cup (5 oz / 155 g) all-purpose (plain) flour

2 tablespoons granulated sugar

½ teaspoon salt

2 tablespoons unsalted butter, at room temperature

1 egg

2 tablespoons grappa

vegetable oil for deep-frying

confectioners' (icing) sugar

※ In a small bowl, stir together the flour, sugar, and salt. In a large bowl, combine the butter, egg, and grappa. Add the dry ingredients and stir until the dough becomes stiff. Transfer to a floured work surface and knead until smooth, about 1 minute. Cover with an inverted bowl and let rest for 30 minutes.

※ Divide the dough in half. Roll out each half as thinly as possible, lifting and turning often to avoid sticking. With a fluted pastry cutter, cut into 4-by-1½-inch (10-by-4-cm) strips.

※ In a deep, heavy saucepan, pour in oil to fill the pan one-third full. Heat the oil to 350°F (180°C) on a deep-frying thermometer. Shake the dough strips to remove any excess flour. Working in batches, slip the strips, a few at a time, into the oil and fry until puffed and golden, about 3 minutes. Using a slotted spoon, transfer to paper towels to drain. Fry the remaining dough strips in the same manner.

※ When completely cool, place confectioners' sugar in a small sieve and dust the cookies generously. Toss them gently to coat evenly. Store in an airtight container at room temperature for up to 1 week.

makes about 3 dozen

Veneto

Baci

chocolate kisses

Chocolate-filled cookie sandwiches are a favorite in Verona, Shakespeare's setting for Romeo and Juliet. In the local bakeries, the cookies are known as baci di Giulietta, or "Juliet's kisses."

1 cup (8 oz/250 g) plus 2 tablespoons unsalted butter, at room temperature

½ cup (2 oz/60 g) confectioners' (icing) sugar

½ teaspoon salt

1 tablespoon rum

2 cups (10 oz/315 g) all-purpose (plain) flour

2 oz (60 g) semisweet (plain) chocolate such as Perugina or Callebaut

❦ In a large bowl, using an electric mixer set on medium speed, beat together the 1 cup (8 oz/250 g) butter, the confectioners' sugar, and the salt until light and fluffy. Beat in the rum. Stir in the flour until smooth and well blended. Cover and chill until firm, about 1 hour.

❦ Preheat an oven to 350°F (180°C).

❦ Scoop up the dough by the teaspoonful and roll each nugget into a ball. Place the balls about 1 inch (2.5 cm) apart on ungreased baking sheets.

❦ Bake until firm but not browned, 10–12 minutes. Transfer to wire racks to cool completely.

❦ Place the chocolate and the remaining 2 table-spoons butter in a small heatproof bowl. Set the bowl over (not touching) simmering water in a saucepan and heat until the chocolate softens. Remove from over the water and stir until smooth. Let cool slightly.

❦ Using a butter knife, spread a small amount of the chocolate on the bottom of a cookie. Place the bottom of a second cookie against the chocolate, sandwich style, and press the halves together. Repeat with the remaining cookies. Let cool on the wire racks until the filling is set. Store in an airtight container in a cool place for up to 1 week.

makes about 2 dozen

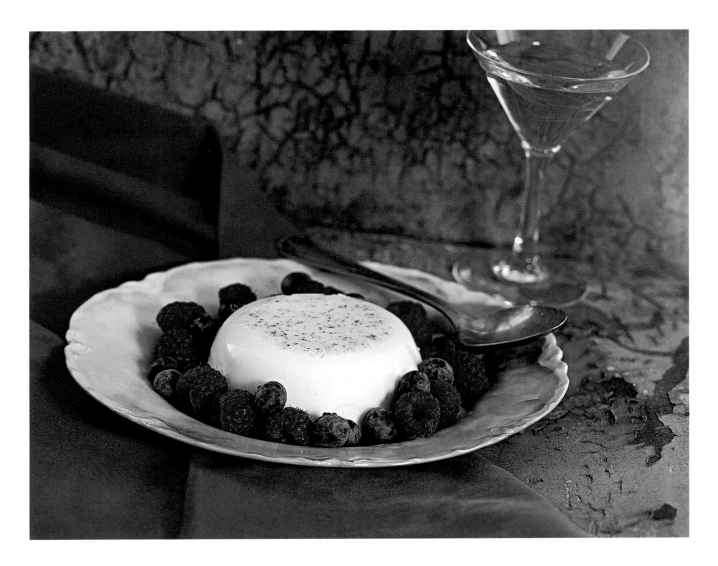

Piemonte

Panna Cotta

cooked cream with mixed berries

These delicate creams are a specialty of Piedmont, where they have been made since medieval times to take advantage of the abundant fresh milk from the region's cows. The name panna cotta, *or "cooked cream," is thought to be a bit of a joke, since the cream is in fact not cooked and never even reaches the boiling point. Serve the cream with fresh fruit, caramel, or warm chocolate sauce.*

2½ teaspoons (1 package) unflavored gelatin

¼ cup (2 fl oz/60 ml) milk

2 cups (16 fl oz/500 ml) heavy (double) cream

¼ cup (2 oz/60 g) sugar

½ vanilla bean

1 small lemon zest strip

4 cups (1 lb/500 g) mixed berries such as blackberries, sliced strawberries, blueberries, and raspberries, in any combination

❦ In a large bowl, sprinkle the gelatin over the milk. Let stand for 2 minutes to soften.

❦ In a saucepan over medium heat, stir together the cream, sugar, vanilla bean, and lemon zest. Cook, stirring occasionally, until small bubbles appear around the edges of the saucepan. Remove from the heat.

❦ Remove the vanilla bean and let cool briefly, then slit it open lengthwise with a sharp knife and scrape the seeds into the cream with the tip of the knife.

❦ Slowly add the cream to the gelatin mixture, stirring until completely dissolved. Pour into four ¾-cup (6–fl oz/180-ml) ramekins or custard cups, dividing evenly. Cover and chill for 4 hours, or for up to overnight.

❦ When ready to serve, run a small knife blade around the inside of each ramekin to loosen the cream. Invert each ramekin onto a serving plate.

❦ Arrange the berries around the creams and serve immediately.

serves 4

Lombardia

Fichi e Gorgonzola al Miele

figs and gorgonzola with honey

Blue-veined Gorgonzola can be stagionato, "aged" or sharp, or dolce, "sweet" or mild. Either type is good with figs and honey, or you can substitute another Italian cheese, such as Lombardy's mild Taleggio.

8–12 ripe black or green figs

about ½ lb (250 g) Gorgonzola cheese, rind trimmed, at room temperature

¼ cup (3 oz/90 g) chestnut or other flavorful honey

¼ cup (1 oz/30 g) chopped pistachios

❦ Score the skin of each fig in 4 or 5 places from the stem end to about halfway to the base. Using a small knife, gently pull the skin down, leaving it attached at the base so that it resembles the petals of a flower.

❦ Cut the cheese into 4 wedges. Arrange the figs and cheese on 4 serving plates.

❦ Drizzle the honey over the cheese, then sprinkle the cheese with the nuts. Serve at once.

serves 4

I Fichi

Figs, or *fichi,* seem to flourish everywhere in Italy. They are cultivated in gardens and also grow wild, pushing their way through crevices in stone fences and ancient parapets. Many varieties ripen twice a year. In southern Italy, the first crop is ready at the end of June. Called *fioroni,* these early fruits are generally larger and softer than the second flush of smaller, sweeter figs that mature later in the summer.

An Italian fable tells the story of a wealthy noble who sent his servant to pick some figs with "a teardrop in their eye," a visible bead of nectar at the base of the fruit, the evidence of a fully ripened specimen. The man became suspicious when the servant returned day after day empty handed, shaking his head as he reported there were none ready for picking. Finally the noble followed his employee, only to find him sitting in the shade of an old fig tree, eating the irresistible—and perfectly ripe—fruits.

Of course, the country's exquisite figs are much sought after for desserts, such as Apulia's *fichi mandorlati,* which calls for warming the dried fruits with almonds, bay, and fennel seeds, and Sicily's Christmas *buccellato* (see page 243), a rich ring cake thick with dried figs and walnuts.

Sicilia

Buccellato

christmas fig ring

Pastries filled with ground figs, nuts, and spices are traditional Christmas sweets found all over Sicily. Sometimes they are formed into ring-shaped cakes, and other times they are made into individual pastries or smaller cookies. During the holiday season, Sicilian women get together to bake, sharing the preparation and vying to see who can make the most elaborate-looking desserts, forming them into flowers, birds, or other fanciful creations.

PASTRY

3 cups (15 oz/470 g) unbleached all-purpose (plain) flour

½ cup (4 oz/125 g) sugar

2½ teaspoons baking powder

½ teaspoon salt

6 tablespoons (3 oz/90 g) unsalted butter, at room temperature, cut into bits

2 eggs

¼ cup (2 fl oz/60 ml) milk

1 teaspoon vanilla extract (essence)

FILLING

2 cups (1 lb/500 g) dried figs, stemmed

½ cup (2 oz/60 g) walnuts, lightly toasted

⅓ cup (4 oz/125 g) honey

¼ cup (2 fl oz/60 ml) fresh orange juice

1 teaspoon grated orange zest

1 teaspoon ground cinnamon

⅛ teaspoon ground cloves

DECORATION

1 egg white, beaten

colored candy sprinkles (optional)

❧ To make the pastry, in the bowl of a stand mixer, stir together the flour, sugar, baking powder, and salt. With the mixer set on medium speed, beat in the butter. In another bowl, whisk together the eggs, milk, and vanilla until blended. Pour it over the flour mixture and mix until blended. Gather the dough into a ball. Place on a sheet of plastic wrap and flatten into a disk. Wrap well and refrigerate for at least 3 hours or for as long as overnight.

❧ To make the filling, in a food processor, combine the figs and walnuts. Pulse to chop coarsely. Add the honey, the orange juice and zest, the cinnamon, and the cloves. Process until blended.

❧ Preheat an oven to 375°F (190°C). Butter a large baking sheet.

❧ On a lightly floured work surface, shape the dough with your hands into a thick rectangle. Roll out into an 18-by-9-inch (45-by-23-cm) rectangle. Using a sharp paring knife or a pastry wheel, trim the edges so they are straight, reserving the scraps. Spoon the filling into an even strip 2 inches (5 cm) wide lengthwise down the center of the rectangle. Lift one long side of the dough over the filling, then fold the other side over the top. Press to seal. Carefully slide the log onto the prepared baking sheet, placing it seam side down. Bring the ends together to form a ring and pinch together to seal.

❧ Reroll the scraps. With a paring knife or cookie cutters, cut out flowers, vines, and leaves. Brush the top and sides of the ring with some of the egg white. Arrange the decorations on top of the ring. Brush the ring and decorations with egg white. Sprinkle with the colored candies, if using.

❧ Bake until golden brown, about 40 minutes. Transfer to a rack and let cool on the baking sheet for 10 minutes. Slide the cake onto the rack and let cool completely.

❧ Serve at room temperature, cut into thin slices. To store, wrap tightly and keep at room temperature for up to 3 days.

serves 16

At Christmastime, Sicilians wrap fruits, nuts, and spices in rich pastry doughs, shape them into birds and rings, flowers and fans, and strew them with candy confetti.

Emilia-Romagna

Semifreddo alle Mandorle

almond semifreddo

Bologna has always been a prosperous city and its residents have the reputation of enjoying the good life. Dining there is considered a special treat, as the cooking is often cited as the best in Italy. Certainly it is the richest, based on meat, cheese, and a trio of fats: butter, olive oil, and more rarely, lard. The banquet is a solid local institution, with wedding dinners historically elaborate affairs.

This semifreddo is a classic Bolognese dessert. Lighter than gelato, a semifreddo is more like a frozen mousse. Because of its airy texture, it never seems as icy cold as ice cream. It can be made with a variety of flavorings, from coffee or rum to praline or fruit.

1 cup (8 fl oz/250 ml) heavy (double) cream

3 egg whites, at room temperature

¼ cup (2 fl oz/60 ml) water

½ cup (4 oz/125 g) plus 6 teaspoons sugar

1 teaspoon vanilla extract (essence)

⅓ cup (1 oz/30 g) crushed amaretti (about 6)

2 tablespoons chopped toasted almonds

2 tablespoons sliced (flaked) almonds, lightly toasted

❦ Line a 6-cup (48–fl oz/1.5-l) loaf pan with plastic wrap and place in the freezer.

❦ In a large chilled bowl, using chilled beaters, whip the cream on medium speed until stiff peaks form. Cover and refrigerate.

❦ Place the egg whites in the large clean bowl of a stand mixer fitted with clean beaters.

❦ In a small, heavy saucepan, combine the water and the ½ cup (4 oz/125 g) sugar. Bring to a simmer over low heat, stirring until the sugar dissolves, then stop stirring. Raise the heat to medium–high and heat, washing down the sugar crystals that form on the sides of the pan with a small brush dipped in cool water, until the liquid reaches 210°F (99°C) on a candy thermometer. At this point, begin beating the egg whites as the syrup continues to boil.

❦ Beat the egg whites on medium speed until frothy. Add 1 teaspoon of the remaining sugar and beat until soft peaks form. Gradually beat in the remaining 5 teaspoons sugar.

❦ When the sugar syrup reaches 238°F (114°C) on the thermometer, turn off the heat. The temperature will continue to rise slightly. As soon as the whites are thick and form soft peaks, begin adding the sugar syrup in a thin stream, beating continuously and pouring it into the whites and not onto the beaters. After adding the syrup, the whites will look glossy and white and triple in volume. Continue to beat them together for several minutes longer until they are at room temperature. They will be very thick and shiny. Beat in the vanilla.

❦ Using a rubber spatula, fold about one-third of the whipped cream into the whites. Gradually fold in the remaining cream until the mixture is smooth. Fold in the amaretti and the chopped almonds.

❦ Scrape the mixture into the prepared pan, smoothing the top. Cover with plastic wrap and freeze for several hours or for as long as overnight.

❦ To unmold, remove the plastic wrap from the surface. Invert a plate over the pan and invert the pan and plate together. Remove the pan and peel off the plastic wrap. Smooth the surface with a rubber spatula, if necessary. Sprinkle with the sliced almonds. Cut into slices to serve.

serves 8

Sicilia

Crema di Ricotta alla Frutta Fresca

cannoli cream with fresh fruit

The cream used to fill cannoli is also a nice accompaniment to fresh fruit. Vary the choices according to the season. For a particularly creamy texture, beat together the ricotta-topping ingredients in a food processor or blender. Also, seek out a vendor who makes his or her own fresh ricotta daily for the best results. It will make a noticeable difference in the final taste. Tangy fresh Sicilian ricotta, traditonally made from the whey of sheep's milk left over from making pecorino cheese, is especially delicious, although cow's milk ricotta is also good.

2 cups (1 lb/500 g) whole-milk ricotta cheese

¼ cup (1 oz/30 g) confectioners' (icing) sugar

1 teaspoon vanilla extract (essence)

½ teaspoon grated lemon zest

pinch of ground cinnamon

6 apricots, pitted and sliced

4 kiwifruits, peeled and sliced

2 tablespoons sugar

2 tablespoons orange- or cherry-flavored liqueur

½ pint (4 oz/125 g) raspberries

3 tablespoons chopped semisweet (plain) chocolate

☙ In a bowl, using a whisk or wooden spoon, beat the ricotta cheese until smooth and creamy. Beat in the confectioners' sugar, vanilla, lemon zest, and cinnamon until blended.

☙ In a small bowl, combine the apricots, kiwifruits, sugar, and liqueur. Using 1 or 2 spoons, toss well, being careful not to bruise the fruit. Scatter the raspberries over the top.

☙ Spoon the fruits into goblets or other attractive serving vessels. Top each serving with an equal amount of the ricotta mixture. Sprinkle with the chocolate and serve at once.

serves 8

GLOSSARIO

The following entries cover key Italian ingredients and basic recipes called for throughout this book. For information on items not found below, please refer to the index.

AMARETTI

Small, crisp macaroons, a specialty of the Lombardy region, amaretti get their name from the ground bitter *(amaro)* almonds that are their key ingredient. The leading brand, widely available in Italian delicatessens, is Lazzaroni di Saronno, in which the cookies are distinctively packaged in tissue-wrapped pairs piled inside an old-fashioned red tin. Serve amaretti with after-dinner coffee and liqueurs or use them crushed as a dessert ingredient. To crush amaretti, place inside a heavy-duty plastic bag and shatter with a rolling pin.

AMARETTO

According to legend, this pale gold sweet liqueur, named for the bitter almonds that, along with apricots, flavor it, was first concocted by a young widow in the Lombardy town of Saronno in the early sixteenth century. She served it to a disciple of Da Vinci, the painter Bernardino Luini, who had come to Saronno to paint a fresco of the nativity in a local *sanctuario*. So enamored was he of the woman and her liqueur, now one of Italy's most popular, that he immortalized her face as that of the Madonna.

ANCHOVIES

These tiny, silver-skinned fish are enjoyed throughout Italy as a flavor element in savory dishes, sometimes strongly evident and sometimes only subtly present. The best-quality, freshest-tasting, and meatiest anchovies are those packed whole layered in salt, sold by weight from large tins in Italian delis.

TO PREPARE SALTED ANCHOVIES for use at home, rinse well under cold running water. Split open along the backbone and cut off the dorsal fins. Pull out the spine, rinse out the interior well, and pat dry with paper towels. Use immediately as directed in recipes or place in a glass or other nonreactive bowl, cover completely with a thin layer of olive oil, and refrigerate. Use within 2 weeks.

If salted anchovies are unavailable, use a good brand of anchovy fillets packed in olive oil. Look for those sold in glass jars rather than tins. The jars permit you to judge easily how firm and meaty the fillets are.

ARUGULA

Throughout Italy, this slender, green leaf vegetable can be found growing wild in the countryside and is valued in both salads and quickly cooked dishes. The finest, most tender young arugula (rocket) leaves have a pleasing delicacy, while the older specimens have a more peppery, slightly bitter taste.

BEANS

Italians sometimes call protein-rich beans the poor man's meat. Whether the beans are gathered and eaten fresh in spring and early summer or dried for use at other times of the year, enthusiastic eaters value such favorites as speckled, pale pink borlotti, similar to cranberry beans; Tuscany's signature cannellini, ivory-colored kidney beans of moderate size; and large, pale green fava (broad) beans, especially popular in central and southern regions.

TO SHELL FRESH BEANS, use your thumbs to split the pods along their seams. When eating fresh favas, all but the youngest and most tender specimens of early spring will also require peeling of their thick skins, a task that can be eased by first briefly blanching the beans.

TO COOK DRIED BEANS, first sort through them to eliminate any debris or misshapen specimens. Presoak in cold water to cover overnight, or quick-soak in a large pot by covering well with cold water, bringing to a boil, then letting stand for 1–2 hours. After soaking, drain the beans, put in a pot with fresh water to cover, bring to a full rolling boil, then simmer until tender, 1–2 hours, depending upon the type of bean. In some recipes that don't require long cooking, you can substitute canned beans. A 15-ounce (470-g) can, rinsed and drained, yields about 2 cups beans, which is equivalent to the yield of about 3 ounces (90 g) dried beans.

BREAD CRUMBS

Used to make crisp toppings for oven-baked dishes or to lend body to fillings and stuffings, bread crumbs should be made from a slightly stale coarse country white loaf.

TO MAKE DRIED BREAD CRUMBS, trim the loaf of its crusts and process in a food processor to form crumbs. Dry the crumbs on a baking sheet in a preheated 325°F (165°C) oven for about 15 minutes; let cool, process again until fine, and then bake, stirring once or twice, until pale gold, about 15 minutes longer.

CAPERS

The preserved green buds of a wild plant that thrives in Italy's sunny climes, capers have been enjoyed at least since the days of ancient Rome. The smallest variety, barely as big as little peas, are known as nonpareil capers and are usually sold pickled in vinegar, which gives them a sharp taste. Italian cooks generally prefer larger capers preserved in salt, available in Italian delicatessens. Before using salted capers, soak in cold water for 15–20 minutes and then rinse them well. Containers of salted capers will keep in the refrigerator for a year or more.

CHICKPEA (GARBANZO BEAN) FLOUR

A rich, nutty-tasting flour ground from dried chickpeas (garbanzo beans), known in Italian as *ceci*. The flour is used to make *panelle*, Sicilan fritters, and *farinata*, a type of crisp flat bread from Liguria. It may be found in specialty Italian shops and health-food stores.

CHEESES

Italians have long savored their distinctive regional cheeses, making them in a variety of ways from the milk of different domesticated animals and enjoying them on their own or as part of cooked dishes.

FONTINA ~ Originating in Val d'Aosta, this rich, firm, and earthy cheese is made from the milk of cows that graze on subalpine slopes.

GORGONZOLA ~ Creamy, tangy, and spicy, this greenish-veined cow's milk cheese originated in its namesake town near Milan, but is now largely produced farther east along the Po River valley. Specimens produced and cave-aged in the traditional way have a captivating pungency. Gorgonzola Dolcelatte (sweet milk) are milder and only lightly veined.

GRANA ~ The term applies to all hard, aged grating cheeses, including Parmigiano-Reggiano (see right). It sometimes more specifically refers to grana padano, a hard grating cheese from Lombardy and Piedmont that is similar to Parmesan.

MASCARPONE ~ A fresh double-cream cow's milk cheese with a spreadable consistency and an edge of tangy acidity. This specialty of Lombardy is used in both savory and sweet recipes.

MONTASIO ~ Traditionally produced in the mountains of Friuli–Venezia Giulia, in Italy's northeast, this cow's milk cheese resembles Switzerland's nutlike Emmentaler when served young. It is also aged to become a hard grating cheese.

MOZZARELLA, FRESH BUFFALO'S MILK AND COW'S MILK ~ The best mozzarella cheese is made fresh from the milk of water buffalo *(mozzarella di bufala)* that graze in and around Campania. Sold floating in watery whey, it has a delicate, tangy flavor and a pleasantly stringy texture that results from kneading the curds during manufacture. Cow's milk is used more often nowadays to make both fresh mozzarella and the drier, firmer, slightly aged varieties.

PARMIGIANO-REGGIANO ~ Intensely aromatic and nutty, with a firm, dry consistency that has excellent melting properties, this renowned cheese, aged for a minimum of 12 months and an average of 18–24, is made exclusively from the milk of cows that graze in specific areas (see page 102). A saying from the region suggests that you should never leave the table without the taste of Parmesan in your mouth.

PECORINO ROMANO ~ A very sharp, hard grating cheese made from the milk of ewes, this was originally produced only in the countryside surrounding Rome. Indeed, legend attributes its invention to Romulus, cofounder of the city with his twin brother Remus. Today, the area of production, defined by law, has been expanded to include Sardinia. Mild, gently aged pecorino is also popular for cooking and eating. Similar pecorino cheeses are produced in other regions, including Sicily, Tuscany, and Sardinia.

RICOTTA ~ Produced by recooking the whey left over from the making of pecorino and other cheeses, ricotta has a fluffy white texture and mild, almost sweet taste when fresh, making it a favorite ingredient for fillings and desserts. Whole-milk ricotta is richer than commercial varieties made from reduced-fat milk. Ricotta salata is a salted and aged version.

TALEGGIO ~ A smooth, semisoft cheese made of cow's milk, this specialty of Lombardy is tangy and pale yellow when young, and ages to a darker color and pungent flavor.

CHILE

Flakes and seeds of the slender dried red chiles known in Italy as *peperoncini* are a popular kitchen seasoning and table condiment in the central and southern regions. They may be bought already crushed in the spice section of food stores and Italian markets or may be crushed at home in a heavy-duty plastic bag with a rolling pin.

COTECHINO

A large fresh pork sausage of Modena made from choice cuts from the shoulder, shank, neck, and ears, ground and mixed with white wine and such seasonings as cloves, cinnamon, nutmeg, salt, and pepper. *Cotechino* is traditionally cooked and eaten with lentils, beans, or potatoes, or as part of a *bollito misto* (mixed boiled meats).

FARRO

Similar to spelt and emmer and eaten as whole berries or finely milled granules, this ancient form of wheat was enjoyed during the Roman Empire and is still popular in Tuscany today.

FENNEL

Known by the Italian *finocchio,* this slightly sweet licorice-flavored bulb is at its best in late autumn and early winter. Native cooks prefer the larger, plumper male bulb raw in salads, and the longer, more slender female bulb for sautéing or braising. Crescent-shaped fennel seeds add a licorice note to stuffings and to sausage mixtures.

HERBS

Italian cooks make the most of a variety of herbs that they gather in the wild, raise at home, or buy at the market. Among the most popular are:

BASIL ~ A member of the mint family, this oval-leafed herb adds a highly aromatic, peppery flavor when used fresh and is the base of Genoa's signature pesto sauce.

BAY LEAF ~ Strong and spicy, the whole glossy leaves of the bay laurel tree are indispensable in long-simmered savory dishes. European bay leaves have a milder, more pleasant taste than the California-grown variety.

MARJORAM ~ More delicate than oregano, a close cousin, this herb is prized fresh as a seasoning for tomato-based dishes.

MINT ~ Italians enjoy several different types from among the over 600 known varieties of this herb, including calamint *(nepitella)*, which has a fresh lemony flavor and leaves resembling basil, leading to its also being known as basil mint or basil thyme; and *mentuccia*, a delicate-tasting variety known in English as pennyroyal and preferred by Romans as a seasoning for artichokes.

OREGANO ~ Related to mint and thyme, this strongly scented herb actually gains in flavor from drying, unlike most herbs. It is the signature seasoning of pizza and is added to many tomato sauces, mushroom dishes, and marinades.

PARSLEY, ITALIAN (FLAT-LEAF) ~ This dark green version of the slightly peppery southern European herb is far more flavorful than the curly-leaf type. It is commonly used as both a seasoning and a garnish.

ROSEMARY ~ Taking its name from the Latin for "dew of the sea," reflecting its love of climates with salt-kissed air, this Mediterranean native contributes powerful but pleasantly aromatic flavor to lamb, veal, chicken, and other dishes.

SAGE ~ An ancient healing herb that takes its name from the Latin *salvus*, "safe," this strong, heady, slightly musty-tasting herb is used fresh and dried to season rich meats and poultry, as well as vegetables and cheeses.

THYME ~ Highly aromatic and yet subtle in flavor, this ancient Mediterranean herb is included in many slow-cooked savory dishes and is especially useful for the digestive properties it contributes to dishes featuring meat or poultry rich in fat.

MARSALA

An amber-colored fortified wine made in the area around the Sicilian city of the same name. Available in sweet and dry forms, it is enjoyed as a dessert wine and is used as a flavoring in savory and sweet dishes.

NUTS

Cooks in Italy make use of many native-grown nuts in both sweet and savory dishes, including almonds, hazelnuts (filberts), pine nuts, pistachios, and walnuts. Toasting nuts deepens their flavor and color and increases their crispiness.

TO TOAST NUTS, spread the shelled nuts in a single layer on a baking sheet and bake in a preheated 325°F (165°C) oven until their color just begins to change, 5–10 minutes. Toasting also loosens the skins of such nuts as hazelnuts and walnuts, which may then be removed while still warm by rubbing the nuts between kitchen towels.

OLIVE OIL

The farther south one travels in Italy, and the sunnier the climes, the more prominently olive oil figures in the cooking. As for wine, the best olive oils come from fruit grown in the best soil, geography, and climate, with those factors affecting the qualities of the final product. Tuscan oils are generally full-bodied and fruity, with a pungent bite. Those of Chianti are particularly noted for their peppery taste. Umbrian oils are fruity and creamy, Ligurian oils sweet and delicate, while those from Lake Garda are prized for their elegance.

Wherever they are produced, the finest olive oils are labeled extra virgin. This indicates that they were mechanically pressed from top-grade olives without use of heat or chemicals, and that the final product has an acidity level of less than 1 percent. Use extra-virgin olive oil as a dressing ingredient, seasoning, or condiment, to highlight its character. Oil extracted using heat or chemicals, then filtered and blended to eliminate much of the olives' character, may be used for general cooking purposes. In the past, such oil was labeled pure olive oil or 100 percent pure olive oil. Today, it is simply labeled olive oil. Store all olive oils in dark glass bottles or tins away from heat and light.

OLIVES

The fruit of the olive tree is enjoyed throughout Italy, whether picked when unripe and green, partially ripe and purple-black, or fully ripened and deep black; cured in brine or salt; and preserved in oil, vinegar, or brine. Among the most popular varieties are the plump, sharp green olives of Sicily and the black olives produced near the coastal town of Gaeta on the Tyrrhenian Sea. The widely available black Niçoise olives of France may be substituted for the latter.

TO PIT OLIVES, place a few at a time on a flat surface and lay the flat side of a chef's knife on top. Smack the knife with the heel of your hand to split the olives and release the pits.

PANCETTA

A form of unsmoked Italian bacon, this long, flat cut of fatty pork belly is seasoned with black pepper, and sometimes garlic, cinnamon, and nutmeg, then rolled up tightly and salt-cured. Pancetta is used thinly sliced as a wrapper for savory dishes and chopped to flavor fillings, stuffings, sauces, and braises.

PASTA

Throughout Italy, scores of different fresh and dried pasta shapes are enjoyed. Pasta should be cooked until it is al dente, literally "to the tooth," which means just cooked through, but still firm and slightly chewy. To achieve that, you must begin to taste the pasta as the end of the cooking time indicated on the package nears. Each brand and shape can have a slightly different cooking time.

Dried pastas, made from doughs of semolina flour and water, are traditionally eaten with tomato- and oil-based sauces. Fresh pasta, or *pasta fresca,* is generally made from egg-and-flour doughs and is best suited to sauces featuring butter, cream, or cheese. Some of the most common pasta shapes called for in this book include:

Bucatini. Hollow, spaghettilike rods of dried pasta; also known as *perciatelli.*

Ditalini. Short, small tubes of dried pasta.

Elbow macaroni. The familiar crooked dried pasta tubes.

Fettuccine. Usually fresh pasta ribbons, the width varies slightly from region to region.

Gnocchi. Small dumpling shapes that can be made from potatoes, cheese, bread, or other doughs.

Linguine. "Small tongues," describing long, thin strands of dried or fresh pasta.

Orecchiette. Small, concave ear shapes of dried or fresh pasta.

Pappardelle. Fresh ribbons about 1 inch (2.5 cm) wide.

Penne. Dried pasta tubes with angle-cut ends resembling quill pens.

Perciatelli. Hollow, spaghettilike rods of dried pasta; also called *bucatini.*

Pizzoccheri. Buckwheat tagliatelle, a specialty of the mountains of Lombardy.

Rigatoni. Moderately sized ridged tubes of dried pasta.

Spaghetti. Classic long, round strands of dried pasta.

Spaghettini. Thin spaghetti.

Tagliatelle. Fresh ribbons about ¼ inch (6 mm) wide.

Trenette. Flat, thin linguine.

Tubetti. Short dried-pasta tubes resembling *ditalini.*

FRESH EGG PASTA DOUGH

about 2 ½ cups (12 ½ oz / 390 g) unbleached all-purpose (plain) flour

4 large eggs

TO MAKE THE DOUGH BY HAND: Pour the flour into a mound on a work surface. Using a fork, make a crater in the center and break in the eggs. Beat the eggs, then gradually incorporate the flour from inside the crater while supporting the wall of flour with your other hand.

When the dough starts to form a ball and becomes firm, sweep any remaining flour to one side. Lightly flour your hands and begin kneading with your fingertips. If the dough continues to feel sticky, gradually incorporate some of the reserved flour until the dough feels moist but not sticky. Do not add more flour than necessary to create a firm ball, or it may become too dry; if it becomes too dry, moisten your hands with a little water and knead it in. The dough is ready when it is smooth and elastic, moist yet not sticky. This should take 8–10 minutes.

Cover the dough with an inverted bowl and let rest at room temperature for at least 30 minutes or for up to 2 hours.

TO MAKE THE DOUGH IN A FOOD PROCESSOR OR STAND MIXER: In a food processor or in a stand mixer fitted with the flat beater attachment, beat the eggs. With the machine running, slowly add the flour by the tablespoonful. When most of the flour has been added and the dough forms a ball on the blade or beater, stop the machine. Pinch the dough. It should feel moist but not sticky and should be fairly smooth. If it is not, turn the machine on again and add more flour as needed. Remove the dough from the machine and knead it on a lightly floured surface for 1 minute to ensure it is firm, smooth, and moist but not sticky. Let rest as directed for dough made by hand.

TO ROLL OUT THE DOUGH BY HAND: Have ready several rimmed trays or baking sheets covered with kitchen towels. Sprinkle the towels with flour.

You will need a long, slender, wooden rolling pin at least 24 inches (60 cm) long and 1½–2 inches (4–5 cm) wide. Lightly dust a large, perfectly flat work surface with flour. Uncover the dough and cut into 4 pieces. It might feel moister and stickier than when you last handled it. While you work with 1 piece of dough, keep the remainder covered with the inverted bowl or plastic wrap. Shape the dough into a round disk and place it on the board. Place the rolling pin in the center of the dough and push it away from you toward the edge. Rotate the dough a quarter turn, center the pin on the dough, and push it toward the edge once more. Repeat rotating the dough a quarter turn and rolling it out from the center 2 more times. Flip the disk over to be sure that it is not sticking; if necessary, dust it with more flour. Working quickly, continue stretching the dough, rotating it, and turning it over from time to time, until very thin and smooth. When it is ready, the dough should be paper-thin so that you can easily see your hand through it when the sheet is held up to a light.

♨ Repeat with the remaining pieces of dough. As you roll out the strips, lay them side by side on the prepared towels without letting them touch one another. Let dry for about 20 minutes, or until firm yet still pliable, turning them at least once before cutting as directed in the individual recipe.

TO ROLL OUT THE DOUGH WITH A PASTA MACHINE: Prepare the trays with towels as directed for rolling by hand. Following the manufacturer's directions, clamp the pasta machine firmly to a countertop or sturdy table. Set the rollers of the pasta machine at the widest opening and dust them lightly with flour. Uncover the dough, and cut into 4 pieces. While you work with 1 piece of dough keep the remainder covered with the inverted bowl or plastic wrap. Flatten the dough into an oval disk. Turning the handle of the pasta machine with one hand, guide the piece of dough through the rollers of the machine. If the dough sticks or tears, dust it lightly with flour. Fold the dough into thirds. Pass the dough through the machine again, flouring if necessary. Repeat folding and passing the dough 5 or 6 times. Move the dial to the next notch. Pass the dough through the rollers. As the dough emerges, lift it out straight so that it stays flat and smooth. Do not fold the dough.

♨ Continue to pass the dough through the machine, moving the dial up 1 notch to narrow the rollers each time, until the dough has reached the thinness you want. It should be thin enough to see your hand through it, but not so thin that it will tear. For stuffed pasta, such as ravioli, the dough should be as thin as possible, so you will probably need to go to the last setting. The second-to-last notch is usually thin enough for fettuccine, *pappardelle,* or other flat pasta.

♨ Repeat with the remaining pieces of dough. As you roll out the strips, lay them on the prepared towels. Proceed as directed for dough rolled out by hand.

PROSCIUTTO

This air-cured raw *(crudo)* ham is dry-salted for 1 month under weights that give it its characteristic flat shape, then air-dried for 6 months or more. The prosciutto develops a deep pink hue, salty-sweet taste, and velvety texture best appreciated in thin slices as an antipasto. *Prosciutto cotto* is a cooked ham, while in Friuli–Venezia Giulia, Trentino, and the Alto Adige, smoked prosciutto is found.

RADICCHIO

Pleasantly astringent, bitter, and crisp, this member of the chicory family may be found in various forms throughout Italy. The most familiar type is a compact, round head of white-ribbed burgundy leaves. In late autumn, markets offer the less bitter Treviso variety, which has spearlike purple leaves the shape of romaine (cos) lettuce leaves.

RICE, MEDIUM-GRAIN WHITE

Three main types of medium-grain white rice are used in Italy to cook the dish known as risotto. Best known is Arborio rice, preferred in the kitchens of Lombardy, Emilia-Romagna, and the Piedmont. Its plump oval grains are very rich in the surface starch that produces risotto's distinctive creamy sauce; the best Arborios are grown in the Po River valley. Vialone Nano rice, a favorite in the Veneto for its smaller grains, has less surface starch and yields firmer-textured, less creamy risotto. The more costly Carnaroli variety is a hybrid of Vialone Nano and a Japanese rice and combines the creaminess of Arborio with the firm texture of Vialone. It is the newest of the trio.

SALT COD AND STOCKFISH

Salted cod is enjoyed by Italians in two distinctive forms; *baccalà,* cod that has been dried in the cold and then preserved with salt, and stockfish, or *stoccafisso,* which has been sun-dried and then salted, producing a much drier, tougher consistency. Before use, both forms must be soaked (see page 164).

SAUSAGES, FRESH ITALIAN

Fresh pork sausages are made throughout Italy, with each region producing a distinctive product. They range from the sweet spiced specimens of Emilia-Romagna to the coriander-spiked links of Lazio to Calabria's fiery-hot variety liberally seasoned with *peperoncini* to Mantua's simple *luganega,* seasoned merely with salt and pepper.

SEMOLINA FLOUR

Milled from the center of the durum (hard) wheat berry, this flour provides the ideal properties for making dried pasta and is also frequently used for bread making. Some of Italy's best wheat is said to grow along the delta of the Po River in Emilia-Romagna.

SQUID

Many seafood merchants sell squid already cleaned and ready to cook. If you need to clean squid yourself, begin by cutting off the tentacles just above the eyes. Grab the tentacles at their base and squeeze to pop out the squid's beak, discarding it. Rinse the tentacles well under running cold water. With your finger, pull out and discard the clear quill (rudimentary shell) from the body, then rinse the body well, discarding all the entrails. Cut as directed in individual recipes.

TOMATOES

During summer, Italian cooks use vine-ripened fresh tomatoes for both uncooked salads and for cooked dishes such as the simple tomato sauce recipe that follows. At other times of year, they use the best-quality canned Italian plum (Roma) tomatoes available, of which the San Marzano variety are considered the finest.

TO PEEL A FRESH TOMATO, use a small, sharp knife to score a shallow X in its flower end. Then, using a slotted spoon, dip the tomato into a saucepan of boiling water for no more than 20 seconds. Submerge the tomatoes in a bowl of ice water to cool. Starting at the X, peel off the loosened skin with your fingertips. To remove the seeds, cut the tomato in half crosswise and squeeze gently.

QUICK TOMATO SAUCE

2 large cloves garlic, minced

¼ cup (2 fl oz/60 ml) olive oil

2 lb (1 kg) ripe plum (Roma) tomatoes, peeled, seeded, and diced

salt and freshly ground pepper to taste

pinch of dried oregano or 6 fresh basil leaves, torn into pieces

In a large, wide saucepan over medium heat, cook the garlic in the olive oil just until fragrant, about 30 seconds. Add the tomatoes and their juice and bring to a simmer. Add salt, pepper, and dried oregano, if using. Cook, crushing the tomatoes with the back of a wooden spoon, and stirring occasionally, until thick and rich, 20–25 minutes. Remove from the heat and stir in the basil.

TRUFFLES

The area around Alba, in Piedmont, is the home of the white truffle, found nowhere else in Europe. Harvested from autumn into winter with the help of specially trained dogs, the truffles are found around the roots of oaks, hazels, poplars, willows, and other trees. The fungi are shaved raw to add intense aroma and flavor to pasta, risotto, and other savory recipes. Slightly milder but still strong and earthy, black truffles are found in Umbria around the towns of Spoleto and Norcia.

VINEGAR

Vinegar, most commonly made from red or white wine, is an indispensable part of the Italian pantry. Italy's most renowned vinegar, *aceto balsamico*, or "balsamic vinegar," is not made from wine, however. This specialty of Modena and Reggio Emilia is based on white grape juice that is reduced by boiling it down to a thick syrup, then aged for many years in a succession of ever-smaller barrels made of different woods, each of which contributes its own taste to the final syrupy, sharp-and-sweet, complex-flavored product.

STOCK

Cooks in Italy use simple homemade broths. For the recipes in this book, use good-quality canned or frozen stock, taking care not to purchase overly salted brands, or prepare one of the following recipes.

CHICKEN STOCK

5 lb (2.5 kg) chicken parts, fat removed

3 qt (3 l) water

1 yellow onion, peeled and chopped

1 carrot, peeled and chopped

12 fresh parsley stems

1 teaspoon minced fresh thyme or ½ teaspoon dried

1 bay leaf

Place the chicken parts in a large stockpot and add all the remaining ingredients. Bring slowly to a boil, regularly skimming off any scum and froth from the surface. Reduce the heat to low and simmer, uncovered, until the meat has fallen off the bones and the stock is fragrant and flavorful, 3–4 hours, periodically adding water to maintain the original level. Line a sieve or colander with cheesecloth (muslin) and strain the stock through it into a large bowl. Refrigerate, uncovered, until cool, then cover tightly. With a spoon, remove the fat that solidifies on top before using. Store for up to 5 days in the refrigerator or for up to 2 months in the freezer.

Makes about 3 qt (3 l)

MEAT STOCK

6 lb (3 kg) meaty beef and veal shanks (shins)

2 yellow onions, coarsely chopped

1 leek, including green tops, coarsely chopped

2 carrots, peeled and coarsely chopped

1 celery stalk, coarsely chopped

6 cloves garlic

4 fresh flat-leaf (Italian) parsley sprigs

10 whole peppercorns

3 fresh thyme sprigs

2 small bay leaves

Place the beef and veal shanks in a large stockpot. Add cold water to cover, bring to a boil, and skim off any scum and froth from the surface. Reduce the heat and simmer, uncovered, for 2 hours, adding water as needed to keep the bones immersed. Skim the scum from the surface occasionally. Add the remaining ingredients to the stockpot. Simmer, uncovered, over low heat for another 2 hours. Remove from the heat and remove the solids with a slotted spoon. Pour the stock through a sieve. Line the strainer with cheesecloth (muslin) and strain the stock again. Refrigerate, uncovered, until cool, then cover tightly. With a spoon, remove the fat that solidifies on the top before using. Store for up to 5 days in the refrigerator or for up to 2 months in the freezer.

Makes 4–5 qt (4–5 l)

ACKNOWLEDGMENTS

Michele Scicolone wishes to thank her agent, Judith Weber, and friend Harriet Bell for their good advice; her husband, Charles, for his inspiration and endless reserves of historical, literary, and wine information; and Nancy Radke of the Consorzio del Parmigiano Reggiano, Linda Russo of Foodcom Inc., and Marina Thompson for help with fact checking.

Noel Barnhurst wishes to thank his assistants, Jessica Martin and Song Repp; Suzanne Cushman, Mary Ann Cleary, and Dave and Bobbie Chapman for their help with props; and Jon Staub and Jeff Finney for generously opening up Sweetwater. George Dolese wishes to thank his assistant, Leslie Busch, for her culinary abilities, patience, and good humor.

Steven Rothfeld wishes to thank the following individuals for their support and assistance: in Paris, Maryse Masse and Isabelle Durighello of Relais & Chateaux; in Modena, the Morandi family of Salumeria da Giusti; in Montefollonico, the Lucherini family of La Chiusa; in Chianti, Lorenzo Righi of the Relais Borgo San Felice; in Liguria, the Segre family of La Meridiana; in Cortona, Susanna Bertollo, manager of Silvia Regi and Riccardo Baracchi's Il Falconiere; and in Florence, Valeria Bosi of the Hotel Regency. In addition, he wishes to express his admiration for Hannah Rahill, the talented editor who skillfully coordinated this complicated project, and Kari Ontko, the sensitive graphic designer who expertly made it flow on the page.

Weldon Owen wishes to thank the following people for their help in creating this book: in San Francisco, Linda Bouchard, Cecilia Brunazzi, Ken DellaPenta, Sandra Eisert, Sharilyn Hovind, Beverly McGuire, Karen Richardson, Kristen Wurz, and Joe Mastrelli of Molinari Delicatessen; in New York, Ann Lenssen of Dufour & Company Ltd.; and in Tuscany, Dott. Rocco Giorgio, Simona Serio, and Anna and Franco Maggi of San Fabbiano Calcinaia.

Photograph pp 22–23 © Paul Solomon/Woodfin Camp & Associates.

OXMOOR HOUSE INC.

Oxmoor House.

Oxmoor House books are distributed by Sunset Books
80 Willow Road, Menlo Park, CA 94025
Telephone: 650-321-3600 Fax: 650-324-1532

Vice President/General Manager: Rich Smeby
Director of Special Sales: Gary Wright

Oxmoor House and Sunset Books are divisions of
Southern Progress Corporation

WILLIAMS-SONOMA INC.

Founder and Vice-Chairman: Chuck Williams
Book Buyer: Cecilia Michaelis

WELDON OWEN INC.

Chief Executive Officer: John Owen
President: Terry Newell
Chief Operating Officer: Larry Partington
Vice President International Sales: Stuart Laurence
Publisher: Wendely Harvey
Associate Publisher: Hannah Rahill
Copy Editor: Sharon Silva
Consulting Editor: Norman Kolpas
Design: Kari Ontko, India Ink
Production: Stephanie Sherman,
Christine DePedro, Chris Hemesath
Editorial Assistant: Lilia Gerberg
Food Stylist: George Dolese
Calligraphy: Jane Dill

THE SAVORING SERIES

conceived and produced by Weldon Owen Inc.
814 Montgomery Street, San Francisco, CA 94133
Telephone: 415-291-0100, Fax: 415-291-8841

In collaboration with Williams-Sonoma Inc.
3250 Van Ness Avenue, San Francisco, CA 94109

Savoring ® is a registered trademark of Weldon Owen Inc.

p 2: *Trenette al pesto,* recipe page 100. pp 4–5: One of the five cliff-side Ligurian villages known collectively as the Cinque Terre, Manarola is a lively fishing port. pp 6–7: Surrounded by three lakes in the Po Valley, Mantua was ruled by the wealthy Gonzaga family dynasty for four centuries. Birthplace of the poet Virgil, this striking city is home to many elaborate *palazzi* of the Gonzaga era, including the vast and splendid Palazzo Ducale. pp 8–9: A road curls through the hills of southern Piedmont, passing through vineyards that produce some of Italy's most celebrated reds. pp 12–13: During Rome's earliest days, the valley between the Palatine and the Capitoline, the city's two most historic hills, was a swamp. But by 200 B.C., construction on countless basilicas, arches, and temples had commenced, creating the ceremonial center of the city, the ruins of which can be viewed today.

A WELDON OWEN PRODUCTION
Copyright © 1999 Weldon Owen Inc.

All rights reserved, including the right of reproduction
in whole or in part in any form.

First printed 1999
15 14 13 12 11 10 9 8

Library of Congress
Cataloging-in-Publication-Data

Scicolone, Michele.
    Savoring Italy : recipes and reflections on Italian cooking /
Michele Scicolone, recipes and text ; Chuck Williams, general editor;
Noel Barnhurst, recipe photography ; Steven Rothfeld, scenic
photography.
        p.   cm. -- (The savoring series)
    ISBN 0-7370-2020-2 (hc.)
    1. Cookery, Italian.   I. Williams, Chuck.   II. Title
III. Series
    TX723.S3664 1999
    641.5945--dc21   99-13546
                                                                      CIP

Separations by Colourscan Overseas Co. Pte. Ltd.
Printed in Singapore by Tien Wah Press (Pte.) Ltd.